How Ireland Voted 2020

October 2022.
Adare.

Helen,

To mark your last election as Returning Officer. John.

Michael Gallagher
Michael Marsh • Theresa Reidy
Editors

How Ireland Voted 2020

The End of an Era

palgrave
macmillan

Editors
Michael Gallagher
Department of Political Science
Trinity College Dublin
Dublin, Ireland

Michael Marsh
Department of Political Science
Trinity College Dublin
Dublin, Ireland

Theresa Reidy
Department of Government and
Politics
University College Cork
Cork, Ireland

ISBN 978-3-030-66404-6   ISBN 978-3-030-66405-3   (eBook)
https://doi.org/10.1007/978-3-030-66405-3

This Palgrave Macmillan imprint is published by the registered company Springer Nature Switzerland AG.
The registered company address is: Gewerbestrasse 11, 6330 Cham, Switzerland

PREFACE

Elections in Ireland used to be rather predictable affairs. Either the country's perennial largest party, Fianna Fáil, would win, going on to form a government on its own or—from 1989 onwards—with a junior coalition partner; or Fine Gael and Labour would win and take the reins of power. These two blocs—one led by Fianna Fáil, the other by Fine Gael—had roughly equal support levels, and whichever could persuade the swing voters to its side in any particular election would come out on top. The party system was defined and structured by the integrity of the quarrel between Fianna Fáil and Fine Gael, even if its origins lay in events of the early 1920s and policy differences between the two parties were increasingly harder to discern. These parties' strengths went up or down a little, new parties came and went, but all change took place within the context of the party system that was created in 1922 and was firmly established by 1932.

It was the economic crash of 2008 that set in motion what seems to be the end of this system. First, at the 2011 election, Fianna Fáil, which had been the strongest party in the country continuously for almost 80 years, suffered a collapse in support and dropped to third position. The ensuing Fine Gael–Labour coalition, at the end of its five-year term in 2016, fared little better, and a stable government could be formed only by an eyebrow-raising arrangement between the largest two parties, Fine Gael and Fianna Fáil, under which the latter sustained in office, through a confidence and supply arrangement (described in Chap. 1), a Fine Gael-dominated government that had the support of barely a third of the Dáil. There were times during the lifetime of this 2016–20 administration when opinion polls suggested that the 'dreary steeples' of the two poles of the pre-2011 party system were re-asserting themselves, but when the election arrived in February 2020 this illusion was shattered by the success of Sinn Féin in winning a plurality of the votes, and the willingness of Fianna Fáil and Fine Gael to form a coalition government four months later seemed to confirm that the structure of the 1932–2008 party system has gone forever.

This government, making the two parties comrades in arms for the first time, came into existence 97 years after the ending of Ireland's bitter civil war between two combatants from which Fianna Fáil and Fine Gael claimed descent and so, not surprisingly, was widely hailed as marking 'the end of civil war politics'. The idea of such a government had occasionally been floated in the past, though there were concerns that a 'grand coalition' would be able to evade parliamentary scrutiny due to its huge size. By 2020, though, this was a decidedly not-so-grand coalition, as the two parties came together because of their joint decline rather than out of a desire to dominate. With the government having a predominantly centre-right complexion and the opposition overwhelmingly left of centre, the scene seems set for the long-predicted emergence of a left versus right party system, though most predictions made after each of Ireland's previous three elections have proved wide of the mark.

This volume in the *How Ireland Voted* series, the ninth, analyses this apparently era-ending election. Chapter 1 provides an account of the term of the incumbent government and assesses its record, while Chap. 2 forensically analyses the degree to which the government fulfilled its pledges. Chapter 3 explores the internal processes within each party, sometimes marked by conflict out of the public eye, through which the parties selected their candidates for the election, and profiles the backgrounds of the 531 contestants.

Chapter 4, which is based on extensive interviews with party strategists and other insiders, recounts the story of the campaign, while Chap. 5 explores the impact, or lack of impact, of Brexit on the election. Social media play an increasing role in elections, and Chap. 6 analyses the parties' activity here, with a focus on Sinn Féin given that party's particular strength among young voters. In Chap. 7 five Dáil candidates give their personal accounts of what it was like to face the voters on doorsteps across the country, and a senator explains the complexities of campaigning in a Seanad election, especially during a pandemic-driven lockdown.

The next three chapters analyse different aspects of the results themselves. Chapter 8 assesses the performances of the parties and analyses the composition of the new parliament, while Chap. 9 illustrates graphically, through detailed maps, the geographical base of candidates' support within constituencies. Chapter 10 analyses survey data to investigate the reasons why people voted as they did, identifying the issues that were most salient to voters and analysing voters' evaluations of the parties on these issues. Chapter 11 is based on a survey of election candidates and explores similarities and differences of views of the nominees of the various parties to present a novel analysis of the Irish policy space as of February 2020.

The upper house, the Seanad, often appears on the verge of fundamental reform, but the 2020 election followed exactly the same form as its predecessors and this is examined in Chap. 12. Chapter 13 analyses the construction of the new government; putting together the 2016 government had taken ten weeks, a then record, but the process in 2020 took exactly twice as long and, as noted above, delivered an unexpected outcome. Finally, Chap. 14 places Ireland's 2020 election outcome in the context of both the country's own political history and the broader European picture. Appendices to the book contain the detailed election results, information on all 160 Teachtaí Dála (TDs) and on government ministers, and other relevant background information.

At the front of the book we have included a chronology of the election campaign, and the book is illustrated by a selection of photographs and campaign literature that capture the spirit of election 2020. We thank a number of Ireland's major media organisations for permission to sample their stock of photographs and reproduce some of them here. *The Irish Times* again gave us access to their rich photo-library, and at the *Irish Independent* we thank Owen Breslin, Kevin Doyle and Fionnán Sheahan for selecting the photos and giving us permission to use them. At the national broadcaster RTÉ, we thank Patricia O'Callaghan for her help in pointing us in the right direction and Vincent Kearney and Fran McNulty for permission to use photos that they took. And our thanks to Áras an Uachtaráin/Maxwell Photography and to Hans Zomer for allowing us to use the photograph of the President of Ireland with the newly appointed government standing suitably socially distanced from each other.

We are pleased that this volume, like its four predecessors, is being published by the major international publisher Springer under the Palgrave Macmillan imprint, and in particular we would like to thank Ambra Finotello for her support for our initial proposal and Rebecca Roberts for her work on taking it through the production process. And as always, we thank our cooperative and patient contributors, who were put under great pressure by the demands of a book being produced on a very tight schedule, exacerbated by the disruptions to their personal and working lives by the Covid-19 lockdown. Coronavirus hardly featured in the Irish media on election day, 8 February, but within a month had become the dominant story on the news agenda with routine political activity virtually suppressed. During the election campaign all parties had made promises as to how they would spend the estimated €11 billion-worth of 'fiscal space' predicted to be available to the next government, but the huge additional expenditure necessitated to address the coronavirus crisis rendered most of these pledges irrelevant and redundant by the time that government was formed.

Finally, we would like to remember two avid followers of Irish elections: Noel Whelan, who died in July 2019, and Jim Farrelly, who passed away at the end of May 2020. Both would have enjoyed watching recent politics unfold. This was the first election for many years not to have been accompanied by one of Noel's publications and his insightful commentary. Jim Farrelly's books were published some time ago, but he also brought two young academics into the *Irish Independent* for the 1987 election and they are still in business.

Dublin and Cork   Michael Gallagher
August 2020   Michael Marsh
                                                        Theresa Reidy

CONTENTS

Notes on Contributors

Duncan Casey recently completed an MA in Politics at the University of Limerick and is currently working as a public affairs consultant in Brussels. His research interests are domestic and European electoral politics and Irish social policy.

John Coakley, MRIA is a professor at the School of History, Anthropology, Philosophy and Politics, Queen's University Belfast, and a fellow in the UCD Geary Institute. Recent publications include *Negotiating a Settlement in Northern Ireland, 1969–2019* (with Jennifer Todd, 2020).

Rory Costello is a senior lecturer in the Department of Politics and Public Administration at the University of Limerick. His research examines legislative and electoral politics in Ireland and the EU. He is co-editor of *Comparative European Politics: Distinctive Democracies, Common Challenges* (2020).

Kevin Cunningham is a lecturer in Politics and Journalism at Technological University Dublin. His academic research focuses on voting behaviour. He runs a public opinion research firm and has worked for several political parties in Ireland, the UK, Australia and across Europe advising on electoral strategy.

Caoilfhionn D'Arcy is a PhD candidate in Maynooth University's Department of Geography. Her research focuses on recent elections across the island of Ireland, specifically focusing on candidate selection and campaigning. She currently teaches 'The Geography of the Eurovision Song Contest' and demonstrates on 'Methods of Geographical Analysis' modules in Maynooth.

William Durkan is a PhD candidate and Irish Research Council Government of Ireland Postgraduate Scholar in Maynooth University's Department of Geography, where he teaches the 'Geographies of Recent Irish Elections' and 'Environmental Politics' modules. His research focuses on voting trends in Irish elections, with a specific focus on the geography of voter turnout.

Michael Gallagher, MRIA is Professor of Comparative Politics at Trinity College Dublin. He is co-editor of *Politics in the Republic of Ireland* (6th edition 2018), has been a visiting professor at City University of Hong Kong and Sciences Po Lille, and has undertaken research on electoral systems, party members and referendums.

Samuel Johnston is a PhD student in the Department of Political Science, Trinity College Dublin. His main areas of research are radical right and ethnoregional political parties in Europe, and Irish politics. More generally, he works in the fields of comparative, European and party politics.

Adrian Kavanagh is a lecturer in the Department of Geography at Maynooth University, where he teaches a range of different modules, including an Electoral Geography module. His main research interests focus on geographical aspects of electoral contests (as well as the Eurovision Song Contest).

Lisa Keenan lectures in the Department of Political Science at Trinity College Dublin. She researches on Irish politics and gender and politics.

Pat Leahy is the political editor of *The Irish Times*. He is the author of two best-selling books, *Showtime: the Inside Story of Irish Politics* and *The Price of Power: Inside Ireland's Crisis Coalition*, and has made a number of television documentaries about politics for RTÉ. Previously deputy editor and political editor of *The Sunday Business Post*, he holds a degree in law from UCD and was a Reuters fellow at Oxford University.

Michael Marsh, MRIA is a professor emeritus of political science at Trinity College Dublin. He has co-edited the *How Ireland Voted* series since 1997, co-authored *The Irish Voter* (2008) and most recently co-edited *The Post-Crisis Irish Voter* (2018).

Gail McElroy is a professor in Political Science at Trinity College, Dublin, and Dean of the Faculty of Arts, Humanities and Social Sciences. Her research interests are in the area of party, electoral and legislative politics.

Claire McGing is a member of the senior management team at the Institute of Art, Design and Technology (IADT), Dún Laoghaire, leading on equality, diversity and inclusion. Her research interests lie in the areas of gender politics and Irish elections. Recent publications include Women doing politics differently: Development of local or regional caucus for women councillors (National Women's Council of Ireland, 2021).

Gary Murphy is Professor of Politics at the School of Law and Government at Dublin City University. He has held visiting professorships at the University of North Carolina, Chapel Hill and the University of Notre Dame. He has published extensively on modern Irish politics and regularly appears in the print and broadcast media.

Mary C. Murphy holds a Jean Monnet Chair in European Integration and is a senior lecturer in the Department of Government and Politics, University College Cork. She is the author of *Europe and Northern Ireland's Future: Negotiating Brexit's Unique Case* (2018) and has published extensively on Brexit and Ireland.

Eoin O'Malley is an associate professor at the School of Law and Government, Dublin City University. He is the author of over 40 peer-reviewed publications, and is finishing a book on Taoisigh and political leadership in Ireland since 1980.

Kirsty Park is a postdoctoral researcher at the Institute for Future Media, Democracy and Society (FuJo) at Dublin City University. She is an Irish Research Council postgraduate scholar with a PhD in Communications.

Theresa Reidy is a senior lecturer in the Department of Government and Politics, University College Cork. Her research interests lie in the areas of political institutions and electoral behaviour. Her recent work has been published in *Electoral Studies, Parliamentary Affairs* and *Politics* and she is also a regular contributor to radio, television and the print media.

Alice Sheridan graduated in 2019 with a Bachelor of Arts in Politics and Public Administration from the University of Limerick, where her work on pledge fulfilment was awarded the prize for the best final year dissertation in politics. She is currently working in the Local Enterprise Office at Galway County Council.

Jane Suiter is a professor at Dublin City University She works at the intersection of political science and communication. She is published in journals including *Electoral Studies, International Political Science Review, Science* and *Journal of Communication*.

GLOSSARY

Áras an Uactharáin, residence of the President of Ireland
ard-fheis (plural ard-fheiseanna), national conference (of a political party)
Ceann Comhairle, speaker or chairperson (of the Dáil)
Dáil Éireann, directly-elected lower house of parliament to which the Irish government is answerable
Fianna Fáil, the largest party in Ireland from 1932 until 2011
Fine Gael, second largest party in Ireland from 1932 to 2011
Leinster House, seat of houses of parliament
Oireachtas, parliament (has two houses: Dáil and Seanad)
Seanad Éireann, indirectly-elected upper house of parliament
Sinn Féin, republican party
Tánaiste, deputy prime minister
Taoiseach, prime minister
TG4, Irish language public service television network
Teachta Dála, Dáil deputy

ABBREVIATIONS

CCS	Comparative Candidate Survey
EU	European Union
FF	Fianna Fáil
FG	Fine Gael
GAA	Gaelic Athletic Association
Grn	Green Party
I4C	Independents 4 Change
INES	Irish National Election Study
IRA	Irish Republican Army
Lab	Labour Party
MEP	Member of the European Parliament
MW	Mid-West
N	North
NC	North-Central
NE	North-East
NUI	National University of Ireland
NW	North-West
PBP	People Before Profit
PDs	Progressive Democrats
PfG	Programme for Government
PR	Proportional representation
RTÉ	Raidió Teilifís Éireann, the national broadcasting station
S	South
S–PBP	Solidarity–People Before Profit
SC	South-Central
SD	Social Democrats

SDLP	Social Democratic and Labour Party, second largest nationalist party in Northern Ireland
SE	South-East
SF	Sinn Féin
Sol	Solidarity
STV	single transferable vote
SW	South-West
TCD	Trinity College Dublin
TD	Teachta Dála, member of the Dáil
UCC	University College Cork
UCD	University College Dublin

CHRONOLOGY OF 2020 ELECTION CAMPAIGN

14 Jan   Taoiseach visits Áras an Uachtaráin and advises President to dissolve the 32nd Dáil. The election date is set for Saturday 8 February, said to be the first Saturday general election since 1918. Fine Gael, the main party in the outgoing government, unveils its campaign slogan 'A future to look forward to', while Fianna Fáil's slogan is 'An Ireland for all'. Sinn Féin declares itself 'On Your Side', for the Green Party 'The Future Belongs to All of Us', while Labour states that it is 'Building an Equal Society'.

17 Jan   Veteran FF TD Pat 'The Cope' Gallagher says that he would favour a post-election coalition between his party and SF, even though party leader Micheál Martin has consistently said that there is no possibility of this. SF itself, which at previous elections has called for the abolition of the non-jury Special Criminal Court (under which many IRA members were convicted in previous years), now says it will merely seek a review of the court and its provisions.

19 Jan   The first poll is published since the start of the campaign; it shows FF with 32 per cent of the votes and FG with only 20 per cent, with SF on 19 per cent, the Greens 7 per cent, Labour 4 per cent and independents 13 per cent. Observers point out that polling was done before the election was called, and at a time when the government was on the defensive because of its handling of a planned commemoration of the pre-independence police force, the RIC, which other parties alleged would be 'celebrating the Black and Tans' (a notorious auxiliary force used by the British administration during the war of independence whose brutal and arbitrary violence towards civilians has not been forgotten or forgiven a century on).

21 Jan   The second poll to be published gives a rather different picture: FF 25 per cent, FG 23 per cent, SF 21 per cent, Greens 8 per cent, Labour 5 per cent, independents 14 per cent.

22 Jan   The same poll shows that respondents cite health and housing as the two most important issues. However, all the parties are finding that pensions is an issue constantly being raised by voters, with resistance to plans to raise the pension age incrementally to 67 by 2021 and to 68 by 2028, especially given that in many jobs the retirement age will remain at 65.

Nominations close at 12 noon. In total 531 candidates are standing for the 159 seats being contested: 369 men and 162 women.

The first televised leaders' debate takes place between Leo Varadkar and Micheál Martin; SF protests that its leader Mary Lou McDonald should also have been a participant. As is almost invariably the case, pundits conclude that neither man landed the proverbial 'killer blow'. Leo Varadkar says his party would be open to a coalition with FF, or to providing confidence and supply to a FF-led government, after the election. Both leaders rule out the possibility of a coalition between their party and SF.

23 Jan   *Irish Times* front page article by Pat Leahy begins: 'Parties scrambled to promise changes to pension rules last night as fears grow of an auction election'. It quotes economists deploring the rash of spending promises, such as University of Limerick's Stephen Kinsella: 'The dramatic escalation in electoral promises—as yet uncosted—risks running a deficit, adding to the national debt, overheating the economy further, and running up against our fiscal rules'.

On behalf of FF, Micheál Martin rules out the possibility of a coalition with FG.

24 Jan   Both FG and FF launch their manifestos, both (like all other parties' manifestos) based on the assumption that additional spending of €11 billion will be available over the five-year term of the incoming government. This is the size of the 'fiscal space', that is, the discretionary spending, that the Department of Finance estimates will be available over the next five years, though some suggest this figure is based on unduly optimistic assumptions. Both parties promise some modest tax cuts and significant increases in spending, with similarities between the manifestoes greater than the differences.

Minister for Foreign Affairs Simon Coveney casts doubt on FF's ability to handle the next stage of the Brexit negotiations, saying, 'I know Micheál Martin better than most. He is not the person I want leading Ireland into the second half of the Brexit challenge'. Coveney denies that he is impugning Martin's character.

25 Jan   Green Party launches its manifesto. It promises a universal basic income, free public transport for students, a wealth tax for those with assets over €10 million and the introduction of a flight tax.

26 Jan   Regarding the two main parties' insistence that they will not enter a coalition with SF, SF leader Mary Lou McDonald says that 'the establishment parties' will do anything and use any excuse to exclude it from power.

Two more polls published. Like the two previous polls, they both find FF ahead of FG and SF not far behind FG. In per cent, one finds FF 26, FG 23, SF 19, Greens 8, Labour 4, independents 14; the other finds FF 27, FG 22, SF 20, Greens 10, Labour 6, independents 11.

27 Jan A TV debate takes place in Galway between the leaders of the seven main parties. Different observers have different impressions as to who fared best, though Mary Lou McDonald of SF is generally agreed to have done well, and the overall assessment seems to be that there was no clear winner and no clear loser.

28 Jan SF launches its manifesto, which promises large spending increases, to be funded by higher taxes on high earners and on corporations, and tax cuts for those on lower incomes, as well as the abolition of property tax. Both FF and FG say these proposals are not financially viable and would cause major damage to the economy, and that the manifesto justifies their stance of refusing to contemplate a post-election coalition government with SF. Mary Lou McDonald again says that 'the political establishment' is 'desperately reaching for any excuse' to keep SF out of government.

 Labour launches its manifesto, promising to freeze rents and build 80,000 social and affordable homes over the next five years, to spend significantly more on the health service, and to establish a citizens' assembly to consider the formulation of a new constitution.

 An FG candidate in Dublin Bay North, Senator Catherine Noone, apologises for calling her party leader 'autistic'.

29 Jan Ireland's EU Commissioner Phil Hogan, a former FG TD and minister, visits Ireland and warns against what he sees as 'complacency' in the country about Brexit, saying that the most difficult part of the negotiations still lies ahead. FF accuses him of a 'coded' partisan intervention in the election campaign designed to assist his former party, which is generally held to want the parties' capacity to handle Brexit to loom larger in the campaign as FG is favourably evaluated by voters on this issue.

30 Jan A second seven-way televised debate between party leaders. Debate co-moderator Ivan Yates starts by accusing all seven party spokespersons of being 'chancers and charlatans' for making promises based on unrealistic economic forecasts, and the event evolves, or degenerates, into what commentators describe as a 'shouting match' or even, metaphorically, a 'bar-room brawl'. The leaders of FF and SF constantly cross swords, while observers speculate as to how much to read into praise from SF leader Mary Lou McDonald for Taoiseach Leo Varadkar's role in helping to achieve the re-establishment of the Northern Ireland power-sharing Executive earlier in the month. Labour's Brendan Howlin is identified by several commentators as the best performer.

31 Jan Social Democrats launch their manifesto, just eight days before polling day. It advocates greater investment in public services and the introduction of flexible working hours.

1 Feb Leo Varadkar and Micheál Martin each accuse the other of being willing to lead his party into coalition with SF despite their commitments to the contrary. Mary Lou McDonald describes the behaviour of both of them as 'childish'.

2 Feb   Opinion poll finds FG now in third position with SF having joined FF in the lead: in per cent, FF 24, SF 24, FG 21, Greens 7, Labour 5, independents 12. Brendan Howlin reiterates Labour policy that it will not enter into any post-election coalition government with SF.

Leo Varadkar, citing the opposition of a majority of FF TDs to the passage of the 2018 referendum on legalising abortion, says that the FF parliamentary party has a lot of 'backwoodsmen' who would slow social progress if FF is returned to government.

3 Feb   RTÉ changes its mind and invites Mary Lou McDonald, as well as Micheál Martin and Leo Varadkar, to take part in the final leaders' debate on 4 February.

4 Feb   Opinion poll finds that SF is now the strongest party; the figures (in per cent) are SF 25, FF 23, FG 20, Greens 8, Labour 4, independents 11.

RTÉ stages televised debate between the leaders of FF, FG and SF; it attracts an average of 658,000 viewers, 54 per cent of all viewership at that time. Mary Lou McDonald is put on the defensive by questions relating to a brutal murder north of the border in 2007 in which there was suspected IRA involvement. She says that Conor Murphy, one of the party's ministers in the Northern Ireland Executive, needs to apologise for having cast a slur on the murder victim, Paul Quinn, recanting her statement in a televised interview the previous day in which she had denied that Murphy had made any such remarks. Leo Varadkar looks uncomfortable when trying to explain why an FG TD, Dara Murphy, was permitted to devote most of his time for over two years after summer 2017 to a job in Brussels while receiving a full TD's salary before finally resigning his seat in December 2019. Micheál Martin appears to avoid any particularly difficult moments.

5 Feb   The continuing fallout from the 2007 murder of Paul Quinn dominates the news agenda. Commentators speculate as to whether this will damage SF or whether it is seen by most voters as irrelevant to the current campaign.

6 Feb   There is a televised debate between the leaders of a number of smaller parties: the Green Party, Labour, Social Democrats, Solidarity–People Before Profit and Aontú.

8 Feb   **Election day**.

10 Feb   The final results are known when the 160th TD, Niamh Smyth from Cavan–Monaghan, is elected. There is much discussion about government formation, as it seems impossible that a majority government, or a stable minority government, can be put together unless one or more of the parties enters coalition with a party that before the election it promised not to go into government with.

11 Feb   Smaller left-wing parties express scepticism as to whether a left-wing government, without any involvement by either FF or FG, can be put together given the Dáil numbers.

12 Feb   Brendan Howlin announces that he will be standing down as leader of the Labour Party.

13 Feb   FF declines SF leader Mary Lou McDonald's invitation to talks. The FF
          parliamentary party endorses, with only a few dissenting voices, the party
          leader's refusal to enter discussions with SF on a possible coalition
          government. There is growing speculation that FF and FG might reach
          agreement on a 'grand coalition'.

14 Feb   SF acknowledges that, given the distribution of seats in the Dáil, it will not
          be possible to form a left-wing coalition government. Its leader berates FF
          and FG for refusing to enter discussions about the formation of a coalition
          with SF. In the following days, some 'preliminary' meetings take place
          between parties, but no serious negotiation has started.

19 Feb   Poll reports that if there were another election, 35 per cent say they would
          vote for SF, with FG at 18 per cent and FF at 19 per cent. Only 20 per cent
          say they want another election.

20 Feb   The 33rd Dáil meets for the first time. It starts by re-electing Seán Ó
          Fearghaíl as Ceann Comhairle (chair of the Dáil) by 130 votes to 28 for his
          only rival, independent TD Denis Naughten. The Dáil then votes on the
          election of a Taoiseach. The largest four parties each nominate their leader,
          and each is defeated: Leo Varadkar (FG) by 36 votes to 107, Micheál Martin
          (FF) by 41 votes to 97, Mary Lou McDonald (SF) by 45 votes to 84, and
          Éamon Ryan (Green) by 12 votes to 115. Media coverage focuses in
          particular on Micheál Martin's strong criticism of SF, including the
          allegation that it continuously tries 'to legitimise [the IRA's] murderous
          sectarian campaign', which observers believe rules out any possibility of a
          coalition between FF and SF, at least under Martin's leadership of his party.
          Varadkar goes to the President and tenders his resignation as Taoiseach,
          though he and the rest of the government will remain in office until a new
          government is voted in.

25 Feb   The leaders of FF and FG meet for the first time since the election. For FF,
          Micheál Martin suggests further talks, while for FG Leo Varadkar, while not
          ruling this out, reiterates his party's belief that FG has been given a mandate
          to go into opposition.

1 Mar   Opinion poll says that if a fresh general election were held, SF would fare
          significantly better than in the February election, gaining the support of 35
          per cent of respondents, almost as many as the combined total for FF (20
          per cent) and FG (18 per cent).

3 Mar   Leo Varadkar says he has written to Mary Lou McDonald offering talks,
          while reiterating that his party is not open to the idea of a coalition between
          their parties.

10 Mar   Leaders of FF and FG issue identical statements saying that their negotiating
          teams should now begin 'in-depth, detailed talks'. This is interpreted as a
          breakthrough and an indication that serious negotiations are finally about to
          start, partly in response to the sense of crisis caused by the coronavirus
          pandemic.

11 Mar   The Covid-19 crisis, hitherto on the fringes of the news agenda, now starts to take centre stage. The Green Party suggests that in response to the need for a government to deal with it, an all-party national government should be formed. The largest three parties all pour cold water on this suggestion.

19 Mar   The Dáil passes, without a vote, the Health (Preservation and Protection and Other Emergency Measures in the Public Interest) Bill 2020, which gives the government sweeping and draconian powers to deal with the coronavirus crisis, including the power to restrict movement and to detain people who are refusing to self-isolate. The following day, the Seanad passes the bill and the President signs it into law.

          An incorporeal meeting of the FG parliamentary party, conducted by teleconference, agrees that party negotiators can continue discussions on government formation with FF, but it does not seem that serious negotiations are taking place despite last week's statements. By now, the coronavirus crisis is completely overshadowing all routine political and other business.

26 Mar   The Green Party reiterates its call for a national government, despite the cool reception this has received from all other parties, and says that it will not engage in talks with SF, FF or FG.

30 Mar   At 11 am polls close in the Seanad election, and the counting of the votes begins at 1 pm. The following morning Seán Kyne, who lost his seat as a TD in the Dáil election, becomes the first senator to be elected.

1 Apr   The six university seats in the Seanad are filled, with all the incumbents securing re-election.

3 Apr   The last of the 49 elected Seanad seats is filled, as Niall Ó Donnghaile wins the final seat on the Administrative panel.

          The votes are counted in the contest to succeed Brendan Howlin as leader of the Labour Party. In a turnout of 87 per cent of the 2,210 eligible voters, Alan Kelly wins 55 per cent of the votes and his only rival Aodhán Ó Ríordáin 45 per cent.

14 Apr   Leo Varadkar and Micheál Martin give their imprimatur to an agreement reached, after several weeks of discussion, between the negotiating teams of their respective parties. This envisages a larger role for the state in several policy areas and also promises no increases in income tax. Once the document has been approved by the two parliamentary parties, the intention is to make it available to other parties in the hope that one or more of the Greens, Labour or the Social Democrats will engage in further negotiations based on the document and will ultimately sign up to an agreed programme for government.

          The following day, the parliamentary party groups of both parties endorse it, albeit with a small number of sceptical voices and some uncertainty as to how the long list of aspirations will be paid for. The document has now been shared with other parties.

23 Apr   After several days during which other parties have reacted in a non-committal and unenthusiastic fashion to the FF–FG document, the Green Party responds with a list of 17 commitments that it asks FF and FG to agree to if it is to enter talks with them.

28 Apr	FF and FG send a joint reply to the Green message of 23 April.
3 May	After several days of discussions, the Greens' parliamentary party agrees to enter detailed negotiations with FF and FG. It subsequently emerges that the party's TDs divided 8–4 on the issue, with deputy leader Catherine Martin among the four TDs opposing the decision.
11 May	FF, FG and the Greens begin formal negotiations on a possible programme for government, 93 days after the general election took place.
13 May	The Social Democrats announce that they have definitely decided not to take part in any discussions with FF and FG on possible government formation.
16 May	News reports say that the government has started to draw up contingency plans as to how a fresh general election could be held under coronavirus restrictions. Two FF front-bench spokespeople react negatively to this news and accuse FG of behaving 'in bad faith', engaging in government formation talks while surreptitiously preparing the ground for a snap election. A conversation between the party leaders on 18 May is said to have resolved the issue.
20 May	Several Green councillors urge deputy leader Catherine Martin to stand against Éamon Ryan in the forthcoming Green party leadership contest; she says she will give 'serious consideration' to the idea.
31 May	Two opinion polls published, both showing a similar picture: if an election were held tomorrow, FG would receive 35–36 per cent of votes, Sinn Féin 27 per cent, FF 15–16 per cent.
6 Jun	Catherine Martin, who is heading the Greens' coalition negotiating team, confirms that she will stand against Éamon Ryan for the position of leader of the Green Party.
14 Jun	In the early hours of the morning, the negotiating teams of FF, FG and Greens complete their work. Remaining unresolved issues are passed up to the party leaders.
15 Jun	In the early afternoon, the leaders of FF, FG and the Greens announce agreement on a programme for government. In the evening, all three parliamentary parties recommend the document for acceptance by their members, who will now vote on it: on a one-member-one-vote basis in FF and the Greens, and by an electoral college in which the votes of TDs and senators carry most weight in FG.
26 Jun	The results of the three parties' internal votes on whether to accept the Programme for Government are announced. FF members have approved it by a 74–26 margin, FG by 80–20 and the Greens by 76–24.
27 Jun	The Dáil meets and elects Micheál Martin as Taoiseach by 93 votes to 63. It later approves his nomination of a government containing six ministers each from Fianna Fáil and Fine Gael and three from the Greens. In addition, three 'super-junior' ministers (with the right to attend cabinet meetings but not to take part in any votes there) are announced. Later in the evening the Taoiseach's 11 senate nominees are announced, thus completing the election of both Houses of the Oireachtas.

29 Jun   In a judgment on a case brought by ten senators before the government took office, the High Court rules that the Seanad would not be validly constituted, and could not meet, until the Taoiseach's 11 nominees have taken up their positions. The case is important for future reference even though the immediate issue has been resolved by the events of 27 June.

1 Jul   The remaining 17 junior ministers (formally, 'ministers of state') are announced. In all, FF and FG each have eight ministers of state while the Greens have four.

14 Jul   The Taoiseach sacks Minister for Agriculture Barry Cowen after only 17 days in his post, the shortest ministerial stint on record, over his refusal to submit himself to questions about a motoring incident several years earlier.

23 Jul   Green leadership result announced; Éamon Ryan is re-elected with 51 per cent of members' votes against 49 per cent for Catherine Martin.

30 Jul   On the last day before the Dáil adjourns for its six-week summer recess, a Green backbench TD votes against a government bill and a Green junior minister abstains. Neither receives a serious sanction, leading to speculation about the prospects of the government's long-term survival.

21 Aug   Barry Cowen's successor as Minister for Agriculture, Dara Calleary, himself resigns following his participation in a dinner of the Oireachtas Golf Society that was held in breach of Covid-19 social distancing guidelines.

Fianna Fáil leader Micheál Martin campaigning in the English Market in Cork, beside the counter made famous by *The Young Offenders*, shaking hands with fishmonger Pat O'Connell as councillor Mary Rose Desmond looks on (Fran McNulty)

Ruairí Ó Murchú (left) campaigns to retain one of the two Sinn Féin seats in Louth, with a little help from the retiring TD and former party leader Gerry Adams himself (*Irish Times*)

Five of the participants in an education debate organised by the Union of Students in Ireland: from left Ivana Bacik (Lab), Donnchadh Ó Laoghaire (SF), Neasa Hourigan (Grn), Richard Boyd Barrett (PBP), Aengus Ó Maoláin (SD) (*Irish Times*)

Taoiseach Leo Varadkar and successful Fine Gael Dublin MW candidate Emer Higgins meet some enthusiastic future voters (*Irish Times*)

Sinn Féin press conference featuring, from left, Mark Ward, Louise O'Reilly, Eoin Ó Broin (partly hidden), Pearse Doherty, David Cullinane, Martin Kenny, John Brady and Claire Kerrane (*Irish Times*)

Social Democrats candidates Gary Gannon and Sarah Durcan pose for the cameras in Dublin's Temple Bar (*Irish Times*)

High-profile though unsuccessful Green candidate Saoirse McHugh campaigns on the doorstep in Mayo. She was to leave the party several months later after it entered coalition with Fianna Fáil and Fine Gael (*Irish Times*)

Brendan Howlin in expansive mood at a Labour press conference, flanked by Ged Nash, Duncan Smith and Annie Hoey (*Irish Times*)

Labour Senator Mark Wall (left), who won the highest percentage vote of any of his party's candidates, campaigns on the farm in Kildare South, accompanied by local party councillor Aoife Breslin (*Irish Independent*)

Veteran Fianna Fáil TD Willie O'Dea canvasses a friendly dog in Limerick City (Willie O'Dea)

Four posters in Dublin NW. As it happened, the candidates finished in the same order as the placement of the posters, Shortall coming second, McAuliffe third, Rock fourth and Montague seventh (editors)

Leo Varadkar, a little apprehensively, holds a dog, flanked by his party's three Dun Laoghaire candidates Jennifer Carroll MacNeill (partly hidden), Mary Mitchell O'Connor and Barry Ward (Vincent Kearney)

The 'walking posters' of Fine Gael candidate Jennifer Carroll MacNeill (see Chap. 7) take a stroll on Dun Laoghaire pier (Jennifer Carroll MacNeill)

Fine Gael poster in Dublin Bay North gives prominence to Senator Catherine Noone ahead of Minister Richard Bruton (editors)

Left-wing posters in Dublin South-Central (editors)

A plethora of posters in Dublin Bay South (editors)

Election literature of the national poll-topper Denise Mitchell in Dublin Bay North

Successful independent candidate Matt Shanahan lays out his priorities

Minister for Business, Enterprise and Innovation Heather Humphreys shows she has not forgotten that 'All politics is local'. The list of constituency projects continues on the other side of the leaflet

Campaign literature of defeated Solidarity TD Ruth Coppinger

Fine Gael literature hints at a dual leadership, and emphasises its team's capacity to deal with Brexit, an issue that voters did not see as salient (see Chap. 5)

AN IMPORTANT MESSAGE
To Government Supporters
From Minister Paschal Donohoe
Fine Gael National Director of Elections

FINE GAEL ⋆

Dear Voter,

May I first take the opportunity to thank you for the courtesy and support you have shown to our candidates and their canvassing teams over the last number of weeks.

If the Government is to be re-elected it is vital that Fine Gael secures two seats in Dublin Bay North. Recent opinion poll research has shown that we can do this, but that we will need to manage our vote.

I am appealing to all supporters of the Government parties in Clontarf, Sutton, Howth, Raheny, Marino, Fairview, Gracepark area to vote

NUMBER 1 Catherine NOONE, and to vote **NUMBER 2 Richard BRUTON**,

☆ **FINE GAEL**	**BRUTON, Richard** (Fine Gael)		**2**
☆ **FINE GAEL**	**NOONE, Catherine** (Fine Gael)		**1**

Richard

Paschal

Minister Richard Bruton TD   **Minister Paschal Donohoe TD**

THIS IS AN OFFICIALLY AUTHORISED VOTER REQUEST ISSUED BY THE FINE GAEL
DIRECTOR OF ELECTIONS IN DUBLIN BAY NORTH.
For confirmation, please telephone Fine Gael HQ at 619 8444

FINE GAEL ⋆

As at previous elections, Fine Gael—this time rather half-heartedly—attempts a vote management exercise in Dublin Bay North. In fact, all 'recent opinion poll research' showed that the party had virtually no chance of winning two seats there, and this was borne out by the result

People Before Profit TD Gino Kenny urges voters to break the cycle

The majority of the Social Democrats' candidates and elected TDs were women, the only party for which this was the case

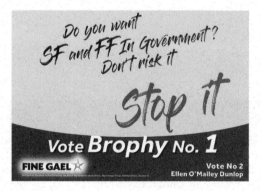

In Dublin SW, outgoing Fine Gael TD Colm Brophy identifies a coalition between the other two larger parties as a real and unwelcome possibility—one that a vote for him can help prevent

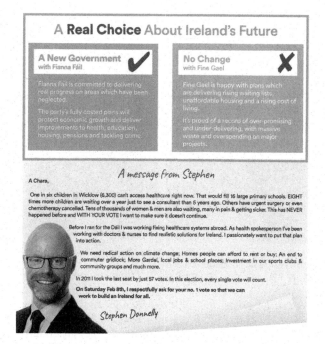

A **Real Choice** About Ireland's Future

A New Government ✔	No Change ✗
with Fianna Fáil	with Fine Gael
Fianna Fáil is committed to delivering real progress on areas which have been neglected.	Fine Gael is happy with plans which are delivering rising waiting lists, unaffordable housing and a rising cost of living.
The party's fully costed plans will protect economic growth and deliver improvements to health, education, housing, pensions and tackling crime.	It's proud of a record of over-promising and under-delivering, with massive waste and overspending on major projects.

A message from Stephen

A Chara,

One in six children in Wicklow (6,300) can't access healthcare right now. That would fill 16 large primary schools. EIGHT times more children are waiting over a year just to see a consultant than 5 years ago. Others have urgent surgery or even chemotherapy cancelled. Tens of thousands of women & men are also waiting, many in pain & getting sicker. This has NEVER happened before and WITH YOUR VOTE I want to make sure it doesn't continue.

Before I ran for the Dáil I was working fixing healthcare systems abroad. As health spokesperson I've been working with doctors & nurses to find realistic solutions for Ireland. I passionately want to put that plan into action.

We need radical action on climate change; Homes people can afford to rent or buy; An end to commuter gridlock; More Gardaí, local jobs & school places; Investment in our sports clubs & community groups and much more.

In 2011 I took the last seat by just 57 votes. In this election, every single vote will count.

On Saturday Feb 8th, I respectfully ask for your no. 1 vote so that we can work to build an Ireland for all.

Stephen Donnelly

Stephen Donnelly warns of the dire consequences of allowing Fine Gael to continue in office. After the election, he became a minister in the Fianna Fáil–Fine Gael–Green coalition government

Polling day arrives. The President casts his vote, as does his wife Sabina Higgins (*Irish Times*)

Tallymen—among them Minister for Communications, Climate Action and Environment Richard Bruton—examine and record the votes as they are counted in Dublin (*Irish Independent*)

Sorca Clarke celebrates with family and supporters as she is elected on the first count in Longford–Westmeath (Shelley Corcoran)

Rose Conway Walsh celebrates with her mother and supporters as she is elected on the first count in Mayo (Keith Heneghan and *Western People*)

On the final count in Dublin Bay South outgoing Fine Gael TD Kate O'Connell loses her seat, while her running mate Eoghan Murphy, with his actor brother Killian Scott on his right, reacts impassively to his own re-election. Jim O'Callaghan (FF), despite standing under the Exit sign, is also re-elected (*Irish Times*)

Social Democrats co-leader Róisín Shortall is congratulated upon her re-election in Dublin North-West to a seventh consecutive term in the Dáil, making her at that time the second longest-serving female TD in the history of the state (*Irish Times*)

Within weeks of the election, the Covid-19 pandemic begins to take over the news agenda and becomes the main issue facing the incumbent caretaker government. Taoiseach Leo Varadkar and Minister for Health Simon Harris make their way back towards Government Buildings (*Irish Independent*)

As dusk falls, Micheál Martin, accompanied by Dara Calleary and Michael McGrath, updates the media on the current state of play in the government formation process (*Irish Times*)

Leader Éamon Ryan speaks at a Green Party press conference. Listening intently is deputy leader Catherine Martin, who is challenging him for the leadership (*Irish Times*)

Party negotiators Simon Coveney (FG), Éamon Ryan (Grn, with bicycle) and Paschal Donohoe (FG) continue the discussions in the courtyard of Government Buildings (*Irish Times*)

After election day, the formation of a government took a further 20 weeks and involved many meetings between negotiating teams and party leaders. The Fianna Fáil team accompanies Micheál Martin to the meeting of party leaders on 14 June that put the final touches on the agreement; from left Anne Rabbitte, Darragh O'Brien, Thomas Byrne, Micheál Martin, Jack Chambers, Dara Calleary and Michael McGrath (*Irish Independent*)

Micheál Martin speaking on 26 June after Fianna Fáil members have voted heavily in favour of entering government, clearing the way for his election as Taoiseach on the following day (*Irish Independent*)

Micheál Martin waves to the media as he heads for his car to be driven to Áras an Uachtaráin to receive his seal of office from the President after his election as Taoiseach on 27 June in the Convention Centre (*Irish Times*)

Mary Lou McDonald walks to the Convention Centre for a sitting of the Dáil
(*Irish Independent*)

The new government, socially distanced, pose for the cameras in Dublin Castle, several ministers holding the seals of office with which they have just been presented by President Michael D. Higgins (Áras an Uachtaráin/Maxwell Photography)

Micheál Martin settles into his seat in the Taoiseach's office, over nine years after becoming leader of Fianna Fáil (*Irish Times*)

LIST OF FIGURES

LIST OF TABLES

The Road to the Election

Gary Murphy

THE END OF THE 32ND DÁIL AND THE CALLING OF THE ELECTION

In the early morning of Tuesday 14 January 2020, the Taoiseach Leo Varadkar informed the Fine Gael ministers of his minority government that their pre-cabinet meeting was cancelled. Since becoming Taoiseach in June 2017, Varadkar, like his predecessor Enda Kenny, had met with his party's ministers prior to the full cabinet meeting. On that morning, however, he told them that the cabinet would be meeting at 9 am instead of its normal time of 10:30.

The news of the cancellation sparked feverish speculation in political circles that Varadkar was set to go to Áras an Uachtaráin to advise President Michael D. Higgins to dissolve the Dáil and call the election. The 32nd Dáil was due to reconvene after its Christmas break on the following day. Varadkar had long let it be known that he had wanted a general election in the early summer of 2020 and had on numerous occasions publicly asked the Fianna Fáil leader Micheál Martin to agree to this. Martin had always refused. The confidence and supply arrangement through which Fianna

G. Murphy (✉)
Dublin City University, Dublin, Ireland
e-mail: Gary.Murphy@dcu.ie

© The Author(s), under exclusive license to Springer Nature Switzerland AG 2021
M. Gallagher et al. (eds.), *How Ireland Voted 2020*,
https://doi.org/10.1007/978-3-030-66405-3_1

1

Fáil had kept the Fine Gael-led minority government in office by agreeing to abstain on budgets and no confidence motions had been difficult for Martin and his party over the previous four years. In that context, he had no interest in agreeing to Varadkar's timetable although he was also personally in favour of a summer election.

The 32nd Dáil had its last sitting on Wednesday 18 December 2019 and it summed up perfectly the woes of Varadkar's minority government, which suffered three defeats in the last votes of the year on a smoky coal ban, pension protection legislation, and pay restoration for workers in not-for-profit disability service organisations. It was an ignominious end to the year for the Taoiseach. As he mulled his electoral options over the Christmas break, he realised that his hope for a summer election was threadbare. Fine Gael had not won any of the four by-elections held the previous month. Wins for the Greens in Dublin Fingal, Sinn Féin in Dublin Mid-West and Fianna Fáil in Cork North-Central and Wexford had strengthened the view of many within all three parties that they could make significant gains in an early election.

In early January, the independent TD for Cork South-West Michael Collins announced his intention to table a no confidence motion in the Minister for Health Simon Harris during his group's Dáil speaking time at the end of the month. Harris had already survived one no confidence motion tabled by Sinn Féin in February 2019 by 58 votes to 53 (with 37 abstentions) in response to the controversy surrounding the increasing costs of constructing the National Children's Hospital. A further problem for Varadkar was that he could no longer be sure that one of his own TDs, Maria Bailey, would vote confidence in Harris after the Fine Gael National Executive voted to deselect her as a candidate in the general election due to a controversial compensation claim she had lodged for a personal injury that she later withdrew (see Chap. 3, p. 51–2). Equally, Micheál Martin could not be sure that all his party TDs would abstain in any no confidence motion with the Kilkenny TD John McGuinness saying before Christmas that he would ignore the confidence and supply deal and vote against the government in any other motions. This was after he had reluctantly abstained, along with all other Fianna Fáil TDs, on a motion against the Minister for Housing, Eoghan Murphy, which was defeated by 56 votes to 53 with 35 abstentions on 3 December 2019.

Given all this political uncertainty, and not wanting to face another motion of no confidence in one of his ministers, Varadkar decided that there was no point in the Dáil reconvening where he would have to 'take several hours of grief' from opposition TDs.[1] He thus informed his cabinet colleagues that the 32nd Dáil would not be not sitting again and that the election for the 33rd Dáil would take place on Saturday 8 February 2020. He then went to brief the leaders of the opposition before addressing the media and the wider public at Government Buildings, where he said that it had been a privilege to serve the country and that a short campaign would let a new government swiftly tackle urgent issues. He lauded his government's record on Brexit, social equality, climate action, jobs and poverty reduction but admitted more needed to be done on a number of issues. Principal among these were housing and health, the two issues that had plagued the government since its formation.

He also extended a special word of thanks to 'the Independent Alliance and the independent ministers and TDs who contributed so much to our country by having the courage to join us in government when others would not.'[2] This was a significant nod to the fact that over a bruising four years in power the independent members of the government had proven themselves to be loyal and reliable members of the minority government, notwithstanding the constant taunts from the opposition that they were nothing but Fine Gael lackeys.

At 1:41 pm, Varadkar took to Twitter to express his hope that the Saturday vote, the first in the history of the Irish state, would cause less inconvenience to parents than a weekday, and make it easier for students and people working away from home to vote. Then in his familiar jaunty style, he declared, 'Next stop the Áras to see the President!'[3] The general election had officially begun.

PARTY COMPETITION UP TO 2016

The result of the February 2016 general election continued the effective sundering of the Irish party system that had begun five years earlier at the 2011 general election. Fianna Fáil, which had dominated the Irish state from when it first took office in 1932 to its collapse to only 17 per cent of the vote in 2011, had made a significant comeback in 2016, winning 44 seats on 24 per cent of the vote. This was still its second worst performance since it began fighting elections over 80 years earlier. As recently as the May 2007 general election, it had won 78 seats on 42 per cent of the vote.

Best described as a catch-all party since its foundation in 1926, Fianna Fáil hovered consistently at above 40 per cent of the vote at election time.

It had a chameleon-like ability to appeal to all social classes, both urban and rural.[4] Once it decided to break one of its core values and enter coalition in 1989 with the Progressive Democrats (PDs), it looked as if Fianna Fáil's centrist appeal could enable the party to govern in perpetuity. The PDs in 1989, 1997, 2002, and 2007, Labour in 1992, the Greens in 2007 had all been persuaded to enter government with Fianna Fáil, and it was also skilled at doing deals with independents. Such coalition-building was based on the assumption of Fianna Fáil polling in its normal 40 per cent range, thus giving it the possibility of choosing alternative coalition partners. After the party's brutal rejection by the electorate in 2011, this was no longer the case.

After its historic vote in 2011 when it won 76 seats on 36 per cent of the vote, Fine Gael's result in 2016 was very disappointing.[5] It is a party mainly of the centre-right with a reputation for being fiscally conservative and economically prudent, although it can also best be described as 'catch-all'.[6] Fine Gael had finished second in every election to Fianna Fáil from its foundation in 1933 until 2011. In 2016, after coalition with Labour it won 50 seats on 25 per cent of the vote, its reduced vote share and seats a direct result of governing during austerity. Still, this was the second election in a row where Fine Gael had won the most votes and most seats. As recently as 2002, it won a historically low 31 seats on just over 22 per cent of the vote and its long term future seemed in grave doubt, particularly as by accepting coalition Fianna Fáil opened itself up to alliances that were once the sole preserve of Fine Gael.

The other half of the 2011–16 government, Labour, was rebuffed by the electorate in even starker terms. It went from winning a historically high 37 seats in 2011 on 19 per cent of the vote to 7 seats on just under 7 per cent in 2016. Again, Labour's failure in 2016 was a direct consequence of governing during austerity. It had to face unmerciful attacks from Sinn Féin and the variety of small left-wing parties and independents over what they saw as a betrayal of Labour's promises in the 2011 campaign to limit austerity. Commonly seen as the half party in Ireland's traditional two and a half party system it went from winning the second largest number of votes and seats in 2011 to clinging to survival in 2016. It quickly changed its leader after the 2016 election, moving from Joan Burton to Brendan Howlin, who had been a TD since 1987 and was Minister for Public Expenditure and Reform in the 2011–16 government.

Sinn Féin received its highest ever vote in 2016, winning 23 seats on 14 per cent of the vote. There was some disappointment within the party that it did not do better given the continued weakness of Fianna Fáil and the collapse of the Labour vote. Sinn Féin's core policy of Irish unity had never played very well with the electorate in the Republic. Instead, it was its increasing focus on left-wing state-led solutions to health and housing that attracted people to it. After a calamitous period in government from 2007 to 2011, the Green party lost all six of its seats at the 2011 election. But its core issues of environmental sustainability and climate change were not going away and it regained two seats in 2016, enabling it at least to voice its policies from within the Dáil. This was crucial to its rebuilding project. Added to this electorally fluid cocktail were a variety of smaller left-wing groups such as the Anti-Austerity Alliance/People Before Profit, and Independents 4 Change, who had won six and four seats respectively in 2016, and the Social Democrats who were basically an offshoot of Labour and won three seats. Ireland has long been characterised by the numbers of independents who run for election and this trend continued in 2016. Twenty-one such independents formed the Independent Alliance in 2015 and they fought the election on a united if very loose set of principles. Six were elected and this group was central to government formation in 2016.[7]

THE NEW MINORITY GOVERNMENT 2016

The government elected in 2016 only had the support of the 50 Fine Gael TDs, 5 members of the Independent Alliance, and a small number of other independents, out of a Dáil of 158 TDs. It faced all sorts of complications due to its minority status. Just six weeks after the new government was formed it was faced with one of the greatest external shocks to ever hit the Irish state when Britain voted on 23 June 2016 to exit the European Union (EU), beginning the process known as Brexit. This cast a long shadow over Irish politics for the duration of the 32nd Dáil.[8] Another external complication came six months later with the collapse of the Northern Ireland Assembly in January 2017 over policy disagreements and trust issues between Sinn Féin and the Democratic Unionist Party (DUP). It took a full three years for the assembly to be restored, by which time Varadkar was on the verge of calling the election.

The closeness of the 2016 general election result inevitably made government formation very difficult. The fact that Fianna Fáil had got to within six seats of Fine Gael meant that it had a reasonable chance at forming a government if Micheál Martin could garner more votes than Enda

Kenny in the first vote for Taoiseach once the Dáil resumed on 10 March. But the fact that Martin had ruled out any form of agreement with Sinn Féin made this impracticable. Eventually on 3 May, after four weeks of tortuous negotiations, the parliamentary parties of Fine Gael and Fianna Fáil unanimously approved an 1800-word agreement by which Fianna Fáil facilitated Fine Gael in forming a government. Confidence and supply was born.

The deal, however, was incumbent on Fine Gael gaining the support of eight independents for its minority government. On 6 May, in a remarkable feat of political dexterity and resilience, Enda Kenny was able to persuade five of the six Independent Alliance TDs, two of the rural alliance (Denis Naughten and Michael Harty), and two others (Michael Lowry and Katherine Zappone) to support him as Taoiseach.[9] Seventy days after the election Kenny was elected Taoiseach by 59 votes to 49, with Fianna Fáil and some other independents abstaining.

The various independents had all stressed during these negotiations that they were interested in national issues and their support was not contingent on local deals. Given the historic nature of the minority government, no fewer than seven independents were rewarded with ministries of some sort, with Naughten, Ross, and Zappone becoming cabinet ministers. Ross was appointed Minister for Transport, Tourism, and Sport but he spent much of his time in office campaigning for the reopening of the Stepaside Garda station in his own constituency of Dublin Rathdown, and for the advancement of the Judicial Appointments Commission bill, which proposed to reform how judges are appointed. While the bill went through the Dáil, it was stalled in the Seanad for almost 18 months after a filibuster led by Independent Senator Michael McDowell, who repeatedly called elements of the legislation unconstitutional. While Fine Gael supported the bill in the Dáil, it was widely believed that many in the party were opposed to it but reluctantly voted in favour of it to keep Ross happy. Moreover, the Attorney General, Séamus Woulfe, was reported in March 2018 as saying that because of a variety of opposition amendments the bill had become a 'complete dog's dinner' and was most probably unconstitutional.[10] Eventually the Seanad voted to pass the bill in December 2019 but it lapsed when the election was called.

The rest of Kenny's cabinet was a conservative affair; he retained all his party's outgoing ministers who had been re-elected. He appointed Frances Fitzgerald as Tánaiste and kept Michael Noonan, although he was in poor health, as Minister for Finance. The two ministers most likely to pose leadership challenges in the future, Simon Coveney and Leo Varadkar, were given Housing, Planning and Local Government, and Social Protection respectively. Kenny appointed two 'super junior' ministers—these are ministers of state (often known as junior ministers), not full cabinet ministers, who are entitled to attend cabinet meetings—and increased the number of junior ministers from 15 to 18.

The new government had barely settled into office when the Brexit vote rocked it to its core. Kenny called an emergency meeting of his cabinet after which he reassured the public that contingency plans for dealing with the situation were well advanced and that Ireland's future lay in remaining a full and active member of the European Union. He later briefed the opposition leaders on those plans and then announced that the Dáil was to be recalled to discuss the impact of Brexit on Ireland. As it turned out Brexit was the glue that held the confidence and supply agreement together. Micheál Martin continually referred to the need to support the government during the Brexit negotiations. Even if at times he complained that the government was not moving quickly enough, he essentially agreed with the core thrust of its strategy. Martin's support for the government's Brexit position was such that in December of 2018 he announced that Fianna Fáil was extending the confidence and supply arrangement for a further twelve months noting that 'Brexit overshadows everything.'[11] According to one Fianna Fáil TD, Martin told that parliamentary meeting, 'he knows what is in the best interests of the party and the country.'[12] Ultimately, Martin decided Fianna Fáil's confidence and supply strategy. The consequences of this were far-reaching when the election was eventually called. Brexit fatigue had exhausted the electorate to such a degree that it was all but irrelevant as an issue come the campaign (see Chaps. 5 and 10).

NEW TAOISEACH, NEW GOVERNMENT

Enda Kenny's tenure as Taoiseach of the minority government lasted barely a year. On his re-election, he said that he would not lead Fine Gael into another election but would serve a full term. He soon found, however, that leading a minority government was much different to heading up the government with the largest majority in the history of the state, as had been his experience between 2011 and 2016. This was due partly to a variety of reforms the new Dáil initiated. Much focus was on the free vote to elect the Ceann Comhairle (speaker), which resulted in Fianna Fáil's

Seán Ó Fearghaíl taking the position. Of more fundamental importance was the decision to remove the Taoiseach's prerogative to set the Dáil's agenda by the establishment of a Business Committee, which was given responsibility for agreeing weekly agendas and planning sessional ones. Each party had one member on this committee, which meant that for the first time in the history of the state a government had lost control of the parliamentary agenda. Other important reforms were pre-legislative scrutiny and the allocation of committee chairs on the basis of proportionality.[13] The era of new politics had begun.

The problem, however, was that while all of these measures strengthened and opened up the business of the Dáil they caused severe difficulties for the government. As the Dáil progressed the government resorted to a sort of old politics and began using the 'money message' device to block a variety of opposition bills from becoming law even when they were not tax or spending bills.[14] This caused significant tensions between government and opposition, and by the time of the Dáil's last sitting over 50 opposition bills had been blocked by the government's use of this device.

There had been constant mutterings about Enda Kenny's leadership of Fine Gael since the disappointing general election results of 2016, but the Brexit crisis had to some extent unified the party. This unity cracked in February 2017 when Alan Farrell, a TD from Dublin Fingal, became the first of the party's TDs to publicly call for Kenny's resignation, stating that he no longer had confidence in the Taoiseach's ability to lead Fine Gael. The backdrop to this call for a change of leadership lay in a disagreement between Kenny and the Minister for Children, Katherine Zappone, as to whether they had a conversation about the Garda whistleblower Maurice McCabe. Kenny, in a live interview on RTÉ radio, stated that he did have a conversation with Zappone before a meeting she had had with Sergeant McCabe just two weeks earlier. It later transpired that this conversation did not happen, with Zappone insisting that she did not tell the Taoiseach about any meeting. This led to Kenny giving two differing accounts to the Dáil of the same incident. McCabe had exposed blatant corruption within the Gardaí in relation to the removal of penalty points from well-known figures for driving offences but had become the victim of a vicious smear campaign including vile and baseless allegations of sexual abuse. On 15 February 2017, Kenny issued an apology on behalf of the state to McCabe in the Dáil stating 'the false allegations against Sergeant Maurice McCabe are simply appalling … I therefore offer a full apology to Maurice McCabe and his family for the treatment meted out to them.'[15] Two days later a tribunal of inquiry, chaired by Justice Peter Charleton, was established to investigate protected disclosures and to report on matters dealing with the conduct of the Health Service Executive, the Child and Family Agency Tusla, RTÉ, Garda Headquarters, and various Garda officers concerning Sergeant McCabe.

Kenny's apology came in a debate on a confidence motion in the government in which it prevailed by 57 votes to 52 with 44 abstentions after Sinn Féin had initially tabled a motion of no confidence. But it was the beginning of the long process of Kenny's leaving. Two opinion polls in this period showed Fine Gael significantly behind Fianna Fáil by 11 and 8 points respectively, although two more taken the following week showed Fine Gael only 1 and 2 points behind (see Fig. 1.1).[16]

A week after winning that confidence motion Enda Kenny told his parliamentary party that he would deal with the question of his future 'effectively and decisively' after his St. Patrick's Day trip to the United States and that he had no time for deadlines and ultimatums.[17] While his brief speech was met with a standing ovation, the writing was on the wall for his leadership. Two months later, he declared that he was retiring as leader of Fine Gael effective from midnight on 17 May 2017 but would remain in a caretaker role until the Fine Gael leadership election concluded on 2

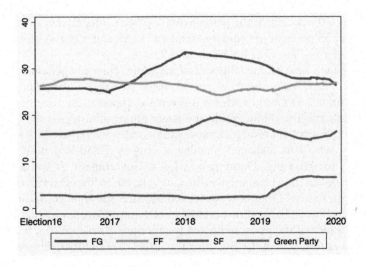

Fig. 1.1   Party support, as measured by opinion polls, 2016–20
Source: Supplied by Prof. Michael Marsh, Trinity College Dublin

June. He had been party leader for 15 years, Taoiseach for over 6 years, and was the only person to ever lead Fine Gael into government on 2 successive occasions.

The race to succeed Kenny as Fine Gael leader, and ultimately Taoiseach, was practically over before it had even begun. The two candidates, Simon Coveney and Leo Varadkar, faced an electoral college consisting of the members of the parliamentary party, councillors, and ordinary party members where 65 per cent of the votes were allocated to the parliamentary party, 25 per cent to ordinary members, and 10 per cent to Fine Gael's councillors. Within a day of the opening of the contest, Varadkar had received the support of five of his fellow cabinet ministers and over a dozen TDs, while Coveney only had the support of the Minister for Health, Simon Harris and a handful of TDs. The contest was as good as over given the weighting of the votes of the parliamentary party. Ultimately, Varadkar received the endorsement of 33 TDs and 11 senators compared to 10 and 8 for Coveney. Varadkar also had a lead in councillor endorsements of 108 to 65.[18] A series of four hustings of ordinary members took place around the country during which Coveney rather dramatically announced that the battle for the leadership was one for the soul of the party. Varadkar struck a more emollient tone safe in the knowledge that he had the leadership sewn up. While Coveney decisively won the membership vote, it was all in vain. Varadkar ultimately won the electoral college by a margin of 60–40, receiving 70 per cent of the parliamentary party's, 55 per cent of councillors', and 35 per cent of ordinary members' votes and was duly elected the 11th leader of Fine Gael on 2 June 2017.

Varadkar's new cabinet was a cautious affair. The only person dropped was the much-maligned Minister for Jobs, Enterprise and Innovation, Mary Mitchell O'Connor who was given the consolation prize of a non-voting place at the cabinet table as a super junior minister, as she became one of no fewer than four such super juniors. She was replaced by Eoghan Murphy, who had managed Varadkar's campaign and was now named Minister for Housing, Planning and Local Government. It was a fateful decision given the prominence housing played in the general election campaign. Paschal Donohoe was named Minister for Finance, adding it to his brief of Public Expenditure and Reform. Simon Coveney was appointed deputy leader of the party and given the foreign affairs ministry, where he played a crucial role in the Brexit negotiations over the following two and a half years.

Six months later Coveney was named Tánaiste (deputy prime minister) after Frances Fitzgerald on 28 November 2017 announced she was resigning as Minister for Business, Enterprise and Innovation in the national interest to prevent a general election. Fianna Fáil and Sinn Féin had placed no confidence motions in Fitzgerald in the Dáil on that very day. Fitzgerald had insisted that, when she was Minister for Justice, she was unaware of a legal strategy by former Garda commissioner Nóirín O'Sullivan in 2015 to question the integrity and credibility of Maurice McCabe at the O'Higgins commission, which was examining allegations of Garda malpractice. It then emerged that Fitzgerald had received three emails on two separate dates advising her of the approach being taken by the Garda Commissioner. This led Fianna Fáil to call for her resignation. Given the importance of Brexit, both Varadkar and Fitzgerald felt she had no choice but to resign as the alternative was a general election.

Fitzgerald's resignation came as the Brexit negotiations were at a critical stage. The British government was on the verge of reaching an agreement with the European Commission that aimed to prevent a hard border between the Republic of Ireland and Northern Ireland after Brexit. This was the so-called 'backstop', which required keeping Northern Ireland in some aspects of the EU's single market until an alternative arrangement was agreed between the Britain and the EU. The government remained in office, and the backstop was secured. The importance of the backstop for Ireland was reinforced by Donald Tusk, the President of the European Council, when he stated that 'Ireland's position will be the European Union's position.'[19] In a domestic context, Fine Gael gained significant political support once the backstop was announced. Government satisfaction at the end of 2017 was at 51 per cent while two opinion polls taken in February 2018 showed Fine Gael at 36 per cent, its highest during the course of the Dáil (see Fig. 1.2).[20]

Some ten months after the backstop was agreed, Justice Charleton's third interim report on 11 October 2018 did accept Fitzgerald's evidence that she had not wished to interfere in the O'Higgins proceedings as an honest appraisal of the situation and a considered response to the information she had available to her rather than a 'lazy dodging of the issues.'[21] While acknowledging that she had probably read the email that highlighted a row between the legal team for the Garda Commissioner and lawyers for Sergeant McCabe, Charleton stated that Fitzgerald and her department rightly did not attempt to direct the Garda commissioner as to how she should approach the O'Higgins Commission. Ultimately, the

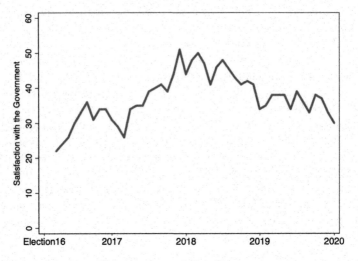

Fig. 1.2 Satisfaction with government, 2016–20
Source: Supplied by Prof. Michael Marsh, Trinity College Dublin

tribunal was satisfied that the Minister and the Garda Commissioner did not speak about the matter. Charleton also fully exonerated McCabe, noting that what had been unnerving about more than 100 days of the tribunal was 'that a person who stood up for better standards in the national police force, Sergeant Maurice McCabe, and who exemplified hard work in his own calling, was repulsively denigrated for being no more than a good citizen and police officer.'[22]

OF ELECTIONS AND REFERENDUMS

One of the earliest decisions taken by the government was to hold a Citizens' Assembly. The Dáil resolution establishing the Assembly gave it five items to consider: abortion, the challenges and opportunities of an ageing population, fixed-term parliaments, the manner in which referendums are held, and how the state can make Ireland a leader in tackling climate change.[23] The Assembly consisted of 99 citizens selected at random by a market research company, and an independent chair, the supreme court justice, Mary Laffoy. Katherine Zappone had insisted on abortion being one of the Assembly's issues in return for supporting Enda Kenny as Taoiseach.[24] The other four were somewhat more eclectic.

Given that there had been no fewer than five referendums on abortion since the passage in 1983 of the eighth amendment (which was intended by its proponents to prevent any future legalisation of abortion), there was much interest in how the Assembly would deal with the issue. In total, it met for nine and half days to discuss abortion and received some 12,200 submissions. In April 2017, it caused some surprise by recommending that abortion should be permitted in the state in a wide range of circumstances including socio-economic ones.[25] There was criticism by various conservative groups that the assembly members were not representative of the general population, but the result of the referendum 13 months later suggested otherwise. An exit poll taken on the day of the referendum, 25 May 2018, found that 66 per cent of voters were aware of the Citizens' Assembly and that around 70 per cent could answer specific questions as to its operation.[26] After the Assembly had reported, an Oireachtas committee was established to consider its recommendations and report to the government. In December 2017, the committee recommended that a straightforward repeal of the eighth amendment was preferable to the Assembly's option of replacing it with an alternative wording. Three of its members, Peter Fitzpatrick—who later resigned from Fine Gael over this issue—Mattie McGrath, and Rónán Mullen, both independents, were resolutely against any change to the amendment and issued their own minority report advocating that the amendment be retained in the constitution.[27]

On 29 January 2018, Leo Varadkar announced that, on the advice of the Attorney General, the government was proposing a referendum to repeal and replace the eighth amendment with an enabling provision. While there was overwhelming support in Fine Gael for repealing the amendment, there was much division in Fianna Fáil. Ten days before Varadkar's announcement Micheál Martin told the Dáil that while he was instinctively on the pro-life side of the abortion debate he had been influenced by expert opinion and by the deliberations of both the Citizens' Assembly and the committee on the eighth amendment and would be voting to repeal the amendment in any referendum.[28] This caused some consternation within Fianna Fáil and ultimately over half its parliamentary party stated they were voting against the proposal, although the party took no collective position. On Friday 25 May 2018, over two thirds of voters opted to repeal the eighth amendment, thus making possible the introduction of legalised abortion.

One consequence of the referendum was that it led to the founding of a new political party. Sinn Féin's Peadar Tóibín had been one of the most prominent opponents of the proposal and was suspended from the parliamentary party for six months in October 2018 after he defied the party whip by voting against the Regulation of Termination of Pregnancy Bill 2018, which gave legislative effect to the referendum result. He then left Sinn Féin and in January 2019 announced he was establishing a new party called Aontú which would contest the forthcoming local elections on a republican and socially conservative platform.

Tóibín had been a thorn in the side of Mary Lou McDonald, who had been elected president of Sinn Féin in February 2018, replacing Gerry Adams. One of McDonald's first major decisions was to decide whether or not Sinn Féin would run a candidate in the presidential election due in October. In July, after some internal discussion, the party announced that it was opposing the incumbent Michael D. Higgins in order that young voters could have a say in who their president should be. The popular Higgins had announced earlier that month that he was seeking re-election. He showed a nimble dexterity in getting out of his original promise to serve only a single term by declaring that, while he did at one stage say getting through one term was the length of his aspirations, he now wanted to build on the foundations of his seven years in office. Higgins's announcement was greeted with approval by the other main parties. Two months later Sinn Féin nominated its Ireland South MEP Liadh Ní Riada, to oppose him. Four other candidates, the independents Peter Casey, Gavin Duffy, Joan Freeman, and Seán Gallagher, made their way on to the ballot by gaining the support of four county or city councils.

Given the widespread popularity of Higgins the campaign was extremely dull until Casey made some incendiary comments about Travellers, arguing that they should not be recognised as an ethnic minority and were 'basically people camping in someone else's land.'[29] These comments generated a welter of publicity for Casey but in the last poll of the campaign, five days before the election, he was at 2 per cent, compared to 12 for Gallagher and a massive 68 for Higgins. As it turned out Casey's comments did have some impact and he caused a huge surprise by receiving 23 per cent of the vote on election day, putting him comfortably in second place behind Higgins who was elected on the first count having received 56 per cent. The turnout at just 43 per cent was the lowest for a presidential election in the history of the state. Politically, the result was disastrous for Sinn Féin; in McDonald's first electoral test as leader, the party had received a paltry 6 per cent. It was an inauspicious beginning and things were to get worse.

In the middle of the presidential campaign the Minister for Communications, Climate Action, and the Environment, the independent TD Denis Naughten, resigned after it was revealed that he had held a series of private dinners with the lead bidder for the National Broadband Plan, David McCourt. Naughten's department was overseeing the tender for the plan. While Naughten's resignation caught the opposition unawares, it was no secret to the Taoiseach, as Naughten in his resignation speech to the Dáil stated that Varadkar 'had asked me to reflect on my position.'[30] For his part, Varadkar said that he had no doubt that Naughten's intentions were honourable, but that he left himself open to allegations of a conflict of interest. And so Naughten fell on his political sword while protesting that he had not interfered in the tender process.

Five successive opinion polls in the two months between the start of January and the first week of March 2019 showed Fine Gael polling over 30 per cent and between 4 and 10 points ahead of Fianna Fáil, and 10 and 19 points ahead of Sinn Féin (see Fig. 1.1).[31] One worrying factor, however, was that satisfaction with the government in this period was between 34 and 38 per cent (see Fig. 1.2), the lowest since Varadkar had become Taoiseach. This pattern held relatively steady until the local and European elections held on 24 May. As there was wide political acceptance that at best the general election was only a year and away and could possibly happen much sooner, these elections were widely seen as a barometer of how the general election might potentially go.

In the local elections turnout was just 50 per cent, the joint lowest in the history of the state (see Table 1.1). As usual, the contest revolved around a mixture of local and national issues and saw Fianna Fáil and Fine Gael consolidate their positions as the two dominant parties in Irish local government. Fine Gael's opinion poll lead did not manifest itself at the local elections where Fianna Fáil won 27 per cent of the vote and Fine Gael 25. Sinn Féin won just under 10 per cent of the vote and lost half of its seats falling from 159 to 81. No other party received over 6 per cent and a plethora of independents were elected.[32]

Things were even worse for Sinn Féin in the European elections where it lost two of its three seats (see Table 1.2). Fine Gael was the big winner of the election, taking 5 of the 13 available seats on 30 per cent of the vote. In contrast, Fianna Fáil saw its overall share of the vote drop to just 17 per cent but it did manage to win 2 seats, as did the Greens and the

Table 1.1   Local election results, May 2019

Party	Seats	Change since 2014	First preference votes	First preference percentage	Change since 2014
Fianna Fáil	279	+12	467,407	26.9	+1.7
Fine Gael	255	+20	438,494	25.2	+1.3
Sinn Féin	81	-78	164,367	9.5	-5.7
Labour	57	+6	99,500	5.7	+1.4
Greens	49	+37	96,315	5.6	+4.0
Social Democrats	19	NA	39,644	2.3	NA
People Before Profit	7	-7	21,972	1.3	-0.4
Solidarity	4	-10	10,911	0.6	-0.6
Aontú	3	NA	25,660	1.5	NA
Independents 4 Change	3	NA	8626	0.5	NA
Independents	185	-7	339,246	19.5	-3.2
Others	7	+2	21,781	1.4	+0.9
Total	949		1,736,139	100.0	

Source: Quinlivan, 'The 2019 local elections' (see note 32)

Note: the election was held on Friday 24 May. 'Others' refer to Independent Left, Irish Democratic Party, Kerry Independent Alliance, Renua, Republican Sinn Féin, United Left, Workers' Party, Workers and Unemployed Action, all of whom won one seat. Various named other groupings were also on ballots across the state but failed to have any candidates elected

left-wing 'Independents 4 Change.' The final seat went to the independent Luke 'Ming' Flanagan, who retained his seat in Midlands North–West.[33] Perhaps the most important thing to note arising out of both elections was that they showed particularly high levels of volatility, in that only half of all voters chose the same party in the two different ballots, which underlined the increasingly shallow nature of party loyalties amongst the Irish electorate.[34]

THE GOVERNMENT'S RECORD: AN OVERVIEW

One consequence of the elections of four TDs (Clare Daly, Frances Fitzgerald, Billy Kelleher, and Mick Wallace) to the European Parliament was a series of by-elections scheduled for November to replace them in the Dáil. Here Varadkar faced an important decision. He could let the by-elections go ahead, with the likelihood that Fine Gael could well fail to

Table 1.2 European Parliament election results, May 2019

Party	Seats	Change since 2014	First preference votes	First preference percentage	Change since 2014
Fianna Fáil	2	+1	277,705	16.5	-5.8
Fine Gael	5	+1	496,459	29.6	+7.3
Sinn Féin	1	-2	196,001	11.7	-7.8
Greens	2	+2	190,755	11.4	+6.5
Labour	0	0	52,743	3.1	-2.2
Inds 4 Change	2	+2	124,085	7.4	+7.4
Solidarity–PBP	0	0	38,771	2.3	-1.0
Social Democrats	0	0	20,331	1.2	+1.2
Independents	1	-2	264,087	15.7	-4.1
Others	0	0	17,056	1.0	-1.5
Total	13	+2	1,678,003	100.0	0

Source: Johnston, 'The 2019 European Parliament elections' (see note 33)

Note: Others refer to Direct Democracy, Identity Ireland, Renua, and Workers' Party, all of whom ran candidates

win any of them, or he could call a general election. As always, Brexit weighed heavily on his mind, as did the continuing lack of an executive in Northern Ireland. Varadkar was not even Taoiseach when the executive had collapsed in January 2017 and multiple efforts to get it back up and running had all failed. Opinion polls between June and November showed Fine Gael support holding steady in the high 20s, a couple of points ahead of Fianna Fáil and anywhere between 10 and 20 points ahead of Sinn Féin (see Fig. 1.1). Mary Lou McDonald had presided over three disastrous elections in a row for Sinn Féin and she had been criticised by some of her own TDs for being a weak leader and for being too tolerant of underperforming colleagues.[35] But Varadkar, who had always been anxious to have an election in the summer, decided to wait and the by-elections went ahead on 29 November. That decision gave Sinn Féin a huge boost, as Dublin Mid-West was a constituency in which it had a superb organisation under the direction of its sitting TD, Eoin Ó Broin. Sinn Féin duly won the seat, giving McDonald a badly needed electoral fillip. Wins in the other contests for the Greens and Fianna Fáil meant that all three opposition parties could look forward to a general election in the new year with a certain degree of confidence. The same could not be said for Fine Gael.

Not only had it lost all four by-elections but also government satisfaction was at just 33 per cent as 2019 ended (see Fig. 1.2).

In one way, Fine Gael had a positive story to tell the electorate. It was generally seen as having performed well in relation to Brexit, and in power it had presided over a surging economy with record numbers in employment. A total of 2,361,200 people were in employment at the end of 2019, up 79,900 and 3.5 per cent on the previous year. The unemployment rate at the end of 2019 was 4.7 per cent, down from 8.4 per cent when the government took office.[36] Its economic growth rates were equally strong. Since Varadkar had become Taoiseach, (modified) Gross National Income had risen, year on year, by over 6 per cent in 2017, 7 per cent in 2018 and by 3 per cent in 2019.[37]

Health and housing, however, remained persistent difficulties that the government could not overcome. In health, the perennial issues of waiting lists for appointments and procedures, and the numbers of hospital patients on trolleys, continued to plague the government. The Department of Health's key trends report for 2019 showed that the 30-day moving average for admitted patients waiting on trolleys in emergency departments was significantly higher than in previous years. At over 300 by the end of 2019, it was twice what it had been when the government took office.[38] Over 150,000 people were on waiting lists for outpatient appointments for over a year in public hospitals in December 2019, and the total number was more than 550,000. The numbers when the government took office were just over 60,000 waiting over a year and slightly less than 450,000 in total.[39]

The government's difficulties in housing were twofold. At one level, it failed to stem record levels of homelessness while at another a whole generation of people felt themselves priced out of ever getting on the housing ladder even as they paid record levels of rent that rose by 8 per cent from 2018 to 2019. House prices also rose across the state throughout the government's period in office, though there was a slight fall off in 2019. The average cost of a property on the eve of the election was €250,766; in Dublin, the figure was €366,153, while in south county Dublin, it was €566,776.[40] When the government took office, there were 3993 homeless adults in the state, 1054 homeless families and 2177 dependents in those families. By the time the Dáil ended the figures had grown to 6697 homeless adults, 1611 families and 3574 dependents.[41] In July 2016 in launching the government's action plan for housing and homelessness, *Rebuilding Ireland*, the Minister for Housing, Planning and Local Government

Simon Coveney pledged that by the summer of 2018 no families would be living in emergency accommodation. Yet by December 2019, the then minister, Eoghan Murphy faced a vote of no confidence due to the ever increasing homeless numbers. By that time, satisfaction with the government had fallen to 30 per cent.

On 1 January 2020, the government unilaterally announced plans to commemorate those who served in the Royal Irish Constabulary and the Dublin Metropolitan Police prior to independence. The announcement by-passed the agreed procedures for getting all-party agreement before taking any such steps and backfired spectacularly when the government was forced to cancel the event just a week later. It had come under sustained pressure from a number of opposition politicians over its hosting of the event after the Fianna Fáil mayor of Clare, Cathal Crowe, declared he would not attend. Micheál Martin described the commemoration as an 'error in judgement' while Mary Lou McDonald said it 'should be cancelled.'[42] The story, which might normally have been seen as rather insignificant in the political sphere, gained wide traction on the cusp of the calling of the election and seemed to have a galvanising effect on Sinn Féin in particular. Ireland's main online news media outlet *The Journal.ie* saw readership figures well over three times the norm with over 170,000 people reading the story of the event's cancellation, up from an average of 49,000 for other political stories.[43] A poll published a week after the calling of the election showed that 73 per cent of respondents disagreed with the government's proposal with 97 per cent of Sinn Féin supporters and 90 per cent of Fianna Fáil supporters against it. Another poll published just days before voting showed that 68 per cent of people thought the government was right to cancel the event.[44] This symbolised what was clearly a significant shift away from the government as the campaign began.

In calling the election, Varadkar's plan was to run on how his government had overseen the economy and the Brexit negotiations. Fianna Fáil hoped to portray itself as the agent of change and continued with its 'Ireland for All' slogan from 2016. Sinn Féin painted Fine Gael and Fianna Fáil as basically the same and argued that it was the only party that could build an alternative Ireland. The Green Party was confident it could build on its positive results in the local and European elections. For the other political parties and independents, it was simply a matter of survival.

NOTES

1. Daniel McConnell, 'General election to take place on February 8; President dissolves 32nd Dáil', *Irish Examiner* 15 January 2020.
2. https://twitter.com/LeoVaradkar/status/1217134722591154177.
3. https://twitter.com/LeoVaradkar/status/1217079356763332609.
4. Gary Murphy, *Electoral Competition in Ireland since 1987: the politics of triumph and despair* (Manchester: Manchester University Press, 2016), pp. 103–5.
5. For a full account of this election, see the previous book in this series: Michael Gallagher and Michael Marsh (eds), *How Ireland Voted 2016: the election that nobody won* (Cham: Palgrave Macmillan, 2016).
6. Liam Weeks, 'Parties and the party system', pp. 111–36 in John Coakley and Michael Gallagher (eds), *Politics in the Republic of Ireland*, 6th ed. (Abingdon: Routledge, 2018), p. 116.
7. Liam Weeks, *Independents in Irish Party Democracy* (Manchester: Manchester University Press, 2017), p. 51.
8. See Mary C. Murphy's Chap. 5 in this book, and the same author's 'The Brexit crisis, Ireland and British–Irish relations: Europeanisation and/or de-Europeanisation?', *Irish Political Studies* 34:4 (2019), pp. 530–50.
9. Weeks, *Independents in Irish Party Democracy*, p. 227.
10. Fiach Kelly, 'Shane Ross's judges Bill a "dog's dinner"', claims Attorney General', *Irish Times* 24 March 2018.
11. Kevin Doyle and Wayne O'Connor, 'Fianna Fáil guarantees no election in 2019 amid Brexit uncertainty as it extends confidence and supply arrangement', *Irish Independent* 13 December 2018.
12. Fiach Kelly, 'Varadkar and Martin discuss confidence and supply extension', *Irish Times* 12 December 2018.
13. Catherine Lynch, Eoin O'Malley, Theresa Reidy, David M. Farrell and Jane Suiter, 'Dáil reforms since 2011: pathway to power for the "puny" parliament?', *Administration* 65:2 (2017), pp. 37–57, at pp. 51, 55.
14. Under Article 17.2 of the constitution, no law entailing the spending of public money shall be enacted unless the purpose of such expenditure has been recommended to the Dáil by the government in a message signed by the Taoiseach.
15. The full debate including Kenny's apology is on the Oireachtas website at https://www.oireachtas.ie/ga/debates/debate/dail/2017-02-15/29/. For a fast paced account of this period see Gavan Reilly, *Enda the Road: nine days that toppled a Taoiseach* (Cork: Mercier Press, 2019). On Maurice McCabe see Michael Clifford, *A Force for Justice: the Maurice McCabe story* (Dublin: Hachette Ireland, 2017).

16. The polls by Behaviour and Attitudes, RED C and IPSOS MRBI had Fianna Fáil between 26 and 33 per cent and Fine Gael between 21 and 28 per cent.
17. Reilly, *Enda the Road*, p. 292.
18. A comprehensive tracker of endorsements was provided by Fiach Kelly in the *Irish Times* and can be seen at https://www.irishtimes.com/news/politics/fg-leadership-race.
19. Nicholas Rees and John O'Brennan, 'The dual crisis in Irish foreign policy: the economic crash and Brexit in a volatile European landscape', *Irish Political Studies* 34:4 (2019), pp. 595–614, at p. 604.
20. Both Behaviour and Attitudes for the *Sunday Times* and Millward Brown for the *Sunday Independent* on 18 February 2018 gave Fine Gael 36 per cent.
21. Mr Justice Peter Charleton, *Third interim report of the tribunal of inquiry into protected disclosures made under the Protected Disclosures Act 2014 and certain other matters* (Dublin: Stationery Office, 2018), p. 165.
22. Charleton, *Tribunal of Inquiry*, p. 330.
23. David M. Farrell, Jane Suiter and Clodagh Harris, '"Systematizing" constitutional deliberation: the 2016–18 citizens' assembly in Ireland', *Irish Political Studies* 34:1 (2019), pp. 113–23, at p. 114. Details of the assembly with recordings from its sessions are at www.citizensassembly.ie.
24. Eoin O'Malley, '70 Days: government formation in 2016', pp. 255–76 in Michael Gallagher and Michael Marsh (eds), *How Ireland Voted 2016: the election that nobody won* (Cham: Palgrave Macmillan, 2016), p. 270.
25. Luke Field, 'The abortion referendum of 2018 and a timeline of abortion politics in Ireland to date', *Irish Political Studies* 33:4 (2018), pp. 608–28, at pp. 614–7.
26. Jane Suiter and Theresa Reidy, 'Does deliberation help deliver informed electorates: evidence from Irish referendum votes', *Representation* 56:4 (2020) pp. 539–57, at p. 543. see also Johan A. Elkink, David M. Farrell, Sofie Marien, Theresa Reidy and Jane Suiter, 'The death of conservative Ireland? The 2018 abortion referendum', *Electoral Studies* 65:3 (2020).
27. The committee's report is at https://www.oireachtas.ie/en/committees/32/eighth-amendment-constitution/. The minority report is at https://www.ronanmullen.ie/wp-content/uploads/2017/12/Joint-Assessment-by-Fitzpatrick-McGrath-and-Mullen-on-the-Committee-of-the-8th-Amendment.pdf.
28. See Martin's tweet https://twitter.com/MichealMartinTD/status/954039065648750593 where he stated that while he was conscious that not everyone would agree with him it was his 'honest view of what I think is the right thing to do'.

29. Alan Duggan, 'Irish presidential election 2018', *Irish Political Studies* 34:2 (2019), pp. 303–14, at p. 310.
30. Marie O'Halloran, 'Surprise gives way to anger in Dáil as Denis Naughten resigns', *Irish Times* 12 October 2018.
31. The polls by Behaviour and Attitudes, Red C, and IPSOS MRBI had Fine Gael between 30 and 32 per cent, Fianna Fáil between 22 and 26 per cent and Sinn Féin between 13 and 21 per cent.
32. Aodh Quinlivan, 'The 2019 local elections in the Republic of Ireland', *Irish Political Studies* 35:1 (2020), pp. 46–60.
33. Samuel A. T. Johnston, 'The 2019 European Parliament elections in Ireland', *Irish Political Studies* 35:1 (2020), pp. 18–28.
34. Michael Marsh, 'The unfaithful Irish voter', *Irish Political Studies* 34:3 (2019), pp. 350–6, at pp. 351, 355.
35. Daniel McConnell, 'Sinn Féin leader McDonald is weak, say rebellious TDs', *Irish Examiner* 17 June 2019.
36. See the Central Statistics Office Labour Force Survey 2019 quarter four at https://www.cso.ie/en/csolatestnews/pressreleases/2020pressreleases/pressstatementlabourforcesurveyq42019/.
37. See the quarterly national accounts from the Central Statistics Office at https://www.cso.ie/en/statistics/nationalaccounts/quarterlynationalaccounts/. I am grateful to Prof Stephen Kinsella of the University of Limerick for his help with this section.
38. See the Department of Health's report: 'Health in Ireland: Key Trends 2019', p. 42. Available at https://www.gov.ie/en/publication/f1bb64-health-in-ireland-key-trends-2019/.
39. Ibid., p. 41. For the 2016 figures, see https://www.gov.ie/en/publication/ede848-health-in-ireland-key-trends-2016/ at p. 38.
40. Cliff Taylor, 'House prices in Ireland decline for first time since 2012', *Irish Times* 30 December 2019.
41. Homelessness figures are available at https://www.housing.gov.ie/housing/homelessness/other/homelessness-data.
42. See https://www.thejournal.ie/ric-cancelled-4956894-Jan2020/.
43. I am grateful to Sinéad O'Carroll, editor of *TheJournal.ie* for providing me with the figures for readership of this story.
44. See https://twitter.com/ireland_thinks/status/1220031442362814466 and Ronan McGreevy, 'Strong support for decision to postpone RIC/DMP commemoration', *Irish Times* 5 February 2020.

CHAPTER 2

Election Pledge Fulfilment Under Minority Government

Rory Costello, Alice Sheridan, and Duncan Casey

The fulfilment of election pledges by governing parties occupies an important place in standard accounts of representative democracy. By setting out their policy commitments in an election campaign, parties make it possible for voters to have their say on how the country should be run. If parties that enter government go on to deliver on these commitments, a clear link between the election outcome and government policy is established.

However, it will come as no surprise to learn that election pledges often go unfulfilled. One factor that can affect pledge fulfilment is a change in circumstances after an election. For example, the coronavirus pandemic that reached Ireland in late February 2020, creating a public health and economic crisis, rendered many of the pledges made for the election earlier that month redundant. Similarly, many pledges made prior to the

The authors are very grateful for the excellent research assistance provided by Frank Fitzgerald and Jadene Davis.

R. Costello (✉) • A. Sheridan • D. Casey
University of Limerick, Limerick, Ireland
e-mail: Rory.Costello@ul.ie

© The Author(s), under exclusive license to Springer Nature Switzerland AG 2021
M. Gallagher et al. (eds.), *How Ireland Voted 2020*,
https://doi.org/10.1007/978-3-030-66405-3_2

23

2007 election became obsolete once the financial crisis struck the following year, and very few were ultimately fulfilled (see Fig. 2.1 below).[1]

The government that was in power between 2016 and 2020 did not face any unexpected changes in circumstances on this scale. The shock result in the Brexit referendum, just two months after the formation of the government, certainly represented a significant challenge that was to occupy the government throughout its term. However, the impacts of Brexit were for the most part anticipated rather than realised during this period (see Chap. 5). Crucially, there was no economic downturn: the economy grew strongly throughout the period as the country continued its recovery from the great recession (see p. 18 above). External conditions should not therefore have been a major obstacle for the government in terms of fulfilling election pledges.

The need to compromise with other parties is another factor that can impede pledge fulfilment. When no party wins a majority of seats, government involves compromise between parties, whether this is in a coalition or—as was the case in the 2016–2020 period—in a minority government relying on support from the opposition. Arguably, the level of compromise required is higher when two parties form a coalition than when one party governs alone with the support of an opposition party. In the former case, both parties will be expected by voters to deliver on their election promises. In contrast, a party that supports a minority government from the outside will be under less pressure to deliver on its promises, reducing the need for compromise between the parties.[2] Furthermore, coalition governments share out cabinet seats among the different parties, further limiting the ability of one party to dominate, while single party minority governments do not.

Comparative research confirms that pledges made by parties that govern alone—even if as a minority government—are significantly more likely to be fulfilled than pledges made by parties that enter a coalition.[3] Controlling for other factors (such as the state of the economy and the duration of government), a pledge made by a party that forms a minority government on its own is found to have on average an 80 per cent likelihood of fulfilment, compared to around 60 per cent for pledges made by parties in coalition governments.

However, as minority governments go, the Fine Gael-led government that formed in 2016 was in a relatively weak position. Fine Gael held only 50 out of 158 Dáil seats. It was a single-party government insofar as there was only one party in government, but Fine Gael did have to share power with a number of independent TDs, who initially held three out of the 15 cabinet seats (dropping to two in 2018). The confidence and supply arrangement with Fianna Fáil meant that the government would not be defeated on key votes such as budgets and no-confidence motions, but on other issues there was no guarantee of success. For these reasons, we should not expect Fine Gael's record of pledge fulfilment to be as high as has been observed for single-party minority governments in other countries. In this chapter, we assess this by conducting a comprehensive analysis of the fulfilment of Fine Gael's election pledges.

We also examine the fulfilment of pledges made by Fianna Fáil. The party was not in government, so it did not contribute to the programme for government or take any ministerial seats. At the same time, it was in a position to influence government policy because the government relied upon its support through the confidence and supply arrangement. The confidence and supply deal also included a number of policy commitments agreed between Fianna Fáil and Fine Gael. Upon signing this deal, Fianna Fáil finance spokesperson Michael McGrath claimed that 'never again will an opposition party have as much influence as Fianna Fáil will in the current Dáil'.[4] We test this claim by comparing Fianna Fáil's election pledge fulfilment record with that of opposition parties in previous governments.

Given the continuing fragmentation of the Irish party system, minority governments and confidence and supply arrangements may become more common. The government of the 32nd Dáil represents an important test case for understanding the influence of both government and opposition parties on the policy agenda under these circumstances.

Measuring Election Pledge Fulfilment

We focus on pledges set out in Fine Gael's and Fianna Fáil's 2016 election manifestos. Other parties, the largest of which was Sinn Féin, may also have been in a position to influence policy and fulfil some of their election pledges, but examining this is beyond the scope of the current study. Identifying what is a pledge is not always straightforward, as manifestos are not a simple list of concrete election pledges. They tend to be very lengthy documents: Fine Gael's manifesto was over 61,000 words long (almost the same length as James Joyce's *Dubliners*—although the similarities end there). Fianna Fáil's manifesto was somewhat shorter, at just over 41,000 words. Manifestos include a mix of general aspirations, criticisms of other parties, details of past policy successes, as well as statements that can be taken as clear policy commitments (often repeated multiple times throughout the document).

In line with previous research, we use a relatively narrow definition of what counts as a pledge. First, it must be a statement of unconditional support for something: in other words, we exclude statements that have caveats such as 'if conditions allow' or 'if possible'. Second, it must refer to a specific action or outcome. So, a statement to 'reform criminal sentencing' is not a specific pledge, while the statement 'introduce mandatory sentencing for violent crimes' is. Third, the statement must be testable. Some statements that at first sight appear to be testable turn out not to be, because the evidence that would be needed to evaluate them is not available. For example, Fianna Fáil set a target for 'an annual 10% increase in e-transactions over the course of the next government'. Upon investigation, we found that no annual figures for e-transactions were available, so the pledge could not be tested. We also disregarded pledges that referred to an implementation period that went beyond the immediate government period. For example, Fianna Fáil set a goal of reducing smoking to five per cent of adults by 2025, which meant that the party did not envisage achieving it during the period of the 32nd Dáil. We count each commitment only once, even if it is made multiple times throughout the manifesto.

In total, we identified 390 Fine Gael pledges and 239 Fianna Fáil pledges. This repeats the pattern from 2011, in that Fine Gael made a substantially higher number of pledges than Fianna Fáil.[5] For each of these pledges, we assessed whether it was fully fulfilled, partially fulfilled or not fulfilled by the time of the 2020 election. Partially fulfilled means that there was policy change in line with the pledge, but either it did not go as far as what was promised, or it did not occur by the date specified in the manifesto. We examined a wide range of sources in order to collect the evidence required to make an assessment on fulfilment for each pledge. Dáil records were a particularly useful source of information, as ministers are regularly questioned on specific aspects of policy and are obliged to respond with detailed information. Other sources included annual budgets, newspaper reports, press releases and reports from government departments, and information from official bodies such as the Central Statistics Office.

In addition to measuring pledge fulfilment, we also looked at a number of other aspects of the pledges. We looked at the relationship between pledges made by Fine Gael and Fianna Fáil, because agreement between parties has been shown to be one of the best predictors of pledge fulfilment. We examined the relationship between the pledges of both parties and the confidence and supply deal that the parties signed up to. For Fine Gael pledges, we also examined whether each pledge was included in the programme for government that was drawn up by Fine Gael and the independent members of government, and we also studied the manifesto costings carried out by government departments in advance of the election.

OVERALL PLEDGE FULFILMENT RATES

Table 2.1 provides the headline findings on pledge fulfilment. Both parties' manifestos included an executive summary highlighting their key pledges, so here we distinguish between these key pledges and other pledges. As expected, a considerably higher percentage of Fine Gael pledges were fulfilled compared to Fianna Fáil pledges. A clear majority (64 per cent) of Fine Gael pledges were at least partially fulfilled. Of the 20 key pledges made by Fine Gael, nearly all (18 out of 20, or 90 per cent) were at least partially fulfilled. These include pledges to reduce unemployment to under six per cent, to balance the budget, and to increase the minimum wage to €10.50 per hour (the latter was partially fulfilled, as it was increased to €10.10 per hour). The two key pledges that were not fulfilled were the commitments to abolish the Universal Social Charge (USC, a tax introduced to raise revenue following the economic crash of

Table 2.1 Pledge fulfilment 2016–2020

	Fine Gael			Fianna Fáil		
	Key	Other	Total	Key	Other	Total
Fulfilled	5	154	159	16	48	64
	(25%)	(42%)	(41%)	(40%)	(24%)	(27%)
Partially fulfilled	13	79	92	10	40	50
	(65%)	(21%)	(24%)	(25%)	(20%)	(21%)
Not fulfilled	2	137	139	14	111	125
	(10%)	(37%)	(36%)	(35%)	(56%)	(52%)
Total	20	370	390	40	199	239
	(100%)	(100%)	(100%)	(100%)	(100%)	(100%)

Note: 'Key' pledges are those that are listed in the summary at the beginning of the manifesto

2008) and to double the number of apprenticeships. The rate of fulfilment for other Fine Gael pledges was lower, but still a majority of these were fulfilled or partially fulfilled.

Just under half (48 per cent) of all Fianna Fáil pledges were partially or fully fulfilled. It is not surprising that the rate of pledge fulfilment is lower for Fianna Fáil than Fine Gael, given that Fianna Fáil did not hold any ministerial seats, did not contribute to the programme for government, and was arguably under less pressure electorally to deliver on its election pledges. However, Fianna Fáil was not without influence: the rate of fulfilment rises when we look at the party's key pledges, of which 65 per cent were fulfilled at least partially. This is lower than the rate of fulfilment for Fine Gael's key pledges, but it should be noted that Fianna Fáil made 40 key pledges compared to Fine Gael's 20 (according to our definition). Some of Fianna Fáil's key commitments that were realised include expanding the number of DEIS schools (these are aimed at addressing the needs of those from disadvantaged communities), creating 250,000 jobs, and scrapping water charges. Key pledges that were not enacted include increasing child benefit by €10 per month, setting up a state enterprise bank, and creating a special savings scheme for first-time house buyers.

To contextualise these figures and test our expectations about fulfilment under different types of government, Fig. 2.1 draws on previous research to show the rate of fulfilment over the last four government periods in Ireland.[6] Each bar represents the percentage of partially and fully fulfilled pledges for a particular party: the senior party in government (Fianna Fáil in 2002 and 2007, Fine Gael in 2011 and 2016), the junior party in government (the Progressive Democrats in 2002, the Green Party in 2007, and Labour in 2011), and the main opposition party (Fine Gael in 2002 and 2007, Fianna Fáil in 2011 and 2016).

Figure 2.1 shows that the rate of fulfilment of Fine Gael pledges in the 2016–2020 period corresponds quite closely to previous fulfilment rates from government parties, if we exclude the 2007–2011 crisis government. For instance, Fine Gael fulfilled 43 per cent and partially fulfilled a further 17 per cent of its pledges during the 2011–2016 government, while its coalition partner Labour fulfilled 43 per cent and partially fulfilled 19 per cent. Comparable rates were also found for Fianna Fáil and the Progressive Democrats during the 2002–2007 period.[7] Being in a single-party minority government (albeit with independents) did not lead to a higher than average rate of pledge fulfilment by Fine Gael.

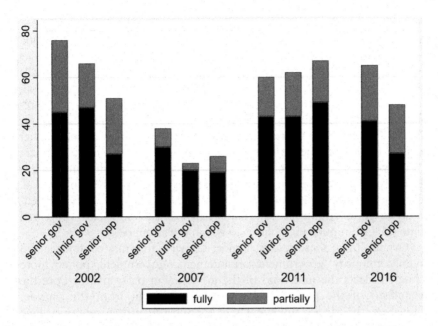

Fig. 2.1 Pledge fulfilment rates by governments elected from 2002 to 2016

Note: 'senior gov' refers to the senior party in government; 'junior gov' refers to the junior partner in government; and 'senior opp' refers to the largest opposition party. The year refers to the date of government formation

As for Fianna Fáil pledges, the fulfilment rate during the 2016–2020 period was not noticeably higher than figures for opposition parties in previous government periods, despite the party having a confidence and supply arrangement with the government. A certain percentage of opposition party pledges are always fulfilled, even under majority government. There are a number of reasons for this: for instance, some opposition pledges will be similar to commitments made by parties that entered government; also, government parties can draw on ideas that originated in other parties' manifestos. If we look back to the 2011–2016 term, when Fianna Fáil was also in opposition, a very high percentage of its pledges were fulfilled (49 per cent, plus 23 per cent partially fulfilled). As discussed in *How Ireland Voted 2016*, there were particular circumstances that led to this high rate of pledge fulfilment for Fianna Fáil at that time (the party had negotiated the terms of the bailout programme to which the incoming Fine Gael–Labour coalition largely adhered).[8] A more appropriate comparison is the fulfilment of Fine Gael pledges during the 2002–2007 period, when it was the main opposition party: 27 per cent of Fine Gael pledges were fulfilled at that time, and a further 25 per cent were partially fulfilled—very similar rates to those of Fianna Fáil in the 2016–2020 period.

Being in a supporting role under confidence and supply does not therefore seem to have resulted in a significant increase in pledge fulfilment for Fianna Fáil, although as previously noted the party did have a much higher rate of fulfilment when it came to its key pledges. Of course, there are other ways apart from fulfilling its election pledges through which Fianna Fáil may have had an influence. Fianna Fáil had a *de facto* veto in the Dáil, because the government needed Fianna Fáil's support (or at least abstention) to get anything passed. Fianna Fáil may therefore have prevented Fine Gael from pursuing policies to which it was opposed.

Overall, then, these results support the view that in a confidence and supply minority government arrangement, government policy more closely reflects the manifesto of the government party than it does the manifesto of the party that supports government from the outside. However, the pledge fulfilment rate for the single-party minority Fine Gael government was not higher than it has been for parties in coalition governments in the past, and indeed was lower than we might expect based on research on minority governments in other countries. The fulfilment rate for Fianna Fáil was not noticeably higher than for opposition parties in previous periods. In the following section we take a closer look at pledge fulfilment for both parties to try and explain these findings.

EXPLAINING PLEDGE FULFILMENT

As we have seen from other countries, parties governing alone (even as a minority government) typically fulfil a higher proportion of their election pledges than parties that govern as part of a coalition. Why, then, did Fine Gael not fulfil more of its pledges? As discussed, the economic conditions were generally favourable, and the government lasted almost its full term, so the explanation does not lie there. In this section, we examine how the ability of Fine Gael to fulfil its pledges was shaped by political obstacles such as the need to compromise with other parties and political actors. We also look at the fulfilment of Fianna Fáil pledges in this light. We then consider the possibility that some pledges were not fulfilled simply because the party was never committed to implementing them to begin with.

Political Obstacles

While minority governments can be quite effective, it was certainly not all plain sailing for this Fine Gael minority administration. The opposition became much more activist during this period, and the number of private member's bills introduced by members of the opposition increased sharply. However, only a small proportion of these were enacted into law, and many were blocked by the government using a procedure known as the 'money message'.[9] Well in excess of 90 per cent of bills that were passed by the Dáil during this period were government bills.[10] We cannot therefore put the non-fulfilment of Fine Gael pledges down to the legislative agenda being hijacked by the opposition.

Another possibility is that the government simply stopped putting forward bills that it knew would be defeated. Evidence for this would be a reduction in the overall productivity of the Dáil, in terms of the number of bills passed during the period. Early on, Labour leader Brendan Howlin categorised it as a 'do-nothing Dáil' where legislation 'has ground to a halt'.[11] However, the record does not support this. Over the three full years of government (2017–2019), an average of 45 bills were passed per year. This lies roughly halfway between the corresponding figures for the two previous governments (both majority administrations), which had annual averages of 54 and 38 bills.[12]

Does the confidence and supply arrangement with Fianna Fáil explain why only 41 per cent of Fine Gael pledges were fully fulfilled? The two parties are generally perceived to be quite close in terms of policy orientations, and a substantial minority of each party's pledges were in agreement with each other: 21 per cent of Fine Gael pledges were in agreement with a pledge made by Fianna Fáil, while 36 per cent of Fianna Fáil pledges were in agreement with a pledge made by Fine Gael.[13] There were also some policy differences between the two parties, however, and a certain amount of compromise was required.

To investigate the compromises reached between the two parties, we examined the text of the confidence and supply deal that was published on 3 May 2016.[14] Much of this agreement was taken up with procedural issues regarding how the relationship would operate, but it also included a relatively short list of policy commitments. Several of these (15 in total) were in line with pledges contained in Fine Gael's manifesto, all of which were subsequently fulfilled at least partially. These include pledges to establish a rainy-day fund, to roll out the housing assistance payment nationwide, and to establish a public service pay commission. In contrast, only two of the policy commitments contained in the confidence and supply agreement were in direct conflict with Fine Gael election pledges, namely a decision to suspend water charges, and an agreement to reform (rather than abolish) the USC. While these were important policy concessions by Fine Gael—the issue of water charges was one of the key differences between the parties in the 2016 election—there were an additional 137 Fine Gael election pledges that were not fulfilled.

As well as compromising with Fianna Fáil, Fine Gael also had to make some concessions to the independents who joined them in government. However, the need to compromise with the independents is likely to account for only a relatively small number of Fine Gael's unfulfilled pledges. As O'Malley points out, the negotiations between Fine Gael and the independents did not concern ideological differences, but just involved the incorporation of some specific concerns of the independents.[15] Most of the independents supporting the government were members of the Independent Alliance grouping. This was not a political party and did not produce a manifesto, but it did issue a ten-point 'Charter for Change' in advance of the 2016 election. Most of these points were very general (such as promising to end political cronyism) and do not count as election pledges according to our definition; but the charter did contain four specific pledges: passing the Seanad Reform bill (not fulfilled), passing the Equality of Access (Down's Syndrome) Bill (not fulfilled); ratifying the UN Convention on the rights of persons with disabilities (fulfilled); denying bail to serial offenders (not fulfilled).

If the independents did exert a significant influence over government policy, we would expect to see it most clearly in the policy areas where they held the ministry. The independent members of government initially held three cabinet seats (Tourism, Transport and Sport; Children and Youth Affairs; and Communications, Climate Action and Environment); this fell to two following the resignation of Denis Naughten in 2018. The fulfilment rate of Fine Gael pledges was not lower for pledges in these three policy areas (41 out of 63, or 65 per cent of Fine Gael pledges in these areas were fulfilled at least partially), suggesting that having independents in government was not a significant policy obstacle for Fine Gael.

As for the fulfilment of pledges made by Fianna Fáil, the relationship between the two parties was an important factor. As Table 2.1 shows, a total of 64 Fianna Fáil pledges were fully fulfilled. Of these, 27 were in consensus with Fine Gael pledges, and a further six of them were included in the confidence and supply deal. So, over half of the fulfilled Fianna Fáil pledges can be explained in this way. A further seven were status quo pledges: that is, pledges to keep things as they were, such as the commitment to continue the sustainable energy grants. As for the remaining Fianna Fáil pledges that were fulfilled, these include pledges to restore the Farm Assist means testing rules, to reduce DIRT (a tax on interest earned) by three per cent, and to increase funding to the child protection agency (Tusla) by €15 million.

Pledges as 'cheap talk'?

An alternative explanation is that a failure to deliver on promises is not just the result of external constraints, such as the need to compromise with other parties, but also because parties make some promises that they are not committed to. Election pledges are sometimes described as 'cheap talk' designed just to win votes, rather than genuine policy intentions.[16] This view is widely held among the public, and it is an accusation that parties often level at their opponents.[17] There is also evidence that parties in Ireland engage in over-pledging, whereby they promise more than they can possibly deliver given what is known about the economic circumstances.[18] The extent to which parties engage in this kind of over-pledging is likely to depend on whether they think that voters will hold them to account for broken promises at the next election.[19]

While we can never know the true intentions behind a pledge, in this case we are presented with an opportunity to compare what Fine Gael presented to the electorate (the manifesto) with what it was actually serious about implementing (the programme for government). Programmes for government are usually produced only when there is a coalition government, because under single-party government the manifesto serves the same purpose. In this case a programme for government was produced, due to the involvement of independent TDs in government.

Comparing Fine Gael's election pledges with the programme for government provides a good way of disentangling the various explanations for broken promises that we have discussed. First, we can be confident that any manifesto pledges that were excluded from the programme were not due to changing circumstances, because it was produced a mere three months after the election. Developments such as Brexit, or the gradual deterioration in the strength of the government as it lost the support of a number of TDs, cannot be blamed for the failure to include pledges in the programme for government.[20] Second, we can be confident that the programme for government was largely the work of Fine Gael, rather than a compromise between parties. Fianna Fáil was not involved in any way in writing it, as is stated clearly in the confidence and supply document; and as we have seen only two Fine Gael pledges were in conflict with the confidence and supply agreement. While the programme for government did involve some input from the independents, this seems to have been relatively marginal, as discussed above.

If the Fine Gael election manifesto was a mix of genuine commitments and 'cheap talk' designed to win votes, then the programme for government is a list of the measures that Fine Gael was serious about implementing, stripped of any electioneering. Table 2.2 presents the relationship between the two documents. We distinguish between pledges that were fully included in the programme for government, pledges that were partially included, and pledges that were not included at all. Looking to the final column, we see that a surprisingly large number of Fine Gael pledges (172, or 44 per cent) were not included at all in the programme for government. A further 65 pledges (17 per cent) were only partially included, which in most cases meant that the original pledge was watered down in the programme for government. For instance, the manifesto pledge to recruit an additional 2800 nurses and 600 medical consultants was modified to 'recruit additional front-line service professionals such as doctors and nurses' in the programme for government; while the manifesto pledge to cut the lower rate of employer's PRSI to 6.5 per cent became a much looser commitment to 'cut employers' PRSI for low-income workers'.

Table 2.2 Inclusion of Fine Gael pledges in Programme for Government, by type of pledge

	Uncosted money pledge	Costed money pledge	Other pledge	Total
Full inclusion	30	25	98	153
	(34%)	(31%)	(44%)	(39%)
Part inclusion	13	35	17	65
	(15%)	(44%)	(8%)	(17%)
Not included	44	20	108	172
	(51%)	(25%)	(48%)	(44%)
Total	87	80	223	390
	(100%)	(100%)	(100%)	(100%)

Note: See text for description of different types of pledges

We argue that non-inclusion in the programme for government indicates, at least in some cases, a lack of commitment to a pledge by Fine Gael. This interpretation is supported when we look at the other columns in Table 2.2, which break down the pledges into three categories. A substantial proportion of the pledges can be categorised as 'money' pledges, as they have a significant financial element. These include pledges to provide funding for particular programmes, and pledges to cut or raise taxes and charges. It is possible to assess the credibility of a money pledge by investigating whether or not it has been costed prior to inclusion in the manifesto. There are two main ways in which a pledge can be considered to have been costed. For pledges that commit to investing money in a programme, the party can state how much money it will invest. An example from the Fine Gael manifesto is the pledge to set up a new active retirement fund of €5m per year; while an example of a vague (uncosted) investment pledge where no amount is specified is the pledge to 'Introduce a new small grants scheme to provide essential upgrades to existing regional arts and cultural centres around the country'.

Many other money pledges are more complicated, as they commit to an action or an outcome that will have financial implications that need to be estimated. Examples include the pledge to 'increase the State Pension and the Living Alone Allowance above the rate of inflation', and the pledge to 'introduce free GP care to under-18s'. To assist parties in estimating the financial implications of their policies, the Department of Public Expenditure and Reform and the Department of Finance provide a costing service. Parties can submit their policy proposals and receive detailed estimates of the financial implications. For each money pledge in the manifesto, we examined whether or not the party had received a costing from the Department of Public Expenditure and Reform or the Department of Finance. An example of a costed pledge from the 2016 Fine Gael manifesto is the pledge to increase the Contributory State Pension by €25 per week. Fine Gael did ask the Department of Public Expenditure and Reform to provide a costing for this, which estimated that it would cost €20.51m for every €1 increase in the Contributory State Pension.[21] Other proposals were submitted for costing and then not included in the manifesto (perhaps because the cost was too high); while yet other proposals with financial implications were not submitted for costing at all. An example of the latter was the pledge to 'fund an additional 114 midwives annually from 2017 for 4 years', which was not costed and subsequently not included in the programme for government.

Table 2.2 reveals a clear difference between costed and uncosted money pledges in terms inclusion in the programme for government. Three-quarters of the costed pledges were included at least partially in the programme for government, compared to less than half of the uncosted money pledges. The fact that many of the pledges that were not included in the programme for government were uncosted suggested that they may have simply been 'cheap talk' that the party was never very serious about implementing.

The Relative Impact of Different Factors on Pledge Fulfilment

We have discussed a number of explanations for the fulfilment or otherwise of Fine Gael and Fianna Fáil pledges. These include the relationship between each party's pledges, and in the case of Fine Gael whether the party held the relevant ministry, whether the pledges were costed, and whether they were included in the programme for government. We now estimate the unique effect (i.e. controlling for other things) that each of these factors had on fulfilment. As most of these explanatory factors relate only to Fine Gael pledges, we restrict this final analysis to that party.

Table 2.3 shows how the likelihood of a pledge being at least partially fulfilled was affected by each of these factors. The first row shows that, controlling for other things, the likelihood of fulfilment was 17 percentage points higher for a costed money pledge than for an uncosted money

Table 2.3 Effect of each factor on probability of pledge fulfilment (Fine Gael pledges)

Type of pledge	Effect
Costed (vs uncosted) money pledge	+17%
Other (non-money) pledge	-12%
Status quo pledge	+26%
Included in Programme for Government	+11%
Agreement with Fianna Fáil	-1%
Relevant ministry	+2%

Note: Figures refer to the difference in the probability of fulfilment (including partial fulfilment) when the relevant variable changes in value, for example from not holding the relevant ministry to holding the relevant ministry. Other variables are held at their mode values. Estimates based on logistic regression models. The number of pledges included in the analysis is 390 pledge. The likelihood of fulfilment for other (non-money) pledges, for instance pledges to introduce legislation, was 12 percentage points lower than for money pledges. Pledges to maintain the status quo had a likelihood of fulfilment that was 26 percentage points higher than for pledges to introduce change. Full inclusion in the programme for government increased the likelihood of fulfilment by 11 percentage points. Somewhat surprisingly, agreement with Fianna Fáil had a negligible effect on fulfilment of Fine Gael pledges when we control for other factors.[22] As mentioned previously, Fine Gael held the vast majority of cabinet positions throughout the period, and pledge fulfilment did not vary significantly between those areas where it held the ministry and those where it did not.

Together, these effects add up to quite substantial differences in the likelihood of fulfilment for different types of pledges. For example, a costed money pledge that was included in the programme for government had a probability of fulfilment (or partial fulfilment) of 83 per cent; this falls to 60 per cent for uncosted money pledges that are not in the programme for government, and to 48 per cent for other pledges that are not in the programme for government.

Conclusion

The question 'Do politicians keep their election promises?' is one that we know quite a lot about, thanks to a growing body of comparative research. Government parties typically fulfil a substantial number of their election pledges, particularly parties that govern alone. Yet many pledges also go unfulfilled, either due to changing circumstances or political obstacles, or because the pledges were not credible or sincerely made to begin with. These broken promises often get a lot of attention at election time, reinforcing public cynicism about politics.

When we compare pledge fulfilment rates across countries, Ireland is towards the lower end of the league table. The main comparative study on pledge fulfilment to date examined 57 elections in 12 countries, and found that the UK, Sweden, Portugal and Spain had the highest rates of government party pledge fulfilment, while the countries with the lowest rates were Ireland, Bulgaria, Austria and Italy.[23] Ireland's relatively poor performance on this measure is due partly to the fact that Irish governments are usually coalitions, which requires a significant degree of compromise between parties. The present study focused on pledge fulfilment during the 2016–2020 period, when there was a minority government consisting of one party plus a number of independents. Evidence from other countries suggests that pledge fulfilment tends to be significantly higher under single party minority governments than coalition governments.

Our findings show that while Fine Gael did implement many important commitments that it made in 2016, including nearly all of the pledges that it highlighted at the start of its manifesto, the overall rate of fulfilment for Fine Gael pledges was not higher than what has been previously observed for coalition governments in Ireland. Overall, 41 per cent of Fine Gael's 2016 manifesto pledges were fulfilled, plus another 24 per cent partially fulfilled, leaving 36 per cent (139 pledges) unfulfilled.

That pledge fulfilment by this Fine Gael-led government was lower than has been observed in minority governments elsewhere is perhaps not surprising, given that the party held fewer than one-third of Dáil seats and had to rely on the support of independent TDs plus a confidence and supply arrangement with Fianna Fáil. However, the analysis presented in this chapter suggests that while the need to compromise with Fianna Fáil and others accounts for some of Fine Gael's unfulfilled promises, this is not the whole story. Many Fine Gael pledges did not conflict with the deal struck with Fianna Fáil, and were unlikely to have caused conflict with the independent TDs in government, yet were not even included in the programme for government that was written a few months after the election. Many of these pledges had not been costed, giving rise to the possibility that they were not priorities for Fine Gael to begin with.

As stated at the outset, pledge fulfilment is a critical part of the representative process. When parties do not endeavour to fulfil their election pledges, manifestos become meaningless, and elections no longer provide voters with a genuine opportunity to have a say on how the country is governed. In Ireland, parties in government continue to implement their core election pledges to a considerable extent. However, manifestos are very lengthy documents, and contain some commitments that are not priorities for the party and are quickly discarded after the election. As long as this continues to happen, pledge fulfilment rates will remain at best modest, regardless of the type of government that forms or the external conditions that it faces.

Notes

1. Robert Thomson and Rory Costello, 'Governing together in good and bad economic times: the fulfilment of election pledges in Ireland', *Irish Political Studies* 31:2 (2016), pp. 182–203.

2. Catherine Moury and Jorge M. Fernandes, 'Minority governments and pledge fulfilment: evidence from Portugal', *Government and Opposition* 53:2 (2018), pp. 335–55.

3. A comparative study of pledge fulfilment across 57 governments in 12 countries found no difference between single-party majority governments and single-party minority governments in terms of pledge fulfilment rates; while parties that governed alone (either in minority or majority governments) fulfilled a significantly higher rate of pledges compared to parties that shared power in a coalition. See Robert Thomson et al., 'The fulfillment of parties' election pledges: A comparative study on the impact of power sharing', *American Journal of Political Science* 61:3 (2017), pp. 527–42.

4. Kevin Doyle and Niall O'Connor, 'How Micheál Martin won the sweetest deal in Fianna Fáil history', *Irish Independent* 5 May 2016.

5. Rory Costello, Paul O'Neill and Robert Thomson, 'The fulfilment of election pledges by the outgoing government', pp. 27–45 in Michael Gallagher and Michael Marsh (eds), *How Ireland Voted 2016: the election that nobody won* (Cham: Palgrave Macmillan, 2016), p. 31.

6. Thomson and Costello, 'Governing together'.

7. Costello, O'Neill and Thomson, 'The fulfilment of election pledges by the outgoing government', p. 34.

8. Costello, O'Neill and Thomson, 'The fulfilment of election pledges by the outgoing government', p. 39.

9. Under the constitution, a bill cannot pass into law unless the government indicates that it supports the necessary expenditure. By refusing to make any such declaration, the government was able to block the enactment of many private member's bills.

10. The *Irish Examiner* reported that by April 2019, 114 bills had been passed by the 32nd Dáil, of which 104 were government bills. Fiachra Ó Cionnaith, 'Opposition bills are stuck in a legislative labyrinth', *Irish Examiner* 23 April 2019.

11. Elaine Loughlin, 'Review of system on the cards amid criticism of "do-nothing Dáil"', *Irish Examiner* 17 April 2017.

12. These figures exclude election years. Figures calculated from the Electronic Irish Statute Book, available: http://www.irishstatutebook.ie/ (accessed 4 May 2020).

13. More specifically, 83 Fine Gael pledges were in agreement with 87 Fianna Fáil pledges. The numbers are not identical because pledges can vary in scope: one broad pledge can be related to two more narrowly-focused pledges.

14. Fiach Kelly, 'The full document: Fine Gael–Fianna Fáil deal for government', *Irish Times* 3 May 2016.

15. Eoin O'Malley, '70 days: government formation in 2016', pp. 255–76 in Michael Gallagher and Michael Marsh (eds), *How Ireland Voted 2016: the election that nobody won* (Cham: Palgrave Macmillan, 2016).

16. Joseph Harrington Jr, 'The impact of reelection pressures on the fulfillment of campaign promises', *Games and Economic Behavior* 5:1 (1993), pp. 71–97.

17. Elin Naurin, *Election Promises, Party Behaviour and Voter Perceptions* (Basingstoke: Palgrave Macmillan, 2011), p. 71. For an example of parties accusing one another of engaging in cheap talk, see Costello, O'Neill and Thomson, 'The fulfilment of election pledges by the outgoing government', pp. 27–8.

18. Thomson and Costello, 'Governing together', p. 199.

19. It is easier for voters to assign responsibility under single-party government than under a coalition. This in turn might imply that parties that expect to enter a coalition government are more likely to include pledges that they are not committed to (but might win them some votes), whereas parties that anticipate governing alone will be more careful about what they pledge, knowing that voters will hold them (and them alone) to account. This line of reasoning may explain why single-party minority governments in other countries, where they are the norm, are associated with higher rates of pledge fulfilment than we have observed for the Fine Gael government of 2016–2020. Prior to 2016, Fine Gael had never formed a single-party executive, and it was not expected to do so then. If over-pledging is something that parties do when they anticipate coalition government, then Fine Gael may have engaged in this.

20. The government's Dáil strength declined from 57 to 53 between 2016 and 2019, due to the loss of Fine Gael TDs Frances Fitzgerald, Peter Fitzpatrick and Dara Murphy, as well as independent TD Denis Naughten.

21. This costing is available on p. 65 of a document entitled 'Fine Gael Costings' available on the Department of Public Expenditure and Reform's website: https://www.gov.ie/en/collection/94a724-party-costings-for-budget-2016/ (accessed 29 May 2020).

22. While the rate of fulfilment for Fine Gael was higher for those pledges that were in agreement with Fianna Fáil pledges, this effect goes away when we control for other factors, such as inclusion in the programme for government.

23. Thomson et al., 'The fulfillment of parties' election pledges', p. 535.

CHAPTER 3

Too Many, Too Few: Candidate Selection in 2020

Theresa Reidy

Candidate selection can be likened to the shortlisting phase of a job inter-view: political parties engage in a pre-screening process choosing the peo-ple who will appear on the ballot paper with their party label. It is not concealed from the electorate, rather it proceeds unnoticed in the political undergrowth.[1] All of the political parties have rules about how they choose their candidates, and power in this shortlisting phase is shared imperfectly between party members and party elites. Party elites determine the criteria for the decisions to be made. Geography, gender, age, succession planning and the number of candidates to contest the election on behalf of the party are all decided in advance. Party staff usually issue a call for potential

I am particularly grateful to all of the political party general secretaries, strategists and candidates who agreed to be interviewed for this chapter. To a person, they were generous with their time and insights. All of the data listed in the tables were sourced from party and candidate websites, social media pages, print and broadcast media and interviews.

T. Reidy (✉)
Department of Government and Politics, University College Cork, Cork, Ireland
e-mail: T.Reidy@ucc.ie

© The Author(s), under exclusive license to Springer Nature   41
Switzerland AG 2021
M. Gallagher et al. (eds.), *How Ireland Voted 2020*,
https://doi.org/10.1007/978-3-030-66405-3_3

candidates to come forward but this is not the only way in which candidates are identified. Party members (elected and unelected) will often approach individuals and encourage them to come forward (see the contribution of James O'Connor in Chap. 7). Parties invest a lot of time and resources in candidate selection.

Though largely overlooked by the media and voters alike, the candidate selection phase for general elections has immeasurable consequences. This stage in the electoral cycle determines much of the electoral choice presented to voters on polling day. Some candidates are non-party (independents) but most (over two-thirds in 2020) come from the ranks of political parties of varying ideologies, interests and sizes. In Ireland, all members of the cabinet must be members of the Oireachtas and the vast majority of ministers come from political parties. Thus candidate selection does not just influence the shape of the Dáil, it also largely determines the choices available to Taoisigh when it comes to picking cabinet members. The party selectorate are often described as gatekeepers; an aspiring TD, minister or Taoiseach needs to gain their endorsement on the path to parliament.

The background and experience of cabinet ministers featured in debates on political reform in the lead-up to the 2011 election. There was much unfavourable commentary on the capabilities of the Fianna Fáil and Green Party government. This led to a debate on the types of people who contest elections and whether the mix of skills and experience found in election candidates was appropriate for the challenges governments would face, a debate that was present in academic analyses of Irish politics dating back to 1981 when R. K. Carty critiqued candidate selection procedures for producing 'decidedly mediocre individuals, handicapping the parties' ability to provide the system with effective political leadership'.[2] As the economic crisis faded, so did the campaign for political reform; but the question of how well political party candidate selection procedures serve the political system remains a pertinent one.

Labelled 'the choice before the choice',[3] candidate selection is an important staging point in understanding the outcomes of an election. This chapter will begin with some summary information on candidate selection for the 2020 election before proceeding to an assessment of the factors that inform candidate selection decisions. The ensuing section will provide an overview of candidate selection processes within the main political parties. It will document the party rules that structure candidate decision making and discuss some informal practices. It will present an account of the strategies devised and deployed by each of the parties and provide an assessment of the balance of power between party elites and ordinary members. A profile of the candidates that contested the election is included in the penultimate section and the chapter concludes with some general findings on how the approach of political parties has evolved over time and the implications of decisions taken in 2020.

CANDIDATE NUMBERS AND DECISIONS IN 2020

The threshold for accessing the ballot at Dáil elections is modest. Prospective candidates have three options. They can present to the returning officer a statutory declaration signed by 30 constituents, or a deposit of €500, or proof that they are the nominee of a registered political party. Independent candidates access the ballot through route one or two. In 2020, almost a quarter of candidates were independents, who cannot use that label but must either describe themselves on the ballot as 'non-party' or simply use no description.

Candidate selection in 2020 was marked by two overlapping dynamics: earlier preparation, and lower key coordination by party strategists, than in 2016. Expectations of another election began to surface within months of the formation of the minority administration in May 2016. This led parties to make election preparations earlier than usual in the election cycle. The eruption of a major scandal regarding the treatment of Garda whistleblower Maurice McCabe prompted intense speculation that a general election was imminent in late 2017 (see Chap. 1, p. 11). A wave of hastily convened selection conventions ensued but the election was averted by the resignation of Minister for Justice Frances Fitzgerald. Ultimately, the government endured far longer than had initially been expected with the result that some of the candidate selection decisions made in 2017 had to be re-visited. A second round of hastily convened national candidate committee meetings and local selection conventions was prompted in the weeks just before the election in early 2020.

Candidate gender quota legislation came into effect at the 2016 general election for the first time.[4] Unless political parties had a minimum of 30 per cent of their candidates from each gender, they faced severe financial penalties, and this led to extensive intervention and monitoring of candidate selection by all party headquarters. In practice, this was a female gender quota given the past record of male dominance of party tickets. For the 2020 election cycle, direct intervention in selection processes on gender grounds was reduced. Some strategists reported that resistance to the gender quota had fizzled out by the time candidate preparations were being put in place and the local elections in 2019 were also mentioned as an important means of normalising discourse around more balanced gender tickets. All of the main parties met the 30 per cent threshold at the general election. However, many parties made limited progress beyond the 30 per cent threshold and some parties showed a disimprovement in their gender balance from 2016. The gender quota is due to rise to 40 per cent, potentially by the next general election.[5]

Political parties provide a lot of practical campaign supports for candidates. All of the main parties arrange for candidates to have their photos taken for use on the ballot paper, posters and election literature (see Chap. 7 for description of individual party supports). Among the larger parties, Fine Gael does much of its election literature printing in-house and it also provided art work and other content for candidates who printed their own literature. The other parties block-purchased election literature and posters. Canvassing workshops for candidates and policy workshops have become more common and some parties provide specific training opportunities for women candidates while others engage groups such as Women for Election and the National Women's Council of Ireland to carry out this work. Social media supports were provided widely in 2020 with parties purchasing digital advertising, supporting candidates with micro-targeting and directly managing social media accounts (see Chaps. 6 and 7 for further discussion).

Candidate selection proceeded without much national media attention for most political parties in the 2020 election cycle, apart from Fine Gael, which had to manage controversial deselections in Wexford and Dún Laoghaire, as well as some reorganisation of its constituency tickets following weak performances in the 2019 local elections by some of its would-be general election candidates. Of the main parties, Fianna Fáil, the Social Democrats and Solidarity–People Before Profit (Sol–PBP) increased their candidate numbers from 2016, creating opportunities for new candidates, while Fine Gael, Sinn Féin and Labour scaled back their party tickets. Individual candidate decisions were only occasionally in the news, but the overall number of candidates contesting the election for many of the parties became a recurrent topic of discussion during the election campaign. As poll figures began to crystallise the emerging new balance in politics, it became apparent that Sinn Féin did not have enough candidates in the field to capitalise on its surge in support while Fianna Fáil and Fine

Gael were both deemed to have over-selected candidates given their flat and at times declining poll numbers.

In total, 531 candidates (plus the outgoing Ceann Comhairle, returned automatically) contested the election. This was a further drop from the 2011 peak in candidate numbers but the total number of candidates contesting elections continues to trend above pre-2008 economic crisis elections. The 2017 Constituency Commission made some changes to electoral boundaries and the 33rd Dáil returned 160 TDs from 39 constituencies. Wicklow had the longest ballot paper with 20 candidates and Cork North-West and Meath West had the lowest number of candidates with nine each. One candidate opted to contest the election in 11 constituencies—5 Cork constituencies, 5 Dublin constituencies and Kerry—while former presidential candidate Peter Casey contested in his native Donegal and also in Dublin West, which he chose on the basis that it was the constituency of the Taoiseach. An overview of candidate numbers from 1997 is provided in Table 3.1.

INTERNAL PARTY DEMOCRACY

Electability is the obvious answer to the question, 'what is the most important factor that political parties consider when choosing candidates for an upcoming election?' But it is not the only factor in play. Nor is there a definitive answer to what makes a candidate politically desirable. Electability is an imprecise concept and undoubtedly varies across political environments and political parties. Party candidates are chosen by party elites and party members who may also differ somewhat in their preferences from

Table 3.1 Candidate numbers 1997–2020

	1997	2002	2007	2011	2016	2020
Fianna Fáil	112	106	107	75	71	84
Fine Gael	90	85	91	104	88	82
Sinn Féin	15	37	41	41	50	42
Green Party	26	31	44	43	40	39
Labour	44	46	50	68	36	31
Sol–PBP	–	12	9	20	31	37
Soc Dems	–	–	–	–	14	20
Ind/Others	197	146	129	215	221	196
Total	484	463	471	566	551	531

the wider electorate. A 2010 study noted that a majority of party members in Europe were men and ageing markedly.[6] Party membership is quite low in Ireland and very little is known about the profile of party members.[7] Political parties are often reluctant to facilitate in-depth studies of their memberships, as they risk poor publicity and sharing inner secrets with their competitors. Thus, the small number of studies that have conducted detailed research on party members and their role in candidate selection are very valuable.

Early research from the UK[8] found that party members chose candidates who they thought would be elected while in a similar vein, a more recent Belgian study[9] found that party members favoured more experienced political candidates, that is, those with a track record of success in politics. There is a large literature on incumbency advantage in elections and a related body of research on how large pools of incumbent male candidates make it more difficult for female candidates to succeed at the candidate selection stage. Research from Belgium has also demonstrated that party selectors lean towards a mix of candidate backgrounds and occupations that is similar to the party's voting base but they favour those with high social and political capital for the seats that they are most likely to win.[10]

The electoral system may also shape the decisions selectors make. PR-STV with its multi-seat constituencies (see Appendix D for full description) means that larger parties will often have more than one candidate in each constituency. Fianna Fáil and Fine Gael ran more than one candidate in most constituencies and Sinn Féin ran two candidates in four constituencies in 2020. This gives rise to decisions on the location and sometimes age of candidates. Having a candidate from the local area is an established preference of voters[11] and this logic leads to a penchant for candidates who live in the constituency and who are spread across it, especially in large rural constituencies. The need for multiple candidates also provides opportunities to manage succession planning, usually resulting in a small number of opportunities for councillors to contest general elections. Political parties approach the process of choosing political candidates in different ways. Rahat and Hazan have presented a two-dimensional framework for evaluating how political parties conduct selection decisions.[12] Dimension one looks at who is empowered to take decisions. At the exclusive end of the spectrum, a party leader may be the sole decision-maker while in the most inclusive scenario, all voters would have a right to vote in selection decisions. The use of 'party primaries', where all party members have a vote, would also be on the inclusive end of the spectrum. The second dimension of the framework looks at the level at which decisions are taken. In a centralised system, decisions are made at the national level while decentralised decision making sees judgements made at the level of the electoral division for the election.

From the following section, it will become clear that all of the main political parties have inclusive and qualified decentralised decision making. Party structures that deal with candidate selection democratised from the 1990s. Selection decisions are taken in constituencies at conventions. Parties use a system known as One Member, One Vote (OMOV) which enfranchises all party members of good standing in their candidate decision making. Crucially though, party elites construct the choices that members vote on. Party elites set the parameters, known as directives, for decisions. They determine how many candidates are to be chosen, what if any gender balance is required and whether there are any geographic criteria to be met. Party members decide which people fill these pre-determined slots. And parties also allow internal bodies to add and deselect candidates as needed. While members are clearly involved in decisions, their power is distinctly moderated by internal regulations.

Party Rules, Strategies and Controversies

Fianna Fáil

Fianna Fáil held a selection convention—which every member had the right to attend—in every constituency and ran 82 candidates in the election. The party revised some of its internal operating procedures relating to the selection of candidates and the election of the party leader in the aftermath of its collapse in support at the 2011 election. Most notably, OMOV was introduced for all candidate selection conventions. Procedures have remained stable since 2012. The party manages the process of candidate selection through its National Constituencies Committee (NCC), which is a permanent sub-committee of the Ard Comhairle (Executive Council). It managed council co-options in the aftermath of the 2016 election[13] and, about six months afterwards, it began to make early preparations for the next general election.

The publication of the 2017 Constituency Commission report led to the escalation of preparations. NCC decision making is informed by national and local opinion polls, local constituency research and feedback from members in the local organisation. Maximising seat gains is the obvious core objective but decisions are also informed by the need to meet the gender quota, to have balanced geographic tickets—especially in two-county constituencies—and to manage the long term prospects of the party by preparing succession plans. It was noted in interviews that all of the party research indicated a reasonably stable outlook for the party and some improvement in the performance from 2016 was expected. This underpinned the decision to run more candidates than in 2016 and reduce the number of constituencies where just one candidate would contest the election.

The NCC provided a candidate directive to each selection convention that outlined the number of candidates to be selected, and any gender or geographic requirements. Selection conventions started with the most straightforward decisions. The first convention took place in Dublin West on 25 July 2017 where one candidate had to be chosen, and there was an incumbent, Jack Chambers. Conventions continued into 2018.

The NCC has the power to add and deselect candidates from the party ticket. It reviewed the slate of candidates on a regular basis at its meetings and added candidates throughout the process. No candidates were deselected and 28 were added to the party ticket. Former minister Mary Hanafin was not selected at her convention in Dún Laoghaire but she was subsequently added to the party ticket in December 2017, a move that caused some annoyance in the constituency, where her attempts to return to national politics had been rebuffed on a couple of occasions. However, party strategists suggested that her high profile meant that she was seen as a viable candidate and being a woman, she also helped with gender balance. Additions continued into January 2020. Orla Leyden, daughter of an incumbent senator, was added to the Fianna Fáil ticket in Roscommon–Galway on 13 January 2020. Again, the move caused some local irritation, especially for incumbent TD, Eugene Murphy who took to Twitter to express his shock at the last-minute decision commenting 'The addition of @OrlaLeyden to the FF ticket in Ros/Galway has quite frankly taken me by surprise as I had been told by Cllr Leyden and @SenatorTerry that she was not going to run.' While the addition of some women to Fianna Fáil tickets did receive comment in the media, the party ran just two candidates without any previous political experience and just one of these was a woman, and internally the party was much happier with its management of the issue than in 2016. The final addition was made in the Limerick County constituency where the party announced on 20 January that councillor Eddie Ryan had agreed to join the party ticket. Ryan withdrew less than 24 hours later amidst allegations of acrimony with the incumbent TD, Niall Collins. With the close of nominations imminent, the party added Michael Collins (no relation of Niall) to the ticket on 22 January. The last-minute changes caused local surprise, comment and mild ridicule but did not make the national news agenda.

There was a degree of unanimity in interviews with both party staff and candidates that candidate selection was managed more smoothly in 2020 and party HQ was less interventionist in its approach than in 2016. Three factors were cited prominently for this: the gender quota was more embedded in decision making, the party had a good election in 2016 and it entered the selection process expecting further growth, which meant opportunities for potential candidates.

Given Fianna Fáil's disappointing election result, there was criticism in post-election commentary of the decision to increase candidate numbers. Commentators pointed to over-selection in Clare, Kildare South, Roscommon–Galway and Wexford as possibly contributing to a poorer outcome for Fianna Fáil than would have occurred if they had fewer candidates in the field. Party strategists remained of the view that its candidate selection strategy was appropriate given the information that shaped it. Their evidence pointed to a possible uptick in support and potential seat gains. Strategists also argued that most losing Fianna Fáil candidates were usually some distance from the competition for final seats (see Chap. 8 for deeper analysis).

Fine Gael

The Minister for Finance Paschal Donohoe was appointed director of elections for Fine Gael and he oversaw co-ordination of the candidate selection process. Decisions on candidate strategy are made by the Executive Council (EC) of the party. The EC (formally on the recommendation of the party leader) has the power to add and deselect candidates and it used both of these tools during the 2020 election cycle. In practice, decisions are heavily influenced by the director of elections and the election strategy committee. The election strategy committee comprises party staff, senior politicians and some party supporters of significant standing with appropriate campaign skills. Members in 2020 included TDs Eoghan Murphy and Michael D'Arcy, Tom Curran (party general secretary) and Olwyn Enright (former TD). The Fine Gael candidate selection strategy was informed by extensive research: the party commissioned constituency and national polls as well as qualitative research. There was a strategy committee in every constituency providing local feedback that fed into the national strategy.

The party was polling between 25 and 28 per cent for much of the early election preparation period in 2017 (see Chap. 1, p. 9) and a 'most favourable scenario' was devised that suggested an upward trajectory for the party and the possibility that extra seats might be won. Gender balance on the party ticket was monitored closely throughout the selection process. Ultimately, the party met the candidate gender quota by the narrowest of margins: 30.5 per cent of its candidates were women. The party had been criticised during the local elections in 2019 (where no candidate gender quotas applied) for having fewer than 30 per cent female candidates. A candidate directive was issued to each constituency and two of those (Dublin West and Longford–Westmeath) included a gender criterion. The EC also added 23 candidates to the party ticket, of whom 13 were women. Ultimately, just two of the 23 candidates added were successful (Frank Feighan and Jennifer Carroll MacNeill).[14] Four Fine Gael candidates had no previous experience of contesting an election at any level and three of these were women (all three were also added to the ticket). The higher election success rate (49 per cent) for candidates selected at convention does indicate that party members add some value to the selection process, even allowing for the fact that incumbents predominate among candidates selected at convention.

Party strategists noted that candidate selection was a smoother process in 2020. They described the approach of party HQ as 'less aggressive' than in 2016 and working more like a partnership. This observation overlooks the party's continuing imbalanced gender profile and the major challenge that lies immediately ahead for the party when the quota rises to 40 per cent. But it also reflects the fact that party elites have far-reaching powers when it comes to candidate selection, and even when candidates preferred by party elites do not progress through selection conventions, they can be added at a later stage through internal procedures. Party HQ does not have to be aggressive to achieve its goals. Mary Newman, a sister of Dublin Bay South TD Kate O'Connell, contested the Tipperary selection convention and missed out by a few votes, and was later added to the party ticket. Deirdre Duffy, a prominent campaigner at the marriage equality referendum of 2015, was also added to the party ticket in Dublin Central, on this occasion without contesting a convention. Parties have long sought out high-profile people and encouraged them to become candidates. For the 2020 election, Fine Gael looked particularly to the ranks of civil society organisations that had been at the forefront of recent referendum campaigns. Duffy was one such candidate, as was Ellen O'Malley Dunlop, who was a candidate in Dublin South-West.[15]

Fine Gael holds selection conventions in each constituency and operates OMOV. The first selection convention took place in November 2017. Quite a few conventions were uncontested. The party ran a reduced slate of candidates in 2020 and there were few opportunities for new candidates. Ninety-five candidates contested conventions, of whom 71 were chosen by vote of the membership. Selection conventions operated according to the party schedule but the party had to adapt its strategy as 12 candidates who had been placed on the party ticket withdrew for reasons that included deselections, poor performance at the local elections, election to the European Parliament and also personal reasons. Julie O'Leary in Cork North-Central is one of those who withdrew following a weak performance in the local elections. Joe O'Reilly left the party ticket in Cavan–Monaghan in a move that was reported in the media as both a voluntary withdrawal and deselection by the EC. Undoubtedly, some candidates faced a choice between voluntary withdrawal and deselection. In Sligo–Leitrim, two of the candidates selected at convention (Gerry Reynolds and Sinéad Maguire) withdrew. Senator Frankie Feighan had withdrawn his name from the contest on the night of the convention. The party tried unsuccessfully to persuade retiring TD Tony McLoughlin to run again. Former MEP Marian Harkin was also asked to join the party as a candidate, but she declined and contested the election as an independent. In July 2019, Feighan was added to the ticket and councillor Thomas Walsh was also added in December 2019. Frances Fitzgerald was elected to the European Parliament in May 2019, creating a vacancy in Dublin Mid-West. And lastly, Maura Hopkins withdrew her candidacy in the Roscommon–Galway constituency in January 2020 for personal reasons following the birth of her first child. Hopkins had contested the constituency in 2016 and had been a senator on the administrative panel from 2016–2020.

It was the deselection of two candidates that drew the greatest attention in the national media. Dún Laoghaire TD Maria Bailey became embroiled in a long running controversy relating to a personal injuries case that she initiated against a Dublin hotel. She engaged in an ill-judged radio interview on the RTÉ radio *Today with Sean O'Rourke* programme that led to a surge in public opprobrium. Her local constituency organisation sought her removal from the party ticket and she was eventually deselected by the party, seemingly the first time an incumbent TD has been explicitly deselected since 1987.[16] Her deselection led to the late addition of Jennifer Carroll MacNeill to the Fine Gael ticket (see Chap. 7 for an account of her campaign and election). Verona Murphy was a candidate for Fine Gael in the Wexford constituency by-election in November 2019. During the campaign, Murphy made a series of remarks that were hostile to migrants and ill-informed. She initially apologised but later reiterated her comments on local radio and released an election-day video that blamed the national media for her campaign problems. Following the election, pressure on Fine Gael grew to deselect her as a candidate and the EC voted to remove her in December 2019. She contested the election as an independent and won a seat.

Fine Gael was disappointed with its election result. The party returned with fewer TDs. Its post-election review found the party had few narrow losses, indicating that quite a number of its candidates were not competitive, especially several of the women candidates who had been added to the ticket. Over-selection was considered to be a factor in some of the poor results, Cavan–Monaghan and Carlow–Kilkenny in particular. However, the general evaluation of the candidate process was that it was managed as well as it could be, given the elongated selection period and the fact that the evidence that informed the initial decisions turned out to be overly optimistic.

Sinn Féin

Decisions on candidate selection are made by the Ard Comhairle (Executive Council) in Sinn Féin. The director of elections submits proposals on strategy for discussion and decision. An election division based in party HQ is responsible for the administrative side of the process. It organises selection conventions and communicates directives to cumainn (branches) around the country. Selection conventions are held in every constituency and each party member (of six months' standing) has a vote. Candidates must be party members and are required to sign the party code of ethics, which the party considers to be comprehensive and rigorous. Some informal vetting of candidates does take place but the party did not hold screening interviews with candidates in 2020, a change from 2016.

The overall candidate strategy for the party was informed by local and national research, private party polling and national polls. The party is very vocal about its all-island status and aims to run a candidate in every constituency, though in the event it had candidates in only 38 of the 39 constituencies in 2020. Gender played a part in selection decisions, but party strategists reported that it did not have the prominence of 2016, when the gender quota laws had come into effect for the first time. Sinn Féin has a reasonable track record on gender. It exceeded the requirements in 2016 and with quite a few female incumbents, a more hands-off approach was adopted in 2020: just three gender directives were issued to selection conventions (in Clare, Kildare North and Kildare South). However, the party's proportion of female candidates did drop slightly.

Unusually among political parties, Sinn Féin selection conventions tend not to be contested. There is a widespread public impression that many decisions in the party are strongly influenced by the preferences of the Ard Comhairle and internal party democracy is more constrained than in other parties. More information was made available for the 2020 election but it remains the case that the party is reluctant to release details of internal organisational matters. Planning for the 2020 election began soon after the 2016 contest and the party had most of its selection conventions completed in 2017. Just three of the 39 conventions were contested, which suggests an element of informal pre-screening prior to conventions. The early completion of conventions posed something of an administrative hiccup as according to party rules, decisions lapse after two years. As a result, Sinn Féin had to hold a second wave of selection conventions in December 2019 and January 2020. In most cases, these conventions served to ratify existing decisions, especially in constituencies where the party had incumbent TDs. However, there were a small number of constituencies where new candidates had to be selected due to changes in personal circumstances, a late retirement or a death. None of the second wave of selection conventions was contested.

In January 2020, Cork North-Central incumbent TD Jonathan O'Brien decided to step down from politics and a new candidate (Thomas Gould) was chosen. In Cork North-West, the candidate selected decided not to contest the election for personal reasons. The party tried to find a replacement and former presidential election candidate Liadh Ní Riada was mooted in media reports but she decided against running, leaving the party with no candidate in the constituency. New candidates were selected at conventions in Clare and Tipperary, while in the Sligo–Leitrim constituency, Sligo based councillor Chris McManus withdrew from the party ticket. He was not replaced, with media reports suggesting that a one-candidate strategy was more likely to secure the seat of the incumbent, Martin Kenny. The decisions not to replace Chris McManus in Sligo–Leitrim and opting for a one-candidate ticket in Clare (over the two-candidate ticket that had been in place) highlight the cautious approach to candidate selection taken by Sinn Féin in the aftermath of its poor performance in the local and European elections of May 2019. Although the party secured an unforeseen victory in the Dublin Mid-West by-election, the wave of Sinn Féin victories in the election was unexpected, and preserving existing seats was a priority that informed many late 2019 decisions.

Sinn Féin ran 42 candidates in 38 constituencies. Cork North-West was the only constituency without a candidate and two candidates contested Cavan–Monaghan, Donegal, Dublin Mid-West and Louth. Party strategists interviewed for the chapter agreed with the widely reported contention that the party did not run enough candidates and that it might have secured up to ten extra seats with a larger slate of candidates (see Chap. 8). The party ended up contesting the election with a carefully calibrated defensive strategy designed to secure the seats of incumbent TDs. It was an electoral miscalculation, unavoidable perhaps due to the dynamic nature of party support, and it restricted the potential growth of the party. Aside from candidate numbers, candidate decision making was a relatively smooth process and there were few controversies in comparison to 2016.[17]

Green Party

The Green Party has an election task force (ETF) that is responsible for managing candidate selection. The committee includes the party chairperson, leader and deputy leader and some members from across the country. The party also has an election steering committee, which is established closer to the start of each election campaign. There is some overlap in the membership of the two committees and they work closely together in some of the final decision making as the election approaches. Preparations for the general election began in 2017 and the party confirmed its all-island approach to elections with its objective to run a candidate in every constituency. Members of the ETF also stressed that the party believes its supporters in every constituency should have the option of voting for a Green candidate. The party relies heavily on national polls, internal analysis and local feedback to develop its strategy. As its poll numbers improved through 2018, preparations intensified and strategists reported there was a strong sense the party could make gains.

Selection conventions were convened across the country starting in 2018. The ETF is responsible for overseeing selection conventions and the party chairperson appoints the returning officer for each convention. The Green Party operates OMOV and requires six months of membership before voting rights are acquired. The process is quite decentralised and a call for nominations is issued at constituency level and remains open for two weeks. Conventions are scheduled for two weeks after the close of nominations. Occasionally, the party engages in a local search for candidates. Strategists reported that this occurs especially when the local branch is small and in predominantly rural constituencies. Where a search committee is convened and asked to identify potential candidates, gender is often emphasised, but otherwise party strategists reported that a relatively hands-off approach to selection is preferred.

The Green Party had a very strong performance in the local and European Parliament elections and strategists reported two important outcomes from this. The number of contested selection conventions increased. Ambitious candidates identified opportunities for success and were more likely to put themselves forward at conventions. The second outcome was the ETF had a discussion about a two-candidate party ticket, which would be a rarity for a minor party. In effect, the discussion related only to Dublin Bay South and the possibility that the popularity of the leader, Éamon Ryan, might provide an opportunity to elect a second candidate. The final decision to stick with a one-candidate strategy was informed by the fact that the party leader was likely to spend a lot of time campaigning nationally and as a result might not be able to spend much time in his own constituency, thereby reducing the chance of success for a second candidate. It was also acknowledged that a second candidate could potentially endanger the seat of the leader and worse, might leave the party with no seat in the constituency. A small number of changes were made to the slate of candidates in early 2020 as the election approached. For example, Karin Dubsky stood down for personal reasons in Wexford and was replaced by Paula Roseingrave.

The post-election strategy review raised a number of important points. Managing success was a new phenomenon and contested selection conventions unusual in the past. The party is now considering how it will manage ambition at future elections. Strategists also noted that the party always had a strong gender balance but some last-minute changes in its candidate slate meant the party became a little concerned about its ticket and closer attention had to be paid to gender in the final decisions. As a result, it is expected that gender may be a more prominent consideration for future selection strategies.

Labour

The Labour Party ran 31 candidates in the election. It was widely remarked in the early stage of the election that this was the smallest field of candidates presented by the party since the 1950s.[18] Perhaps the most notable reflection of its electoral woes was the absence of a candidate in the Kerry constituency, which had been a stronghold for the party and produced one of its more significant party leaders, Dick Spring.

A sub-committee of the party's executive board is responsible for managing candidate selection. The group includes the party chair, party leader (who does not usually attend), national organiser, three members from the executive board and three appointees made by the party leader. Planning for the general election started immediately after government formation and two selection conventions were held in 2016. The party devised a plan to get young candidates onto the party ticket, in large part because of the older age profile of the Oireachtas members. Once candidates were on the ticket, they were deemed to have a quasi-electoral status and could participate more prominently in public debates. Selections accelerated in late 2017 in the lead-up to the resignation of Frances Fitzgerald. The pace of decision making slowed thereafter.

Candidate nominations are sought through a mail shot to all members. Nominees who come forward are asked to attend an interview with a selection panel made up of an Oireachtas member and two other party members. Incumbent Oireachtas members do not have to go through this process. The interview is generally informal and serves to evaluate compatibility with party values and policies. If a nomination is approved, the candidate goes forward to a selection convention. Selection conventions are held at constituency level and each member has a vote once they have been a member in the constituency branch for at least six months. Just one selection convention (Kildare North) was contested.

The decision not to contest every constituency was an uncomfortable if pragmatic one according to strategists. The party felt it did not have the members and organisation on the ground to support candidates in a number of constituencies and the gender quota was also a factor. With a smaller overall number of candidates, the party had to manage its final decisions carefully to ensure that it met the 30 per cent threshold. For example, the party had potential candidates (both male) in Cavan–Monaghan and Dublin South-West, but they were not formally ratified until the party was certain that it had sufficient women on the ticket. There were a number of additions to the party ticket in late 2019 as the party reviewed its local election performance and finalised its general election slate. The process involves the national organiser making a recommendation to the party chair and party leader, who approve or reject it. Late additions included Annie Hoey, Juliet O'Connell, Ciarán Ahern, Liam van der Spek and Ciara Kennedy.

Labour had a poor general election; its plan for recovery was up-ended. The party returned with one TD fewer and notable casualties from its senior ranks (Joan Burton, Jan O'Sullivan) but its difficulties are deep-rooted and were clearly visible in the pre-election phase. The absence of Labour candidates on ballots in some constituencies and the lack of competition at selection conventions reinforce the impression of long term decline.

Social Democrats

The Social Democrats were formed in 2015 and have a shared leadership structure with Catherine Murphy and Róisín Shortall acting as co-leaders. The party had temporary candidate selection procedures in place for the 2016 general election and internal party procedures were formalised in a party constitution after that election. The party has a Candidate Selection and Development Committee (CSDC) which is a sub-committee of the party's national executive. The CSDC has eight to ten members and it includes members outside of the national executive with specialist expertise relevant to election planning. The party leaders are members of the national executive but they have no specific powers in relation to candidate selection. The party has 30 branches around the country but strategists admitted that some of these are quite small and involve just a few members.

The CSDC devised the party's candidate strategy and managed the process. At an early point, the party took a realistic approach and decided that it would not contest constituencies where the party had no branches. Candidate selections were accelerated in 2018 and 15 candidates were chosen by the end of that year. Following successful local elections, the party increased its number of target constituencies and began to focus more resources in those areas.

The candidate selection process involved the CSDC issuing a call for candidates through the party network and also approaching potential candidates. The CSDC interviewed all candidates and made recommendations on nominations for constituency-level selection conventions. Strategists pointed out that while more than one candidate was interviewed in quite a few constituencies, frequently just one nomination was put forward to selection conventions. Some candidates who were interviewed as potential general election candidates were encouraged to run instead as local election candidates. Indeed, most of the party's general election candidates also contested the local elections. The CSDC was also managing candidate selection for the 2019 local election. Policy compatibility was a priority for the CSDC in its interviews with candidates, along with electability. The CSDC became interested in the social media track record of candidates towards the end of 2019, largely arising from scandals in the November 2019 by-elections, although its own candidates were not involved. No specific policy in relation to the social media profiles of candidates was adopted but this is an area where strategists expect that new party requirements may emerge. The Social Democrats were the only party to raise social media concerns in relation to candidate selection. Ill-judged social media comments of candidates were a particular feature of media coverage of the November 2019 by-elections and emerged again after the general election for both the Social Democrats and Sinn Féin. Their experiences may lead to incorporation of a social media profile review of candidates by all parties at future elections.

Selection conventions were held in all cases as party rules stipulate that the CSDC makes recommendations and not decisions on candidate selection. OMOV applies and members must have at least six months' membership to be eligible to vote in their constituency selection convention. Some later selection conventions doubled as candidate launches.

The Social Democrats have two female co-leaders and had a strong female slate of candidates at the 2016 general elections and again at the 2019 local elections. Strategists admitted that gender balance was discussed at CSDC meetings and at one point, somewhat flippantly, it was suggested that male candidates might need to be added to the ticket but this never arose.

A small number of candidates withdrew from the party ticket citing personal and financial reasons, in constituencies including Dublin Fingal, Dún Laoghaire and Limerick City. Prior to conventions, withdrawals were managed easily but some of these withdrawals led to last-minute decisions in early 2020 such as the addition of Jenny Blake as a candidate in Limerick City. In Dublin Mid-West, Anne-Marie McNally, a prominent party activist, decided not to run after a weak showing in the local elections and the November by-election while in Dún Laoghaire, Sinéad Gibney withdrew at a very late point and was replaced by councillor Dave Quinn.

Party strategists noted that the party was more focused on its candidates and providing direct support to their campaigns in 2020 compared with 2016, when building the party brand had been the over-riding objective. In 2020, the party top-line strategy was to prioritise candidates.

Solidarity–People Before Profit

Sol–PBP previously contested elections under the banner Anti-Austerity Alliance–People Before Profit (AAA–PBP). It is a loose electoral coalition that comprises three groups: Solidarity (whose members are also part of the Socialist Party), RISE (a group founded by Paul Murphy, formerly of AAA and the Socialist Party) and PBP. It is a far-left political movement. Twenty-seven of its candidates came from PBP, nine from Solidarity and Murphy was the only RISE candidate.

The parties maintain separate organisations and candidate selection was managed within the party groups. Efforts are made to reduce the number of constituencies where candidates within the alliance compete against each other. However, this is managed informally, on a case-by-case basis, and strategists indicated that there was a degree of 'horse-trading' to the negotiations and it was not always possible to get agreement. In Dublin Bay North, Solidarity and PBP both ran candidates alongside John Lyons, an independent candidate who had contested the 2016 election for PBP, which was deemed less than ideal by one of the party candidates. Similarly, in Dublin South-West, Solidarity ran a candidate in the same constituency as RISE's only candidate.

In PBP, the national steering committee oversees candidate selection. The committee is elected annually and has 12 members. The committee can also co-opt additional members, as needed. In 2019, the steering committee instructed branches to hold selection conventions. The party has strong branches in a number of constituencies and these held meetings to select candidates. Only a small number were contested. Each selection convention is attended by a member of the steering committee. All members are entitled to a vote although a strategist indicated that the approach is generally informal and membership details are not always checked. Candidates selected are ratified by the steering committee. In areas where the party has some party members but a weak branch structure, the steering committee approaches new candidates and these are added to the ticket.

Adding candidates in areas where the party does not generally have a strong profile was identified as meeting three objectives. It assisted the party in its goal of meeting the 2 per cent national vote threshold required to secure party funding under electoral law, it allowed the party to manage its gender profile in a low key manner and it also provided opportunities for the party to develop its structure.

PBP dealt with a controversy in Galway West when one of its candidates, Joe Loughnane, was suspended and later expelled from the party amidst allegations of assault. The party entered the election with a defensive strategy. The core aims were to protect the seats of its three incumbent TDs and maintain its state funding. It did not anticipate the surge in support for Sinn Féin and the spill-over advantage for PBP. At the post-election national committee meeting, the party reviewed its performance and a key aim for future elections is to build a more stable candidate base. The party runs a notable proportion of new candidates at every election.

PROFILING THE CANDIDATES

This section provides a profile of the candidates who contested the 2020 general election. The occupational background, gender breakdown, political experience and family political connections of candidates are set out for each party and for independents. As highlighted above, party selectors often lean towards candidates with more experience and prestigious occupational backgrounds. The chapter uses the *How Ireland Voted* classification system, first adopted in 1987. Seven categories of occupations are used. First on the list are farmers. The second group is commerce and this includes business people, the self-employed, financial consultants, auctioneers, agricultural contractors and web designers. Higher professional includes barristers, pharmacists, architects and doctors while lower professional comprises mainly teachers, nurses and therapists. Non-manual includes secretaries, sales persons, public sector employees, political staff and trade union officials while manual employee covers occupations such as tradespersons, bus drivers and manufacturing workers. The 'other' category is the most varied and includes students, the unemployed, retired persons, full-time activists, and occupations as varying as carers, performance artist and bodyguard. Candidates are classified according to their occupation prior to entering full-time politics and the data are presented in Table 3.2. Candidate occupations are listed on the notice of poll issued by each constituency returning office and are also often included in campaign literature, websites and on social media sites, especially LinkedIn. A small number of candidates were contacted directly by phone or email.

The largest group of candidates (24 per cent) have an occupational background in commerce. Business owners cover a wide spectrum of enterprises, from those who own medium sized firms employing hundreds of staff to smaller companies with a few people employed. Thirty-eight per cent of independent candidates have a commerce background and there are also significant numbers from a commerce background in Fianna Fáil, Fine Gael and the Green Party. The concentration of people from a business background is interesting more broadly as there is a general perception that there are few business people in politics. The absence of business people in the cabinet during the 2008 economic crisis was the subject of a great deal of comment.[19] The data from 2020 show that voters have a choice of people from different business backgrounds for whom they can vote.

Non-manual employees account for the second largest group of candidates. There is a diverse range of roles within this category. Since 2016, there has been a notable increase in the number of candidates who work in community and social development roles with public sector organisations and social enterprises. Parties on the left of the spectrum draw a large share of their candidates from this category and it accounts for the largest occupational group of candidates in Sinn Féin and Labour.

The professions have been prominent for some time. Twenty per cent of candidates are drawn from lower professional backgrounds and the Social Democrats, Green Party, Solidarity–PBP and Labour have a high concentration of candidates with this background. The higher professional group accounts for just 12 per cent of all candidates. The Green Party has the highest share of candidates from this group and, within this, there is an unusual cluster of architects.

The percentage of manual employees is low overall and Sinn Féin has the highest share of candidates from this occupational category at ten per cent. Farmers account for just five per cent of total candidates: this group,

Table 3.2 Occupational backgrounds of candidates, 2020

	Farmer	Commerce	Higher professional	Lower professional	Non-manual employee	Manual employee	Others	Unknown	Total candidates (%)	Total candidates (N)
Fianna Fáil	6	27	20	21	18	2	5	0	100	82
Fine Gael	13	23	17	17	21	4	5	0	100	84
Sinn Féin	0	12	5	17	38	10	17	2	100	42
Greens	0	21	23	31	21	0	5	0	100	39
Labour	0	16	10	29	32	6	6	0	100	31
Sol–PBP	0	5	0	30	27	8	30	0	100	37
Soc Dems	5	15	10	35	25	0	10	0	100	20
Other	3	22	13	9	10	9	16	1	100	68
Ind	7	38	5	20	17	6	17	0	100	128
% Total	*5*	*24*	*12*	*20*	*21*	*5*	*12*	*0*	*100*	*—*
Total (N)	*28*	*128*	*63*	*107*	*109*	*29*	*65*	*2*	*—*	*531*

Note: Figures within each party are expressed in percentages and the total N (and percentage) for occupations are included and listed in italics in the two end rows once a dominant force in Irish politics, has seen its numbers contract over many elections. Interestingly, even for those who do list farmer as their occupation, quite a few combine it with another role. Farmer is listed in the data for this chapter where it is the first occupation provided by a candidate. The growth in part-time farmers is a trend highlighted regularly by farming organisations in the media and it is also evident in political data now.

When combined, the lower and higher professions have the most candidates, but when these are separated, there are now more candidates from commerce and non-manual occupations. This marks the continuation of a trend where the professions are less dominant than they once were and politics has become more diverse with a greater share of non-manual employees and business people contesting elections. Interestingly, candidates from the Green Party share a more similar occupational background with Fianna Fáil and Fine Gael than with the other parties of the left.

One hundred and thirty eight TDs sought re-election in 2020, a slight decrease on the 2016 number (145). And in a pattern typical of other elections, 23 senators sought election to the lower house. Table 3.3 provides an overview of the political experience of candidates contesting the 2020 election.

Table 3.3 Political experience of candidates, 2020

Party	TD	Senator	Cllr/MEP	Other electoral experience	New candidate	Total
Fianna Fáil	54	5	35	5	2	100
Fine Gael	49	16	26	5	5	100
Sinn Féin	43	5	23	29	0	100
Green Party	8	3	49	21	21	100
Labour	16	10	45	23	6	100
Sol–PBP	16	0	8	51	24	100
Soc Dems	10	0	45	20	25	100
Others	3	0	9	46	43	100
Independents	13	0	20	32	35	100
Total (%)	*26*	*4*	*25*	*25*	*20*	100
Total (N)	*138*	*23*	*136*	*130*	*104*	*531*

Note: Numbers in rows are percentages. In the 'Cllr/MEP' column, all are councillors apart from one Sinn Féin candidate who was an MEP. 'Other electoral experience' refers to candidates who were not public representatives when selected but had previously contested elections at either local, Seanad, Dáil or European level. A new candidate is defined as a person with no previous experience as an election candidate

Fianna Fáil, Fine Gael and Sinn Féin presented experienced candidate
tickets to the electorate with incumbent TDs and senators making up 59,
65 and 48 per cent respectively of their candidates. These parties also drew
heavily from their councillor ranks as can be seen in Table 3.3. Succession
planning is important for parties and most aim to have a pipeline of potential candidates available from local government level, preferably with experience of contesting general elections, as vacancies emerge. The larger
parties tend to run very few candidates with no political experience at
general elections. Smaller parties (Green Party, Labour, Social Democrats)
had fewer Oireachtas members and relied more heavily on their councillor
ranks for election candidates. There is a clear preference for experienced
political candidates in the main parties. The 'Other' category consists of a
number of small and micro-parties. Competition for candidacy tends to be
quite limited in these parties: interest is lower and likelihood of success
also much reduced. As a result, the parties often see a high turnover of
candidates and field many new candidates at each election. The category
'other electoral experience' includes quite a diverse group of people. Some
have contested elections over many decades, while a small number made
their debut in the May 2019 local elections. The category also includes
those with political experience outside of the state. Anne McCloskey of
Aontú contested in the Sligo–Leitrim constituency but she is also a councillor in Derry (Northern Ireland); the same party's James Hope has also
contested parliamentary elections in Northern Ireland. And John Bowler
of the Irish Freedom Party was a city councillor and mayor in Hermosa
Beach City (USA).

Finally, turning to the personal backgrounds of candidates, Table 3.4
provides an overview of the gender breakdown of party tickets and family
connections in politics. All of the main parties reached the 30 per cent
quota required to receive full state funding, though just barely in the cases
of Fianna Fáil, Fine Gael, Labour and Sinn Féin. As discussed earlier, gender presented fewer controversies at selection conventions than in 2016
and party strategists had been working to meet the quota since the preceding election but the data show that many of the parties did not substantively improve their gender profile. While 33 per cent of Sinn Féin
candidates were women, this was a reduction on the 36 per cent figure in
2016. Gender balance on the party ticket also disimproved for Labour,
whose percentage share of women candidates dropped from 36 per cent
to 32 per cent. The quota is due to increase to 40 per cent at any general
election in 2023 or thereafter. The data highlighted here suggest that

Table 3.4   Gender and family links of candidates, 2020

Party	Total	Women	%	Family link	%
Fianna Fáil	84	26	31.0	29	34.5
Fine Gael	82	25	30.5	27	32.9
Sinn Féin	42	14	33.3	3	7.1
Green Party	39	16	41.0	3	7.7
Labour	31	10	32.2	3	9.7
Sol–PBP	37	15	40.5	1	2.7
Soc Dems	20	11	55.0	0	0
Others	68	21	30.8	3	4.4
Independents	128	24	18.8	9	7.0
Total	531	162	30.5	78	14.7

Note: Family link in politics is defined as where a family relation has held, or holds, office at either local or national level

many parties will have to invest considerable further effort in their gender initiatives if they are to meet the higher threshold. The reported light-touch efforts essentially resulted in a no change outcome in gender balance for the two bigger parties (Fianna Fáil and Fine Gael). Just 19 per cent of independent candidates were women. No quota applies to independent candidates and the group remains overwhelmingly male.

Political dynasties have been a longstanding feature of politics in Ireland and the data in Table 3.4 show that 15 per cent of candidates had a family link in politics. Family political link includes parent, aunt, uncle, brother or sister and spouse was added to the list in 2016. The percentage of candidates with such a link has averaged close to 15 per cent for at least four elections. Two family political pathways have been common for many years: candidates who succeeded a family member (often a parent) into politics and candidates who have a family member who is a local councillor and operates within the political family business. The second type has grown sharply since the abolition of the dual mandate at the 2004 local elections. A high-profile example is senior Fianna Fáil TD Michael McGrath and his brother Séamus McGrath, who is a well-known councillor in Cork. Of the first type, Seán Haughey is the son of former Taoiseach Charles Haughey, Éamon Ó Cuív a grandson of former Taoiseach Éamon de Valera, Charlie Flanagan a son of former Fine Gael minister Oliver J. Flanagan and Richard Bruton a brother of former Taoiseach John Bruton. Emer Currie is the daughter of Austin Currie, who was a founding member of the SDLP in Northern Ireland and later served as a Fine

Gael TD. Having a family link in politics is much more common among Fianna Fáil and Fine Gael candidates.

Smaller parties and independents more typically have family members in politics at the same time. The Greens' Catherine Martin and Francis Noel Duffy are the only married couple elected to the 33rd Dáil and Catherine Martin's brother Vincent P. Martin also contested the election for the party, and he was later appointed to the Seanad as one of the Taoiseach's 11 nominees (see Chap. 12). Michael Healy-Rae and Danny Healy-Rae were both re-elected in the Kerry constituency. The Healy-Rae brothers were the only successful sibling pairing, but there were a few others who contested the elections as well. James Byrne contested the Louth constituency for Fianna Fáil and is a brother of Fianna Fáil TD Thomas Byrne. And three members of the Tóibín family contested the election on behalf of Aontú.

CONCLUSION

Political parties in Ireland operate an inclusive approach to candidate selection. Party members have voting rights and decision making is shared with party elites. Decisions are taken at constituency level, which implies decentralised decision making, but the picture is more complex. There are crucial differences between the larger and smaller parties. In smaller parties, just one candidate is chosen and party members often have greater latitude in the decisions that are taken. Larger parties (Fianna Fáil, Fine Gael and Sinn Féin) have more candidates and also more incumbents so a more intrusive approach is adopted. When more than one candidate is to be selected, party elites decide on the numbers and any other qualifying criteria that must be met. In all parties, elites have the power to add and deselect candidates. Larger parties use this power tactically, often adding candidates who may not have come through a convention, or chose not to contest a convention knowing they would not emerge as a candidate even though they were preferred by the leadership. Small parties add candidates where they have no branch network and no-one is very interested in being the candidate. These candidates, often known as paper candidates, fly the party flag on the ballot but there is little expectation they will win or even be competitive in a race. The need for parties to meet the gender quota also leads to greater structuring of decision making by party elites. Many parties added female candidates as the election approached to ensure the

30 per cent quota was met; larger parties, because of a predominantly male incumbent profile, require greater use of these powers.

Candidate selection strategies resulted in sub-optimal outcomes for Fianna Fáil, Fine Gael and Sinn Féin in 2020. To some extent, over-selection by Fianna Fáil and Fine Gael, and under-selection by Sinn Féin, was unavoidable. Fianna Fáil and Fine Gael over-estimated their final support and operated expansive candidate strategies while Sinn Féin managed a defensive process that aimed to protect incumbents. Polls during the campaign suggest there were notable movements in support levels for the three parties (see Chap. 10). Ultimately, Fianna Fáil and Fine Gael had too many candidates, while Sinn Féin had too few. The strategic mis-alignment of the three parties underlines the fluid electoral context of the election.

Parties faced the prospect of a snap election from an early point in the election cycle and this led to early preparation for an election that did not materialise. Party tickets are rarely fixed until the days before an election and parties had to deal with considerable fluidity in their candidate lists for this election cycle due to the long preparation phase. Ensuring that party tickets complied with the gender quota contributed to uncertainty about tickets until the close of nominations. The last-minute addition of women candidates indicates that meeting the gender quota continues to challenge parties.

Two High Court cases relating to candidate selection arose during the 2016 election cycle. In contrast, the 2020 cycle passed off with only a small number of low-level controversies. Deselection of Fine Gael candidates were the most notable episodes, while most other disputes were resolved at constituency level.

Returning to the question of who gets selected and why that matters, it is clear that the profile of candidates has been changing incrementally at elections. Commerce, non-manual and professional occupational backgrounds are the most common, while farmers have all but faded from national politics. 2020 marked a further small change in these trends rather than any notable departure. More women are now selected and there are fewer dynastic candidates. But parties have also retained their decisive role in ensuring that their preferred personnel make it to the ballot paper. It is an open question as to whether the 2020 candidate cohort provided fewer 'mediocre' candidates, as Carty termed them in 1981.

NOTES

1. For an extensive discussion and a slightly different metaphor, see Michael Gallagher and Michael Marsh (eds), *Candidate Selection in Comparative Perspective: the secret garden of politics* (London: Sage, 1988).
2. R. Kenneth Carty, *Party and Parish Pump: Electoral Politics in Ireland* (Waterloo, Ontario: Wilfrid Laurier University Press, 1981), p. 137.
3. Gideon Rahat, 'Candidate selection: the choice before the choice', *Journal of Democracy* 18:1 (2007), pp. 157–70.
4. See Fiona Buckley, Yvonne Galligan and Claire McGing, 'Women and the election: assessing the impact of gender quotas', pp. 185–206 in Michael Gallagher and Michael Marsh (eds), *How Ireland Voted 2016: the election that nobody won* (Cham: Palgrave Macmillan, 2016).
5. Under the relevant legislation, candidate gender quotas rise to 40 per cent seven years after the first general election at which they were implemented.
6. See Susan E. Scarrow and Burcu Gezgor, 'Declining memberships, changing members? European political party members in a new era,' *Party Politics* 16: 6 (2010), pp. 823–43.
7. Fine Gael is a notable exception to this; see Michael Gallagher and Michael Marsh, *Days of Blue Loyalty: the politics of membership of the Fine Gael party* (Dublin: PSAI Press, 2002).
8. John Bochel and David Denver, 'Candidate selection in the Labour Party: what the selectors seek', *British Journal of Political Science* 13: 1 (1983), pp. 45–69.
9. Audrey Vandeleene, Jérémy Dodeigne, and Lieven De Winter, 'What do selectorates seek? A comparative analysis of Belgian federal and regional candidate selection processes in 2014', *American Behavioral Scientist* 60:7 (2016), pp. 889–908.
10. Audrey Vandeleene and Giulia Sandri, 'The more, the smoother? Candidate selection and intraparty competition,' pp. 77–103 in Audrey Vandeleene, Lieven De Winter and Pierre Baudewyns (eds), *Candidates, Parties and Voters in the Belgian Partitocracy* (Basingstoke: Palgrave Macmillan, 2019).
11. David M. Farrell, Michael Gallagher and David Barrett, 'What do Irish voters want from and think of their politicians?' pp. 190–208 in Michael Marsh, David M. Farrell and Theresa Reidy (eds), *The Post-Crisis Irish Voter: voting behaviour in the Irish 2016 general election* (Manchester: Manchester University Press, 2018), pp. 192–3.
12. Gideon Rahat and Reuven Y. Hazan, 'Candidate selection methods: an analytical framework', *Party Politics* 7:3 (2001), pp. 297–322.
13. TDs may not hold a seat in a city or county council concurrently with being a member of the Dáil. Thus, newly elected TDs are deemed to have vacated council seats they held. These vacancies are filled by co-option

rather than by-elections; in practice, each party chooses the replacements for its own departing councillors.

14. This number requires some qualification as Verona Murphy was added to, and then deselected from, the party ticket. She was subsequently elected as an independent.

15. For a discussion, see Elaine Loughlin, 'Fine Gael courting the campaigners as election candidates', *Irish Examiner*, 25 March 2019.

16. The deselection of an incumbent TD by a party is quite rare. It seems that the most recent examples prior to 2020 date from 1987 and were Fine Gael TDs Alice Glenn and Liam Skelly and Fianna Fáil TD Tom Leonard (data provided by Michael Gallagher, TCD).

17. For a discussion of candidate selection at the 2016 general selection, see Theresa Reidy, 'Candidate selection and the illusion of grass-roots democracy', pp. 47–74 in Gallagher and Marsh (eds), *How Ireland Voted 2016*.

18. For a discussion see Daniel McConnell, 'Kerry constituency profile: no Labour candidate for first time in 87 years', *Irish Examiner*, 3 February 2020.

19. This point is discussed in more detail in Theresa Reidy, 'Candidate selection', pp. 47–67 in Michael Gallagher and Michael Marsh (eds), *How Ireland Voted 2011: the full story of Ireland's earthquake election* (Basingstoke: Palgrave Macmillan, 2011).

CHAPTER 4

Campaign Strategies: The Inside Story of How the Election was Fought

Pat Leahy

The only constant now, it seems, is change. Where once Ireland's politics was a byword for predictability and consistency, with the leadership of government changing hands occasionally between two similar parties and government policy changing almost not at all, the great retreat from traditional loyalties and voting patterns begun by the financial crash of 2008 and period of austerity that followed has continued apace in the elections since. The 2020 general election followed the contests in 2011 and 2016 in further remaking the political landscape, ending the dominance of the big two parties and further fracturing the political system. The old

---

This chapter relies heavily on the author's coverage of the campaign (and that of his colleagues) in *The Irish Times*. In addition, conversations and background interviews were held after the election with a series of people closely involved in the campaign. Where possible, sources have been cited.

P. Leahy (✉)
The Irish Times, Dublin, Ireland
e-mail: pleahy@irishtimes.com

© The Author(s), under exclusive license to Springer Nature   71
Switzerland AG 2021
M. Gallagher et al. (eds.), *How Ireland Voted 2020*,
https://doi.org/10.1007/978-3-030-66405-3_4

politics is truly gone. What shape the new politics takes is not yet clear but volatility seems certain to mark it.

If there is one word to describe the campaign of 2020, it is this: unpredictable. It was preceded by a long period of deep uncertainty about the future because of the threat of Brexit—a concern that ultimately decided the timing of the general election. The incumbent government was a novel arrangement: a minority administration comprising Fine Gael and independent TDs facilitated by a confidence and supply arrangement with Fianna Fáil. To add further to the complications, Fine Gael had changed its leader in 2017, with Leo Varadkar replacing Enda Kenny, and like all new leaders, Varadkar was eyeing his own mandate. Fianna Fáil sat impatiently on the opposition benches, ever more critical of the Fine Gael-led government that it was keeping in office, while elsewhere the opposition critiques—especially on housing, where a major social crisis was developing—grew in volume and intensity. Sinn Féin had also changed its leader; Gerry Adams stood down after 35 years in which he led the party first through a brutal and bloody war, then, eventually, to peace. The party he left as leader was unrecognisable to the one he first led, but as the election approached, after reverses in local and European elections in the Republic and under increasing pressure for its failure to revive the power-sharing institutions in Northern Ireland, it was caught in a sense of deep uncertainty about its future and its mission.

Brexit overshadowed everything in the run-in to the election; indeed, the contest would have taken place well before 2020 if it hadn't been for the UK's lengthy and convoluted exit from the EU. In the light of the Covid-19 pandemic that would convulse the world, Brexit seems almost trivial. But for the two years before the 2020 election, it was the biggest issue in Irish politics (see Chap. 5).

But that was not the only issue. The domestic problem that would dominate much of the election debate was a chronic shortage of housing, leading to a mushrooming of the numbers of people experiencing homelessness and seeking emergency accommodation. By the run-in to the 2020 election, the numbers in emergency accommodation had reached 10,000; government efforts to tackle the crisis by providing new forms of accommodation and building more social and affordable housing, while not entirely ineffectual, never managed to get ahead of the problem.

Along with housing, the Government most often found itself under pressure on health. It wasn't, for sure, the first government to experience public dissatisfaction with the state of the health service, and won't be the last. But at a time of strong economic growth and a buoyant exchequer, many voters were particularly agitated about it. A million people were on waiting lists; emergency units were perpetually overcrowded; the system seemed not to be fit for purpose. Along with housing, health topped the list of issues of concern for voters (see Chap. 10).

There was more than just public dissatisfaction with the government's performance on health and housing at play, though. There was a sort of underlying national grumpiness bubbling beneath the surface of public opinion. It was different from the anger at austerity that had infused the election of 2016, but no less politically potent. Polls showed that many people believed that Varadkar and Simon Coveney (Minister for Foreign Affairs) were doing a good job on Brexit; but they also believed that while things were clearly better for the country than they had been in 2016—and vastly better than they were in the depth of the economic crisis of the few years before—very many voters were still finding it hard to manage, hard to get a break. They were, to coin a phrase, running to a standstill. In a Life and Times survey for *The Irish Times* in 2019 (as distinct from the newspaper's regular political polling), the responses showed that 49 per cent of people said they were 'getting by'; almost a third (32 per cent) said they did not see the benefit of the economic recovery; 14 per cent said they were struggling. Commenting on the data, Fintan O'Toole wrote that Ireland was now 'safely harboured in the port of global ordinariness: urban, wired-up, consumeristic, aspirational. But beneath the waters there are deep currents of uncertainty.'[1]

Ireland, O'Toole said, was 'rather like a swimming duck—an apparently smooth glide on the surface hides a great deal of frantic paddling below'. This uncertainty, this tension, this stress of paddling furiously would unleash itself spectacularly at the ballot box in the shape of a vote for change that was as momentous as it was unfocussed. None of that was apparent before the election campaign commenced. It was the campaign that did the job of focussing that inchoate mood among many voters into a desire for political change. In that respect at least, it was one of the most consequential general election campaigns ever.

THE PARTIES PREPARE THEIR CAMPAIGNS

Sinn Féin

Sinn Féin's approach to the general election was different to any it had previously contested. For a start, it was no longer led by Gerry Adams: after a long apprenticeship and a carefully managed process, Mary Lou McDonald had replaced her mentor (without a contest) in early 2018. Though McDonald had put years into cultivating the organisation in the North as part of her preparation to assume the role, the privately-educated, Trinity graduate was capable of reaching into cohorts of the southern electorate that had proved off-limits to Adams, the old warhorse.

That, at least, was the theory. But McDonald had a difficult opening period as leader. Against the advice of some party colleagues, she insisted on running Liadh Ní Riada in the presidential election against the enormously popular incumbent Michael D. Higgins; she flopped. Far more serious were the local and European elections of May 2019, which produced the worst result Sinn Féin had seen since it entered southern politics seriously (see Chap. 1). The story was the same almost everywhere—in the urban heartlands in Dublin and Cork, the rural towns where candidates had chiselled out political bases, places where the party had strong organisations, and where it did not, where it had strong candidates, and where it did not.

It would be hard to overstate the shock to the organisation. 'Sinn Féin aren't crybabies,' McDonald defiantly told reporters when she turned up to face the music at the count in the RDS, but she and the rest of the party leadership were reeling. 'We realised quickly there was a very big problem,' says one party insider.[2]

The party embarked on a 'very, very sharp' review of the campaign and the state of the organisation. It was 'very thorough, very scathing, very critical', says one party figure; 'there was a lot of tough talking'.[3] The exercise was conducted at all levels of the party, and encompassed discussions, interviews and written submissions. TDs and other party figures conducted their own researches among party members and activists. One of the things that worried the party leadership was not just that the results of the elections were so bad, but that they did not see it coming. 'Why did we not pick up the signal that the election would be so bad? Why were we deaf and blind to where the voters were?'[4]

They went to people and said, 'Right, gloves off, tell us what went wrong'. The results were sobering. They found that for all the much-vaunted level of volunteerism in the party the organisation in many parts of the country 'just wasn't functioning'. Individual parts of the organisation had become riven with divisions—this element of the party's dysfunction was visible to the outside world because of a series of resignations from the party, with many of the departing members (who included several local representatives) alleging campaigns of bullying and intimidation against them. They found that voters were not hearing what the party thought it was saying to them.

There was also a 'very frank discussion' about the performance of the new leader, which aroused significant criticism in a party with a stronger than usual culture of loyalty to the leadership. Participants in the exercise found her 'too shouty', 'too negative', and prone to 'too much attacking'.[5]

There was also a strategic problem: the point of the McDonald leadership was to broaden the party's appeal in the Republic, but while her attempts to move the party towards the mainstream in search of new voters had not, apparently, been successful, her attempts to do so had alienated some of her core voters. It was not a good place to be.

Faced with this frank assessment of the party's—and the leadership's—failures, and staring an imminent general election in the face, party chiefs made a series of changes in the way the party was preparing for the contest. A number of organisational changes were put in place; research was improved; there was a focus on better local political and electoral intelligence. There was, says one person involved, an effort to professionalise many aspects of the party's operations.

Externally, the party sought to ensure that its political messages became more consistent, clearer, more ruthless. There was a focus on 'solutions', rather than complaints: health, housing, giving families a break. They sought to 'soften' the image of McDonald, seeking to show her to voters in a variety of 'non-combative' poses.[6] At the same time, prominent party TDs such as Pearse Doherty, Louise O'Reilly, David Cullinane and Eoin Ó Broin began to present themselves as possible ministers in a future government. Doherty and Ó Broin were especially effective in the finance and housing briefs, with strong Dáil and media performances.[7]

In late November, the party gave itself a shot in the arm with a by-election victory in Dublin Mid-West, one of four contests held on the day. Mark Ward, a councillor in Clondalkin, took the seat ahead of the independent councillor and former Green TD, Paul Gogarty and the Fine Gael candidate Emer Higgins. His victory was a huge morale boost for a party desperately in need of one—'We had won again; that was very important'[8]—but it also showed that the combination of an improved 'ground game' and better message discipline could be a winning combination. The local messaging concentrated heavily on the idea that ordinary families needed a break—a refrain that would become familiar during the general election campaign. As a result of the by-election victory—and the changes that had been made in the party's approach—it was in far better shape as the year ended. Sinn Féin didn't expect to win big; but it believed it had a fighting chance not to lose big.

The Green Party

If Sinn Féin had endured a nightmare at the local and European elections in May, the Green Party had its best electoral outing ever. 'It's more than a surge,' wrote Harry McGee in *The Irish Times*,[9] when the results of the RTÉ exit poll were published. A more common description was the 'Green tsunami'.

Actually, this overstated things somewhat. The Greens had an outstanding day, winning six per cent of the vote and gaining 37 seats in the local elections and returning two MEPs (narrowly missing out on a third), but the party still ended up behind the Labour Party on every measure—seat numbers, share of the vote, number of votes cast. Nonetheless, the Greens' transformative performance was the story of the day, and the party leadership immediately began to look forward to the possibilities of the general election.

The local and European election campaign had marked a step change for the Greens in every way—volunteers, donations, media share, political clout. From an early stage, this was visible on the ground: Green candidates who had previously plodded the pavements with a handful of committed volunteers noticed that they now had dozens turning up every night. The rise in activism that Green candidates had seen during the local election campaign continued afterwards; the party saw its membership rolls swell from 1200 to 2500 in a couple of months. The growing public concerns about climate change—as school climate strikes and other activism gained strength—also helped the party build its reach and capacity, and added to the sense of growing momentum. When the colleges returned in the autumn, the numbers attending events run by the party's youth wing, the Young Greens, shot up. The question for party managers was the same as always: how do we best turn this support into seats? The party's electoral task force—the body charged with overseeing the preparations for the election—worked throughout the autumn on professionalising the party's preparations, with a greater use of data and a tighter focus on supporting the constituencies where they reckoned there was a strong chance of a seat. These were ranked in order of winnability, and therefore priority for support from party headquarters. At one stage, the number of target seats expanded to 20, but contracted to more realistic estimates as the election came closer. (Party leader Eamon Ryan maintained publicly the party could win six seats, but his private expectation was considerably higher.) Each candidate was given help designing and refining campaign plans tailored for individual constituencies. 'It was a different type of support [to the candidates],' says a person involved. 'More support and a different type of support. More management. More strategic ... It was a complete change in the way we operated previously.'[10]

There was some unease in the party, some of whose members tended to interpret its volunteerist ethos as a licence for amateurism. It certainly represented a somewhat cultural shift. 'There was unease ... I wouldn't call it opposition,' says one senior party figure.[11] The party reckoned it was ready to fight an election with a few weeks' notice in September; by October, the candidates were canvassing regularly. Candidates were encouraged to raise money over the Christmas period. By January, 'we were in a holding pattern—we were ready to go.'

Fianna Fáil

Fianna Fáil approached the 2020 general election with reasons to be confident, and reasons to be nervous. It believed—correctly—that the Fine Gael government was unpopular, especially outside Dublin, and that its strong ground game in the constituencies could help it take seats from its old rivals.

Some influential people in Fianna Fáil also suspected the longer Leo Varadkar spent in office, the greater the chances that voters would lose confidence in him. Party leader Micheál Martin and his advisers did not hold a flattering view of the Fine Gael leader, constantly attacked him for being 'obsessed with spin' and believed that he would be 'found out' by voters.[12] And while senior Fianna Fáil figures sought to understand Varadkar's method and motivations—on the military maxim of 'know your enemy'—they never really got a handle on him or his inner circle. There was always a measure of nervousness in their judgements on the man they assumed would be their chief opponent. They were wary of him.

Fianna Fáil also looked at Sinn Féin's difficulties and saw opportunity. With several targets in Dublin, and Sinn Féin's weakness in the local elections making that party apparently vulnerable, Fianna Fáil nurtured hopes of regaining much of the working-class and lower-middle class vote that had been its traditional bedrock in Dublin before the financial crisis.

The party drew some encouragement from the local election results, especially in Dublin, where it won top spot on Dublin City Council for the first time in 20 years. With the party desperately needing to recover in the capital, the local results seemed to be a sign that things were on track. Nationally it won 12 new council seats, retaining its status as the largest party of local government. But the European elections were less successful.

A much greater worry for Fianna Fáil TDs was the confidence and supply arrangement under which they had facilitated the Fine Gael government since 2016, and which, they feared (correctly, as it turned out) would hamper their ability to campaign against the Fine Gael government. Every time they raised the shortcomings of the Fine Gael-led government—on housing, on health, on broadband, on overspending at the National Children's Hospital—they faced the accusation: but you are keeping them in government. They heard it as much in television and radio studios as they did on the doorsteps. And it was, they knew, true. Fianna Fáil was keeping them in government.

As it prepared for the campaign, Fianna Fáil sought to hone a message of reliability and responsibility. It had said it would facilitate the Fine Gael-led government for three budgets; it did. 'We did what we said we would do,' said Seán Dorgan, the party's long-time general secretary.[13] After that, it extended the facility—a unilateral move by Martin that caused some considerable grumbling in his parliamentary party—for another, final budget in the autumn of 2019 because of the ongoing Brexit crisis-drama, a move it hoped voters would recognise as responsible politics.

Martin and his tight-knit group of officials and advisers hoped and planned that this campaign would be the culmination of the remarkable journey on which they had led their decimated party since 2011. Then, the very future of Fianna Fáil was widely held to be in the balance. Martin and his team led Fianna Fáil back from the brink, through the comeback election in 2016 and now, they hoped, they could achieve the impossible by making it once again the largest party in the Dáil, and the anchor of the next government. In this context, the fact that the Fianna Fáil campaign team chose to repeat the slogan of 2016—'An Ireland for all'—for the 2020 election was entirely consistent with their approach. Their message about investment in public services and 'fairness' in health and housing, with the background music of Martin's increasingly overtly social democratic positioning, was also the same as 2016. With polling and feedback from TDs telling them that Fine Gael was—once Brexit was left aside—increasingly unpopular, they hoped it was a message whose time had come.

Fianna Fáil also realised that the mood for change in the country was strong. 'The government was unpopular, Varadkar was unpopular, people were unhappy with their lot, they wanted change,' was the summary offered by one of Martin's advisers of the public mood before the election.[14] But Fianna Fáil didn't believe the people wanted radical change, that they would risk the benefits of the economic recovery that was now so much more palpable to voters than it had been in 2016. Fianna Fáil reckoned the country was ready for moderate and considered—not radical—change. It was a reasonable expectation. It would not, however, survive contact with the white heat of a general election campaign.

Labour

Labour approached the general election campaign struggling—as it had done for much of the previous four years since the electoral massacre of 2016—for relevance, attention and distinctiveness. The party's decision to eschew government in 2016 was intended to allow it to rebuild in opposition but the opposition benches—crowded with Fianna Fáil, Sinn Féin, the Greens and Social Democrats, along with independents and the small parties of the radical left—left little room for Labour's introspection. Its leader Brendan Howlin was a quintessential politician of government—indeed, he had probably been the best minister, in the toughest job, in the 2011–2016 cabinet—and he was unsuited to the political dogfight necessary after that. Beyond the successful campaigning of health spokesman Alan Kelly on the Cervical Check and children's hospital scandals, it was hard to think of one issue on which Labour had made the running in opposition. In truth, the party had never really recovered, politically or psychologically, from the trauma of its time in government and its bloody denouement.

But Howlin was a canny enough politician to know that Labour's future—and he knew the party was fighting for its future—depended not

on having a say on the great issues of the day, but on securing seats in a
handful of key constituencies. If Labour's next generation of leaders—
Kelly, Ged Nash, Aodhán Ó Riordáin, Seán Sherlock—could not hold or
gain seats then it was hard to see a viable future for the party in the next
Dáil. The great cull of 2016 had left it with the oldest parliamentary party
in the Dáil and with retirements on the cards (though some veteran TDs,
such as Joan Burton and Jan O'Sullivan, bravely vowed to soldier on)
generational replacement was imperative. Winning those seats became
Labour's overriding priority, and it was given significant encouragement
by a decent local elections result in the May 2019 contests. In the autumn,
it appointed Trinity senator Ivana Bacik to be its director of elections, and
the party received a boost when Duncan Smith performed strongly in the
Dublin Fingal by-election in late November. At a national level, the party's
message was about increased funding for public services, especially housing and healthcare—but so was everyone else's. Labour hoped that its
experience in government would convince voters it could implement its
policies; on the other hand, it didn't want to talk too much about its time
in government, either. In any event, its focus would be on the handful of
do-or-die constituencies.

Social Democrats

Once touted as the coming thing in Irish politics the Social Democrats
prepared for the 2020 general election with more modest expectations
than once might have been the case; but this prompted a realism and focus
that would pay dividends. The party's only two TDs, Róisín Shortall and
Catherine Murphy, were 'co-leaders' (the third of its original co-leaders,
Stephen Donnelly, had left the party in 2016 and subsequently joined
Fianna Fáil) and the party punched above its weight with a particularly
strong voice on the health issue, stemming from Shortall's leadership of a
Dáil committee that produced the Sláintecare reform plan. The party also
benefited from a strong backroom team.

Like other parties, the Social Democrats were on election watch for
most of 2019 and were preparing for an imminent contest from the start
of 2020, bringing all their candidates together early in January for advice
on messaging, slogans and on managing their campaigns. Although some
last-minute changes to the tickets were necessary, the party ran 20 candidates, of which it reckoned ten were seriously in the running for seats.

Independents and Small Parties

Ireland's archipelago of micro-parties and independents had become, if anything, more diffuse than it was in 2016, when independents and small parties won nearly 30 per cent of the vote and a group of independents—styling themselves the Independent Alliance—entered government to take up a variety of ministerial posts. Some independent alliance ministers—John Halligan and Finian McGrath—decided not to stand again, as did the Clare independent Dr Michael Harty. Clare Daly and Mick Wallace had departed to the European Parliament. But elsewhere the profusion of independents continued in every constituency. The former Sinn Féin TD Peadar Tóibín, who split with the party on the issue of abortion, founded a new party, Aontú, after a series of well-attended public meetings around the country.

Solidarity–People Before Profit, despite having some of the Dáil's most high profile TDs among its members, approached the general election with some trepidation. It had suffered a disappointing local election in 2019, and feared that its candidates would be squeezed out, though at least it had managed to keep the radical left's customary splits and infighting to a minimum (if not eliminate them completely). TDs such as Richard Boyd Barrett, Paul Murphy and Ruth Coppinger were strong media performers—but they knew that might not save them in their constituencies in tight counts. Their message was to offer a 'radical alternative' to Fine Gael and Fianna Fáil. But there was a queue for that ride.

Fine Gael

Fine Gael had started working in earnest on election planning in the spring of 2018. Though there had been a general election 'scare' in November–December 2017 over revelations—reverberations from a decade and more of Garda misdeeds—which led to the departure of Frances Fitzgerald from the government,[15] an election then was never likely, despite much huffing and puffing from all sides (see Chap. 1). Varadkar was just six months in office then; but that is long enough to know that no prime minister ever sacrifices his government to save a minister. The opposite always happens.

Nonetheless, the affair did prompt urgency from Fine Gael about its election preparations. From then on, the sound of the election drums would never be far distant; election speculation came and went with the changing of the seasons. After the election, senior figures in Fine Gael acknowledged that the optimum timing for an election would have been in the summer after the passage of the constitutional referendum that liberalised Ireland's abortion laws in May 2018. They say Varadkar realised it too at the time; but it was too late to spring an election on voters who had not been prepared for such a move, and in any event, though preparations had been ongoing for months, they were substantially incomplete.[16] 'The practicalities take time,' said Mark Mortell, a party adviser.[17] Senior figures in the party—including but not limited to the decisive triumvirate of Varadkar, finance minister Paschal Donohoe and Tánaiste Simon Coveney—were by turns bullish and cautious. In the end, the brief flurry of election fever in the summer of 2018 amounted to just another series of news cycles dominated by election speculation, with nothing at the end of it all. There would be many others before the poll was eventually called a year and a half later.

Brexit came to dominate Irish politics, and to overshadow the question of election timing (see Chap. 5). And while the Fine Gael-led government was generally judged, by pundits and public alike, to be performing well on Brexit, other aspects of the government's performance had produced exactly the effect that Fianna Fáil hoped. In particular, controversies about the escalating cost of major projects, including the National Broadband Plan and the National Children's Hospital, had damaged the administration's credibility as a competent manager of the national finances. And the government seemed incapable of addressing the problem. When social protection minister Regina Doherty told RTÉ presenter Seán O'Rourke at the height of the controversy about the children's hospital that the 'problem with Fine Gael' was that it was too prudent and too careful with the public finances,[18] she was articulating the party's true sense of itself; she was also demonstrating how far removed it had become from the public's rather less rosy judgement. All parties in government eventually become remote from the voters; Fine Gael was no different. It would never quite get over that problem.

The party had also suffered a series of self-inflicted wounds from its own TDs and candidates throughout 2019, most notably those concerning incumbent TD Maria Bailey and election candidate Verona Murphy (see Chap. 3, p. 51–2). In December, the Cork TD and former junior minister for European Affairs Dara Murphy resigned his seat after it was reported that he continued to claim attendance expenses at Leinster House whilst working principally in Brussels for the European People's

Party. The Taoiseach mumbled about an inquiry in the Dáil, but the damage had been done.

By the end of 2019, with the UK due to leave the EU as soon as possible (though with a transition period until the end of 2020), there was now nothing standing in the way of a general election in Ireland. If Fine Gael could see that, the Dáil could too. On 9 December, the government scraped through a motion of no confidence in the housing minister Eoghan Murphy, winning by just three votes. Independent TDs on whom the government relied muttered privately that they would not be able to continue their support in the new year. The jig was up, and everyone knew it.

There was time, early in 2020, for Fine Gael to take aim at its own foot one more time. A proposed government commemoration of the Royal Irish Constabulary (RIC), the police force that upheld British rule in Ireland prior to independence, was planned as an inclusive gesture and part of the 'decade of commemorations'. Accusations that the government was paying tribute to the Black and Tans, the notorious paramilitary force created by the British to assist the RIC, led to a huge public controversy. The government made the classic mistake of first defending, then abandoning its position.[19] It stuck in many voters' minds, giving them another reason to dislike the Fine Gael-led government.

Fine Gael was under no illusions about the nature of the task it faced. It knew it would receive tremendous criticism on health and housing, the two areas where public concern was strongly anti-government. And Varadkar knew that it would be an extraordinary feat for any party to win three consecutive terms in government. Yet Fine Gael brought to the campaign an undeniably strong economy, and dextrous handling of Brexit that had avoided the worst possible outcome of a hard, crash-out Brexit—a prospect that had terrified the country for the past year. We will lose on housing, one minister told the present writer at the time. We can get 'a draw on health' (it was a strong view in the leadership of Fine Gael at the time that while the public were habitually despairing of the health service, they didn't necessarily believe anyone could fix the problems). We win on the economy, and we win on Brexit.[20] 'Brexit was the strongest card,' said a key figure of the backroom team.[21] The party also felt that its team of ministers—high profile compared to a little-known Fianna Fáil front bench—gave it a significant advantage over Fianna Fáil (all governments think this). And there was no mistaking it: Fine Gael believed its rivals were Fianna Fáil. Beat Fianna Fáil, and they won the election. It wouldn't quite turn out like that.

THE CAMPAIGN

The Larger Parties

On the morning of 14 January, Taoiseach Leo Varadkar, declaring that now was the 'best time for the country' to choose its next government, called a general election for Saturday, 8 February.

Varadkar said his government had achieved agreements on Brexit and in Northern Ireland and 'modernised our society', but acknowledged that many people were frustrated about housing and health services. He promised to use the fruits of economic recovery for 'health, housing, climate action and tax reform'. 'Now I seek a fresh mandate so we can continue to build a better future,' he said at Government Buildings, before departing for Áras an Uachtaráin to seek a formal dissolution of the Dáil from President Michael D. Higgins. 'Opposition leaders immediately sought to draw the campaign battle lines on the issues of health and housing,' *The Irish Times* reported.[22]

From the outset, Fine Gael targeted Fianna Fáil, reflecting the political and media consensus that the election campaign would be a shoot-out between the big two. On the first full day of campaigning, Varadkar launched the Fine Gael campaign in a forklift factory in Monaghan. Local TD and business minister Heather Humphreys declared: 'This is not the time for the Fianna Fáil junior B team,' beginning a series of GAA metaphors that refused to die throughout the campaign. Varadkar attacked the Fianna Fáil MEP Billy Kelleher, who had suggested he might vote against the Brexit withdrawal agreement, then awaiting ratification in the European Parliament. 'Fianna Fáil can't be trusted on the big issue of Brexit,' he told reporters. The other news of the day was that a homeless man had been seriously injured during an operation to remove his tent, pitched beside the Grand Canal in Dublin. It would become a familiar pattern throughout the campaign—Fine Gael seeking to talk about Fianna Fáil and about Brexit, while public attention was focussed elsewhere, frequently on housing or healthcare. Sinn Féin had other ideas. In Mary Lou McDonald's first major intervention in the campaign, she pledged to reverse the pension age increases of recent years, restoring the full old age pension to people who turned 65. The big parties paid little heed at first, but it was dynamite on the doorsteps. They didn't know it yet, but something was afoot.

The first polls of the campaign showed a three-horse race between Fine Gael, Fianna Fáil and Sinn Féin. For both Fine Gael and Fianna Fáil, this was not entirely unexpected, nor unduly worrying; they thought that Sinn Féin support would fall off towards the end of the campaign, as it always had before. The assumption was not an unreasonable one, but it would turn out to be very wrong. Something different was happening on the doorsteps with Sinn Féin candidates. The party's canvass reports—collated every night and fed back to the central organisation—were 'off the Richter scale', according to one successful TD. 'We kept saying to ourselves, "It's overestimating us", but it wasn't. It was 100 per cent accurate.'[23]

There were a few elements contributing to this dynamic. Crucially—and this move seemed to some observers, including this one, to be the whole point of McDonald's leadership—the change in the party's position on coalition was making it a viable contender for government in a way that it hadn't been in previous campaigns. In 2016, the party had ruled out supporting a government led by either Fine Gael or Fianna Fáil, pledging only to take part in a left-led government—a goal endorsed by lots of voters, but nowhere near enough to make it a realistic proposition. But now Sinn Féin was saying 'We are in the business of forming a government—we will implement these promises' and that made the party a more potent political alternative. The change of position 'opened up lots and lots of voters to us,' recalled Dublin TD Eoin Ó Broin.[24] 'People were saying to us, "We want you in government",' Ó Broin says. 'We were in the frame for government formation in a way we weren't previously.' Significantly, though, at the same time, Fine Gael and Fianna Fáil kept ruling out Sinn Féin—which, says Ó Broin, reassured the party's traditional supporters, because it meant that McDonald and co were not selling out. It was a narrow enough sweet spot, but the party hit it bang on.

Most importantly, Sinn Féin hit its stride with a strong message of change—it promised radical new solutions to the problems of health and housing, an end to the desiccated old establishment's stranglehold on power, a break with the past. Indeed, the determination of the old duopoly parties to rule out Sinn Féin only made the point for McDonald. They want to keep us out; they're afraid of change. RTÉ's position that the Sinn Féin leader should not take part in the final televised debate of the campaign—which it planned between Martin and Varadkar in the final week of campaigning—further bolstered the Sinn Féin case that it was the victim of an establishment stitch-up. 'RTÉ excluding us was priceless',[25] says a senior party figure simply. RTÉ would later reverse the decision.

The first *Irish Times* poll of the campaign asked about the country's appetite for change: it was overwhelming.[26] Over half of all voters (55 per cent) said that country was going in the wrong direction; 38 per cent agreed that 'the Government has not made enough progress in important areas and it is time for a change'; while a further 37 per cent agreed, 'it is time for a radical change of direction for the country'. That made 75 per cent of all voters who wanted a change. The question of whether this was a change election was answered definitively.

Fianna Fáil also figured it could get into the change business, though. Martin talked constantly about the need to change the government, emphasising again and again that the country needed a change from Fine Gael after nine years. On exactly what would change, though, the Fianna Fáil leader had a less sharp message. The idea that a Fianna Fáil-led government would represent a huge change from a Fine Gael-led one was one that Sinn Féin and others didn't have a great deal of difficulty knocking down. Fianna Fáil's pitch was to that 38 per cent of the electorate who were in the mood for moderate change. But it was a difficult sell, to be fair. It was about to get a lot more difficult.

The first televised debate between the two putative leaders of the next government took place on the Virgin Media television channel, still mostly referred to as TV3 by those involved. It was perhaps a score draw between Varadkar and Martin, with the presenter Pat Kenny apparently just as keen to hog his share of the limelight. The most important moment, one of the most important in the campaign, came when Varadkar, under questioning about his coalition options—and specifically the possibility of a grand coalition—said that the two party leaders 'have to be grown-ups'. 'My preference would be to form a coalition with old partners like Labour and independents,' he said. 'Maybe new partners like the Greens'. 'But if it's the case that people voted in a certain way, and the only way we could form a stable government is for Fianna Fáil and Fine Gael to work together, well I'm willing to do that.'

In the hospitality room where senior Fianna Fáil staff were watching one of their number shouted 'You stupid bastard Leo!' at the screen.[27] They knew exactly what had just happened; so did Fine Gael. By opening the door to a possible Fine Gael–Fianna Fáil coalition after the election, Varadkar was pulling the ground from under Fianna Fáil's pitch to 'change' voters. 'That changed everything,' says a senior Fianna Fáil figure.[28] They knew immediately this was damaging to the Fianna Fáil campaign—and a massive gift to Sinn Féin. Afterwards, Martin scrambled to shut it down.

He would spend much of the remainder of the campaign trying to do so. But it was hopeless. 'Varadkar opens the door to grand coalition with Fianna Fáil' blared the *Examiner*'s headline.[29]

It was also entirely deliberate on Varadkar's part. 'For us to hold our own, we needed to stop the drift to Fianna Fáil. So that's what that was about,' said Mark Mortell, reflecting on the incident after the election. He was unaware of Varadkar's plans to drop the bomb. But he immediately understood its significance.[30] At the time, and subsequently, other senior Fine Gael figures admitted to the present writer that the manoeuvre was intended to damage Fianna Fáil, in the full knowledge that it would work to the advantage of Sinn Féin. They were so focussed on suppressing the Fianna Fáil vote, that it did not occur to them that Sinn Féin could possibly beat both of them. Or perhaps that was a risk they were prepared to take.

Sinn Féin didn't believe it either. But it was sure making progress on the ground. The row over the age at which people qualified for the state pension quickly turned into a rout. As a result of trade union pressure the issue had first been raised by the Labour Party—whose leader Brendan Howlin had actually helped introduce the changes when Minister for Public Expenditure in the 2011–2016 government—but was quickly seized on by Sinn Féin, which had been making patient efforts over several years to woo the trade union movement, and to promote its members within it. The pension age had been increased from 65 to 66 as far back as 2014 (without much opposition, and broad political consensus) and was due to rise further to 67 in 2021 and to 68 in 2028. But because many private employers required people to retire at 65, they were left seeking unemployment assistance during the intervening period. Now they were looking at two years of unemployment benefit and suddenly, it was an election issue. Fine Gael was first to crumble and Fianna Fáil followed. Privately, politicians in both parties admitted it was a retrograde step that stored up trouble for the future.[31] Neither party was willing to die on that particular hill, though. It was a sign of where the momentum was in the election campaign. In *The Irish Times*, several prominent economists warned about the dangers of an auction election.[32]

Sinn Féin launched its manifesto in an art gallery in Temple Bar—a document Miriam Lord in *The Irish Times* dubbed the 'Everybody can have Everything' manifesto.[33] Where Fianna Fáil and Fine Gael both confined themselves to the 11 billion euro in discretionary spending that Department of Finance figures suggested would be available to the next government, Sinn Féin said it would raise new revenues and made spending pledges estimated at around twice that figure. Record investment in healthcare, housing and childcare; tax cuts for the lower paid ('putting money back in people's pockets'); and the abolition of the property tax—all paid for by tax increases on businesses and the better-off. It was a dramatically redistributionist document, promising a massive transfer of resources from people that Sinn Féin believed would never vote for the party to those who might. It was immediately assailed by Fine Gael and Fianna Fáil as dangerous, reckless, economically illiterate—to predictably little effect. 'Tweedledum and Tweedledee', Mary Lou McDonald replied. They've had it their own way for 100 years. They've done nothing for ordinary people. We'll put an end to all that. Time for a change.

The Smaller Parties

The small parties tried desperately to get into the debate. Broadcasters were obliged to cover them proportionately and most newspapers tried to give them a reasonable crack of the whip. But there was never a sense that any of the smaller parties was central to the election debate, or its defining issues. The idea that this would be the first election in which climate change was a central issue hardly got off the ground. Everyone expected the Greens to have a good election, and some suspected there could be a historic breakthrough that catapulted the party into the 20-seat range, driven by growing public concern about the climate and global warming. But while the public did say that it cared about global warming—the polls were clear about that—few voters cared enough about it to make it their most important issue when choosing whom to vote for. In fact, pre- and post-election polls would show that climate change ranked very far down the list of priorities for voters. Although the Greens were on course to have their best ever election, there was no paradigm shift in sight.

Things were even tougher for Labour and the Social Democrats. Even in the ordeal of the 2016 campaign, Labour was accustomed to a large share of the available media attention. This time, the party was a minnow and struggled to elbow its way into the debate. In fact, its leader Brendan Howlin put in a decent performance during the campaign, while the party's big guns fought for their lives in the constituencies. But as the party's sparsely attended press events, in a small room in an anonymous building, attested, Labour was only ever going to be a bit-player in this campaign.

The Social Democrats suffered from the same small-party handicap but also had another, unusual disadvantage: everyone agreed with their signature policy, the Sláintecare health reform plan, drawn up in 2016, which had been paid lip service by both government and Fianna Fáil since that time. With health issues central to the election debates, everyone promised to implement this plan (though in truth, many had misgivings about it) for want of anything better to say. It left the Social Democrats sounding like everyone else on arguably their most important issue.

By the end of the penultimate week of campaigning, the Sinn Féin surge was undeniable. 'The anti-Fine Gael feeling on the doors was stronger than we thought and it just seemed to grow throughout the campaign,' said Dermot Looney, campaign manager for the Social Democrats.[34] 'The discontent, the general disgruntlement, the desire for change—I think it was quite fluid, but it just settled on Sinn Féin,' reflected Ivana Bacik, the Labour director of elections.[35] A round of focus groups for *The Irish Times* a week from polling showed the mood for change was as strong as ever;[36] a few days later the final campaign poll showed that Sinn Féin was poised to win the largest share of the vote. The country was on course for a political earthquake.

The Final Days

On the Monday before polling, RTÉ bowed to the reality of the campaign and performed a U-turn on the shape of its final leaders' debate: it announced that the Sinn Féin leader Mary Lou McDonald would, after all, be admitted to the event, previously intended to feature only Leo Varadkar and Micheál Martin. The debate over the debate illustrated perfectly how the structure and momentum of the campaign had arranged itself in Sinn Féin's favour. Excluded, she could rail against the establishment stitch-up (Sinn Féin—or at least many of its vocal band of online supporters—counted RTÉ as part of that dastardly establishment); included, she could throw her Tweedledum and Tweedledee zingers at her two rivals all night.

In the event, McDonald did not get things her own way at all, shipping some damage on Sinn Féin's attitude to the 2007 murder of Paul Quinn, a young County Armagh man beaten to death by a gang of men, in which IRA involvement was suspected. Quinn's grieving parents succeeded in making their son's death an election issue in the final week, with Fine Gael and Fianna Fáil especially giving the issue as much airtime as they could manage (see Chap. 6). Sinn Féin's treatment of the Quinn case, and others, Micheál Martin said in a string of interviews, raised 'fundamental moral issues' about the party's participation in government. Martin wasn't just attacking his rivals before an election; he was laying down red lines on moral issues from which it would be impossible to retreat after an election. The Fine Gael and Fianna Fáil assaults on Sinn Féin in the final week may have changed the result of the election somewhat; they certainly changed the subsequent landscape of government formation.

Fine Gael ended the election in a welter of negative campaigning—not just about Sinn Féin, but also, more pointedly, about Fianna Fáil. Varadkar started the week with a walkabout in a rainy Athlone, accusing Martin's party of 'being opposed to social progress'. More pungently, he repeatedly asserted that Fianna Fáil was likely to do a coalition deal with Sinn Féin after the election. If there was an edge of desperation about all this, it was because Fine Gael was desperate. Private polling was showing the party below 20 per cent.[37] Ministers feared they would lose their seats; even Paschal Donohoe scrambled for survival. 'The guns were turned on Micheál Martin personally,' one Fine Gael figure who was centrally involved said.[38] This had been part of Fine Gael's message throughout the campaign—the party sought to attack Martin's credentials as a credible candidate of change. At one meeting of Fine Gael politicians and staff, one voice asked, 'Is there a single figure in Irish politics that looks less like change than Micheál Martin?'[39] Meanwhile, in the constituencies, its candidates hammered home a 'Vote FF, get SF' message.

It might not have been pretty; but it was effective. In the final days of this most unpredictable of campaigns, the pendulum swung away from Fianna Fáil, and Fine Gael avoided the meltdown it feared. The party had endured another torrid election, and its project of selling Leo Varadkar to the electorate as the embodiment of the new progressive Ireland, which had greatly propelled his rise to the leadership of his party, was in ruins. And yet the party also heaved a sigh of relief that it wasn't worse. Fianna Fáil stumbled in the last week, and Sinn Féin soared. When the exit poll on election night predicted a three-way dead heat in the share of the vote, Sinn Féin could scarcely believe it; in the event, when the votes were counted, the result was even better for the party. Fianna Fáil ended up with the largest number of seats in the new Dáil (just about) but it was Sinn Féin that had won the election campaign. Irish politics now looked vastly different than it did three weeks before.

NOTES

1. *The Irish Times*, 27 April 2019
2. Interview with author.
3. Interview with author.
4. Party source, interview with author.
5. Private information.
6. Private information.
7. Ó Broin's publication of a book on the housing crisis added additional authority to his contributions, and Sinn Féin's army of online supporters were always keen to present him as the man who 'wrote the book' on the housing crisis; his opponents pointed out that he had written 'a book' on the housing crisis—not quite the same thing. *Home: Why Public Housing is the Answer* (Dublin: Irish Academic Press, 2019).
8. Interview with party source.
9. *The Irish Times*, 25 May 2019.
10. Interview with party source.
11. Interview with author.
12. Private information.
13. Interview with author.
14. Interview with author.
15. Fitzgerald was largely vindicated by a subsequent inquiry, though like Alan Shatter before her, she was forced from office because of the quick judgements and rough justice of politics, not because she had been found guilty of any wrongdoing (nor could she be) in a court or tribunal. It was a distinction lost on both of them.
16. Private information.
17. Interview with author.
18. Today with Seán O'Rourke, RTÉ Radio 1, 6 February 2019.
19. Rather like the Royal Irish Constabulary, actually.
20. Private information.
21. Interview with author.
22. *The Irish Times*, 15 January 2020.
23. Interview with author.
24. Interview with author.
25. Interview with author.
26. *The Irish Times*, 21 January 2020.
27. Private information.
28. Interview with author.
29. *Irish Examiner*, 23 January 2020.
30. Interview with author.
31. Private information.

32. *The Irish Times*, 23 January 2020.
33. *The Irish Times*, 28 January 2020.
34. Interview with author.
35. Interview with author.
36. *The Irish Times*, 1 February 2020.
37. Private information.
38. Interview with author.
39. Private information.

CHAPTER 5

Brexit and the Election: The Issue That Wasn't

Mary C. Murphy

In the UK's December 2019 Westminster election, a sizeable 22 per cent of Northern Ireland voters indicated that Brexit would influence their choice of candidate and/or party. No such similar pattern is evident for the 2020 Irish general election that took place just two months later. In fact, despite its far-reaching consequences for Ireland, Brexit merited little substantive mention during the election campaign and, as we will see, the election exit poll revealed that Brexit had a negligible impact on voter choice. Fine Gael was the only political party that sought to mobilise electoral support around its record on Brexit and its capacity to steer the country through the next phase of negotiations on the future relationship between the UK and the European Union (EU). Voters, however, were decidedly unreceptive to this election narrative.

There are various historic and contemporary explanations as to why Brexit was not an issue during the 2020 general election. These are related to traditionally high levels of public support for the EU in Ireland based

M. C. Murphy (✉)
University College Cork, Cork, Ireland
e-mail: maryc.murphy@ucc.ie

M. Gallagher et al. (eds.), *How Ireland Voted 2020*,
https://doi.org/10.1007/978-3-030-66405-3_5

on a broad appreciation of the (economic) benefits of EU membership. What opposition there is to the EU in Ireland is largely confined to periods when the issue is publicly salient, namely during EU treaty referendum campaigns. Outside of these episodes, Euroscepticism is a marginal force in Irish politics, a trend confirmed by the results of the 2020 election.

The UK decision to leave the EU, however, impacts very directly and profoundly on Ireland. During the UK's 2016 Brexit referendum, all of Ireland's main political parties made clear their hope for a Remain decision. The parties subsequently shared a similar perspective on how the Irish government should approach the UK–EU negotiations after 2016. In essence, Brexit has been quite remarkable for having generated so little division and disagreement in Ireland. This produced an election campaign in 2020 where differences on Brexit were minimal and so there was little for Irish parties and candidates to debate and argue about.

Although the UK's departure from the EU was not front and centre of this election campaign, its shadow nevertheless lingered in the political ether. Brexit's significance crystallised in the context of Sinn Féin's remarkable electoral performance. The party's core political objective is Irish unity, an ambition that, as Sinn Féin sees it, has been abetted by Brexit. According to the party, Brexit challenges the logic for partition and simultaneously strengthens the case for Irish unification by providing a pathway for Northern Ireland to remain in the EU as part of a united Ireland. Enabled by Brexit and emboldened by its electoral gains, Sinn Féin's post-election narrative confirms its intention to pursue its constitutional agenda. The 2020 Irish general election may not have been a 'Brexit election', but the election outcome has clear Brexit undertones that have the potential to stimulate transformative constitutional change in Ireland and the UK.

This chapter begins by outlining the multitude of ways in which Brexit challenged and disrupted the Irish political system, economy and society after 2016. This is followed by an overview of the 2020 election, which demonstrates the limited traction that Brexit gained on the campaign trail. The lack of a Brexit election narrative is explained with reference to relatively strong patterns of Irish support for the EU influenced by a largely positive experience of EU membership. Episodes of opposition to EU integration are contextualised to reveal a shallow form of Euroscepticism among the Irish electorate, while the Brexit period post-2016 is marked by a high degree of cross-party consensus that undermined any basis for electoral contestation. The chapter concludes by considering the indirect impact of Brexit on Ireland's future, and in particular what the rise of Sinn Féin means for the emerging constitutional opportunities that Brexit presents.

IRISH POLITICS AND THE BREXIT DISRUPTION

The UK's decision to leave the EU following a referendum on 23 June 2016 dealt a considerable blow to the EU and its member states. Given its geographic proximity and strong economic and political links to the UK, Ireland was markedly exposed to the fallout from the referendum decision. In the lead-up to the referendum, the Economic and Social Research Institute (ESRI) warned about the potentially large-scale economic impact of a Leave vote for the Republic of Ireland.[1] There were also pronounced concerns about the impact of Brexit on the stability of the Northern Ireland peace process, the implications for the Belfast/Good Friday Agreement, and the consequences for relationships on the island of Ireland, and between Ireland and the UK.

The triggering of Article 50 in March 2017 by UK Prime Minister Theresa May set in train a two-stage negotiation process to facilitate, firstly, an orderly UK exit from the EU and, secondly, agreement on a future UK–EU trading relationship. Issues related to Ireland constituted one of three core agenda items that required resolution before the EU would move to phase two of the negotiations.[2] The most challenging aspect of the negotiations between the UK and the European Commission concerned the so-called Irish border issue. From the outset, the negotiating mandate agreed between the EU and the UK committed to ensure that Brexit would not create a hard border between north and south on the island of Ireland. This meant protecting and maintaining the free and unfettered movement of products and people across the Irish border. As the most vexed issue confronting the negotiating teams, the core problem centred on the incompatibility between the UK's intention to leave both the EU customs union and single market and the maintenance of an open border on the island of Ireland. The challenge was exacerbated by Northern Ireland unionist objections to any proposal that Northern Ireland should be treated differently from the rest of the UK. This opposition was largely channelled through the ten Westminster MPs of the Democratic Unionist Party (DUP) who supported May's minority government through a confidence and supply agreement following her (ill-advised) decision to call a UK general election in June

2017. This position gave unionism a period of unrivalled political leverage during the early negotiation period. None of these developments, however, smoothed the passage of the withdrawal deal through Westminster. On a number of occasions, both May and her successor Boris Johnson faced hurdles in securing support for different iterations of the deal.

A political breakthrough was finally achieved in October 2019 when the bones of a revised deal were agreed between Johnson and Taoiseach Leo Varadkar at a meeting on the Wirral in north-west England. However, the renegotiated deal again failed to secure majority support in Westminster. The stalemate was decisively broken only following a UK general election on 12 December 2019 that returned a large Conservative Party majority. The *European Union (Withdrawal Agreement) Bill* subsequently secured parliamentary support and paved the way for the UK to formally exit the EU on 31 January 2020. This withdrawal deal includes a *Protocol on Ireland and Northern Ireland* that is designed to prevent a hard border on the island of Ireland. The protocol details a creative and complex system that allows Northern Ireland both to remain in the UK customs territory and to benefit from access to the EU single market.

The sheer complexity and sensitivity of the Irish border issue, and related economic and political risks, meant that Ireland's Brexit effort consumed a vast swathe of resources across every facet of the state, economy and society. Extensive contingency planning and preparation involved: financial and budgetary preparations; business supports (€300 million Brexit Loan Scheme and €300 million Future Growth Loan Scheme); the passing of the *Brexit Omnibus Act 2019* (the largest single piece of legislation ever agreed by the Oireachtas comprising 15 parts and amending almost 60 pieces of legislation across a multitude of policy areas); the redeploying of civil servants and expansion of Ireland's diplomatic missions in EU capitals; a nationwide communication and stakeholder engagement programme; and extensive bilateral contact with the EU negotiating team.[3] To a discernible extent, this focus on Brexit dictated the pattern and focus of Irish politics after 2016 and distracted attention from other domestic policy priorities and consequential wider global developments. Indeed the reason the 2020 Irish general election had not happened sooner was largely down to Brexit. Fianna Fáil, which supported the minority Fine Gael–led government through a confidence and supply agreement (see Chap. 1), ruled out triggering an election until such time as the Brexit landscape stabilised. By January 2020, the successful passage of the *European Union (Withdrawal Agreement) Bill* through Westminster offered a form of (temporary) stability deemed appropriate to an Irish electoral contest.

BREXIT: THE ELECTION ISSUE THAT WASN'T

On 14 January 2020, Taoiseach Leo Varadkar announced the general election. The content of his statement was Brexit-heavy. He noted that an orderly UK exit was now assured and that key Irish Brexit priorities had been met. However, the Taoiseach also included a note of caution when he said: 'Brexit is not done yet. In fact, it's only half-time'.[4] This theme was echoed in the Fine Gael election manifesto, where an emphasis on Brexit was front and centre. The party claimed that it offered: 'The right team; the right relationships; the right strategy; and the right results for Ireland' in navigating the past Brexit challenge and in influencing the future UK–EU trade talks. The party kicked off its election campaign in Monaghan, a border county exposed to Brexit, and used the opportunity to speak at length about the party's contribution to the Brexit negotiations. At the manifesto launch, Minister for Foreign Affairs and Trade Simon Coveney stated: 'This comes down to one question: who do you trust to lead Ireland forward?' This emphasis and messaging was to become a central feature of Fine Gael's election strategy and was repeated and rehearsed throughout the early weeks of the election campaign.

Fine Gael's election campaign was also animated by support and praise from senior EU officials. When he visited Dublin and Belfast midway through the election campaign, EU chief Brexit negotiator Michel Barnier suggested that it would not have been possible to reach agreement on a withdrawal deal 'without the work of the government, you Leo, Simon Coveney and Helen McEntee, and politicians in the Dáil and the Seanad'.[5] An intervention by EU Trade Commissioner Phil Hogan (a former Fine Gael TD and minister) was heavily criticised by Fianna Fáil leader Micheál Martin. He accused the commissioner of interfering in the Irish general election by making a 'coded partisan intervention' on behalf of Fine Gael and politicising Brexit during the final week of the campaign.[6] At a later press briefing on the economy and Brexit, Fianna Fáil accused its confidence and supply partner of cynically using Brexit to win votes and of completely ignoring the mechanics of how the Irish government had approached Brexit, especially the constructive cross-party support that had enabled Fine Gael to pursue a strategic national response to Brexit. This view was echoed by Labour Party leader Brendan Howlin. In a pointed tweet, he urged: 'Time for a little Fine Gael humility on Brexit. They have received consistent all party support and the backing of some of the finest public servants in Europe'.[7]

For its part, Fianna Fáil was less focused on Brexit than Fine Gael. However, the party did highlight its approach to Brexit, suggesting that its analysis and core strategy had been consistently validated by events. The party also claimed credit for the terms of the Ireland/Northern Ireland protocol which it claimed were similar to the party's proposal for Northern Ireland to become a Special Economic Zone (a position that Micheál Martin had first outlined in September 2017).

Sinn Féin was less vocal on Brexit. The party's election manifesto contained no dedicated section on Brexit. Having endured damaging electoral losses in the 2019 EU and local elections, the party's 2020 general election strategy was based on a determined effort to connect more effectively with the key concerns of voters and to positivise the tone and content of the party's messaging.[8] Given how non-salient an issue Brexit was for voters, it made little sense for the party to focus on it during the election campaign. Instead Sinn Féin concentrated its campaigning and canvassing efforts on those non-Brexit-related bread-and-butter issues that were most exercising Irish voters. Insofar as the party did engage with Brexit, it did so through a constitutional, as opposed to a policy lens, presenting it as a development that rationalises and strengthens Sinn Féin's Irish unity agenda. But even this appeal to nationalism was not a prominent feature of Sinn Féin's electoral campaign strategy and narrative.

Other smaller parties did not engage substantively with Brexit during the election campaign. The Green Party's opposition to Brexit was more narrowly framed in the context of a commitment to ensure that the UK's existing environmental commitments were respected and enforced. The Social Democrats' election manifesto looked beyond Brexit and committed to fostering a close future relationship with the UK and to achieving a united Ireland by consent. The Labour Party proposed the creation of a Brexit contingency fund to support economic sectors affected by Brexit, referenced the post-Brexit pressures facing the marine sector, and vowed to nurture Irish relations with EU member states and the UK. None of these issues constituted important talking points during the election campaign.

The limited interest in Brexit extended to the televised flagship leaders' debates. In total there were three leadership debates aired on two national television stations (see Chap. 4). In the first head-to-head debate between the leaders of the then largest two parties, Fine Gael leader Leo Varadkar clashed with Micheál Martin on a number of issues but their exchanges on Brexit were limited and tame. In the next debate a week later, which included all party leaders, the Brexit issue warranted no substantive mention. The final leaders' debate included Varadkar, Martin and Sinn Féin leader Mary Lou McDonald. Here again, Brexit was sidelined. This absence of discussion and debate was in keeping with the wider public mood, which pointed to an electorate with little interest in Brexit.

An *Irish Times* Ipsos MRBI poll published one week into the election campaign indicated that just 3 per cent of voters would choose to support a party or candidate on the basis of their position on the 'management of Brexit'.[9] Of the six policies put to respondents, Brexit ranked last. This hid some minor distinctions among voters based on their social class, party choice and geography. For example, 11 per cent of farmers were concerned about the management of Brexit, whereas just 1 per cent of Dublin voters indicated Brexit was a priority election issue.

A lack of interest in Brexit was also discernible on the campaign trail. Although Fine Gael candidates, including Neale Richmond, Jerry Buttimer and Maria Byrne, suggested that voters were raising Brexit on the doorsteps, this was disputed by other politicians and journalists: 'Fine Gael candidates have been at pains to argue that Brexit has been coming up regularly on the doorsteps but anecdotal evidence, and the claims of countless non-FG candidates, would suggest otherwise'.[10] Politicians such as Willie O'Dea (Fianna Fáil) were adamant that during their canvassing efforts, no-one mentioned Brexit on the doorsteps.[11] During the early days of the campaign, Simon Coveney advised that Brexit was being raised with him every day by voters.[12] However, later in the campaign, he acknowledged that the issue had not featured on the doorsteps and that voters were 'tired' and 'fed up' of the Brexit narrative.[13] In his native Cork city, Coveney's Brexit efforts did not enjoy widespread resonance. In a radio vox-pop, one Cork voter noted that the minister's work on Brexit was 'no good to us'; instead, the Tánaiste was judged on how little he was perceived to have delivered for his home city.[14] A Business Post RedC opinion poll conducted three weeks before the general election confirmed this view. The poll found that Brexit (and the economy) were not as relevant or as important to voters as policies on housing and health. There was a sense among voters that the economic recovery was advancing and that the pressures of Brexit had eased with the completion of phase one of the negotiations. This revealed a fundamental flaw in Fine Gael's election strategy: 'The ... core strengths that Fine Gael have relied on to see itself lead in the polls for the last number of years, have simply become less important to voters as the election was called'.[15]

In the aftermath of the election, the exit poll confirmed a near complete lack of interest in Brexit among Irish voters. Just 1 per cent of respondents advised that Brexit was the most important issue impacting on their vote.[16] Across all other indicators—gender, age and region—a score of 1–2 per cent was consistently the case. The only distinction was in relation to party choice: for 5 per cent of Fine Gael voters Brexit was a determining factor.

WHY DID BREXIT NOT FEATURE MORE?

Brexit poses serious risks and threats for Ireland and its impact is potentially substantial. This includes a predicted negative impact on the Irish economy[17]; potential destabilisation of political and community relations in Northern Ireland[18]; adverse consequences for British–Irish relations[19]; and pressures for future constitutional change in the direction of Irish unity.[20] Despite a broad sweep of challenging and possibly even transformative Brexit consequences, the Irish general election campaign was not animated or influenced by the issue. So what explains the absence of debate and discussion during the 2020 general election on one of the most significant and consequential political developments for Ireland in recent times?

A History of Irish Support for the EU

The crude answer is that, unlike for the UK, 'Europe' is simply not an issue that mobilises Irish voters or political parties. As Sinnott notes: 'Issues having to do with the European Union are a minority interest in Ireland'.[21] Ireland is, in fact, one of the member states most enthusiastic about EU membership. Simpson notes that Irish support has been consistently above the EU average between 1987 and 2018.[22] In the autumn 2019 Eurobarometer poll, the pattern was reaffirmed, with the EU conjuring up a positive image for 63 per cent of Irish respondents: the highest proportion in any EU member state and 21 points above the EU average.[23] A 2020 European Movement Ireland/RedC poll recorded similarly positive views with an 84 per cent approval rate for Ireland remaining in the EU.[24]

Coakley notes that these generalised pro-EU attitudes among Irish voters extend to broadly positive perceptions about specific aspects of the EU integration project, including the single currency, foreign policy and EU enlargement.[25] Other positive Irish perceptions of the EU include above average levels of trust in the EU and strong agreement that Irish interests are well taken account of by the EU.

There is, however, an interesting (and curious) disconnect in Ireland between positive perceptions of the EU and low levels of knowledge.[26] The EU knowledge base in Ireland remains relatively low despite opportunities for discussion and debate during EU referendums (Ireland has held referendums on seven EU treaties) and despite experimentation with different forms of deliberation including the National Forum on Europe[27] and a series of citizens' dialogues.[28] This underlines that Irish support for the EU is based on more complex judgements and perceptions than knowledge alone. Kennedy and Sinnott find that Irish individuals' knowledge of the EU does not affect the relationship between opinion of EU support and evaluations of domestic and European institutions.[29] Marsh notes that attitudes to EU integration, party cues and measures of satisfaction with government have played a role in determining Irish voters' attitudes towards EU treaty change.[30]

Voters typically take their cues from political actors including political leaders, parties, interest groups and movements. In Ireland, Fianna Fáil and Fine Gael—historically the largest two parties in Irish politics—have been consistently pro-EU. Both supported EU membership in 1973 and have subsequently supported every treaty reform during the intervening period. The Labour Party was initially opposed to Ireland's membership of the EU. However, from the late 1970s, the party gradually adopted a more pro-EU outlook and aligned itself with the socialist grouping in the European Parliament. The Green Party has also shifted from a position of opposition to critical support. Sinn Féin's position on the EU has been more complex. At the time of Ireland's accession to the EU in 1973, the party was virulently anti-EU. It equated membership with an unacceptable loss of national sovereignty and judged the EU to be an anti-democratic 'rich man's club' designed to privilege capitalist powers. The intensity of the party's opposition to the EU, however, has moderated to the point where today Sinn Féin takes the view that Ireland's place is in the EU. Since the 1990s, the party's approach to the EU has shifted towards a policy of 'critical engagement'.[31] This combines support for continued EU membership with a core element of soft Euroscepticism, including opposition to the EU's economic and social agenda, and calls for reform of EU institutions and key policies. This has been most emphatically evident in the context of the party having campaigned against all EU treaty referendums in Ireland.

Ireland's Episodic Opposition to Deeper EU Integration

Despite positive attitudes towards the EU, Irish voters have episodically demonstrated their dissatisfaction and frustration with the decisions, operation and machinations of the EU. On two occasions, the Irish electorate rejected EU treaties. In 2001 voters opposed the Treaty of Nice, and in 2008 the electorate rejected the Treaty of Lisbon. The No votes were delivered despite strong cross-party and cross-sectoral support. However, there was also an anti-EU and Euro-critical narrative that was largely channelled through Sinn Féin, a small number of independent Eurosceptic MEPs and a variety of anti-EU movements with a single-issue focus.

Fitzgibbon notes that civic society organisations that campaigned for a No vote during the first Treaty of Lisbon referendum did not advocate Irish withdrawal, but were clearly opposed to different facets of the EU.[32] Opposition ranged from calls for reform of EU institutions as articulated by Libertas to claims that the EU constituted an attack on traditional Catholic values as projected by Cóir. Groups such as the Irish National Platform, the Peace and Neutrality Alliance (PANA) and Action from Ireland (Afri) were specifically opposed to the alleged militarisation ambitions of the EU while minor parties such as People Before Profit were against what they termed the EU's neoliberal agenda. The success of these groups in mobilising and motivating voters to reject EU treaties in 2001 and 2008 signals the existence of some reservations about EU integration among the Irish electorate. Closer analysis, however, reveals that the depth and intensity of opposition to the EU in Ireland is not deep-rooted.

In 2001, 54 per cent of Irish voters voted against the Treaty of Nice. Turnout for the referendum was particularly low at 35 per cent. Research concluded that voters were discouraged from turning out to vote because of a lack of information and understanding. This knowledge deficit was also an explanatory factor for the No vote and, at 39 per cent, it was the most cited reason among those who voted against the treaty.[33] Using the campaign slogan 'If you don't know, vote No', a well-organised No campaign focused explicitly on the issue of poor voter information and knowledge. Hayward noted the failures of official Irish discourse in combating this pronounced knowledge vacuum that the No side sought to exploit.[34]

Turnout for the first Treaty of Lisbon referendum was considerably higher at 53 per cent with a 53 per cent vote against the treaty. The explanation for the No vote reiterated the conclusions from 2001: of those who abstained, 46 per cent cited lack of knowledge or information as their main reason for not voting, while, crucially, 42 per cent of those who voted No also cited lack of knowledge and/or information.[35]

Both referendum questions were put to voters a second time following agreement between Ireland and the EU on a series of clarifications, concessions and guarantees. On each occasion, and following more determined and strategic campaigns by the Yes side, the treaties were supported by increased turnouts and healthy majorities of 63 per cent for the Treaty of Nice and 67 per cent for the Treaty of Lisbon.

A Broadly Positive Irish Experience of EU Membership

Signs of Irish dissatisfaction with the EU during referendums nevertheless coexist with persistently higher than average levels of public support for the integration process. That support is generally understood to be linked to a broadly positive experience of EU membership and an appreciation, in particular, of the economic benefits that the single market has brought. Economically, EU membership has been a key factor in the modernisation, diversification and growth of the Irish economy, particularly since the 1980s and 1990s. This produced a marked shift in the geographic pattern of trade between Ireland and the UK. For example, in 1971 (two years before accession to the EU), 61 per cent of Irish exports went to the UK. By 2013, that figure had fallen to 17 per cent. In tandem, Irish exports to the rest of the EU increased from 13 per cent to over 50 per cent.[36] Ireland's reduced reliance on the UK was manifest in its decision to join the single currency in 1999 notwithstanding the UK opting to remain outside the monetary union. Ireland has also benefited to the tune of over €50 billion from the EU structural funds.[37] In addition, receipts from the EU's Common Agricultural Policy (CAP) play a role in sustaining and supporting Ireland's agri-food sector. Ireland's shift from being a net beneficiary of the EU budget to being a net contributor has not altered positive Irish perceptions of the benefits of EU membership. A majority of Irish voters appear comfortable with paying more into the EU budget because this is deemed a price worth paying for the broader advantages of EU membership.[38] By 2016, this combination of dynamics meant that Irish economic dependency on the UK was substantially less significant than the more valuable trade relationship and economic links between Ireland and the rest of the EU. The rationale for severing Irish ties with the EU and following the UK out of the EU, therefore, simply did not support core economic interests.

The benefits of EU membership, however, have been more than just economic for Ireland. Speaking in 2013, Taoiseach Enda Kenny characterised Ireland's membership of the EU as 'a story of transformation', one that has impacted not just on the Irish economy, but on the state, society and British–Irish relations. As Laffan and O'Mahony note: '[Ireland's] focus on the United Kingdom for economic and policy templates slowly gave way to a wider interdependence'.[39] And importantly, as equal partners within the wider EU framework, membership helped to disrupt and dilute the historically asymmetrical relationship between Ireland and the UK.

The Hollowness of Irish Euroscepticism

Irish public support for the EU is heavily based on utilitarianism and transactionalism with little evidence of any real internalisation of Europe among Irish voters. In other words, among Irish voters the EU is not conceived in normative terms, which would entail membership being regarded a good in itself, but instead is narrowly linked to perceived benefits. Moreover, an exclusivist Irish national identity and nationalist values limit attachment to a broader and more inclusive European identity.[40] Despite its thin character, however, Irish support for the EU has been sufficient in resisting hostility towards the EU. This is evident in that there has been no substantial destabilisation of the Irish political system as a consequence of anti-EU sentiment. In Ireland, Eurosceptic activists and movements tend to fade from public discourse and the public conscience outside referendum periods. They have not become embedded or permanent staples of the Irish political system, and this was again evident in Ireland's 2020 general election.

A renewed burgeoning of populist, right-wing, anti-immigrant and anti-EU movements in Ireland in reaction to both Brexit and, perhaps more particularly, the EU refugee crisis contested the general election. The right-wing and Eurosceptic Irish Freedom Party was created in 2018 and calls for Ireland to follow the UK's example and leave the EU. It is one of a number of very small and disparate groups that also includes the National Party and Anti-Corruption Ireland. These parties and movements have garnered little traction in Ireland, particularly in first-order elections. In 2020, their platform and messaging did not find a receptive Irish electorate. The parties failed to return a single candidate to the 33rd Dáil and polled a tiny percentage of two per cent or less of first preference votes in every constituency in which they ran. In fact, not a single candidate from any of these fringe parties received more than 1000 first preference votes.

The 2016 Eurobarometer country report confirmed the rejection of anti-EU sentiment in Ireland and notes specifically that there has been no mushrooming of Euroscepticism as a consequence of Brexit.[41] It may even be the case that the Brexit crisis is in fact contributing to some latent internalisation of the EU among some Irish voters. The EM Ireland/Red C poll 2019 notes that for 58 per cent of respondents, Brexit has improved their opinion of the EU.[42] Regardless of the UK's decision to exit the EU, continued Irish membership of the EU is taken for granted by the vast majority of the electorate in Ireland.

Cross-party Consensus on Brexit

All of Ireland's main political parties supported the UK remaining in the EU. This extended to the Euro-critical Sinn Féin campaigning in Northern Ireland for Remain during the 2016 referendum. Admittedly, the party's canvassing efforts were not vigorous. An element of election fatigue following two earlier elections (the election to the Northern Ireland Assembly in May 2016 and the Irish general election in February 2016) and the expectation of a Remain vote undermined the intensity of the party's campaign machine. Sinn Féin's position on the referendum question was motivated primarily by domestic political factors rather than wholesale support for the EU. The party was concerned by the potential for Brexit to reintroduce a (hard) border between north and south, to compromise key features of the Belfast/Good Friday Agreement and to deepen partition on the island.

Sinn Féin's opposition to a UK exit from the EU meant that all of Ireland's main political parties adopted the same position, albeit for a range of motivations. The broader effect of this alignment was a high degree of cross-party consensus in Ireland in support of the UK's membership of the EU and, following the referendum, shared cross-party support for the least disruptive Brexit. Throughout the initial Brexit negotiation phase, there was a perceptible absence of opposition, criticism and grandstanding. This was facilitated by the lack of a dedicated anti-EU party in the Irish party system (although some independent TDs, MEPs and minor parties are more critical of the EU than the mainstream) and also by a widespread absence of civic support for Brexit across Ireland. Even though the EU is a mildly disputed issue in Ireland, this was not an obstacle to the emergence of a shared approach on Brexit. Indeed the widespread conception of Brexit, as a narrow form of English nationalism, meant it was unlikely that the UK decision to leave the EU would ever win support in Ireland.

The Indirect Brexit Impact

Brexit may not have been a mobilising issue during the 2020 Irish general election, but its shadow lingered over the election campaign and especially over the result. This relates specifically to the overriding story of the 2020 Irish general election, namely the rise and remarkable electoral performance of Sinn Féin. The party's core political aim is to achieve Irish unity and although there was no ostensible discussion of unification during the general election campaign, the issue is to the forefront in the Sinn Féin election manifesto. The drive for Irish unity is specifically linked to 'the controversy and chaos around Brexit' that the party claims has increased support for a border poll (that is, a referendum on Irish unity).[43] In a speech to the Institute for International and European Affairs during the election campaign, party leader Mary Lou McDonald proposed that a referendum on Irish unity be held within five years. She has also suggested that Irish unity would be a component of government formation talks: 'We are United Irelanders. So, be assured that in all of our discussions with other parties about agreeing a programme for a government, the desire and demand for unity is a priority'.[44]

The election result has been interpreted by Sinn Féin as legitimising and invigorating the party's flagship manifesto commitment to Irish unity. The discussion and/or future achievement of Irish unity is far-reaching not just for Ireland, but also for the UK. Other political parties in Ireland are resistant to calls for a united Ireland debate to begin at this juncture due to the risk of serious economic and political fallout resulting from a potentially divisive and bitter constitutional conversation. The risks are perhaps even more pronounced for the UK. Brexit has already challenged and undermined some of the core tenets and conventions of the UK constitutional order. Sinn Féin's mobilisation around Irish unity adds to the potential unravelling of the status quo in the UK by playing into Scottish calls for a second independence referendum. At the intersection of Brexit and Sinn Féin's election victory, the future of the British and Irish states is exposed to the possibility of momentous constitutional change.

CONCLUSION

Despite the potentially enormous changes that Brexit heralds for Ireland, the 2020 Irish general election was fought and won solely on domestic policy issues with little substantive mention of Brexit, despite the best efforts of Fine Gael. Tacit Irish public support for the EU integration project, cross-party consensus on how best to approach Brexit and an absence of contestation on core Brexit issues negated the need for debate and discussion. Nevertheless, the influence and impact of Brexit hung over the election result and played into Sinn Féin's united Ireland ambitions. The combination of Brexit and electoral success empowered the party to pursue a debate about the prospects of Irish unity, to push for a referendum and to campaign for that constitutional objective. By enabling this set of responses and actions, the 2020 general election may conceivably set in train a process that leads towards future constitutional change. This prospect is not just important for Ireland's future, it is also consequential for the UK. Sinn Féin's electoral success in 2020 heightens the prospect of a post-Brexit period animated by ever more complex challenges related not just to the future UK–EU relationship but also to the constitutional future of Ireland and the UK.

The 2020 Irish general election campaign was in full swing on 31 January 2020, the day when the UK formally left the EU and the second phase of the Brexit process commenced. Phase two of Brexit involved difficult and complex discussions on the terms of a UK–EU free trade deal and the implementation of the *Ireland/Northern Ireland Protocol*. Ireland's economic, political and constitutional stability was at stake and so the calibre and skills of Ireland's political negotiators were tested. There was a twist of irony in the fact that the 2020 general election overlooked one of the issues that would in fact dictate and dominate the agenda and priorities of Ireland's next government.

NOTES

1. Alan Barrett et al., *Scoping the Possible Economic Implications of Brexit on Ireland* (Dublin: ESRI, November 2015), available at: https://www.esri. ie/system/files?file=media/file-uploads/2015-11/RS48.pdf.
2. The other two areas were (1) a budgetary settlement and (2) the status of UK citizens in the EU and EU citizens in the UK.
3. See Government of Ireland, *Preparing for the withdrawal of the United Kingdom from the European Union: Contingency Action Plan Update* (Dublin: Government of Ireland, July 2019), available at: https://www. dfa.ie/media/dfa/eu/brexit/keydocuments/Contingency-Action-Plan-Update.-July-2019.pdf.
4. *Statement of Taoiseach Leo Varadkar*, 14 January 2020, available at: https://www.rte.ie/news/politics/2020/0114/1107371-leo-varadkar-statement/.
5. 'Barnier praises government for work during Brexit negotiations', *Newstalk* 27 January 2020, available at: https://www.newstalk.com/news/barnier-meet-varadkar-dublin-today-brexit-day-approaches-956949.
6. 'Micheál Martin attacks Phil Hogan over "partisan" election intervention', *Irish Independent* 20 January 2020.
7. Brendan Howlin, 15 January 2020, available at: https://twitter.com/BrendanHowlin/status/1217531294256713728.
8. Gráinne Ní Aodha, 'How did they do it? Sinn Féin's historic 24% win was built on learnt lessons and a fed-up electorate', *thejournal.ie*, 12 February 2020, available at: https://www.thejournal.ie/sinn-fein-comeback-5001379-Feb2020/. See also Chap. 4 above.
9. Pat Leahy, 'Irish Times poll: health and housing are most important issues for voters', *Irish Times* 21 January 2020.
10. 'Has team Varadkar backed the wrong horse with their focus on Brexit?', *The Kerryman*, 22 January 2020, available at: https://www.pressreader. com/ireland/the-kerryman-south-kerry-edition/20200122/281913070073606.
11. Willie O'Dea, 15 January 2020, available at: https://twitter.com/willieodeaLIVE/status/1217556241838419968.
12. See Simon Coveney tweet in response to journalist Vincent Kearney, 22 January 2020, available at: https://twitter.com/simoncoveney.
13. '"We're not trying to scare people": Coveney says Brexit not coming up on the doorsteps, but that might change', *thejournal. ie*, 29 January 2020, available at: https://www.thejournal.ie/simon-coveney-brexit-6-4985087-Jan2020/.
14. Drivetime, *RTÉ Radio 1*, 31 January 2020, available at: https://www.rte. ie/radio/radioplayer/html5/#/radio1/11148590.

15. The Business Post/Red C, *General election campaign opinion poll*, January 2020, p. 3, available at: https://www.redcresearch.com/wp-content/uploads/2020/01/SBP-January-2020-Poll-Report.pdf.
16. Ipsos MRBI, *Exit poll: General election 2020* (on behalf of RTÉ/*The Irish Times*/TG4/UCD), at p. 12.
17. See Adele Bergin et al., *Ireland and Brexit: Modelling the impact of deal and no-deal scenarios*, ESRI Special Article (Dublin: ESRI 2019), available at: https://www.esri.ie/system/files/publications/QEC2019SPR_SA_Bergin.pdf.
18. See Mary C. Murphy, *Europe and Northern Ireland's Future: Negotiating Brexit's Unique Case* (Newcastle-upon-Tyne: Agenda Publishing, 2018).
19. See Etain Tannam, 'The future of UK–Irish relations', *European Journal of Legal Studies* (Special Issue), 29 October 2019, available at: https://ejls.eui.eu/wp-content/uploads/sites/32/2019/10/10-Tannam-final.pdf.
20. See Eileen Connolly and John Doyle, 'Brexit and the changing international and domestic perspectives of sovereignty over Northern Ireland', *Irish Studies in International Affairs* 30 (2019), pp. 217–33.
21. Richard Sinnott, *Attitudes and behaviour of the Irish Electorate in the referendum on the Treaty of Nice: Results of a survey of public opinion carried out for the European Commission Representation in Ireland*, 2001, p. 5, available at: https://www.cvce.eu/content/publication/2013/7/30/c96e12c8-503c-4e7d-9b4b-8dee6f269194/publishable_en.pdf.
22. Kathryn Simpson, 'European Union crises and Irish public opinion: continuity and change in patterns of support', *Irish Political Studies* 34:4 (2019), pp. 514–15.
23. European Commission, *Standard Eurobarometer 92 (Autumn 2019)*, November 2019, p. 9, available at: https://ec.europa.eu/commfrontoffice/publicopinion/index.cfm/Survey/getSurveyDetail/instruments/STANDARD/surveyKy/2255.
24. EM Ireland/RedC, *Ireland and the EU 2020*, available at: https://www.europeanmovement.ie/programmes/ireland-and-the-eu-poll/.
25. John Coakley, 'Irish public opinion and the new Europe', pp. 94–113 in Michael Holmes (ed.), *Ireland and the European Union: Nice, enlargement and the future of Europe* (Manchester: Manchester University Press, 2005), at p. 103. See also successive EM Ireland/RedC polls 2013–2020, available at: https://www.europeanmovement.ie/programmes/ireland-and-the-eu-poll/.
26. European Commission, *Standard Eurobarometer 74 (Autumn 2010)*, February 2011, available at: https://ec.europa.eu/commfrontoffice/publicopinion/index.cfm/Survey/getSurveyDetail/search/information/surveyKy/918. For earlier survey data see Richard Sinnott, *Knowledge of*

the European Union in Irish Public Opinion: Sources and Implications (Dublin: Institute for European Affairs, 1995).

27. The National Forum on Europe, which was established following the first rejection of the Treaty of Nice in 2001 (but later disbanded in 2009), operated as a means for informing the Irish public in a non-partisan and neutral manner about the EU and as a basis for greater public participation on EU issues and developments.

28. For example, in 2018, the Irish government supported a series of Citizens' Dialogues on the Future of Europe (facilitated by European Movement Ireland). This exercise was motivated by the publication of the European Commission's *White Paper on the Future of Europe* published in 2017.

29. Fiachra Kennedy and Richard Sinnott, 'Irish public opinion towards European integration', *Irish Political Studies* 22:1 (2007), pp. 61–81.

30. Michael Marsh, 'Voting on Europe, again and again: stability and change in the Irish experience with EU referendums', *Electoral Studies* 38:2 (2015), pp. 170–82.

31. Martyn Frampton, 'Sinn Féin and the European arena: "ourselves alone" or "critical engagement"?', *Irish Studies in International Affairs* 16 (2005), pp. 235–53.

32. John Fitzgibbon, 'Citizens against Europe? Civil society and Eurosceptic protest in Ireland, the United Kingdom and Denmark', *JCMS Journal of Common Market Studies* 51:1 (2013), pp. 105–21, at p. 113.

33. Sinnott, *Attitudes and behaviour of the Irish electorate*.

34. Katy Hayward, 'Not a nice surprise: an analysis of the debate surrounding the 2001 referendum on the Treaty of Nice in the Republic of Ireland', *Irish Studies in International Affairs* 13 (2002), pp. 167–86.

35. Millward Brown IMS, *Post Lisbon Treaty Referendum Research Findings* (Conducted by Millward Brown IMS on behalf of the Department of Foreign Affairs), September 2008, pp. i–ii, available at: http://www.proyectos.cchs.csic.es/euroconstitution/library/working%20papers/Millward%20Brown%202008.pdf.

36. Mary C. Murphy and John O'Brennan, 'Ireland and the EU at forty: pragmatic incrementalism and differential policy convergence within a transformative European landscape', *Administration* 62:2 (2014), p. 10.

37. Jonathan Haughton, 'Historical background 1690 to present', in John O'Hagan and Francis O'Toole (eds), *The Economy of Ireland: policy-making in a global context* (London: Palgrave, 2017), p. 24.

38. For example, in both 2018 and 2019, 58 per cent of respondents to the European Movement Ireland/RedC research poll agreed: 'Ireland

should contribute more to the EU budget to continue to get [these] benefits', available at: https://www.europeanmovement.ie/programmes/ireland-and-the-eu-poll/.

39. Brigid Laffan and Jane O'Mahony, *Ireland and the European Union* (Basingstoke: Palgrave Macmillan, 2008), pp. 28–9.
40. John O'Brennan, 'Ireland says No (again): the 12 June 2008 referendum on the Lisbon Treaty', *Parliamentary Affairs* 62:2 (2009), pp. 258–77, at p. 271. See also Coakley, 'Irish public opinion and the new Europe', at pp. 109–10.
41. European Commission, *Standard Eurobarometer: National Report (Ireland)*, Autumn 2019, p. 4, available at: https://ec.europa.eu/commfrontoffice/publicopinion/index.cfm/Survey/getSurveyDetail/instruments/STANDARD/surveyKy/2255.
42. EM Ireland/Red C, *Ireland and the EU 2019*, available at: https://www.europeanmovement.ie/programmes/ireland-and-the-eu-poll/.
43. Sinn Féin, *Giving workers and families a break: A manifesto for change* (Dublin: Sinn Féin, 2020), p. 11, available at: https://www.sinnfein.ie/files/2020/SF_GE2020_Manifesto.pdf.
44. Amanda Ferguson and Gerry Moriarty, 'McDonald emphasises Sinn Féin's desire for Irish unity', *Irish Times* 15 February 2019.

CHAPTER 6

Media and the Election: Social and Traditional Media Narratives in the Campaign

Kirsty Park and Jane Suiter

This chapter explores how the campaign was covered on mainstream media and social media and draws on data including content of media coverage and party posts. Throughout this chapter we place a strong focus on Sinn Féin. The party outperformed the expectations of pre-election opinion polls, and this became a major part of the campaign story in mainstream and social media. It also ran a successful social media campaign and set a strong narrative as the party representing 'change' and, perhaps relatedly, according to the MRBI exit poll (see Chap. 10, p. 221), captured a significant proportion of votes among those under 35. For these reasons, we have chosen to centre our analysis of the media campaign on Sinn Féin, although we highlight key trends in the coverage of all the other major parties where appropriate.

K. Park (✉) • J. Suiter
Dublin City University, Dublin, Ireland
e-mail: kirsty.park@dcu.ie

© The Author(s), under exclusive license to Springer Nature
Switzerland AG 2021
M. Gallagher et al. (eds.), *How Ireland Voted 2020*,
https://doi.org/10.1007/978-3-030-66405-3_6

113

This chapter is organised around a number of questions. The first asks how the campaign was covered in the mainstream media. Specifically, in what ways did the media focus its attention in terms of parties and topics, and how much of this focus was on polling or electioneering rather than more substantive coverage of issues? Of course, media framing of the parties and their campaigns is only part of the story. In this hybrid media age we must also look to the framing of the parties on social media. This leads to our second question which goes behind the gatekeepers in the media to ask: who won the battle for attention and engagement on social media? Third, we look at the intersection of the mainstream and social media, examining how Sinn Féin set its own agenda and how this was received by other parties and the mainstream media.

We first turn our attention to coverage of the parties during the campaign on mainstream media including in *The Irish Times*, the *Irish Independent* and *TheJournal.ie* with a particular focus on game or issue framing. Second, we examine the attention paid to the parties on social media with a look at the campaign on Twitter and Facebook, followed by Google Trends data. Finally, we discuss what this means in terms of the parties' media campaigns, with a particular focus on Sinn Féin.

THE CAMPAIGN IN THE MAINSTREAM MEDIA

At the start of the campaign, there was something of a feeling of 'business as usual'. The expectation within the mainstream media was that the 2020 election would result in a win for either Fianna Fáil leader Micheál Martin or Fine Gael leader Leo Varadkar. Early campaign articles framed it as such with headlines like 'Big two to slug it out in most open election for years' (14 January 2020) from *The Irish Times* or 'Election 2020: A date with destiny for Varadkar and Martin' (18 January 2020) from the *Irish Independent*, giving the impression that this would be a straightforward contest between the two. This sentiment was reflected in the announcements from RTÉ and Virgin Media at the beginning of the campaign that they would conduct leaders' debates between Martin and Varadkar without including Sinn Féin leader Mary Lou McDonald. This probably inadvertently reinforced Sinn Féin messaging around change and the establishment.

All that was to change over the course of the campaign. In this chapter our attention and focus is on the media and its role in the campaign. In order to uncover the focus of the mainstream media, we analysed 625 election articles from the two main broadsheet newspapers *The Irish Times* (354) and the *Irish Independent* (144) and from *TheJournal.ie* (127). Both *The Irish Times* and the *Irish Independent* were chosen as they represent traditional print media as well as having active websites to disseminate their articles. *TheJournal.ie* is an online only outlet. It was the second most popular brand for online news in Ireland in 2019 and considering that younger people are more likely to consume news only online, its inclusion helps to ensure that our understanding of mainstream media is shaped by both print and online consumption.[1] The *Irish Independent* put up a paywall following the election, and thus in our data only *The Irish Times* was paywalled during the campaign period.

The articles were collected by scraping the contents of the political or election sections of each website from the date the election was called, 14 January, until 7 February, the day before polling. Any article that addressed the general election was included, with the exception of live polls, live blogs or landing pages for podcasts. We can generally separate the media frames of a campaign into two broad categories: game and issue frames. The game frame reports the party strategies, has a focus on polling and is concerned with the so-called horse race.[2] The issue or policy frame by contrast focusses on policy priorities and examines how the candidates or parties deal with societal problems, sometimes with a focus on manifestos.[3] Each article was coded for its dominant topic, which party it focussed on if it addressed one party specifically and whether it utilised a game/strategy frame or an issue-based frame.

We found that over half of all articles (54 per cent) focussed on a party, generally focussing attention on an individual party's leader, a candidate, campaign strategy or manifesto/policy position. By singling out an individual party, newspapers are choosing to specifically shine a spotlight, positively or negatively, on that party. They do this through framing or on occasion agenda setting, creating the narrative of how that party is seen within an election campaign. If we compare the individual party-focussed articles with the percentage of first preference votes (see Table 6.1), we can see that Fine Gael received the most individual party coverage, which we might expect as it was the governing party before the election and therefore likely to receive the most coverage.[4] While Sinn Féin received more individual coverage than Fianna Fáil, overall the focus was over-representative of Fine Gael and some of the smaller parties, and under-representative of the vote share for Sinn Féin, Fianna Fáil, independents, the Green Party and the Labour Party.

Table 6.1   Mainstream media coverage and vote share

Individual party focus	Percentage share of articles	Vote share in election	Difference in article focus
Fine Gael	30	21	+9
Sinn Féin	22	25	-3
Fianna Fáil	16	22	-6
Independent	10	15	-5
Green Party	6	7	-1
Labour	6	4	+2
Solidarity–PBP	5	3	+2
Social Democrats	4	3	+1
Other	1	1	0

If we focus on the three main parties, which each received a similar share of first preference votes and seats, we can see that individual coverage varied, with Fianna Fáil receiving the least party-focussed coverage across each of the outlets. The *Irish Independent* had a significantly higher focus on Fine Gael (56 per cent) followed by Sinn Féin (25 per cent); *The Irish Times* had the most focus on Sinn Féin (37 per cent), although the spread was very close between the parties; and *TheJournal.ie* prioritised Fine Gael (48 per cent) followed by Sinn Féin (33 per cent). It is notable that all three titles focussed to a much greater extent on Fine Gael, the outgoing party of government, rather than Fianna Fáil, its partner in the confidence and supply arrangement, perhaps due to incumbency bias. We also assessed individual articles more qualitatively, particularly the coverage in the later part of the campaign, and we have highlighted examples of how the different parties were treated throughout this chapter.

Almost half (46 per cent) of all the articles did not have a clear party focus and instead were coded as addressing either multiple parties, such as a conflict between two party leaders, or no party, such as an overview of a specific issue. In terms of framing, 62 per cent of these were strategy/game based and 36 per cent were issue based, with the remainder coded as unsure.

These figures are averaged over the course of the campaign, but we also expect longitudinal differences. We might expect coverage to vary over time, driven by events and, particularly, opinion polling, which changed significantly a week or so into the campaign. The general election was called on Tuesday, 14 January, with the vote taking place on Saturday, 8

February 2020. To analyse the change over time, we have broken this time period into four weekly blocks with each Saturday in the campaign period marking the beginning of a new block. The biggest shifts between the three main parties occurred in weeks three and four. The coverage in week three focussed heavily on Fine Gael and showed a reduction for the other two parties. Some of this increase in Fine Gael coverage involved comments made about Leo Varadkar by Fine Gael Senator Catherine Noone (see Chronology, p. xxi), which did provide a minor controversy during its campaign, and a smaller amount involved reaction to opinion polls and a rejection of a potential coalition with Sinn Féin.

Week four provided one of the most interesting points of analysis, as the beginning of this week coincided with a number of opinion polls that showed a Sinn Féin surge, putting it second behind Fianna Fáil in public support, followed by others later in the week that showed it leading. We can see this change reflected in the party-focussed coverage (see Fig. 6.1). Some 24 per cent of voters in the exit poll reported that they made their minds up only in the last few days of the campaign (see Chap. 10, p. 223), so this last week was a critical time from a campaign perspective.

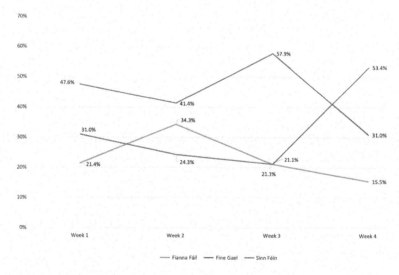

Fig. 6.1 Weekly coverage of the three main parties in mainstream media

While there was a steady climb in support for Sinn Féin, arguably the opinion polls in week four led to a change in narrative. While Sinn Féin did not run enough candidates to capitalise on its popularity with a Dáil majority, the opinion polls raised the possibility that a new majority government could include Sinn Féin at the expense of Fine Gael, a scenario that seemed less likely when the election was called.

Sinn Féin coverage steadily declined over the first three weeks and then spiked in week four. This coincides with a controversy around comments previously made by Conor Murphy, a senior Sinn Féin politician in Northern Ireland and former Provisional IRA member, regarding the murder of a young man named Paul Quinn in 2007. Quinn's death has been linked to members of the IRA and the controversy put a spotlight on Sinn Féin's ties to the IRA. If we look at the 31 Sinn Féin-focussed articles in week four, 22 (71 per cent) of them were about the murder of Paul Quinn. If we remove any articles focussed on Paul Quinn and look again at the coverage for the three parties during week four, then the coverage of Sinn Féin in terms of issues or party politics was significantly lower than Fine Gael at 50 per cent and equal to Fianna Fáil at 25 per cent. This suggests that the spike in coverage for Sinn Féin reflects an editorial focus on the suitability and credibility of Sinn Féin as a leading party, a focus made through the lens of the party's reaction to Paul Quinn's murder. For instance, one article in *The Irish Times* that was entirely focussed on Paul Quinn began as follows: 'Sinn Féin's surge in the opinion polls has raised questions about how it would perform in government were Fine Gael or Fianna Fáil to reverse their stance of refusing to go into coalition with them.'[5] There was also an extended back-and-forth between presenter Miriam O'Callaghan and Mary Lou McDonald in the final RTÉ debate about Sinn Féin's response to the murder, a segment that was quoted verbatim in *The Irish Times*. This coverage reflected more of an ideological opposition to Sinn Féin as a party as opposed to more substantive coverage that could have addressed policy positions, such as analysing the viability of its economic proposals. This is consistent with previous, sometimes, hostile coverage of Sinn Féin.[6]

But, of course, not all coverage is equal. For as long as there have been journalists (or indeed writers or storytellers), they have attempted to frame things in a way that suits their own logics whether storytelling, commercial or other. Frames promote the salience of a topic, organising the discourses and appearance of topics,[7] particularly telling readers what the important element to focus on is.[8] Through the repeated use of frames, the media can set the agenda.

The post-election polls (see Chap. 10) demonstrate that health and housing were the most important topics in voters' minds when casting their vote. But were these the topics that the media had set in its election coverage? Game/strategy articles were coded as such if the primary focus in the article was tactics or strategy, speculation on winners and losers, opinion polls, power formations, and perceptions of performance in debates or on the campaign trail. In contrast, issue-based articles put the primary focus on policies, issue positions or what politicians say or do in relation to issues. We find that overall 43 per cent of articles were issue-focussed and 54 per cent were strategy/game-focussed, with the final 3 per cent being indeterminate.

Across the three outlets, after removing the unclear articles, *The Irish Times* had the largest focus on strategy/game frame in its coverage at 60 per cent, followed by the *Irish Independent* at 56 per cent, while *TheJournal. ie* had a greater focus on issues as only 43 per cent of its coverage was strategy/game-based. These numbers did not change significantly throughout the weeks, with the exception of a rise in strategy/game articles for week two in *The Irish Times*, which is largely attributed to the fact it did a profile of candidates and likely seats for every constituency. If we look at how the framing varied for the party-focussed articles, Fine Gael articles had the highest proportion of strategy/game framing at 56 per cent compared to 43 and 40 per cent for Sinn Féin and Fianna Fáil, respectively. This probably reflects Fine Gael's position as the largest party during the election as well as the strategic considerations a Taoiseach has in choosing when to call an election.

In the next step of the analysis, each article, whether strategy/game- or issue-based, was coded according to the dominant issue that it focussed on. This coding took place using an initial 21 categories covering a range of topic areas such as agriculture, education and housing, and including one 'Other' category for anything that did not match one of these. At the end of the coding some issues within the social affairs category were recoded and split into additional categories to address prominent issues that emerged during the campaign, namely the pension age, healthcare and childcare, bringing the total number of categories to 24. A full list is available in the Appendix (see p. 132). Some articles covered more than one issue, and in these instances, the issue that received the most coverage within the article was chosen for coding purposes.

The most common topic by far, at 51 per cent, concerned electioneering such as party politics, election strategy or campaigning. This represents significantly higher coverage than any other individual topic or issue, including those that received the most coverage such as housing (6 per cent), tax/spending (5 per cent) and the pension age (5 per cent). If we remove electioneering from this analysis and focus only on the remaining issues, we can see a little more clearly which topics were prioritised. Table 6.2 shows the results of the MRBI exit poll, indicating which issues voters were most concerned about, alongside how those same issues ranked for topic focus within the articles.[9] The main topic that the media articles significantly under-reported on was health, the top concern of voters in the exit poll, along with housing/homelessness to a lesser extent. One explanation for this may be that health has been an important issue for countless elections, while the housing crisis and rise in homelessness were relatively new and thereby more newsworthy.

If we take the top two topics in the exit poll, health and housing, and look at how each outlet prioritised these in its coverage, we can see how the amount of coverage given to important topics also reflects individual editorial decisions. In the *Irish Independent* housing was the second most covered while health was fourth, *The Irish Times* prioritised housing with

Table 6.2 Preponderance of topic coverage in mainstream media and exit poll focus

	Exit poll percentage	Media percentage excluding electioneering	Difference in article coverage
Health	34	7	-27
Housing/Homelessness	27	12	-15
Pension age	9	10	+1
Jobs	6	6	0
Climate change	6	8	+2
Taxation	5	10	+5
Crime	3	4	+1
Childcare	3	3	0
Immigration	1	1	0
Brexit	1	3	+2
Others	6	36	+30
Total	100	100	100

the most coverage while health was eighth and *TheJournal.ie* gave housing the second most coverage followed by health in eighth.

If we look at how coverage of the major topics was spread across each week, housing coverage was relatively consistent throughout the campaign. Healthcare started low in week one at 9 per cent but received similar coverage through weeks two, three and four at around 30 per cent each week. However, coverage of the pension age significantly spiked in week two, with 69 per cent of pension age articles occurring in this week. Early articles spoke about how the pension age was 'becoming an issue', suggesting that this was not something anticipated by parties or commentators in advance. As journalist Miriam Lord wrote in *The Irish Times* in the middle of week two: 'Everyone is jumping on the old age pension bandwagon now',[10] although lowering the pension age to 65 had been one of Sinn Féin's initial election pledges. Coverage in week two focussed on party reactions, analysis of the issue and explanations of what the various parties were promising in their manifestos, before continuing on at a lower level. It does not seem that such coverage drove the narrative, but rather that it was responsive, with articles recognising factors such as canvassers' reports that this was becoming a prominent issue and, most notably, a highly discussed episode of RTÉ's *Liveline* radio show in which callers approaching the retirement age spoke about how the issue was affecting them.

THE CAMPAIGN ON SOCIAL MEDIA

There are two dominant fields of study in social media and campaigns: one focussed on the use of social media by voters and the other its use by parties and candidates. Much prior research has focussed on Twitter political campaigns, probably because of the relative ease of access to the Twitter API (Application Programming Interface) for collecting data. We gathered data through Newswhip, a social media analytics platform, for the last week of the campaign when campaigns would have been busiest including the Twitter accounts of all the parties, party leaders and prominent deputies held on that database. Indeed if we look at the tweets of the parties and candidates in the last week, we can see that the most popular tweets were from Mary Lou McDonald and Micheál Martin and were largely uncontentious, announcing the beginning and end of the campaign or lamenting the untimely death of RTÉ journalist Keelin Shanley.

The number of tweets in the last week is relatively small with the Sinn Féin party and candidates tweeting the most (304), followed by Fine Gael (294), Fianna Fáil (177), Greens (85), independents and small parties (299) and Labour (176). But far and away the most popular by both likes and retweets was one from Sinn Féin leader Mary Lou MacDonald, thanking supporters for their vote with 2167 retweets and 17,720 likes in that week. This is almost ten times the numbers for Fianna Fáil leader Michael Micheál's most popular tweet, one from outside his childhood home with the words 'Where it all began', which attracted some 172 retweets and 1730 likes in that week. Sinn Féin again attracted orders of magnitude more than all the other parties and independents, underlining Sinn Féin's number of supporters on Twitter, often referred to somewhat disparagingly as 'Shinnerbots' given their proclivity to be quick to denounce and attack any post not to their liking. Sinn Féin performs very well with younger voters and so its success on social media fits with international evidence where on average social media users are younger and pay more attention to politics than those who do not use social media.[11] Given the high vote for Sinn Féin in this election, it might be that the large number of Twitter followers did indeed turn out to vote for the party.

Facebook, however, is a different environment where politicians are more likely to engage in dialogue with voters and use the platform for marketing,[12] as this is the arena where voters rather than media and political activists spend more of their time. Our data here, also from the Newswhip API, runs for the entire duration of the campaign from 14 January to 8 February and is made up of all the public pages of the political parties amounting to 728 posts in total. Again we find a similar pattern: Sinn Féin had around ten times the engagements of the other parties on Facebook with 567,020 total interactions on posts compared to 49,358 for Fianna Fáil and 55,152 for Fine Gael. The top 15 posts of all parties were all Sinn Féin posts. Fine Gael's top post: 'This Saturday, ask yourself one question: Who do you trust? http://finegael.ie #Look Forward' was in 16th place overall with some 5013 interactions, far below Sinn Féin's top post at 13,742 total interactions.

Of course not all interactions are the same; since February 2016, Facebook users have been able to add a 'reaction' (with an emoji icon). Thus Facebook users can click on reactions such as 'Love', 'Haha', 'Wow', 'Sad' and 'Angry'. Previous research has shown that these kinds of mentions and reactions can mobilise the vote[13] or encourage voters to pay more attention to campaign communications[14] or to seek out information.[15] The reactions differ greatly between Fianna Fáil and Fine Gael posts and those of Sinn Féin. 'Haha' or 'Angry' constituted 94 per cent of emoji reactions for Fine Gael and 90 per cent for Fianna Fáil. In contrast, only 7 per cent of Sinn Féin's emoji reactions were 'Haha' or 'Angry', with 91 per cent being 'Love'. This may be partly the result of a change of campaign emphasis following the local and European elections when the internal Sinn Féin diagnosis was that it needed to produce solutions and not just focus on angry denunciation, as well as reflecting the large numbers of Sinn Féin activists online (see Chap. 4). For comparison, this is in marked contrast to an analysis of parties' Facebook pages during the 2017 Austrian parliamentary election. This found that 'Anger' was the most common reaction for the candidate with the highest level of overall reactions, former Austrian vice-chancellor Heinz-Christian Strache, and his most engaged-with posts focussed on dire migration warnings as part of a populist negative campaign.[16]

A further way to understand how voters are engaging with the key messages or framing from a political party is to examine the Google Trends data, which provides access to a largely unfiltered sample of actual search requests made to Google. It normalises search data, and each data point is divided by the total searches of the geography and time range it represents to compare relative popularity. The resulting numbers are then scaled on a range of 0–100 based on a topic's proportion of all searches on all topics. It can thus be used to determine the focus of voters' attention. For example, Google Trends data from the last seven days of the 2015 Greek bailout referendum was used to predict the results with a high level of accuracy.[17] Of course, we do not seek to predict the vote, but nonetheless think that the Trends data may indeed be an advance indication of a surge in support for a party leading up to an election. We searched for all Irish political parties in the week before the election. In the last week of the campaign in Ireland, Sinn Féin was one of the most popular search terms for those searching on Google News in Ireland. In the seven days leading up to the election, Sinn Féin was the party most searched for, again by a factor of about ten. Lower value searches were also all dominated by Sinn Féin, including Sinn Féin policies, Sinn Féin leader, Sinn Féin special criminal court and Conor Murphy Sinn Féin. If we look over time (Fig. 6.2), we can see that this spike of interest in searching for Sinn Féin manifested itself in the last week or ten days of the campaign.

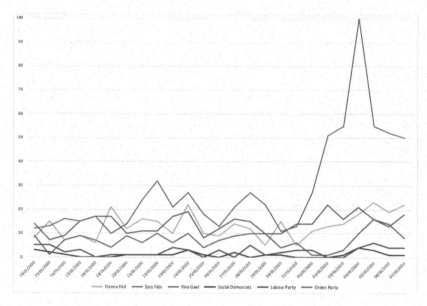

Fig. 6.2 Google Trends (web searches) for all Irish political parties over the course of the campaign

The Sinn Féin Agenda and (Social) Media

As this section will explore, Sinn Féin set a populist, anti-establishment agenda as being a party of change, through its interactions with mainstream media and its social media presence, as well as through participating in a voting strategy with left-leaning parties. The reaction of mainstream media towards Sinn Féin, perhaps inadvertently, served to reinforce its messaging.

One significant media event early in the campaign was the exclusion of Mary Lou McDonald from leaders' debates between Micheál Martin and Leo Varadkar, particularly RTÉ's *Prime Time* leaders' debate, scheduled for the last week of the campaign. This was an early opportunity for Sinn Féin to define itself as an underdog fighting for change against both a political and media status quo. Sinn Féin finance spokesperson Pearse Doherty was quoted in articles as saying that RTÉ was 'facilitating the game plan of Fine Gael and Fianna Fáil', and as the Facebook post in Fig. 6.3 indicates, Sinn Féin used this as an opportunity to further blur the lines of separation that Micheál Martin sought to draw between Fianna Fáil and Fine Gael, positioning Sinn Féin as the main alternative if voters wanted to see something different. While RTÉ later included McDonald

Fig. 6.3 Sinn Féin Facebook post regarding the RTÉ leaders' debate

on the basis of Sinn Féin's continued opinion poll successes, this early interaction between the party and the media set the tone for Sinn Féin's approach throughout the campaign, positioning itself as an underdog and main challenger to the establishment.

As the governing party, Fine Gael's strategy initially appeared to focus on positioning itself as the party with the experience to guide Ireland through Brexit, with its campaign launch describing itself as the 'winning team' to complete the negotiations. However, as discussed, voters cared most about issues such as health and housing. These were long-standing yet pressing problems that existed under the Fine Gael-led minority government that was able to govern through its confidence and supply agreement with Fianna Fáil. It was in this political context that Sinn Féin positioned itself. McDonald was quoted on the day the election was called as saying that Sinn Féin would 'give people an opportunity to make a change' and its first Facebook post spoke of 'the biggest public housing building programme in the history of the state' and 'real solutions to the health crisis'. The party would focus relentlessly on the message of 'change' on Facebook. Over 20 per cent of its posts contained phrases such as 'Vote change. Vote Sinn Féin' or 'Vote for change. Transfer for change'. Indeed Sinn Féin accounts for some two-thirds of all mentions of 'change' by all parties on Facebook.

The distinction between a coalition and a confidence and supply agreement may have been less obvious to voters, a point that Sinn Féin took advantage of, leaving both Fianna Fáil and Fine Gael vulnerable to negative framing from Sinn Féin. For example, an early Sinn Féin Facebook post with over 4000 interactions spoke of the 'phoney war' between the two main parties stating that 'Fianna Fáil and Fine Gael are the Establishment. They want to maintain the status quo.'

In its communications Sinn Féin pursued an anti-elite populist narrative, a type of populism that was identified among Irish voters in a study of the 2016 general election.[18] This was not largely evident within the mainstream articles, presumably because the party cannot fully set its own narrative when relying on journalists' coverage. This anti-elite narrative is most clearly reflected in the arena where it vastly outperformed its rivals: its social media messaging. The party's most popular Facebook posts used phrases like 'put ordinary people first', 'government for the people' and 'serves the people'. It also extended into the positioning of party members and leaders as ordinary people, such as when Pearse Doherty used the phrase 'posh boys and girls' in critiquing those creating the current government's housing policy, a somewhat ironic phrasing given the private education of both the leader Mary Lou McDonald and housing spokesperson Eoin Ó Broin.

Sinn Féin was able to capture a left-wing, anti-establishment sentiment that extended beyond the party, and this was reflected in social media. Left-leaning parties and candidates promoted voting for left-leaning parties to allow for the possibility of a left coalition led by Sinn Féin in a 'Vote Left, Transfer Left' strategy. The example in Fig. 6.4 shows a local People Before Profit Twitter account sharing an image that suggests voting Sinn Féin number two on the ballot as it is 'the only party who can lead a left wing coalition'.

This strategy provided a strong 'get out the vote' cross-party message that further established Sinn Féin's image as a party leading the fight for leftist change. In the exit poll data, 48 per cent of voters thought it best to have a change in government, while 31 per cent believed the country needed a radical change in direction. The desire for change, paired with a 'transfer left' strategy and a framing of Fianna Fáil as the establishment, left Sinn Féin ideally placed to capitalise upon this sentiment in its communications (Fig. 6.5), particularly with the boost from the later opinion polls.

By the end of the campaign, it was clear that Sinn Féin had successfully themed the election to be about change, and the reaction from other

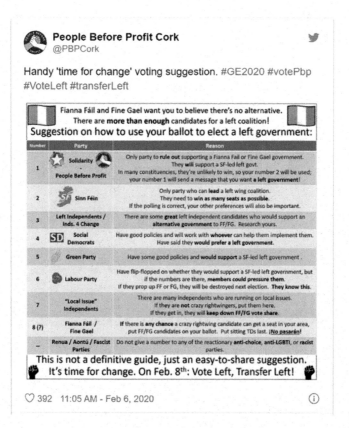

Fig. 6.4   #Vote Left Transfer Left social media strategy

parties and the mainstream media both co-opted and, at times, countered this messaging by focussing on the credibility and suitability of the party to lead in government. It was at this point in the campaign that the mainstream outlets put a major focus on Sinn Féin and its suitability for government, through the controversy surrounding Paul Quinn's murder. Additionally, some coverage focussed on the qualities of McDonald as a leader, with one editorial from the *Irish Independent* suggesting that she was the new Donald Trump and that Sinn Féin was 'an outlet for the disillusioned to lash out at the establishment'.[19] It could be argued that the mainstream media eventually recognised that Sinn Féin had successfully themed the election to be about change, leaving the response to focus on

Fig. 6.5 Sinn Féin Facebook post in the final week of the campaign

whether this change could be trusted in the hands of Sinn Féin, rather than trying to defend a negatively framed concept of the status quo that Sinn Féin had developed. In the last week, the articles also reflected the framing of change, particularly in coverage of the opinion polls. These articles featured quotes from leaders in the three parties positioning themselves as parties of change, such as when Varadkar stated, 'Other parties talk about change, but we are the ones who have been driving it though'[20] or Martin's describing Fianna Fáil as the only party 'that can create real change and a different government'.[21] In the final debate Varadkar even characterised the election itself as being a 'change election', reflecting that the parties were competing under the change agenda that Sinn Féin had pushed strongly from the start. In the final week, we can see (Fig. 6.6)

Fine Gael
6 February · 🌐

We are change. This Saturday, vote No. 1 Fine Gael. #LookForward

👍😮😢 551   269 comments 63 shares

Fianna Fáil
4 February at 21:26 · ⊙ · 🌐

Ireland can fix its problems.
It's time for change.
Vote Fianna Fáil

#GE2020 #AnIrelandForAll

For more visit: www.fiannafail.ie

👍😮❤ 128   108 comments 31 shares 4.3K views

Fig. 6.6   Framing change

Sinn Féin Ireland
8 February ·

Today's the day for change BUT only if you vote Sinn Féin. Polls are open 7am-10pm. You DON'T need a polling card, just Photo ID.
Vote Sinn Féin, vote for change, vote for unity.

TODAY'S
THE DAY FOR
CHANGE!

Fatmir Trezhnjeva and 2.1K others   227 comments 1K shares

Fig. 6.6 (continued)

how the three main parties had incorporated the framing of change and were using social media to promote a message that they would be the agents of that change.

CONCLUSION

The key story in the 2019 local and European elections had been the 'green wave' that saw a surge in support for the Green party and a collapse of the Sinn Féin vote after a previously strong showing in 2014 (see Chap. 1). However, the major story in the 2020 general election campaign was the rise in popularity of Sinn Féin through its platform of 'change', which culminated in the party having the second highest number of seats and the largest percentage of the popular vote. Our first question asked how the campaign was covered in mainstream media. The mainstream media coverage took what we could consider a status quo approach to the campaign, with a large focus on the governing party, Fine Gael, and most coverage utilising a game frame in discussing electioneering or party politics. It is difficult to ascertain for certain whether the mainstream media sets the agenda or responds to it, but it would appear that they did underestimate the importance of health to voters and covered the pension age in a way that did not seem to chime with voters' concerns during the campaign.

Our second question asked who won the battle for attention and engagement on social media. It is clear from the data that Sinn Féin dominated on social media, vastly outperforming Fine Gael and Fianna Fáil on Twitter and Facebook. While this may be attributable to higher social media use among Sinn Féin supporters, the Google Trends data suggest that it may reflect a wider interest in Sinn Féin during this general election campaign. Sinn Féin's success on social media provided it with a strong platform to set its own narrative and counter the other parties without relying on the gatekeepers of journalism.

Our third question built upon the analysis of the previous sections and examined the agenda set by Sinn Féin and how it was received. By centring its campaign on the issues that connected with voters and establishing itself as the leader of a left, anti-establishment movement, Sinn Féin was able to successfully communicate a message of change, leaving Fine Gael and Fianna Fáil to try and co-opt that message into their own campaigns, a significant departure from the 'stability to finish Brexit' messaging with which Fine Gael had started the campaign. Additionally, while the coverage percentages suggest that Sinn Féin was reasonably well represented in the media, the large increase in the last week was mostly through the lens of the Paul Quinn controversy. This was a largely negative frame, leading us to ask the question of whether this was the mainstream media's reaction to Sinn Féin's successful framing of itself as the party of change.

The dynamics of the 2020 election make it difficult to definitively declare any party a 'winner', but the improvement in Sinn Féin's performance between the 2019 and 2020 elections clearly represents a success in its revised communication strategy during the 2020 campaign.

Appendix: Coding Categories for Dominant Topic

1. Macro economics	13. Defence
2. Civil rights, freedoms	14. Culture/Media
3. Social affairs	15. Foreign affairs
4. Agriculture	16. Democracy/Governance
5. Employment	17. Party politics/Election strategy/Campaigning
6. Education	18. Other
7. Climate/Energy	19. Emigration
8. Immigration	20. Opinion polls
9. Traffic/Transport	21. Brexit
10. Justice/Crime	22. Healthcare (added during recoding)
11. Housing	23. Pension age (added during recoding)
12. Micro economics (Tax/Spending)	24. Childcare (added during recoding)

Notes

1. Niamh Kirk et al., *Digital News Report Ireland 2019* (DCU FuJo & Broadcasting Authority of Ireland, 2019).

2. See Doris A. Graber, 'Making campaign news user friendly: the lessons of 1992 and beyond', *American Behavioral Scientist* 37:2 (1993), pp. 328–36; Thomas E. Patterson, 'The 1976 horserace', *The Wilson Quarterly* 1:3 (1977), pp. 73–9; Shanto Iyengar, Helmut Norpoth, and Kyu S. Hahn, 'Consumer demand for election news: the horserace sells', *The Journal of Politics* 66: 1 (2004), pp. 157–75.

3. Kathleen Jamieson and Joseph Cappella, 'The effect of a strategy-based political news schema: a Markle Foundation Project Report', paper delivered at the American Political Science Association Convention, Washington DC, 1993; Thomas E. Patterson, 'Of polls, mountains: U.S. journalists and their use of election surveys', *The Public Opinion Quarterly* 69:5 (2005), pp. 716–24.

4. Heinz Brandenburg, 'Political bias in the Irish media: a quantitative study of campaign coverage during the 2002 general election', *Irish Political Studies* 20:3 (2005), pp. 297–322.

5. Gerry Moriarty, 'Old question of who pulls the strings comes back to haunt Sinn Féin', *The Irish Times* 6 February 2020.

6. Pat Leahy, 'Campaign strategies: how the campaign was won and lost', pp. 75–97 in Michael Gallagher and Michael Marsh (eds), *How Ireland Voted 2016: the election that nobody won* (Cham: Palgrave Macmillan, 2016), p. 91.

7. Robert M. Entman, 'Framing: toward clarification of a fractured paradigm', *Journal of Communication* 43:4 (1993), pp. 51–8.

8. William A. Gamson and Andre Modigliani, 'Media discourse and public opinion on nuclear power: a constructionist approach', *American Journal of Sociology* 95:1 (1989), pp. 1–37.

9. The mainstream media percentages reported here include all topics for which we coded with the exception of electioneering. Thirty-six per cent of the articles addressed topics that were not covered in the exit poll and so the figures for mainstream media coverage total to 64. While this does not enable a direct comparison between the two sets of figures, it does allow us to see the degree of under- or over-representation among the topics reported.

10. Miriam Lord, 'The left woos Mary Lou as FG tries to keep Ireland's nanas and granddads happy,' *Irish Times* 22 January 2020.

11. Kristoffer Holt et al., 'Age and the effects of news media attention and social media use on political interest and participation: do social media function as leveller?', *European Journal of Communication* 28:1 (2013), pp. 19–34.

12. Gunn Sara Enli and Eli Skogerbø, 'Personalized campaigns in party-centred politics', *Information, Communication & Society* 16:5 (2013), pp. 757–74.

13. Nicholas A. Valentino et al., 'Election night's alright for fighting: the role of emotions in political participation,' *The Journal of Politics* 73:1 (2011), pp. 156–70.

14. Michael B. MacKuen et al., 'Affective signatures and attention: the persistent impact of emotional responses to the news', paper delivered at the Midwest Political Science Association Annual Meeting, Chicago, 2013.

15. Nicholas A. Valentino et al., 'Is a worried citizen a good citizen? Emotions, political information seeking, and learning via the internet,' *Political Psychology* 29:2 (2008), pp. 247–73.

16. Jakob-Moritz Eberl et al., 'Emotional reactions on Austrian parties' Facebook pages during the 2017 Austrian parliamentary election' (University of Vienna: Computational Communication Science Lab, 2017).

17. Nikos Askitas, 'Calling the Greek referendum on the nose with Google Trends'. Bonn: IZA Institute for the Study of Labor, IZA Discussion Paper No. 9569 (2015).

18. See Theresa Reidy and Jane Suiter, 'Who is the populist Irish voter?', *Journal of the Statistical and Social Inquiry Society of Ireland* 46 (2016–17) pp. 117–31, and Jane Suiter et al., 'Hybrid media and populist currents in Ireland's 2016 general election', *European Journal of Communication* 33:4 (2018), pp. 396–412.

19. Philip Ryan, 'Mary Lou McDonald could well be the Irish version of Donald Trump', *Irish Independent* 2 February 2020.

20. Fiach Kelly et al., 'Sinn Féin "will talk to all parties" on forming a government', *Irish Times* 2 February 2020.

21. Rónán Duffy, 'Micheál Martin again rules out Sinn Féin coalition, saying party would "destroy enterprise"', *TheJournal.ie* 3 February, 2020.

CHAPTER 7

On the Campaign Trail

Mairéad Farrell, James O'Connor,
Jennifer Carroll MacNeill, Roderic O'Gorman,
Marie Sherlock, and Jennifer Whitmore

MAIRÉAD FARRELL (SINN FÉIN, GALWAY WEST)

Mairéad Farrell served a term on Galway City Council from 2014 to 2019. She was elected to Dáil Éireann on her first attempt in 2020, taking the third seat in the five-seat constituency on the eighth count. She has a BA in Economics and History from the National University of Ireland, Galway, and an MSc in Finance from Queen's University Belfast. She worked in financial services before entering politics full time.

M. Farrell (✉) • J. O'Connor • J. C. MacNeill • R. O'Gorman • J. Whitmore
Dáil Éireann, Dublin, Ireland
e-mail: T.Reidy@ucc.ie

M. Sherlock
Seanad Éireann, Dublin, Ireland

M. Gallagher et al. (eds.), *How Ireland Voted 2020*,
https://doi.org/10.1007/978-3-030-66405-3_7

135

An election seemed to be on the cards from the day a Leinster House government was formed in the aftermath of the 2016 general election. The confidence and supply arrangement between Fianna Fáil and Fine Gael never seemed as stable as they would have liked it to be. There is no doubt that this instability was the cause of all political parties and independents being on constant election footing. Sinn Féin was no different. In fact, our party's Ard Chomhairle (governing body) initiated a general election candidate selection process at the end of 2017, meaning that the Galway West–South Mayo Dáilcheantar (constituency) candidate selection convention took place on Sunday 3 December 2017. The convention itself was uncontested due to the fact that I was the only name submitted by members to go before convention at the close of nominations, 72 hours before the event. Nonetheless, over 150 members turned up to endorse my candidacy and to hear guest speaker Pat Doherty, former MP for West Tyrone, deliver the main address.

I have contested three elections, but each time it has been a source of immense pride for me to be selected by my peers to represent Sinn Féin. It undoubtedly brings a whole host of challenges and responsibilities, but it also gives you a platform that you can use to articulate the concerns and voices of people in your community; an opportunity to be part of a process that could bring about a better world for us all. It is often said of people involved in politics that they are 'only in it for themselves' and that it is ultimately an exercise in self-aggrandisement. For me, the basis of my involvement in politics is very much the opposite. It is about giving a voice to the marginalised, the impoverished and those most disenfranchised from the structures of power and wealth in society. It is, and always will be, about realising the republic declared in 1916, and no less.

For those who are unaware of the structures within Sinn Féin that lead to a member being selected to run for election, I will expand on my own experience of this process. Sinn Féin's leadership is its membership-led governing body, the Ard Chomhairle. An Ard Chomhairle is elected by a members' conference every year known as an ard fheis. Delegates from each cumann (branch), comhairle ceantair (regional body) and cúige (provincial body) are given a vote at an ard fheis along with outgoing members of the national officer board and an Ard Comhairle itself. Many more hundreds attend the ard fheis in the form of ordinary members, visitors, international guests, press and more besides. The national officer board and the Ard Chomhairle are elected from the floor of the ard fheis, and the newly constituted Ard Chomhairle then has the power to subsequently co-opt small numbers of members for specific work.

One of the responsibilities of an Ard Chomhairle is to discuss and agree a plan for our election cycles. As soon as the broad parameters for the holding of candidate selection conventions were agreed, our comhairle ceantair forged ahead with the logistics. As it happened, the selection conventions held in winter 2017/spring 2018 were quite early and the period during which their results remained valid (until autumn 2019) had passed before an election was called. So we were then required to initiate another set of conventions in late 2019 and I was delighted that our current leas uachtarán (deputy president) Shinn Féin Michelle O'Neill MLA was in a position to attend my second convention held in Galway during November 2019, with the same outcome.

The 2020 general election campaign for me could be best described as a whirlwind. Although we had been anticipating an election for the guts of four years, when outgoing Taoiseach Leo Varadkar announced the dissolution of Dáil Éireann on 14 January and an election date of 8 February there was a mixture of relief and overwhelming stress. We had just over three weeks to speak to as many as possible of the more than 100,000 voters in Galway West–South Mayo. My campaign team are fantastic and I genuinely couldn't ask for better. It's probably a truism to say, but there's no way I would be where I am today without them. Once a date was set, we all kicked into action. That means getting the campaign leaflet designed and off to print, getting posters organised and putting specific people in charge of the various responsibilities from social media, graphic design and press to canvass, postering and communications. We broke the Dáilcheantar down into manageable geographic clusters: Galway City, south Connemara, north Connemara, south Mayo and the Oranmore/Claregalway area.

I met my core team regularly to discuss various aspects of the campaign. I would be telling a lie if I said that I'm a candidate who takes it all in my stride. I have a tendency to put all my energies into whatever task is in front of me, and election campaigns are unbelievably busy, you're in campaign mode 24 hours a day, seven days a week. For candidates, it can be very draining mentally and physically. You are often dealing with people who are in really distressing social and economic circumstances and that takes its toll on you. I have no doubt that those closest to me get the brunt of my frustration and exhaustion as a campaign develops. You need to have people who you can bounce ideas off and get advice from, but like anyone engaged with something as intense as an election campaign, you also need people to vent to when you're having a bad day. I am lucky to have such long-suffering friends on my team who have gone through more than one election with me. They will remain nameless, but they know my deep appreciation for all they do. Elections forge deep bonds of friendship with people due to the fast-paced and consuming nature of a campaign and all that it entails, from late night and early morning meetings to long drives down country lanes or long walks in and out of housing estates. I remember a conversation at the end of one particularly long night of canvassing; it was getting dark and the man was surprised yet quite happy to see us arriving at his house. The man was very supportive and chatty, so my canvassing partner admitted that he thought he recognised him from somewhere and asked what he worked at. The man replied that he was actually out of work, to which my friend said enthusiastically, 'Ah, that's how I know you, I'm in the same vocation myself'. Laughter and good humour have an amazing capacity to make life seem so much more enjoyable and human.

Interviews and debates hosted by print media and radio are a crucial part of any election campaign, and at the start, it can be extraordinarily nerve-wracking. It's probably the fear of the unknown, if you're asked a technical question to which you don't have an answer, if you trip over your words and don't get your message across as clearly as you know you can. It's also something that you find your groove with and different people have different ways of overcoming the stress involved with media appearances. I think it's a bit like playing sport, no matter how much preparation or training you do beforehand, there's always a healthy anxiety about what you will face when you get down to it and whether you will get an opportunity to really put your knowledge or skills effectively to use.

I have said that for me general election 2020 could be best described as a whirlwind. At the outset, it seemed as though nationally Sinn Féin would perform ok overall; we would hold our seats and possibly gain one or two extra. In Galway West–South Mayo, for a variety of reasons, I felt that we had an outside chance, but the local and European elections of May 2019 were very much a disappointment and we all quietly limited our expectations with that in mind. Having said that, as a party we learned much in the aftermath of those elections. We went back to our supporter base and asked them what we could be doing better, and they told us. We needed to sharpen our message, be clear on our alternatives and engage more effectively with our grassroots. That's what we did, and as we began to canvass the homes of voters in my constituency, the increased sense of hope and optimism for our political alternative was palpable. Each and every day of the campaign brought new energy and new volunteers. I have no doubt that there were more people involved in that general election campaign for Sinn Féin than any other Galway election in my memory.

I have to say that the stand-out moment of the election from my perspective was the visit of uachtarán (president) Shinn Féin Mary Lou McDonald to my home community of Mervue on the east side of Galway city. I was born on McBride Avenue and currently live on Wolfe Tone Avenue in the home of my late grandmother, both located in Old Mervue and named after two significant figures in Irish Republican history. Built in the 1950s as a council estate to house the growing population of Galway City, Mervue is an incredibly proud community. The response they gave to Mary Lou lifted my heart. While she was there she met small business owners, workers, nurses, neighbours of mine and elderly residents who were close to my late grandmother and who raised me as a kid. People who epitomise that famous phrase 'Salt of the Earth'.

As I sat in a café with one of my team on 9 February 2020 sipping a cup of tea to calm my nerves, the tallies began to come through from the count centre on Threadneedle Road showing that I was in with a shout for a Dáil seat. All the long meetings, slagging, chats and phone calls late into the night, endless canvassing and postering, they all come down to that count day. On 10 February 2020, the returning officer announced my election to the 33rd Dáil and an Irish tricolour flag that had draped the coffin of my late aunt and namesake, murdered by undercover SAS operatives in Gibraltar 32 years previous, was raised aloft in Salthill, Galway City.

JAMES O'CONNOR (FIANNA FÁIL, CORK EAST)

James O'Connor TD was elected to Cork County Council in May 2019 at the age of 21. It was his first electoral contest, and he took the fourth seat of seven in the Midleton local electoral area (East Cork). Just nine months later, he was elected to the Dáil on his first attempt, taking the fourth seat on the eighth count; the incumbent Fianna Fáil TD lost his seat in the constituency. James took a leave of absence from his degree in Business, Economics and Social Studies (BESS) at Trinity College Dublin following his election to Cork County Council. He is the youngest member of the 33rd Dáil.

My journey to Dáil Éireann really got under way while I was in secondary school. I became involved in Pobalscoil na Tríonóide's student council during my first year when I was elected as a class captain. Three years later I became the youngest chairperson of the student council in the school's relatively short history. It was the first election I contested and thankfully I was successful.

During transition year, I applied for a one-week work experience placement in Micheál Martin's office in 2013. Luckily, I was accepted despite not being in Micheál's constituency. It was a great experience for a young teenager with a keen interest in politics and it brought me to Leinster House for the first time. I went to the viewing gallery for leaders' questions and shortly after I had the opportunity to meet with Micheál. We had a conversation about his life in politics. I always had great admiration for Micheál. I briefly met him when he visited Kyle National School to officially open a newly renovated school building. He had just been appointed as Minister for Foreign Affairs by then newly elected Taoiseach, Brian Cowen.

I grew up on a family farm where I still live with my parents. I was the only person in our house that had an interest in politics. Both my parents work in the dairy industry, and no member of our immediate family was ever elected to public office. I developed my interest in politics through Comhairle na nÓg which is an organisation representing young people in local government. We campaigned to change the fare structure on public transport for young people by lobbying the Minister for Transport who subsequently became Taoiseach following the resignation of Enda Kenny. Having developed a taste for campaigning I decided to pursue a degree in Business, Economics and Social Studies at Trinity College Dublin. It was a popular course amongst members of Dáil Éireann.

When I started in Trinity, I had secured a work placement in Jim O'Callaghan's office by Christmas of 2016. I spent most Fridays in Leinster House throughout the college term helping out in any way that I could. I was offered an internship by the Minister of State for Higher Education, Mary Mitchell O'Connor, which was also a very insightful experience. I deferred my studies around Christmas in 2018. I was hospitalised and underwent surgery in the run-up to my summer exams earlier in the year, and I wanted to take some time out from university.

I returned home to Youghal, and it did not take long before I was approached by Councillor Frank O'Flynn who was the Fianna Fáil whip in Cork County Hall. He asked if I had any interest in contesting the local elections. I can most definitely say that I had no intention of running in the local elections at that stage of my life. Perhaps I flirted with the idea, but I never thought about it in a meaningful way. I started to seriously consider contesting the locals during February, but my parents were not receptive, to say the least. We had all planned that I would resume my degree in September of 2019.

I decided to go to County Hall to meet Frank to discuss this matter further. We agreed that I would have a particularly good chance. The Fianna Fáil local election candidates were already selected by the members. These included Dr Rosarii Griffin, a staff member in UCC, and former Minister of State and incumbent councillor, Michael Ahern. Michael was co-opted following the resignation of Youghal's Aaron O'Sullivan, which had come as a huge surprise. Both Michael and Rosarii were based on the western side of the constituency in the Midleton area, which left a huge opening in Youghal. The town and surrounding area were left with just one councillor out of six. An additional seat was to be added bringing the total number to seven, and this significantly boosted my chances. I went for an interview at Fianna Fáil HQ in March, and ten days later I was added to the ticket.

The major challenge my campaign faced was competing against Councillor Mary Linehan Foley who had left Fianna Fáil after she was unsuccessful in a selection process in the run-up to the 2014 local elections. Mary also enjoyed the support of several former Fianna Fáil town councillors and had extensive connections in the local media. In hindsight, it was a difficult and unnecessarily dirty campaign. I personally felt exploited by the local media in the Youghal area, who attempted to drum up hysteria about my studies in Trinity. Mary was on the board of directors at the local radio station which was particularly brutal and hostile towards my campaign. During the local election campaign, I started to walk into the radio station unannounced during shows where there was an opportunity to discuss community issues. This was a successful strategy of combating set-ups that I previously had to endure.

I set up an election office in Youghal soon after being added to the ticket and we organised a launch event. My parents and family friends assembled a large crowd, and we invited Cork North-Central TD Billy Kelleher (elected an MEP in May 2019) and Waterford TD Mary Butler to attend. Cork East TD Kevin O'Keeffe showed up as well. A well-organised campaign launch is particularly important. It gives energy and momentum to a campaign, which is needed when you are new. Due to the close proximity of the 2020 general election and the 2019 local election, my campaigns almost overlapped.

As soon as the campaign posters could go up, we arranged for a small army of volunteers to erect posters throughout my side of the municipal district. This was done swiftly and was highly effective. Our canvasses were well organised, and I backed this up with a strong presence on social media. Michael Ahern withdrew from the race and decided to retire from politics shortly after, so it was now down to two Fianna Fáil candidates. I was very grateful to the Ahern family for their support. I was confident that we would both get elected, but Rosarii had the backing of the sitting Fianna Fáil TD, Kevin O'Keeffe. Mary was also closely aligned with the O'Keeffe family, which created its own issues. Although there was no agreement on territory, we were both advised to stick to our own areas. My campaign team focused on the east of the electoral area, but towards the final days of the campaign, we moved into the Midleton area following several encroachments by my running mate. We completed a thorough campaign of both Youghal and Midleton along with several key villages and rural communities in my home patch.

I was delighted to take the fourth seat out of seven. It was a fantastic result considering I was a candidate for only nine weeks. Fianna Fáil figures were pleasantly surprised, and shortly after the locals, Padraig O'Sullivan successfully contested the Cork North-Central by-election. Padraig was added to the Fianna Fáil ticket in Cork East before Billy Kelleher decided to run for the European Parliament. When Padraig was elected, an opening arose in Cork East and I was the only sitting Fianna Fáil elected representative in the south of the constituency from Cobh to Youghal. In comparison, the party had taken six seats on the northern side of Cork East between Mallow municipal district (3) and Fermoy municipal district (3).

There was a fast lead into the general election, and I had just eight months to prepare. I engaged in several high-profile issues across Cork East. I developed a habit of conducting radio interviews on a regular basis to keep people updated on the work I was undertaking on Cork County Council. I would also write articles in the local papers, and before long, I noticed a considerable improvement in people's attitude towards me. People appreciated that I was trying my best and fortunately I managed to get some local issues resolved.

I phoned the party's general secretary to officially outline my interest in becoming a candidate for the upcoming general election. I did not have to go through any interview process to become the Dáil candidate. One candidate had already been selected by Fianna Fáil members. I was aware that HQ were closely monitoring the situation to gauge what was happening on the ground. I received a call from the local organiser who informed me that I was added to the ticket.

As a 22-year-old, my candidacy was naturally going to attract some attention, and this was beneficial during the election. I did receive remarks from constituents about lacking experience and being too young to contest a general election, but I did not let it faze me. I knew we had a significant chance to take a seat as Fianna Fáil had a surprisingly good result in the constituency in 2016.

My general election was remarkably similar to the local elections except the general election was on a much larger scale. We put up large numbers of posters and stuck to our home base as much as we could. I did not want to overly encroach on the O'Keeffes' territory, but we spent time in

Mallow and Fermoy due to my family connections in the area. Mary Linehan Foley entering the race did not come as a surprise. I was going into the general election in a very good place as I had worked extremely hard in the months leading up to Christmas. I utilised social media to a much greater extent to better connect with younger voters. I truly feel that this was the first general election in Ireland that was heavily influenced by social media platforms such as Facebook and Instagram. It is certainly an area that is under-regulated at present and more must be done to allow fact-checking of information. Door-to-door canvassing and leaflet drops were important. In my own view, I was elected because we ran a strong campaign on all fronts.

Throughout the period of time approaching the general election, I always held the view that I was in a good position to secure a seat but my thinking was that this would be the second seat for Fianna Fáil. When Fianna Fáil's performance started to weaken in the polls, I did feel that it significantly lowered my chances of getting elected. We were really taken by surprise that Kevin was unsuccessful. I also underestimated my own support in the election. Perhaps there were more factors working in my favour than I realised. I credit my win to the momentum of winning a seat at the local elections a few months earlier and having a campaign that was fit for twenty-first-century politics. In conclusion, I would like to express my gratitude to my family, campaign team and friends who I could not have done this without.

Jennifer Carroll MacNeill (Fine Gael, Dún Laoghaire)

Jennifer Carroll MacNeill was first elected to Dún Laoghaire County Council in May 2019. She was elected to the Dáil on her first attempt taking the third seat on the eighth count. She was added to the Fine Gael election ticket in November 2019. The late addition arose from a vacancy caused by the deselection of then incumbent Fine Gael TD Maria Bailey. Jennifer has a PhD in politics from University College Dublin and, in 2015, won the Basil Chubb prize for the best PhD in Politics. She is a qualified solicitor and barrister, and author of a legal and political textbook on Irish political and judicial institutions. Jennifer worked as a legal advisor to a former leader of Fine Gael and as a senior legal and policy advisor to four Fine Gael ministers between 2008 and 2019.

I was selected in November 2019 for what turned out to be a February 2020 election, following a late change to the Fine Gael ticket in Dún Laoghaire. Having run in the 2019 local elections, I knew the importance of a great team and I was lucky they were still able to help me for the general election. For a general election, that group grows from a personal team to a bigger party membership-based team with significant support from local councillors. That new input is invaluable—the additional political and local insight from a team of really experienced political campaigners. In my case, this broader team gelled very quickly, giving me a large supportive base to run a campaign. I needed it because we had a lot of work to do. It's fair to say that the wind was against government candidates in the early part of 2020 and, as a new candidate with not much profile outside my immediate local electoral area, it was going to be a tough ask to make it over the line.

Fine Gael headquarters supported my team with graphic design as well as providing advice on useful applications for editing videos. We took a number of early steps to build profile locally, with letters and leaflets, local advertising and some national media pieces where possible. But nothing, absolutely nothing, is more important than meeting people face to face. People like to see their representatives, on good days and bad, windswept or pristine, foibles and head colds and half-frozen or blown away. Nothing is more important than meeting people and giving them the opportunity to speak to you as much or as little as they wish, at nearly any hour of the night or day. Really the campaign was built from and expanded on the work we had put in during the local election a few months previously.

Winter elections are different of course. Yes, you go out in any weather but, in my area at least, people don't answer the door much after 8 pm in the dark. In the summer, canvassing could go on until nearly 9 pm but with the universal caveat of the danger of waking a baby or young child by ringing the wrong door at the wrong time. You need constant canvasser vigilance for prams, tricycles and car seats! The impact of the darkness is that it truncates your canvass significantly, which isn't good for anyone but is particularly bad for a new candidate trying to make some headway in a competitive constituency.

From all sides of the political spectrum, it was quite a crowded field. The overall assessment, based on what was going on nationally and from previous elections, was that a seat each would go to the Green Party, People Before Profit and Fine Gael. The last seat was a close call between Fine Gael and Fianna Fáil, and in the end the seat went to Fianna Fáil based on transfers. I always thought I stood a competitive chance of being elected but I thought it might be in the fourth or fifth position overall in the constituency. It would have been difficult for me as a candidate, and for my team, to run in the election without some belief we could win. The reaction on the doors also gave me the sense that it was possible, if I could only achieve sufficient scale in the short campaign period. Some days, I would walk away more confident than others. That's when you really rely on the team around you, to stay positive and keep the energy up.

In both the local and general elections, I came to the competition a little late as it were and had to find new ways of campaigning to help build some recognition. People can't have an opinion of you if they've never heard of you. So, one thing we did in both campaigns was 'walking posters'. This is where you keep some posters back and, instead of putting them on poles, you tie a ribbon through them and put it around a good friend's neck and send them off walking in pairs. Send them all up to the park together at the same time and take a good picture. Have them go drink coffee outdoors or walk on the pier (see Photo section at front of book). Conveniently, the poster is just nearly person-sized and so is really very impactful walking around the place. It is eye-catching, a little silly, fun and very effective in increasing the profile of a new candidate with very little time to win an election. Naturally, it is more effective in a summer local election campaign where you have much longer daylight hours, more people outdoors and a much more concentrated geographical area within which you can have a colourful vibrant impact. But even on the cold winter mornings of a general election, it can at least lighten a morning commute to see a couple of smiling posters bobbing along the path doing no one any harm at all.

Posters are somewhat contentious, with people reasonably looking for alternatives to the creation of new plastic products. I would greatly prefer a durable but compostable poster. Some people complain about them, some see them as a necessary evil and some people generally welcome them and the event as long as they're cleared up. Kids ask their parents about them and it begins conversations about politics. They are up for three weeks and then gone. Candidates take their removal seriously, though it was quite the game to find new ones in brand new places for a week or so after the deadline for their removal. Crucially, posters are a reasonably low-cost barrier to entry for new candidates in the political process. Getting rid of them overnight risks favouring incumbents with already established profiles.

We are lucky in Ireland to have an electoral system that enables a broad range of people to be elected—multiple seats, proportional representation constituencies, as opposed to the first past the post system in the UK. A political culture that favours low-cost participation with posters and leaflets, as opposed to the television advertising-based system in the United States. With the establishment of an electoral commission we can look at ways of further improving every aspect of our election process. Yet, even as it is, people can enter and compete and have a real chance based on transfers. We would always ask for a transfer if possible. People might be committed to an individual or party colleague, but they might consider giving you a number two or three and these can be essential depending on what your overall first preference vote is. The reality of the PR-STV system is that transfers, both inter-party and from other candidates of your own party are, more often than not, absolutely crucial. I was running with two other party candidates, Mary Mitchell O'Connor, who was Minister of State for Higher Education, and Barry Ward, a long-standing councillor who was subsequently elected to the Seanad. There was a weekly Fine Gael meeting in which the campaign managers would meet with the director of elections. Although there were no official territorial divisions, we always knew where the other Fine Gael candidates were canvassing so as to try not to get in each other's way.

One of the best things that happened in my campaign, quite organically, was the development a team of much younger people, and particularly young women, who wanted to be involved. That team grew and grew, helping me with social media, canvassing and ideas. They complemented a growing team of party members, family and friends without whom I could not have been elected. No one knows how hard it is until you do it, how totally and utterly practical it is and how much work it is. Letters, stickers, leaflet drops, poster walkers, social media, text messages, emails—you could work all day and night and not have done enough. So, every meal cooked, leaflet dropped, poster walked, child collected from crèche, bit of housework done, everything from everyone around you is needed to be able to compete at all. And I am very grateful for it.

In my view, the single most important factor in any election campaign is the canvass. The opportunity and privilege to call to someone's door and ask to speak to them. At their door, in their time, asking for their most precious gift in a modern liberal democracy, their vote. Almost immediately in the local election campaign I learned the true enjoyment of the canvass. There is no other reason, really, to be able to call to a stranger's door and ask to speak to them. There were a range of issues that came up on the door, and that varied greatly depending on areas within the constituency. It also depended on who answered the door; younger constituents were concerned about housing, more specifically the affordability of it. With families who already owned their homes, the concerns were more centred on access to childcare and schools. There were also a high number of local and personal issues. What is astonishing, and the true privilege of trying to become a public representative, is that many people use the moment to tell you some of the deepest troubles they have.

Of course, there are differences between the local election and a general election. For the general election there is less time, more area to try to get to, more people to try to meet. Otherwise you have simply no hope of being elected. That comes at the cost of being the one to wait for the door to open in anticipation of meeting the unknown life and experience behind. It comes at the cost of being able to spend the same time with people that you would like and it also comes with the horrible realisation that there will be doors that you cannot get to, no matter how bouncy the new canvas Nikes might be.

Whether I got elected or not, I would never forget meeting the people of my area. Meeting them properly. Now I know who lives where, what happened to them, what the tree across the road means—planted for their deceased spouse, for the benefit of their children. Now I think of them when something relevant pops up in the media. Or I ask my ever-forgiving secretarial assistant what is so-and-so's address who I met in Blackrock one night and her name is definitely Miriam and she was interested in autism and did we have her address so I could ask her about ... Politics is absolutely about people. It operates within the framework of national and international rules and domestic institutions to execute policy. But only to serve the people, to deliver on the multiplicity of needs and wants within limited resources. The canvasser sees all the doors, sees into all the halls and kitchens, all the lives and competing interests. The canvasser sees the level of interest or disinterest, the patterns, the reactions, the tones. It is the best political education possible.

The day of the count starts with a tally, which gives a very basic, but frequently accurate, outlook. My position looked fairly positive; however, nothing was guaranteed. It's all down to transfers. In my own case, I won the most first preference votes (12.4 per cent; 7754 votes) of the three Fine Gael candidates. Then, I secured a healthy enough transfer (4307 votes) from other candidates, I was the third candidate elected, on the eighth count. On the day of the count, I stayed at home with my husband, young son, my dad (who travelled from Spain to be with me) and two friends from the USA. The only person allowed to contact me with updates was my campaign manager; not even my mum or sister, who were at the count, could breach this rule! This mostly filtered out any possibility of false information and, more importantly, false hope. As evening approached, my chances were looking quite good, so I came to the count centre. Tensions were quite high by that time, as the people remaining at the centre were mostly those who had personal vested interest in being there: campaign teams, family members, candidates. After another while, and with two candidates already elected, word went round that the third seat wouldn't be filled until the next day. So we all headed home, all very nervous and facing a sleepless night. But then, in the final hour, we got a call to come back in. I was elected about an hour later at half past ten. What followed was a whirlwind of radio and television interviews that went on until about 3 am, something that set the pace for what would follow in the coming months.

In the week after I was elected, I went to the Dart (suburban rail) stations at Killiney, Shankill, Glenageary, Blackrock and Monkstown each morning to say thank you. Having been there the week before to ask for support and then having been elected I thought it was the obvious thing to do. But it was funny, after just a few days people had quickly moved on. Naturally enough! But it was nice to do and I'm glad I did.

Roderic O'Gorman (Green Party, Dublin West)

Roderic O'Gorman was first elected to Fingal County Council in 2014, and he was re-elected in May 2019. He unsuccessfully contested Dáil elections in 2007, 2011 and 2016 (and by-elections in 2011 and 2014). O'Gorman has been a member of the Greens since being a student of Law at Trinity College Dublin in the early 2000s. He served as party chair from 2011 to 2019. He was the last TD elected in Dublin West and was more than 600 votes ahead of Ruth Coppinger of S–PBP, who lost her seat. Roderic O'Gorman was a lecturer in the School of Law and Government at Dublin City University until his election in February 2020. In June 2020 he was appointed Minister for Children, Disability, Equality and Integration.

The 2020 general election was my tenth election campaign—four general elections, four local elections and two by-elections. It was the first time in a general election we felt we had a real chance of taking a seat. I had a really strong result in the local elections in May 2019 and we had councillors elected in two other wards within the constituency. That being said, the sitting TDs in the constituency—An Taoiseach Leo Varadkar, Joan Burton, Ruth Coppinger and Jack Chambers—were all really strong and Sinn Féin's Paul Donnelly had narrowly missed out on election in 2016. We were never under any illusion that this would be anything but a tough campaign.

The campaign was far more organised than in previous elections. I had a campaign manager, and different members of my team were assigned to different roles. We had far more volunteers than we had in previous elections. And our team was amazing. From the first night after the election was called, the group really came together and we put in a comprehensive canvassing campaign. Most nights we had at least ten canvassers out; some evenings it was closer to 20. There was an active WhatsApp group coordinating locations and for keeping track of people who got stuck on doors. My uncle used to arrive with a big bag of chocolate bars every night to provide a sugar-rush for the team. The size of the team and the degree of camaraderie that built up around it was a big difference from my earlier elections.

Alongside the evening canvass, we had all the other elements of the campaign. I did a train station or school almost every morning, followed by a mid-morning canvass. We did regular static canvasses at shops across the constituency. It was freezing for the entire campaign. I don't think I got warm once across the three weeks. But it only rained once during the campaign, which made things a lot easier.

Our postering operation was great. We had eight teams of two out on the first day, and we got all 450 posters up in the initial 24 hours after the election was called. I had 150 posters from the local elections and 300 new ones. We did about 100 'diamonds' (small diamond-shaped posters that take up less space than the larger image-based campaign posters) on the last week too. It was a lot fewer than the other candidates, but the public's patience with huge numbers of posters is really decreasing. I had a good presence on social media too, using Twitter, Facebook and Instagram. I used these to provide updates on where I was canvassing and what issues were coming up, with pictures and regular videos too. One of my tweets, which was a picture of me giving a belly-rub to a cute little dog, ended up on the front page of the *Irish Mirror* under the caption 'Paws to Vote'. I would have had some involvement in the national campaign, attending our manifesto launch and speaking at the launch of a policy paper on air pollution. But for the most part, I just kept the head down and focused on Dublin West.

The initial week of the campaign was really strong. I was out doing static canvasses on the first Saturday and the response was as good as during the 2019 local elections. Then in week two, we started to notice a change. People started to say things like 'We need a change' and 'I'm not voting for either of the big two', but not saying they were voting for me No. 1. I remember similar language being used in the local and European election in 2014, when they were voting Sinn Féin. In the last week, we were canvassing in strong Fine Gael areas and even there, people were flat out saying they were voting Sinn Féin. I knew at that stage that Paul

Donnelly was going to top the poll, though even I was shocked by the sheer size of the vote. From week two on, we understood that it was between myself and Ruth Coppinger for the final seat, and this shaped our message. Ruth knew that we were in that battle too, and she pushed out a huge campaign over the last two weeks, buses, multiple posters, volunteers in from other areas. Support for me was still strong in my core areas, though I could feel the Sinn Féin vote everywhere.

On polling day, we went out to vote and the vibe was positive, a lot of people shaking my hand on the street or beeping at me from their cars. I was feeling fairly good about my chances. That night, myself and Ray went out to a show as we'd missed his birthday during the campaign. During the second half, my mind began to wander a bit to what the exit poll would look like. When we came out, the exit polled showed Fianna Fáil, Sinn Féin and Fine Gael all about even in the early 20s and the Greens on 7.8 per cent. I was feeling good on those numbers, though saw that S–PBP were doing ok in Dublin too.

My count was in Phibblestown Community Centre. In my nine previous elections, I have always been there from the start to do the tally. I couldn't cope with not being there. Counting the votes slowly allows me to understand how I am doing and, usually, come to terms with the fact that I wasn't going to get elected. There were about 20 of my team there with me. The tallying quickly showed a huge vote for Donnelly. My vote was ok. Ruth was ahead at first, though I was doing ok in Mulhuddart, which in previous elections would have been a weak area. Then I caught up and passed her out as the Carpenterstown and Castleknock votes were counted. On the tally, I had 11 per cent and was in fourth place, 1 per cent ahead of Ruth Coppinger. While my vote was up in all parts of the constituency, it was still mainly concentrated in my local election ward.

As I watched the first count, I became worried as I could see that the Sinn Féin votes were transferring strongly to Ruth. When it was announced, I was on 4900 and Ruth was on 4400. My vote was lower than I hoped. I had always said that if I was on 5500 on the first count, I would be ok with transfers. After Paul Donnelly's surplus of 3700 had been distributed, Ruth was comfortably ahead of me and went further ahead when Peter Casey and other independents were eliminated. The next two eliminations favoured me and allowed me to narrow the gap. Myself and Ray had taken a break from the count around dinner-time and got some food. I started to brace myself for defeat. I thought about going back to DCU and work I could do on the Council. I thought about running for the Seanad and told myself I wouldn't put myself through that.

After the fifth count, it was announced that both Joan Burton (Labour) and Emer Currie (Fine Gael) would be eliminated together. Ruth was 720 votes ahead of me with 4400 votes to distribute and Jack Chambers still in the race. Ruth got 590 transfers, so I needed to get over 1300. I went over to my pile of transfers to watch. I had done the exact same thing in 2016, when I had watched Catherine Martin overtake Alan Shatter on transfers in the last count in Dublin Rathdown. Ruth's people were all there too. It was incredibly tense for everyone. The counters started to put the transfers to me into the bundles of 100. We could see about nine or ten bundles, and more votes still to be counted. Then, two counters arrived over with huge armfuls of transfers. I got this surge of hope, which I tried to keep down. We counted 1000 votes that had gone over, and there were definitely more than 300 remaining. We felt we had it. At the same time, you could see the Solidarity team visibly deflate.

The returning officer declared Jack elected and then he declared me elected without reaching the quota. I was so deeply in shock about the scale of the turnaround, that I could barely react. I kissed Ray, hugged my parents and then did a big round of hugs around all the team. I went over to sympathise with Ruth Coppinger. As soon as I was elected, RTÉ asked me to speak to Bryan Dobson. As I stood on their platform, as I was about to go on, they were replaying my election announcement and I really had to struggle not to start tearing up on live TV. I took a few breaths and answered Dobbo's questions. At the same time, the entire count centre was being deconstructed around us. It was a surreal end to a surreal day.

The 2020 election was a strange one—as a party we went into it with high expectations, and achieved our best ever result, but were still eclipsed by Sinn Féin. In terms of lessons learned, with elections, the temptation is always to fight the last war. The Sinn Féin surge changed everything, but it's difficult to know whether this will become the norm. In the meantime, my focus will be on developing a constituency organisation that works effectively for my constituents across Dublin West, as well using the platform the Dáil provides to advocate for key Green Party policies.

MARIE SHERLOCK (LABOUR PARTY, SEANAD ELECTION CANDIDATE)

Marie Sherlock worked as an economic adviser for over a decade at SIPTU, Ireland's largest trade union. She later served as the union's Head of Equality and Policy. She holds a degree in economics and political science from Trinity College Dublin and a master's degree from the University of Cambridge. She was first elected to Dublin City Council in May 2019 from the Cabra–Glasnevin local electoral area. She did not contest the 2020 Dáil election and was elected on her first attempt to Seanad Éireann on the Labour panel.

If I had been asked previously would I consider running for the Seanad, I would have taken the proverbial right hand off to get the opportunity. However, when that question was posed early in 2020, the answer was far from a foregone conclusion. I had been elected to Dublin City Council less than a year earlier. After an arduous journey to get there, I had finally carved out a path in electoral politics for myself. My head was spinning with ideas I wanted to progress across my local electoral area and I loved being active and delivering for my community. In contrast, the world of the Seanad seemed much more detached and less effective. I loved my day job as head of equality and policy in SIPTU, I loved being a councillor and I obviously love my family. Balancing all three could be done, albeit with many challenges, but the chance to do politics on a full-time basis was too appealing to pass-up.

Since I was a small child and avidly following the political fortunes of my uncle Joe Sherlock (Labour Party TD, Cork), I learned a stark lesson that success in politics frequently depends on tight margins. Merit and hard work will only get a candidate so far. So much depends on being in the right place at the right time. Election 2020 saw the Labour Party return with six TDs. On paper, this was the party's worst ever electoral performance, although the new parliamentary party was relatively fresh-faced and there was a real sense that the future would be better. However, the optics of an all-male line-up was very much at odds with the party's proud history of advancing women and being in the vanguard of fighting for equality. As one of the party's newly elected councillors, I found myself in the right place at the right time.

With women accounting for just 24 per cent of the combined Dáil and Seanad in 2016, there had been a growing focus on getting more women into politics. Ironically, it was getting elected to Dublin City Council that opened up my chance to run for the Seanad. In order to get that chance though, many first have to survive by doing the near impossible: in my case, that meant balancing my day job, family and council work. If we are to increase the number of women in the Seanad and Dáil, we must crack the nut of getting more women into local politics. And once elected, women need to be supported to stay the course.

While the Labour Party had a volatile electoral performance over the past 20 years, it has unusually punched above its weight in Seanad elections. Much of this is due to the election wizardry of former Dublin Central TD Joe Costello who has acted as director of elections for Seanad elections and has ensured that at the last two Seanad elections Labour's 6 per cent of the votes at the panel elections has translated into 9 per cent of the seats.[1] While I still had to go out and work extremely hard to win votes, it was good to know that there would be some help in securing support. Seanad elections are truly like none other. General and local election rules of thumb with regard to getting two-thirds of an electoral quota do not apply. Candidates do not pick up preferences by osmosis, high preferences need to be actively sought out. My husband Ciarán, a veteran observer of Seanad elections, liked to regale me with horror stories of candidates getting great first preferences, only to then sit like a duck for subsequent counts and get no transfers.

And policy platforms are almost meaningless as many of the votes are already promised because of party, gene pool or other allegiances. Ironically, while the electorate is highly politicised, there is little or no policy involved. Electoral politics has a great way of shattering illusions about ambitions to change the world. I quickly realised from all the election literature coming into me that improvement of councillors' pay and conditions was the only policy proposal most candidates wanted to talk about.

I took a different tack and decided to set down my policy priorities in a bid to win over the first preferences of independent councillors who were left-leaning. After all I was running on the Labour panel and the improvement of the rights of workers; the low-paid, women and those with a disability were key issues for me. Added to that, I targeted the transfers of Fine Gael female councillors. I had detected some disillusionment with their all-male line-up in the Labour panel, but this was to be shattered later on in the campaign when Taoiseach Leo Varadkar used a little known legislative provision after the deadline for nominations to add Mary Seery Kearney to the ticket.

Until 2016, independent councillors had tended to be a fairly disparate bunch and were love-bombed by many a Seanad candidate going after the coveted number one vote. That year represented a significant breakthrough where a coordinated effort saw independents win four seats. Early on in the 2020 campaign, it became clear that Gerard Craughwell had effectively hoovered up many independents of all political hues across the country. The coordinated campaign to see Traveller activist Eileen Flynn elected was less visible, but I quickly became aware she was going to take a lot of the left-leaning votes I was chasing.

The Seanad campaign itself is a bizarre mix of the new and the old. Mobile technology played a huge part in the logistics of the campaign as I was able to use GPS to get to the townlands of councillors. Although I did also revert to the old way of tracking down a person by calling into a random house in the locality and getting directions. There was no point ringing to announce your arrival—councillors are busy people! My late uncle Joe contested the Seanad election successfully in 1992 and unsuccessfully in 1997 and I spent much time on my own campaign trying to imagine how difficult it must have been for him and the many others who have contested over the years without the benefit of the technology and the better roads we enjoy today.

I was in a little place called Croaghlin, close to the base of Slieve League in west Donegal when I wondered was it worth all this effort. Six hours on the road, I had just realised that the townland I had arrived at was not where my intended councillor lived, I had yet to meet one councillor that day and I was already two days away from my baby. Back home were my five-year-old, three-year-old and five-month-old baby. Although the baby had been brought almost everywhere with me since birth while I was conducting my council work, long days on the Seanad campaign trail were no place for a small baby. At the start of the campaign I found myself having to invest in a 'bustier'—for hands-free breastmilk pumping. There were many surreal moments on the campaign—driving along some remote country road, glancing at the map on my car screen, talking via bluetooth and hands-free pumping (discreetly under a jumper)—most definitely a twenty-first-century female politician!

It was after some 70 hours' driving over eight days and 2500 km covered across the country that the closure of primary schools due to Covid-19 was announced. Unfortunately, this brought face-to-face campaigning to an abrupt halt, and I had to resort to ringing councillors, which felt like a far less effective means of campaigning. Those eight days were a stark insight into how diverse councillors in Ireland are—from the councillor living in a mobile home at the side of a road, to the councillor advertising his services from his front window and the councillor who shuns a mobile phone and computer and uses a typewriter.

By 1 April, the day of the Labour panel count, public health crisis restrictions meant that all hopes of physically attending the count were dashed. We had to make do with live updates broadcast via Twitter by the clerk of the Seanad. With a combined 65 votes between Labour councillors, TDs and outgoing Senators, I had 29 votes to make up to get to the quota of 94 for the Labour panel. To many looking on, I had a much easier job to do relative to candidates in the Administrative or Industrial panels. Nine hours into the count, it was a different story. I started off well, in fifth place with 79 votes. The trouble began on the fifth count—no transfers for me from the Army Wives' candidate Sarah Walshe and over 40 per cent went to Eileen Flynn. By the 11th count, our young sons had been thankfully packed off to bed while our baby daughter sat on my knee gazing at her parents glued to their phones and the elaborate spreadsheet on the laptop. At that stage, there were ten of us left in the field for nine seats and I was 4.383 votes behind Eileen Flynn with Sinn Féin's Paul Gavan also looking to be in serious trouble.

It is worth saying at this stage that I've become something of a veteran of tight counts. The local elections in 2019 were my own first electoral outing and I eventually got elected after three days of counting and just six votes separating me from the next candidate. As a good friend tweeted after the Seanad count, there are easy counts, there are tight counts and then there are Marie Sherlock counts. In the final count there were just 1.215 votes to redistribute, with me just 0.961 ahead of Eileen for the final seat—the tension in our kitchen was nearly unbearable. The baby was dutifully asleep. There was no reason to believe the surplus of outgoing independent Senator Gerard Craughwell would transfer to me as the trend until then had been largely in favour of Eileen Flynn.

The Clerk rose; Sherlock 1.215. The disbelief. The relief!

In 2019, I won by 0.03 per cent of the vote. In 2020, that gap widened to 0.19 per cent. Elections frequently throw up all sorts of seemingly unfair results. There was a certain irony that in the Labour panel, the panel established to represent the interests of workers in this country, it was the final count before those of the left eventually got elected. Fianna Fáil and Fine Gael hoovered up a combined 7 seats in the first 13 counts, with Sinn Féin's Paul Gavan, the Green Party's Pauline O'Reilly and myself elected on the 17th and final count. After the initial relief and joy, the feeling soon turned to a sense of guilt. I was in and Eileen had come so close. To my great delight and relief, that situation was made right with Eileen's appointment to the Seanad (see Chap. 12, p. 290). This was a huge milestone for Travellers and particularly Traveller women and an intensely proud day for all of us driven to tackling inequality in our country.

JENNIFER WHITMORE (SOCIAL DEMOCRATS, WICKLOW)

Jennifer Whitmore was elected to Wicklow County Council as an independent in 2014. She was a founding member of the Social Democrats in 2015. She was re-elected to the council in 2019, having topped the poll in Greystones. She was elected to the Dáil in 2020 on her first attempt, taking the second seat at the 14th count. She has a BSc in Biological Science and Ecology from the University of Ulster, and she studied environmental law at the University of Sydney. For ten years she lived in Australia, where she worked as a policy analyst in the fields of ecology and environmental science.

When the starting gun was fired on general election 2020, my overriding emotions were ones of excitement and relief. This was an election campaign for which I had been preparing for quite a while, and the three and a half weeks between the calling of the election and polling day really only represented the final sprint in what felt like a marathon. I was eager to get out on the doors, talk to the voters of Wicklow and ask for their vote on the fast-approaching 8 February. I think the county was also ready for an election. Over the previous few months of engaging with people I had a real sense that many people were eager for the opportunity to have an election and opt for change.

My selection as the candidate for the Social Democrats had happened in late 2017. As the only public representative at the time for the Social Democrats in Wicklow (I was a councillor on Wicklow County Council, first elected as an independent), and as a co-founder of the party in 2015, my selection was pretty straightforward and had the full support of my branch and of party HQ. I'd spent 10 years in Australia working in the New South Wales government in the area of policy development and I had seen how decisions in government could be made differently and could help to reshape the country for the better. It made me want to get into politics myself and try to shape the future where key decisions were made. I'd run for election to the county council for that reason, and from there had been involved in setting up the Social Democrats to bring those ideas to the national level. This election was my first chance to bring that before the voters of Wicklow.

This early nomination by the party in 2017 was crucial to enable me to build up a county-wide profile. Whilst I was very well known in my local district of Greystones, having topped the poll in the local elections in 2014 and having achieved the one of the highest votes in the country at the time, I wasn't a well-known face outside of that area. That, coupled with the fact that the Social Democrats were a new party and were still quite an unknown entity, even though we had very high-profile co-leaders in Catherine Murphy and Róisín Shortall TDs, meant that I had a lot of work ahead of me to build up both my branch and my profile.

I used this time to do what I love best, and that is working with communities on the ground to get local projects delivered. I had a small team of people working with me over this time. It was very much a family and friends affair, with my husband Tony, friend Orla Finn and many others, working hand-in-hand with me on this work. Our successful projects impacted a lot on families, and people began to associate my name with my ability to get things done. But my nomination as the Social Democrats candidate for Wicklow now meant I had a county-wide remit and I could expand that work beyond my district boundaries.

My professional background is in environmental law, fisheries and water management, and I was keen to mesh my passion for the environment with the political opportunities to bring about progress that my role on the council offered. I became heavily involved in environmental work across County Wicklow, such as protecting the Vartry River. The work I did there led me to build up networks across the county and created opportunities to work with other communities on similar type projects. I was also heavily involved in policy development with the Social Democrats, and my role as spokesperson for Children ensured that I was getting some exposure at the national level.

In late 2019, it was clear that an election would happen in the next six to nine months. The public were getting progressively frustrated at the lack of real, tangible improvements in their lives, despite the seemingly improved economic situation. The lack of investment by successive governments in public services was now hitting home, with many people across the country wondering if there was ever going to be more to their lives than commuting long hours and paying impossibly high rents, mortgages and childcare costs. This was especially true for my constituents, with one person saying to me that they didn't 'live in Wicklow, but only slept there'.

In expectation of an election, we switched from our 'light-touch' campaign in late 2019, where we were doing a small amount of canvassing and leaflet dropping, to our 'short campaign' mode. That involved moving beyond our core team and expanding into a broader team to get our campaign under way in earnest. Building this larger campaign team came relatively easily. I was very lucky with the number, and the skills, of people that wanted to help get me elected.

My campaign and canvassing teams looked very different from most other political teams, in that they were made up primarily of women. I remember looking around during one of our first team meetings and seeing 12 women and two men in attendance. It really struck me then how different our way of doing politics was, in that we were reaching many women who had never been involved in politics before and who had seen politics as something other people did. This was similar to the change that was seen in recent referendums, and it was exciting to see this shift happen in my own campaign. This more representative and balanced kind of politics, which has been driven over the last number of years by organisations such as Women for Election, was now, thankfully, coming into national politics. There was rarely a meeting or canvass where we didn't have a baby or a child tagging along. My work on issues locally that are important to women such as the Repeal campaign, my work to lobby to keep religious influence out of our new National Maternity Hospital, and fighting for school places for children meant that many women were keen to help me continue with that work. And that was a real strength in my campaign, because there is nothing more determined than a woman looking for change.

The job of overseeing this expanded team fell to my campaign manager Joe O'Connor, who came on board for the short campaign. I was lucky to have Joe leading the team, as his expertise in campaigning was invaluable. He assessed the skill sets among our volunteers and established teams charged with specific tasks. This led to the establishment of a media campaign team, canvassing teams, poster and office team, all constantly interacting with each other with updates and suggestions.

Parallel to my Wicklow team, I also had great support from the Social Democrats' head office. They were always available on the other end of the phone and did what they could to coordinate literature design and policy support. Head office did phenomenal work in disseminating the Social Democrats' brand and messaging throughout the campaign on a national level. However, it was up to ourselves to manage the day-to-day campaigning and messaging at county-level.

We were under no illusion that this was going to be an easy campaign. Wicklow is a competitive county, and I was up against some very high-profile candidates, such as Simon Harris (Minister for Health) and Stephen Donnelly (Fianna Fáil health spokesperson). Barely a day would go by without hearing or seeing my competition on the radio or television. And the national media and pollsters were not giving me a chance. I usually only featured as an afterthought, if at all, when candidates were being discussed.

But, despite this, I knew I had a lot of positives going for me. I was one of only four women running in the county and the only female public representative. My track record of getting things done and achieving outcomes for the community stood to me, as did my environmental expertise—the appetite that was shown in the previous local elections for environmental issues was still there, albeit not to the same extent. Issues like housing, health and work–life balance came up very strongly as well.

As a Social Democrat, our policies are very strong in those areas, and I could point to the excellent work that has been done by our two co-leaders Róisín Shortall and Catherine Murphy. Their names resonated positively with voters on the doors across the county.

Unlike my competitors, who had high national media profiles, I knew I had to look at alternative ways to get my message across Wicklow. Social media offered me that platform. I already had a size-able following on Facebook, through which I've long engaged with communities, campaigns and people all across Wicklow, which I could use to reach further out across the county. Video messaging was hugely impactful and was successful in bringing across the unique aspects of my candidacy and of the values and principles on which I was standing. Some key media interactions did set me apart from the other candi-dates and one very important one was my participation on The Tonight Show with Matt Cooper and Ivan Yates. I performed well and was the only female candidate on the main platform. Speaking to my audience base, and in contrast to the political in-fighting on show that night, my performance solidified my candidacy going into the final week of the campaign.

But central to my campaign was door-to-door canvassing. With lim-ited time and resources available to us we had to decide where to focus our canvassing efforts and we chose to stick to the major towns in Wicklow. I was delighted with the number of people who made them-selves available for canvassing. The numbers on the canvass team that showed up each day were consistent, with up to 30 canvassers on the weekend. Again, the strength of my team shone through when they were on the doors canvassing. My canvassers weren't the normal 'political' types. They were women, with children in tow; they were eager students; they were older men and women who were tired of the status quo—all with very little political experience but whose passion and authenticity spoke to those being canvassed.

As we progressed through the final three and a half weeks of the cam-paign, even though I was still not featuring in the minds of the media for a seat in Wicklow, my team and I felt that I was in with a very realistic chance of being elected. There was an appetite for something different, and the feedback I was getting on the doors was very positive. I'm an optimist by nature and I had always thought I was in with a chance to win a seat in Wicklow. But I had always thought I would end up in a fight for the last seat. Over the course of the campaign, though, listening to people on the doors and getting a feel for the level of change that people wanted, I had a sense that I might do better than my original expectation. The mainstream media were slow to pick up on the appetite for change, but it was becoming visible to me from the early part of the campaign. But you never can tell and the fear was always there that I was reading the voters' intentions incorrectly and that the media's low expectation for me were, in fact, correct.

On polling day, I surprised myself with how relaxed and calm I felt. I remember thinking that no matter what result came in, there was absolutely nothing else myself or my team could have done. We had pulled out all the stops and had spoken with thousands of people all across the county. The result was now in their hands, and if I was not the candidate for them, that was ok, that was democracy.

Thankfully, on 8 February, the people of Wicklow entrusted me with their vote and I claimed the second seat for the county. The moment I was formally elected, as I stood in the count centre with my husband and children, my campaign team and the Social Democrats' co-leaders Róisín Shortall and Catherine Murphy beside me, was an incredibly proud one. It was made even sweeter when I realised that there were six Social Democrats TDs elected that day across the country, which represented a huge win for the party. From small beginnings in 2015, through a lot of hard work and difficult times, we were now a team that could make real, tangible changes on a national level. The purple tide was rising.

Note

1. For a full explanation of the Seanad electoral rules, see Chap. 12.

CHAPTER 8

The Results Analysed: The Definitive End of the Traditional Party System?

Michael Gallagher

With the benefit of hindsight, elections over the period from 1932 to 2007 inclusive showed a picture of remarkable stability. Three parties—Fianna Fáil, Fine Gael and Labour, always in that order—dominated the party system, and while there were occasional upheavals and other parties flared briefly before disappearing, the status quo established in 1932 invariably more or less re-emerged. The mould was broken in 2011, when Fianna Fáil plummeted to a historic low and to third position in the party system, though even then the three main parties collectively retained their dominant position. In 2016 Fianna Fáil regained a little of its former strength, but Fine Gael and Labour both fell sharply back, and for the first time ever, Fianna Fáil and Fine Gael together received fewer than half the votes cast. At times between the elections of 2016 and 2020, polls suggested that these two parties were reasserting themselves and that something like pre-2011 normalcy might be restored. However, the 2020 election results, and even more the post-election coalition government formed by these two parties, confirmed that there is no going back and that a new reality reigns.

M. Gallagher (✉)
Department of Political Science, Trinity College Dublin, Dublin, Ireland
e-mail: mgllgher@tcd.ie

165
M. Gallagher et al. (eds.), *How Ireland Voted 2020*,
https://doi.org/10.1007/978-3-030-66405-3_8

VOTES, SEATS AND CANDIDATES

In the early 1980s and at many previous elections, Fianna Fáil, Fine Gael and Labour won over 90 per cent of the votes; by 2011, their share had dropped to 73 per cent; and in 2020, it fell below the 50 per cent mark in both votes and seats. In 2020, those three parties together reached the 60 per cent level in only four constituencies (Carlow–Kilkenny, Cork NW, Limerick County and Mayo), while in eight, including four Dublin constituencies, they fell below 40 per cent. In Dublin, they won only 42 per cent of the votes, not much above what Fianna Fáil on its own was accustomed to winning there prior to 2011. There were two constituencies where none of these three parties won a seat (Dublin SC and Roscommon–Galway), and just one where they won all the seats (Cork NW, the only constituency where Sinn Féin did not run a candidate). Whereas at the previous election in 2016 the traditional party system seemed to be just about hanging on outside Dublin, while no longer dominant in the capital,[1] in 2020 it was a thing of the past virtually everywhere.

This disappearance of the traditional hegemony of those three parties was brought about by a degree of volatility that, while high, was below what was witnessed in both 2011 and 2016, when Irish elections entered the post-war European record books.[2] Volatility in 2020, calculated by the standard Pedersen index (simply adding the percentage gains of the parties that made gains, and the losses of the parties that lost, and dividing the total by 2), was 17.4—the sixth highest figure ever recorded in Ireland but well below the 2011 and 2016 levels.[3] Its impact was great, though, because of the direction rather than just the size of the change in voting behaviour. It was uniformly away from the traditional mainstays of the party system—Fianna Fáil, Fine Gael and Labour all lost votes—and towards challengers, primarily Sinn Féin and the Green Party (see Table 8.1). As usual, volatility was higher within Dublin (an average of 22 per cent per constituency) than in the rest of the country (an average of 15 per cent per constituency), and in only one constituency, Tipperary, was it below 10 per cent.

The significant gains for Sinn Féin together with the losses for Fianna Fáil and Fine Gael brought about a situation where the leading three parties are very closely bunched in terms of both votes and seats, and none of them commands even a quarter of either the votes or the seats. This is reflected in a highly fragmented party system. The concept of fragmentation is conventionally measured by the idea of the 'effective number of

Table 8.1 Result of the 2020 election, with changes since 2016

	Per cent vote	Change since 2016	Seats	Change since 2016	Per cent seats
Sinn Féin	24.5	+10.7	37	+14	23.3
Fianna Fáil	22.2	-2.2	37	-7	23.3
Fine Gael	20.9	-4.7	35	-14	22.0
Green Party	7.1	+4.4	12	+10	7.5
Labour	4.4	-2.2	6	-1	3.8
Social Democrats	2.9	-0.1	6	+3	3.8
Solidarity–PBP	2.6	-1.3	5	-1	3.1
Aontú	1.9	+1.9	1	+1	0.6
Independents and others	13.5	-6.5	20	-3	12.6
Total	100.0	0	159	+2	100.0

Note: For detailed results, see Appendix A. Table refers to contested seats; Fianna Fáil also won the one uncontested seat (automatic re-election of Ceann Comhairle), giving it 38 seats out of 160 in the 33rd Dáil

parties' devised by Laakso and Taagepera.[4] In 2020 the effective number of parties at electoral level (based on the distribution of votes) was 6.16 and the effective number at parliamentary level (based on the distribution of seats) was 5.98; the latter is by some way the highest ever in Ireland (see Fig. 8.1), while the former is the second highest, exceeded only in 2016. While the degree of legislative fragmentation is still well short of the levels in Belgium (around 10), let alone Brazil (around 18), it is now comparable to some archetypal multi-party systems such as Denmark (effective number of legislative parties between 5.5 and 6.0 at each of the elections in the 2010s) or Finland (close to 6.0 at each election in the 2010s), and higher than most of the elections held since 1945 in Israel, Italy and the Netherlands, for example. This 'Balkanisation' of the party system, and the fact that no two parties together had enough seats to secure an overall majority, had obvious implications for the process of government formation, as discussed in detail in Chap. 13.

The 2020 election also stands out for the high level of proportionality it displayed; that is, the very close correspondence between vote shares and seat shares (see Table 8.1). Given that the average district magnitude (number of seats per constituency) is only 4, which is exceptionally low for any proportional representation system, disproportionality could be expected to be relatively high, and indeed the 1997 election, then the 2002 election and again the 2011 election, generated new record levels of

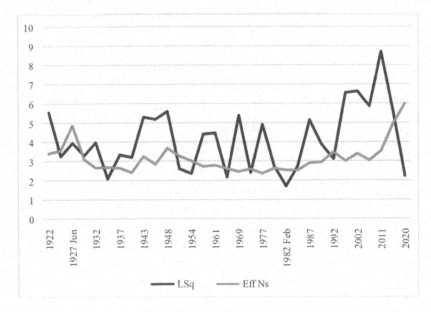

Fig. 8.1 Disproportionality and level of fragmentation in parliament at elections 1922–2020
Source: Election indices dataset at http://www.tcd.ie/Political_Science/people/
michael_gallagher/ElSystems/index.php
Note: LSq refers to the least squares index, which measures disproportionality. Eff Ns refers to the effective number of parliamentary parties in the Dáil; the higher the figure, the more fragmented the parliament

disproportionality. In 2020, though, every party won a seat share very close to its vote share, which in Sinn Féin's case resulted from its misjudging its support level and significantly under-nominating candidates, as elaborated below. As a result, Sinn Féin was slightly under-represented in terms of seats, an unusual outcome for the party that wins most votes at an election. The 2020 election produced a score of just 2.22 on the widely used least squares index, the fourth lowest ever for an Irish election and lower than the figures for the most recent elections in, for example, Denmark, Finland and Norway. Had Sinn Féin run sufficient candidates to capitalise on its support and won an additional 14 seats, as it might have (see below), the index would have been 5.78, much the same as in 2016.

A total of 531 candidates contested the election, the third highest number ever. Around 30 per cent were elected, a further 30 per cent were not

Table 8.2   Fate of candidates at the 2020 election

	Number	Average vote	Average Droop quotas	Per cent elected	Per cent not elected but qualifying for reimbursement of expenses	Per cent not qualifying for reimbursement of expenses
All candidates	531	4112	0.37	29.9	30.1	39.9
Sinn Féin	42	12,752	1.17	88.1	11.9	0
Fianna Fáil	84	5766	0.51	44.0	47.6	8.3
Fine Gael	82	5556	0.50	42.7	46.3	11.0
Green Party	39	3992	0.38	30.8	43.6	25.6
Labour	31	3083	0.28	19.4	41.9	38.7
Soc Dems	20	3170	0.32	30.0	40.0	30.0
Solidarity–PBP	37	1552	0.15	13.5	27.0	59.5
Aontú	26	1599	0.14	3.8	15.4	80.8
Others	170	1732	0.15	11.8	14.7	73.5
Cabinet minister	15	7805	0.72	80.0	20.0	0
Junior minister	15	6800	0.60	60.0	40.0	0
Other TD	108	8521	0.78	75.9	24.1	0
Senator	23	5527	0.49	39.1	47.8	13.0
Councillor	135	4142	0.38	24.4	60.7	14.8
MEP/former TD	5	7332	0.61	60.0	20.0	20.0
None of above	230	1397	0.12	4.8	13.5	81.7
Male	369	4334	0.39	33.3	27.6	39.0
Female	162	3606	0.33	22.2	35.8	42.0

Note: Candidates qualify for some reimbursement of campaign expenses provided their vote total at some stage of the count reaches a quarter of the Droop quota (for explanation of the Droop quota, see Appendix D). Voting figures refer to first preference votes. 'Councillor' refers to those candidates who at the time of the election were members of a county or city council. 'Former TD' category is applied only to those former TDs with no current elected status. One candidate stood in seven constituencies and another in two, but each candidate in each constituency is treated as a separate unit

but managed to qualify for reimbursement of expenses, and the remaining 40 per cent did not even achieve that (see Table 8.2). Sinn Féin's large vote, combined with its inadequate number of candidates, meant that on average each of its candidates, exceptionally, received over 12,000 votes and more than a Droop quota (the Droop quota equals the number of votes that guarantees election; for full explanation, see Appendix D, p. 357). The expectations of the two major parties, in contrast, were pitched too high, so they over-nominated, and on average each of their candidates received only around half a quota, comparable with other low points in those parties' recent history: Fianna Fáil's 2011 figure was 0.48, and Fine Gael's 2002 figure was 0.53.

Unsurprisingly, current elective status is strongly related to a candidate's fate. Of the 138 TDs to contest the election, 103 (75 per cent) were re-elected, though unusually ministerial TDs fared less well than other TDs. Senators and councillors had a respectable election rate, with only a small minority failing at least to qualify for reimbursement of expenses. Those with no elective status fared poorly, as always, and 147 of these (64 per cent) received fewer than 1000 first preferences. The Sinn Féin surge meant more success than usual for such candidates, though: 11 were elected, eight from Sinn Féin along with two independents and a Fine Gael candidate who was already a household name in his constituency (Mayo) due to his achievements as a county footballer. Male candidates won, on average, more votes than female candidates, but this is not the result of any gender effect; when elective status and party label are controlled for, the difference between the performance of men and of women is not statistically significant. As we saw earlier in the book (see Chap. 3, p. 64–5), several parties only just managed to reach the candidate gender quota of 30 per cent; in particular, if Fianna Fáil and Fine Gael had run just one or two fewer women, they would have failed to reach the threshold and would have lost significant amounts of state funding. There are signs that both parties ran some female candidates more in order to reach the 30 per cent level than with any expectation that the candidates might win a seat; in Fianna Fáil all seven candidates whose first preference votes came to less than a fifth of a quota, and in Fine Gael six of the seven candidates in this category, were female.

As at most elections, the tipping point for success for a candidate was around the figure of half a quota of first preferences. Of the 343 candidates whose votes came to less than 0.45 of a quota, only 4 per cent were elected, while among those winning at least 0.55 quotas, 88 per cent were elected. Those whose first preferences fell between 0.45 and 0.55 quotas had a 51 per cent success rate. Only one was elected with less than a third of a quota (Joan Collins of I4C, who was also one of only two candidates elected with fewer than 3000 first preferences and who benefited greatly from the transfer of Sinn Féin surplus votes), and only two of those who won at least two-thirds of a quota failed to be elected. The number of votes at play at Irish elections is relatively small, one of the factors that accounts for the salience of individual candidates and the close links between TDs and their constituencies. The median number of votes for all candidates was 3170, the median number with which a candidate was elected was 7940 and only seven candidates received as many as 7000 first preferences without being elected, the highest being Fianna Fáil's Timmy Dooley in Clare with 7763 first preferences.

Finally, we should note that turnout (valid votes as a percentage of electorate), at 62 per cent, was one of the lowest ever recorded. It was very slightly higher than the 2002 figure (62.2 per cent compared with 62.1 per cent) but below every other election since 1923. Any analysis of turnout trends must take into account widespread concerns about the accuracy of the electoral register, but even allowing for this, and given that there is no reason to believe that the register was any worse in 2020 than it was in 2016, the apparent decline in turnout casts doubt on any perception that the result, and in particular the surge in Sinn Féin support, came about because of a large-scale mobilisation of previous non-voters, though there was a positive correlation between Sinn Féin gains in share of the votes and increases in turnout ($r = 0.34$).

Party Performances

Along with the unprecedented level of fragmentation in the party system, the headline story, and the one that gained international news coverage, was the rise of Sinn Féin, which became the best supported party in the state for the first time in its current incarnation.[5] The Greens also advanced, but all other parties lost votes. While Green success had been expected following electoral gains in 2019, most of the other parties had anticipated results very different from what materialised.

Sinn Féin

This is particularly true of Sinn Féin, which had won 23 seats in 2016 but had sustained a series of setbacks since then, as outlined in Chaps. 1 and 4. It entered the campaign in defensive mode, sharing the widespread expectation that it would lose seats, which led it to field just 42 candidates, 8 fewer than in 2016. Once the first polls of the campaign appeared, it became apparent that this was a serious misjudgement and that the party was likely to miss out on seats by under-nomination. Apart from Cork NW, the only constituency where the party did not run a candidate, it failed to reach at least 10 per cent of the votes in just one constituency (Dun Laoghaire), and in nine it exceeded 30 per cent (a level it had never before reached in any constituency since an earlier Sinn Féin party won a majority of the votes in 1922), peaking at 45 per cent in Donegal. Its candidates headed the poll in 26 of the 39 constituencies, and 27 of them exceeded the quota on the first count. Denise Mitchell in Dublin Bay N was the nationwide poll-topper with 21,344 votes, and three other Sinn Féin candidates also achieved the rare feat of exceeding 20,000 first preferences. Only five of its candidates were unsuccessful, and one of these, Louis O'Hara in Galway E, came within 400 votes of winning a seat.

The party's gains were nationwide, with increases of over 10 per cent in 22 constituencies, spread across all four regions.[6] It made the largest advance in Dublin (up by 13 per cent). The party's gains do not correlate especially strongly with losses of any other party (the Pearson correlations are 0.31 for Solidarity–PBP, 0.21 for Fianna Fáil and 0.11 for Fine Gael), and the survey evidence shows that it made significant gains among all demographics (see Chap. 10, p. 249). Class tends to have a greater impact in Dublin than elsewhere, and in the capital there was a marked difference between the most middle-class constituencies (its support grew by only 4 per cent in Dun Laoghaire, 5 per cent in Dublin Rathdown and 6 per cent in Dublin Bay S) and the most working-class constituencies (up by 20 per cent in Dublin MW, 18 per cent in Dublin Bay N, 17 per cent in Dublin NW and 16 per cent in Dublin SC). All the indications are that the additional votes came to Sinn Féin almost regardless of who its candidates were. Several of its successful candidates—Martin Browne (Tipperary), Sorca Clarke (Longford–Westmeath), Réada Cronin (Kildare N), Mairéad Farrell (Galway W), Johnny Mythen (Wexford) and Violet-Anne Wynne (Clare)—had been defeated in the May 2019 local elections, while another, Patricia Ryan (Kildare S), spent much of the campaign away on a pre-booked holiday.

Sinn Féin ran two candidates in only four constituencies: in two of these, it held two seats at the dissolution, and in another (Donegal) it had won two in 2011. As the results came in on 9 February, it became apparent that the party had missed out on a number of seats due to under-nomination, as many of its candidates comfortably exceeded the quota but had no running mate available to receive their transferred surplus votes (for an explanation of the electoral system, see Appendix D). Under-nomination is rare at Irish elections and is likely to arise only when the electoral environment is fluid or uncertain. In several cases, Sinn Féin's sole candidate achieved almost two quotas—over 1.9 quotas in Dublin SC and Waterford, over 1.7 also in Dublin Bay N, Dublin Central, Dublin SW and Dublin NW—so even if a second candidate had brought in very few votes of their own, he or she would almost certainly have been elected, thanks to the surplus votes of the lead candidate. As Table 8.3 shows, there are ten constituencies where Sinn Féin would probably or almost

Table 8.3 Constituencies where Sinn Féin could have won an additional seat with an additional candidate

Constituency	SF quotas	Seat was actually won by
Probable		
Carlow–Kilkenny	1.43	Malcolm Noonan (Green)
Cork NC	1.33	Mick Barry (Solidarity)
Donegal	2.71	Thomas Pringle (Ind)
Dublin Bay N	1.79	Cian O'Callaghan (SD)
Dublin Cen	1.78	Gary Gannon (SD)
Dublin Fingal	1.49	Duncan Smith (Lab)
Dublin NW	1.78	Paul McAuliffe (FF)
Dublin SC	1.97	Joan Collins (I4C)
Dublin SW	1.78	Paul Murphy (Solidarity)
Waterford	1.91	Marc Ó Cathasaigh (Green)
Possible		
Laois–Offaly	1.44	Carol Nolan (Ind)
Louth	2.52	Ged Nash (Lab) or Peter Fitzpatrick (Ind)
Wexford	1.50	Verona Murphy (Ind)
Wicklow	1.46	Steven Matthews (Grn)

Note: Assuming reasonably efficient vote management by Sinn Féin—that is, a fairly even spread of votes between its candidates

certainly have won an additional seat had it run one more candidate, and a further four where it would have had a reasonable chance of doing so. The main beneficiaries of Sinn Féin's under-nomination were independents (four or five seats), the Greens (three seats), Solidarity–PBP (two seats), the Social Democrats (two seats), Labour (one or two seats) and Fianna Fáil (one seat). Had Sinn Féin taken those 14 additional seats—though, given that we are talking about probabilities rather than certainties, it could be expected not to have won every one of them—it would have won 51 in total. Fianna Fáil would have taken 37, Fine Gael 35, Greens 9, Labour 4 or 5, Social Democrats 4, Solidarity–PBP 3 and independents 15 or 16, an outcome that would have given, for example, a Sinn Féin–Fianna Fáil coalition a comfortable overall majority.

Fianna Fáil

Fianna Fáil too had not expected the eventual outcome. The plan had been very different. When Micheál Martin became leader in the dark days of early 2011, his challenge was, first, to ensure the party's survival at the imminent election, which was achieved albeit with massive losses; second, to bring the party back to contention at the next election, a target that was more than met with a better than expected 44 seats in 2016; and third, to re-establish Fianna Fáil as the leading party at the following election, with more than 50 seats, making it the indisputable core of the next government. To this end, Fianna Fáil ran 84 candidates, exactly twice as many as Sinn Féin. A loss of both votes and seats was not envisaged, but that was the outcome. The party's vote share went up in just 11 of the 39 constituencies, nowhere by as much as 5 per cent compared with its 2016 performance, and dropped in the other 28. It lost votes right across the country, with no strong regional patterns; of the four regions conventionally used for analysis (see Appendix A), its losses were greatest in Connacht–Ulster (down 4.7 per cent) and lowest in Munster (down 0.2 per cent). Its overall level of support is the second lowest ever—only in 2011 did it fare worse—and in eight constituencies it has no TD, a virtually unthinkable prospect prior to 2011. It did not reach 40 per cent of the votes, which prior to 2011 was considered its baseline national level, in any constituency.

Dublin remains a particularly problematic area for the party; its strength there, at 15 per cent, is well below its national level of 22 per cent, though it made two of its three seat gains in Dublin constituencies and lost only one seat there. With nearly 25 per cent of the votes, it was, just, the strongest party outside Dublin, but in Dublin it came third, well behind both Sinn Féin and Fine Gael, losing out to the former among working-class voters and to the latter among middle-class voters. It was the strongest party (disregarding independents) in 15 of the 28 constituencies outside Dublin, but not in any constituency in the capital.

Its number of candidates proved wildly out of kilter with its eventual vote total, and in four constituencies (Clare, Kildare S, Louth and Roscommon–Galway, where the incumbent made clear his displeasure at having a second candidate added to the ticket at the last minute, as discussed on p. 48) it is at least possible that running one candidate fewer would have saved a seat. Four of its seats (in Dublin Bay S, Dun Laoghaire, Galway E and Longford–Westmeath) were won by fewer than 1000 votes, but it also missed out on four others by similar narrow margins (in Carlow–Kilkenny, Clare, Dublin Rathdown and Kildare S), so overall, the random nature of close finishes worked neither for nor against it. Vote management—the art of trying to allocate support evenly among a party's leading x candidates, where x is the number of seats it aims to win—did not prove especially important; in only one constituency (Carlow–Kilkenny) did it miss out on a seat that could have been won through better vote management, and there was only one (Longford–Westmeath) where good management of its votes proved essential to winning a seat. The party did enter government after the election, but in a minority position rather than being the dominant partner as it had hoped.

Fine Gael

Like Fianna Fáil, Fine Gael entered the election with hopes that were not fulfilled, and was ultimately surprised to find itself back in government. It too ran what proved to be an inappropriately high number of candidates (82), and it too ended up losing votes and seats. Having been, for the first time since the 1920s, the strongest party at the two previous elections, it was now relegated, for the first time in its history, to third position, despite having led in the opinion polls for much of the inter-election period (see Fig. 1.1, p. 9) and having won almost twice as many votes as any other party at the European Parliament elections just nine months earlier. Fine Gael's share of the votes, at 21 per cent, was only marginally above its worst ever result (20 per cent in 1948), and its slippage of nearly 5 per cent of the votes followed a loss of almost 11 per cent at the previous election, leaving the party with fewer than half the number of seats it had won just two elections earlier. It did not reach 40 per cent of the votes in any constituency and reached 30 per cent in just five. Perhaps due to having a Dublin leader, or due to the combination there of Fianna Fáil's continuing weakness and the absence of many non-left-wing independents, its losses in the capital, at 3 per cent, were only half of those outside Dublin, leaving its support remarkably evenly spread among the four regions (see Appendix A). Its nine years in government appear to have alienated rural voters more than urban ones; since 2011, Fine Gael support has dropped by only 9 percentage points in the capital but by 17 points in the rest of the country.

It gained votes in only 6 of the 39 constituencies and gained a seat in just one, Dublin Rathdown, one of only two constituencies, the other being Mayo, where it won more than one seat. Since 1948, only once, in 2002, has it won so few seats. A total of 12 Fine Gael TDs lost their seats, a figure that includes five junior ministers and one cabinet minister, Regina Doherty. The party could consider itself slightly unfortunate in that it quite narrowly missed out on seats in five constituencies (Cork SW, Dublin Bay S, Dublin SC, Dun Laoghaire and Wicklow) while only two of its own seats (in Clare and Dublin Rathdown) were won by narrow margins, though, since overall it won its 'fair share' of seats,[7] and a couple more besides, it has no real cause for complaint. With better vote management, it could have taken additional seats in Dun Laoghaire and in Wicklow and possibly in Cavan–Monaghan, while excellent vote management was crucial to its seat gain in Dublin Rathdown. In three constituencies (Cork SW, Tipperary and Waterford) it ran two candidates but did not win a seat, and while there is no guarantee that it would have taken a seat had all of the constituency focus been on just one candidate, splitting the vote fairly evenly between two candidates certainly did not help.

Green Party

Along with Sinn Féin, the Greens were the other winners of the election, and unlike that party they became a part of the ensuing government. Pro rata their gains were larger than those of Sinn Féin, as they more than doubled their votes and returned with six times as many seats as in 2016 and twice as many as their previous peak. Whereas most observers were surprised by the performance of the three larger parties, the Greens' 2020 result matched expectations. In May 2019 the party had doubled its vote in the European Parliament elections and won two of Ireland's 13 seats, and it quadrupled its number of seats in the simultaneous local elections, going on to record its first ever Dáil by-election victory, in Dublin Fingal, in November 2019. In 2020 it delivered on these promising signs even though, in the event, climate change did not prove to be as prominent an election issue as some had anticipated in 2019 (see Chap. 10). As has become its practice, it ran precisely one candidate in every constituency, and whereas just two elections ago 91 per cent of its candidate had failed even to qualify for the reimbursement of expenses, in 2020 only a quarter met that fate. As usual, it fared best in Dublin—its support there was twice as high as the level outside Dublin—which was the base of 8 of its 12 TDs. Of its other four seats, one came from the overwhelmingly urban Limerick City and two from largely urbanised Waterford and Wicklow, with Carlow–Kilkenny, where it also had a seat from 2007 to 2011, the only primarily rural constituency where it won a seat. Within Dublin its strongest areas remained the better-off constituencies on the south side, though it also won seats for the first time in inner-city Dublin Central and Dublin SC. Green gains were strongly related to the strength of the Yes vote in the May 2018 referendum on removing the 'pro-life' eighth amendment from the constitution (see Chap. 1, p. 13). The Pearson correlation coefficient (r) is 0.68, indicating that the stronger the Yes vote in 2018, the greater the gains made by the Greens in 2020, as might be expected given the Greens' consistently liberal stance on moral issues.

The party gained votes in every constituency and made its strongest advances in Dublin, where it added over 7 per cent to its 2016 level of support. Whereas Green candidates in the past in many constituencies have tended to lack any elective status and, after one unsuccessful run, retired from the fray and were replaced by a new batch of hopefuls, the party's success in the 2019 local elections meant that it could field a much more battle-hardened team: over half of its candidates were either councillors or incumbent TDs, and all 12 of its TDs were elected to a local council before reaching the Dáil. As usual, Green candidates proved very transfer-friendly, and six of its TDs owed their election to transfers from other parties' candidates (see later discussion). To some degree the party benefited from the bounce of the ball, in that in three constituencies (Carlow–Kilkenny, Dublin W and Wicklow) it won a seat fairly narrowly, compared with only one (Louth) where it narrowly lost out, but overall its seat total closely reflects its national share of the vote.

Labour

Labour has lost its place in the Irish party system. At every election in the independent Irish state, up to and including 2007, it was invariably either the third or, temporarily, the fourth party, sometimes characterised as the 'half' party in the two-and-a-half-party system. It broke the mould in a positive direction in 2011, becoming the second strongest party for the first time ever, but unmoored from the anchor of a secure if subordinate role within the party system, in 2020 it sank to fifth position. It won only 4 per cent of the votes, its lowest ever, and its total number of votes fell below the 100,000 mark for the first time since 1933 despite the record size of the electorate. It exceeded 10 per cent of the votes in only four constituencies. Sinn Féin's five leading vote-getters together won more votes than Labour. Similarly, its total of just six seats was a historic low. After its disastrous result in 2016, when it dropped from 37 seats to just 7, it had hoped that the only way was up, but its slide towards possible oblivion continued in 2020. Veteran incumbents such as Joan Burton (first elected in 1992) and Jan O'Sullivan (first elected in 1998), along with former incumbents seeking to make a comeback such as Joe Costello (first elected in 1992), Emmet Stagg (first elected in 1987) and Joanna Tuffy, were humiliated at the polls, each receiving fewer than 3000 first preferences. The party did not even run a candidate in several constituencies where it had won seats as recently as 2011, including Clare and Cork SW—as well as Kerry, where it had held a seat almost continuously since 1943.

Labour's remaining seats seem very dependent on the appeal of its incumbent TDs, as was illustrated by its experience in Longford–Westmeath; its long-serving incumbent Willie Penrose retired and his successor as the Labour candidate did not even qualify for reimbursement of election expenses. Three of its six seats were retained by incumbents, two were reclaimed by former TDs returning to the Dáil, and the only newcomer was Duncan Smith in Dublin Fingal, the only new Labour TD elected since 2011, and this was the retention of a Labour seat held by a retiring TD rather than a Labour gain. Smith had also benefited by gaining exposure as the party's candidate in a by-election held less than three months before the general election. In no constituency was the Labour candidate the runner-up, and only in Kildare S (its strongest constituency in terms of percentage vote) did an unsuccessful Labour candidate make a serious challenge for a seat. Moreover, two of its seats were won by fewer than 200 votes, Ged Nash edging out the Green candidate in Louth by only 141 votes and Duncan Smith finishing just 188 votes ahead of an independent in Dublin Fingal. As noted in the previous volume in this series, some of the factors that in the past have guaranteed that the party would eventually recover from any setback—its position as the sole or dominant standard-bearer of the left, its bedrock in the trade union movement—are no longer applicable.[8] Transfer analysis (see below) suggests that many voters on the left see Labour as just another 'establishment party' rather than a radical alternative to the status quo. Its struggles mirror those of social democratic parties around Europe, and even the combined strength of Labour and the Social Democrats is well below the level that Labour averaged prior to 2016. Labour was encouraged by a good result in the Seanad election (see Chap. 12), but its new leader Alan Kelly faces a major challenge.

Social Democrats

The Social Democrats won the same number of seats as Labour, but unlike that party, they regarded this outcome as a success. At their first general election in 2016 they had won three seats, but each was held by a high-profile incumbent who would probably have been elected anyway if standing as an independent. One of these three, Stephen Donnelly, subsequently left the party and moved to Fianna Fáil. The party made no impression at the European Parliament elections of May 2019 and took just 19 of the 949 seats at the local elections held at the same time. Nonetheless, in 2020 it reached seat parity with Labour, despite receiving only two-thirds as many votes; indeed, the Social Democrats' share of the votes was very marginally down on the 2016 figure.

Like all the other left-wing parties it is strongest in Dublin in terms of both votes and seats; three of its TDs represent constituencies in the capital and another two have seats in commuter counties adjacent to Dublin. Its sixth seat was the unexpected success of Holly Cairns in Cork SW; she narrowly edged out the leading Fine Gael candidate on the last count, and similarly, Gary Gannon in Dublin Central was also a fairly narrow winner of the final seat. As a result, the party was slightly over-represented (its 'fair share' would have been five seats compared with seven for Labour).

Solidarity–People Before Profit

The far-left alliance also had reason to be pleased with its result, as at the May 2019 local elections it had lost both votes and seats and won just 11 of the 949 seats available. Indeed, in the 2020 election it lost around a third of its 2016 support. Nonetheless, it came back with five seats, just one fewer than in 2016, with Ruth Coppinger in Dublin W its only defeated incumbent. At one stage during the count it looked as if it might make an unexpected gain in Dublin NW, as its candidate Conor Reddy, despite winning less than 4 per cent of the first preferences, quintupled his number of votes over the course of the count, thanks to transfers from Sinn Féin in particular, only to miss out on the final count.

The balance within the alliance has changed greatly since 2016. Then, the two component parts, the Anti-Austerity Alliance (AAA) and People Before Profit (PBP), had won almost exactly the same number of votes, and both saw three of their candidates elected. Since then, the AAA had renamed itself Solidarity, and in September 2019 one of its TDs, Paul Murphy, announced that he was leaving Solidarity (while remaining part of the Solidarity–People Before Profit alliance) and founding his own organisation, to be called Rise. Of the 37 candidates run by the alliance in 2020, 27 were from PBP and only 9 represented Solidarity, with Murphy as the other candidate. PBP's dominance within the alliance was reinforced in March 2021 when Murphy announced that he and Rise would in future operate within PBP. PBP won 70 per cent of the votes of the alliance and retained its three seats, with Solidarity and Rise now having one each.

Others

The only other party to win a seat was Aontú, founded in early 2019 by Peadar Tóibín, who left Sinn Féin over its refusal to accommodate his opposition to the legalisation of abortion (see Chap. 1). Tóibín was comfortably re-elected, but none of the party's other candidates came close; only two others won even 4 per cent of the votes in their constituency, and four-fifths of Aontú candidates did not qualify for reimbursement of expenses. Three other parties included opposition to abortion among their policies, which also included concerns about immigration and, in the case of the last two, strong Euroscepticism: Renua, the Irish Freedom Party (which advocates Ireland exiting the European Union) and the National Party. Of the 32 candidates run by these three parties between them, none received even 1000 first preferences, and all failed to reach the threshold needed for reimbursement of election expenses. The Workers' Party lingers on despite not having won a Dáil seat since most of its TDs left it to form Democratic Left in February 1992, but each of its four candidates received fewer than 500 first preferences.

As ever, there was no shortage of independent candidates entering the lists; there were more than the number of candidates put forward by Fianna Fáil and Fine Gael together. The loosely organised Independent Alliance that had won six seats in 2016 had completely disintegrated; some of the TDs elected under that banner retired in 2020, while the others stood as sole traders. Twenty, amounting to one in eight of all TDs, were elected, slightly down on the 2016 figure but still the second highest ever. Fourteen of these were incumbents who were re-elected, and one was a former TD who had stepped down in 2007 and then served three terms as an MEP. Of the remaining five, three had previous records within parties. Michael McNamara, elected in Clare, had lost his seat as a Labour TD in 2016; Verona Murphy had been selected as a Fine Gael candidate in Wexford, but after some off-message comments about immigration she made while running for the party in a by-election in November 2019 (see Chap. 3), she was deselected by the party, stood as an independent and won a seat at the expense of a Fine Gael incumbent, and Richard O'Donoghue had been elected as a Fianna Fáil councillor in 2014 before leaving the party in the run-up to the 2016 election.

VOTE TRANSFERS

As explained in detail in Appendix D, the proportional representation by the single transferable vote (PR-STV) electoral system offers voters the opportunity to rank order all candidates on the ballot paper in order of their preference. During the course of the count, as candidates are elected or eliminated, their votes are transferred to the remaining candidates in line with the next preferences marked. By examining patterns in vote transfers, we can draw inferences about how warmly or coldly supporters of each party regard other parties, and indeed how far voters seem to be thinking in party terms at all when deciding how to vote.

An indication of the latter is the solidarity of intra-party transfers: that is, the proportion of votes that remain within the party fold when one candidate of a party is eliminated and at least one other candidate of that party is available to receive transfers. Prior to the 1990s, when party identification was higher than it is now and when the range of parties on offer was much more restricted, for the major parties such internal solidarity

Table 8.4 Transfer patterns at the 2020 election, in per cent

From	Available	N cases	FF	FG	SF	Sol–PBP
Internal solidarity						
FF	FF	24	54.3			
FG	FG	35		56.8		
SF	SF	2			77.9	
Inter-party terminal transfers						
FF	FG	6		28.5		
FG	FF	5	33.7			
SF	Sol–PBP	23				37.1
Sol–PBP	SF	3			34.4	

Note: The 'Available' column shows those parties that had candidates available in each case to receive transfers. 'Inter-party terminal transfers' refer to cases where the party whose votes were being distributed had no candidates of its own left in the count. Thus, for example, in the six cases where a terminal Fianna Fáil transfer took place and a Fine Gael candidate was available to receive transfers, 28.5 per cent of those transfers passed to a Fine Gael candidate or candidates. Figures for other parties are not given since these would be meaningless in the absence of information as to the number of cases in which these parties had a candidate available to receive transfers. The cases analysed exclude surpluses that were based on the distribution of a package of votes from a candidate of another party was high; in November 1982, over 80 per cent of transfers from both Fianna Fáil and Fine Gael candidates went to other candidates of the same party when such candidates were available to receive transfers. These figures have been in decline ever since, and in 2016, the figure for both parties was below 60 per cent. The percentages declined slightly again in 2020, marking new record lows for both parties (see Table 8.4).[9] Sinn Féin's solidarity was much higher, though the figure is based on only two cases. The implication is that not much more than a half of those who cast a vote for a candidate of Fianna Fáil or of Fine Gael were strong partisans or perhaps any kind of partisans at all, as their next preference went to a candidate of another party or to an independent even though it could have gone to a candidate of the same party. In the case of Fianna Fáil, seven of the 24 cases exhibited an internal solidarity rate below 50 per cent and only one was higher than 70 per cent, while for Fine Gael the respective figures were six and three out of the 35 cases. The lowest for either party was Fianna Fáil's figure of just 36 per cent in Tipperary. In Wexford an internal Fianna Fáil transfer was only 38 per cent, and an independent candidate, who was eventually elected, who came from the same town as the eliminated Fianna Fáil candidate received over 500 more transfers than a Fianna Fáil incumbent, who was eventually the runner-up, a rare case of an intra-party transfer helping a rival candidate to overtake a running mate (see Table 8.5). Fianna Fáil would have taken four or five additional seats (in Clare, Kildare S, Louth, Wexford and possibly Roscommon–Galway) had its internal transfer rate still been around 80 per cent, and Fine Gael would have won an additional seat in Tipperary, Waterford and Wicklow.

There is some tendency for such internal solidarity to be lower outside Dublin, not surprisingly given that geographical factors play a bigger part in large rural constituencies than in compact urban ones. As an example, Fine Gael's second lowest internal rate of transfer came in the two-county Longford–Westmeath constituency, when on the tenth count its Longford-based candidate Micheál Carrigy was eliminated. Of his 6981 votes, 2709 (only 39 per cent) went to his Westmeath-based running mate Peter Burke, while 2828 (41 per cent) passed to the Longford-based Fianna Fáil candidate Joe Flaherty. The salience of geography is illustrated strikingly by a couple of other examples. In Mayo, over a third of the votes of Ballina-based Fine Gael candidate Michelle Mulherin transferred to Ballina-based Fianna Fáil candidate Dara Calleary, while in Kerry, upon the elimination of Fianna Fáil's Norma Moriarty, 994 of her 4217 votes went to a Fine Gael candidate whose base was near her own in the south

Table 8.5   Constituencies where inter-party transfers affected the outcome

Constituency	Seat won by	At the expense of	Due to transfers from
Carlow–Kilkenny	Malcolm Noonan (Grn)	Bobby Aylward (FF)	SF, Ind, PBP
Clare	Michael McNamara (Ind)	Timmy Dooley (FF)	Grn, Ind
Cork E	Seán Sherlock (Lab)	Kevin O'Keeffe (FF)	Grn, Ind
Cork NC	Mick Barry (Sol)	Kenneth O'Flynn (Ind)	SF, Grn
Cork SW	Holly Cairns (SD)	Tim Lombard (FG)	SF, Grn
Donegal	Thomas Pringle (Ind)	Pat Cope Gallagher (FF)	SF, Ind, Grn
Dublin Central	Gary Gannon (SD)	Mary Fitzpatrick (FF)	SF, PBP
Dublin Fingal	Duncan Smith (Lab)	Dean Mulligan (I4C)	FF, FG
Dublin MW	Gino Kelly (PBP)	John Curran (FF)	SF, Ind, Grn
Dublin NW	Paul McAuliffe (FF)	Conor Reddy (PBP)	FG
Dublin SC	Joan Collins (I4C)	Catherine Byrne (FG)	SF, PBP, Inds
	Patrick Costello (Grn)	Catherine Byrne (FG)	Lab, Soc Dems
Dublin W	Roderic O'Gorman (Grn)	Ruth Coppinger (Sol)	Lab, FG
Dun Laoghaire	Cormac Devlin (FF)	Mary Mitchell O'Connor (FG)	SF, Aontú
Galway E	Anne Rabbitte (FF)	Louis O'Dea (SF)	FG
Kildare S	Cathal Berry (Ind)	Fiona O'Loughlin (FF)	Ind, Lab
Limerick City	Brian Leddin (Grn)	Frankie Daly (Ind)	Lab, Soc Dems
Limerick County	Richard O'Donoghue (Ind)	Séighin Ó Ceallaigh (SF)	FG
Longfd–Wmeath	Joe Carrigy (FF)	Kevin 'Boxer' Moran (Ind)	FG
Louth	Ged Nash (Lab)	Declan Breathnach (FF)	SF, PBP, Grn
	Ged Nash (Lab)	Mark Dearey (Grn)	FF
Waterford	Marc Ó Cathasaigh (Grn)	John Cummins (FG)	SF, PBP
Wexford	Verona Murphy (Ind)	Malcolm Byrne (FF)	SF, Ind, PBP, FF
Wicklow	Stephen Matthews (Grn)	Andrew Doyle (FG)	SF, PBP, Ind

Note: The counter-factual scenario is one where the votes transferred from the party or parties in the final column went equally to the two candidates in the previous columns, in which case the candidate in the third column would have taken the seat

of the constituency and only 40 to the Fine Gael candidate based in north Kerry. (See Chap. 9 for a fuller discussion of the impact of geographical factors.)

When a vote transfer takes place from a candidate who has no running mate still available to receive votes, we refer to these as terminal transfers, and these can shed light on inter-party relationships. There are more parties now contesting elections than in most earlier decades, and political alliances are much more fluid, with pre-election agreements rare. As a result, we would not expect to find strong inter-party transfers between any two parties of the sort that used to characterise, say, transfer rates between Fine Gael and Labour in the 1970s and 1980s, or even in 2016, when over 50 per cent of terminal transfers from Fine Gael and Labour went to the other party when it still had a candidate in the running.[10]

In 2020, there were no inter-party transfer rates above 40 per cent. The strongest relationship was that between Sinn Féin and Solidarity–PBP, with over a third of terminal transfers passing between these two parties in both directions. This was encouraged by the slogan 'Vote Left, Transfer Left' used by candidates of both parties (e.g. see Fig. 6.4). The closeness between these parties is perhaps understated by these figures. In the case of transfers from Sinn Féin to Solidarity–PBP, many of the latter's candidates won few first preferences and would not have been well known to Sinn Féin voters; in some cases the transfers these candidates received from Sinn Féin surpluses dwarfed their own first preference tally, most notably in Waterford where the PBP candidate won only 1153 first preferences but received 3208 votes from the distribution of the Sinn Féin candidate's surplus. In the six cases where Solidarity–PBP had an incumbent TD, the transfer rate from Solidarity–PBP was over 40 per cent, rising to an astonishing 82 per cent in Dun Laoghaire, where PBP TD Richard Boyd Barrett received 5245 votes on the elimination of the Sinn Féin candidate, the largest transfer in the country in both numerical and percentage terms, even including intra-party transfers. Likewise, in each of the three cases where terminal Solidarity–PBP transfers were made when a Sinn Féin candidate was still available to receive transfers, the Solidarity–PBP candidate had received fewer than 2000 first preferences and there may have been a significant personal element in the vote they received.

Terminal transfers between the two parties that subsequently went into coalition together, Fianna Fáil and Fine Gael, were not strong, though at around 30 per cent the mutual feeling could be considered lukewarm rather than as chilly as the familiar label 'the civil war parties' might imply. The figures were virtually unchanged from 2016, when the Fianna Fáil to Fine Gael terminal transfer rate had been 29 per cent and the rate in the other direction 35 per cent. These in turn were higher than had been the case at previous elections; in 1997, for example, the respective percentages were 15 and 23. In Dublin NW, transfers from Fine Gael secured a seat for Fianna Fáil at the expense of PBP, an irony given that the pre-election speculation had been that Fianna Fáil and Fine Gael would be in contention for the final seat there. In Longford–Westmeath, too, transfers from Fine Gael brought about a seat gain for Fianna Fáil, though as discussed above geography was the main factor here. In another two constituencies, though, stronger transfers between these two parties would have secured a seat for one of them but did not materialise, Fine Gael missing out in Dublin SC and Fianna Fáil in Roscommon–Galway.

Overall, inter-party transfers affected the outcome in more than half of the 39 constituencies, an unusually high proportion (see Table 8.5). The largest three parties all suffered at the expense of smaller parties. Fianna Fáil (which won four seats due to transfers but was deprived of nine) and Fine Gael (which did not gain any seats this way and was deprived of five) were the most adversely affected, while Sinn Féin was deprived of two seats this way. In contrast, the Greens as usual proved themselves to be the most transfer-friendly party, with half of their 12 seats owing to favourable transfers from candidates of other parties and only one seat slipping away due to inter-party transfers. Labour, with a net 'profit' of three seats (it too was dependent on transfers from other parties for half of the seats it won), as well as the Social Democrats and independents, both with a profit of two, were the other main beneficiaries. Given the huge number of Sinn Féin surplus votes that had to pass to candidates of other parties because Sinn Féin had not nominated running mates for their lead candidates (see Table 8.3), it is not surprising that transfers from Sinn Féin were instrumental in determining 12 of the seats in Table 8.5. Almost invariably, Sinn Féin's transfers assisted parties of the left (broadly defined) at the expense of what it branded the establishment parties, Fianna Fáil and Fine Gael.

THE BETTING MARKET AS RESULTS PREDICTOR

Betting markets operate on several aspects of Irish general elections: the number of seats and votes each party will win, turnout, the fate of individual candidates, the composition of the next government and others. While for national-level predictions the markets tend to follow opinion poll findings rather than constituting an independent pool of informed judgement,[11] at constituency level there are few if any opinion polls, and thus, the betting markets offer a unique and accessible snapshot of which candidates are, at any given moment, expected by the market to win seats. How useful they are as predictors of the result depends on how accurately the market is reading voting intentions. The markets' failure to foresee the success of Donald Trump or Brexit in 2016 emphasised that they should not be regarded as infallible guides to political outcomes.

In terms of the national outcome, the betting market had successes and failures. Its assessment of Fine Gael's likely fortunes was very accurate; having predicted on 14 January, the day the Dáil was dissolved, that the party would win 49.5 seats, its prediction dropped steadily over the ensuing three weeks and by election day, 8 February, it stood at 35.5 seats, the party's actual total being 35.[12] The market also did well when it came to the seats that would be won by the Greens (it predicted 10.5 against an actual 12) and Labour (it predicted 5.5 against an actual 6). It performed poorly with regard to the strongest two parties, though, consistently over-estimating Fianna Fáil and under-estimating Sinn Féin. On 14 January, the seat prediction for Fianna Fáil stood at 50.5, and over the course of the campaign this figure actually rose to 54.5 by election day, a far cry from the 38 seats the party won. In the case of Sinn Féin the trend was at least in the correct direction, its predicted number rising from 18.5 when the Dáil was dissolved to 29 on election day, but this was still well short of its actual tally of 37. While the betting market, even on polling day, expected Fianna Fáil to win nearly twice as many seats as Sinn Féin, in fact the two parties ended up virtually level. Of course, most political observers, with a few notable exceptions,[13] and election participants also failed to foresee the actual outcome. In fact, the polls turned out to be very accurate, but, perhaps because the polls at the May 2019 local elections had systematically over-estimated support for the Greens and under-estimated that for Fianna Fáil and Fine Gael, there was an unjustified scepticism as to whether Sinn Féin was really doing as well as the polls suggested.

When it comes to assessing the likelihood of individual candidates winning a seat, the betting markets in effect provide a perceived probability for each candidate by offering odds on whether he or she will be elected.[14] As we would expect, the higher a candidate's probability of winning a seat, as assigned by the betting market, the higher was his or her vote as a proportion of the Droop quota in their constituency ($r = 0.820$, $n = 460$).[15] The relationship remains strong if we confine the analysis to candidates of the seven main parties ($r = 0.771$, $n = 330$). If only those candidates receiving at least a fifth of the quota are included, the correlation is still strong ($r = 0.671$, $n = 305$) but is quite a bit lower than at the 2016 election, when it was 0.795, an indication that the market was less accurate in 2020 than in 2016.[16]

This particular betting market is not, of course, about how many votes each candidate will win but about whether they will or will not be elected. Reassuringly, the higher the betting market's expectation that a candidate

Table 8.6 Fate of candidates, by probability assigned by betting market

Betting market perceived likelihood of election	Elected	Not elected but qualifying for reimbursement of expenses	Not qualifying for reimbursement of expenses	Per cent elected	Average Droop quotas	N
<0.101	0	31	134	0	0.11	165
0.101–0.2	4	37	8	8.2	0.31	49
0.201–0.3	6	15	0	28.6	0.45	21
0.301–0.4	12	27	1	30.0	0.40	40
0.401–0.5	8	10	0	44.4	0.59	18
0.501–0.6	4	12	0	25.0	0.44	16
0.601–0.7	11	5	0	68.8	0.58	16
0.701–0.8	24	8	0	75.0	0.59	32
0.801–0.9	34	8	0	81.0	0.69	42
0.901–1	56	5	0	91.8	1.04	61
All	159	158	143	34.5	0.42	460

Source: paddypower.com. Probabilities based on odds offered on 7 February 2020, the day before election day, not taking account of overround, that is the bookmakers' margin, the amount by which the sum of probabilities of the options exceeds 1

Note: The 71 candidates for whom no odds were offered are excluded; nearly all of those candidates fared very poorly (see text)

will be elected, the more likely they indeed are to be elected, as shown by Table 8.6, so whereas no candidate given less than a 10 per cent chance was elected, 92 per cent of those seen as having a greater than 90 per cent chance did win a seat. The relationship is almost monotonic, though with a lapse in the band 0.501–0.6 (representing in practice odds lying between 10–11 and 4–6 inclusive), who overall fared much less well than the betting market expected.

Given that the betting market for national seats seriously underestimated Sinn Féin's prospects, it is not surprising that several of the elected Sinn Féin candidates in effect defied the odds in securing a seat; of the ten longest-priced winners, five were Sinn Féin candidates. The longest-priced winner was Holly Cairns (SD, Cork SW, 6–1), followed by Jennifer Carroll MacNeill (Fine Gael, Dun Laoghaire—see her account in Chap. 7), Carol Nolan (Ind, Laois–Offaly) and Violet-Anne Wynne (Sinn Féin, Clare), all at 4–1. Similarly, the market's over-estimation of how Fianna Fáil would fare resulted in 15 Fianna Fáil candidates being among the 20 shortest-priced losing candidates. Five candidates who were assigned a probability greater than 90 per cent were not elected: John Curran (Fianna Fáil, Dublin MW, 1–50), Bobby Aylward (Fianna Fáil, Carlow–Kilkenny, 1–20), Timmy Dooley (Fianna Fáil, Clare, 1–14), Shane Cassells (Fianna Fáil, Meath W, 1–10) and Kevin 'Boxer' Moran (Ind, Longford–Westmeath, 1–10). As in 2016, there seemed to be some tendency for female candidates' chances to be under-estimated: seven of the ten longest-priced winners were female, compared with only two of the ten shortest-priced losers, as if there is a degree of gender bias in the market. Overall, the betting market in 2020 confirmed its reputation as a useful, though far from infallible, guide as to the election outcome, both nationally and at constituency level.

The Members of the 33rd Dáil

Turnover and Experience

After exceptionally high levels of turnover at the previous two elections— in 2011 only a minority of those elected had been members of the previous Dáil—turnover subsided to a more normal level. Of the 158 members of the 32nd Dáil at the start of December 2019, one resigned his seat later that month amidst some controversy (see Chronology under 4 February) and a further 18 retired once the election was called. Notable retirees included former Taoiseach Enda Kenny, the longest-serving member of the 32nd Dáil, who had first been elected in 1975; Michael Noonan, a former Fine Gael leader, who had played a central role in government as Minister for Finance in the 2011–2016 government that took office during the dark days following the economic crash; Gerry Adams, who became leader of Sinn Féin in 1983 and held the position for over 30 years; former Ceann Comhairle Seán Barrett; and current ministers of state Jim Daly, John Halligan and Finian McGrath (see full list in Appendix E). As would be expected, those retiring were older (an average age of 65) than those who fought again (average age 53).

In addition to these 19 departures, 35 incumbents were defeated at the election, and these were slightly older than those re-elected (57 compared with 52), a familiar pattern and one that suggests that some TDs may, consciously or otherwise, start winding down as they get older. Another familiar pattern is that defeated TDs had fared less well at the 2016 election (their first preferences on average amounted to 0.69 quotas) than had their re-elected counterparts (an average of 0.79 quotas), so the 2020 outcome was to some extent foreshadowed by the 2016 result. Retiring TDs had polled even less well in 2016 (an average of 0.68 quotas), suggesting that some at least of the retirees pre-empted their ejection by the electorate by standing down voluntarily. The defeated TDs included former cabinet ministers Joan Burton, Mary Mitchell O'Connor and Jan O'Sullivan as well as current cabinet members Regina Doherty, Shane Ross and Katherine Zappone. Malcolm Byrne's defeat in Wexford put an end, temporarily at least, to a uniquely short Dáil career, as he had been elected just over two months earlier in a by-election. The great majority of the defeats were inter-party, but six were intra-party, as an incumbent was ousted by one of their own running mates; five Fianna Fáil TDs suffered this fate, as did one Fine Gael TD, Mary Mitchell O'Connor being replaced in Dun Laoghaire by Jennifer Carroll MacNeill, who gives an account of her campaign in Chap. 7. The increased fragmentation of the party system has meant that intra-party competition, one of the most highlighted aspects of PR-STV, is not as salient as it used to be when Fianna Fáil and Fine Gael were dominant. A majority of the TDs in the 33rd Dáil (84 out of 160) are either independents or stood as the sole candidate of their party, and hence may not be subject to the same degree to the pressures and incentive structure faced by TDs who foresee a threat to their seat from a running mate at the next election.

The size of the Dáil increased slightly in 2020, a response to population growth. Just over a third (56 out of 160) of the members of the 33rd Dáil had not belonged to the previous Dáil, with eight of these being former TDs returning after an absence and the other 48 (30 per cent) being first-time TDs. Of these first-time TDs half were first-time candidates as well, while at the other end of the scale Colm Burke of Fine Gael established a new record by being elected over 37 years after his first Dáil candidacy, which had been back in November 1982. Overall, 92 of the 160 TDs were elected the first time they stood and only 13 were elected after three or more defeats. Two, Paul Donnelly and Roderic O'Gorman, both coincidentally from the same constituency, were finally elected after five unsuccessful attempts (see the latter's account in Chap. 7). Leaving aside the 48 first-time TDs, only 15 of the other 112 have tasted any defeat after their initial election, meaning that once a TD does lose their seat, they rarely come back. Eight TDs were first elected in the 1980s; Bernard Durkan was first elected in 1981, but he lost his seat at the following election and the TDs with the longest continuous Dáil membership are Richard Bruton and Willie O'Dea, both first elected in February 1982. Only 19 TDs were first elected in the twentieth century, and only 43, not much more than a quarter, were in the Dáil prior to 2011. The median TD was first elected in 2016; political generations come and go rapidly.

Backgrounds of Deputies

Before the election of 2016 candidate gender quotas were introduced, entailing a reduction in state funding for parties that failed to achieve at least a 70–30 gender balance among their candidates. This led to an increase in the number of female TDs, though the Dáil was still markedly less gender-balanced than most parliaments across Europe.[17] With no change in the quotas in 2020, the main parties evidently saw no incentive to increase their proportion above the threshold required to avoid financial penalties and, as discussed in Chap. 3, they complied with the requirement in minimalist fashion; Sinn Féin, Fianna Fáil, Fine Gael and Labour all selected candidate lists that were at least two-thirds male. The main parties continue to comply with the letter of the legislation, but it is open to question whether they are complying with its spirit. The result in overall terms was no change in the gender balance of the Dáil, the proportion of female TDs rising from 35 out of 158 in 2016 (22.2 per cent) to 36 out of 160 in 2020 (22.5 per cent). Of the main parties, Sinn Féin's Dáil group is by some way the most gender-balanced: 34 per cent of its TDs are women, compared with only 17 per cent for both Fine Gael and the Greens and 13 per cent for Fianna Fáil. Among the smaller groups the Social Democrats, uniquely, have a predominantly female Dáil group (four women out of six TDs), with Solidarity–PBP at 20 per cent and Labour bringing up the rear with no female TDs at all. Among the independents, to whom no candidate gender balance requirements apply, 25 per cent of elected TDs were women, a higher proportion than for all but two of the parties.

Three constituencies returned a majority of female TDs, and in another three there was an equal gender balance, but there were 12, seven of them in Munster, that did not elect any female TDs at all. Exactly a third of the first-time TDs were female, compared with 18 per cent of the re-elected incumbents. On the other hand, female incumbents did less well than their male counterparts (39 per cent of the women who stood for re-election were defeated compared with only 21 per cent of the men), though as discussed at the start of this chapter women do not receive fewer votes than men once account is taken of the effect of party and

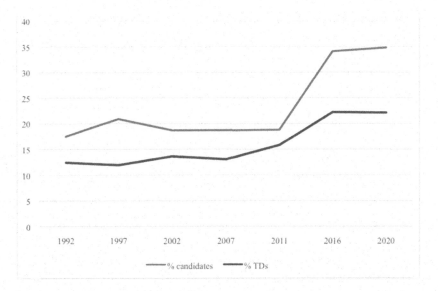

Fig. 8.2   Percentage women among candidates and TDs of seat-winning parties, 1992–2020
Note: Figures show the percentage of female candidates, and of female TDs, in parties that won at least one seat in the Dáil

elective status. The impact of the candidate gender quota law can be seen in Fig. 8.2, which displays the pattern with independent and micro-parties omitted. In 2016, there was a marked increase in the proportion of women among the *candidates* of the parties that won seats, but the increase among the TDs was much more muted. The candidate gender quota is set to rise from 30 per cent to 40 per cent in 2023, but on the evidence of the 2020 election, without a significant change of approach such as the introduction of gender quotas at local elections, we can expect most of the parties to pick scarcely more than the required minimum proportion of female candidates, with the overall proportion of female TDs rising to only around 30 per cent, if even that.[18]

Approximately 60 per cent of TDs have a university degree, with particularly high proportions among the smaller parties (over three quarters of the TDs of the Greens, Labour and the Social Democrats) and Fine Gael (almost 70 per cent). As at recent elections, slightly under half of all TDs had professional occupations, with nearly a quarter in 'commercial' roles such as running a small business. The proportion of farmers continued its steady decline, interrupted briefly in 2016, and now stands at just

6 per cent. The average age of the TDs of the 33rd Dáil is 49, very much in line with the norm for recent Dála. TDs are predominantly middle-aged; two-thirds are in their 40s or 50s. Only two are in their 70s, the oldest being Bernard Durkan of Fine Gael, who was two months short of his 75th birthday on election day, and in all 24 were over 60. A further 28 were aged under 40, with just three in their twenties, the youngest being 22-year-old James O'Connor (see his account in Chap. 7).

Routes to the Dáil

As in every Dáil, the most well-trodden route to the national parliament is via local government. Of the 48 new TDs, two-thirds were sitting councillors, and only five had never belonged to a city or county council. Altogether only 23 of the 160 TDs have never been councillors. The great majority (132, or 82 per cent, the same proportion as in the previous Dáil) were elected to a council en route to becoming a TD. The remaining five reversed the sequence, but all five were first elected prior to 2004, since when the law has prevented anyone being simultaneously a TD and a councillor. Establishing a base through local government is especially important for smaller party TDs: all of the Green and Social Democrat TDs, and all but one of Labour's, were councillors before entering the Dáil.

Another well-established route to the Dáil lies in following in the foot-steps of a relative. In the 33rd Dáil, 26 TDs were preceded by a relative, and on a subjective judgement, this was a significant factor in the first elec-tion of 22 of them (14 per cent), a relatively low figure by the Dáil's his-toric standards. This applies mainly to TDs of the traditional major parties (ten are from Fianna Fáil and seven from Fine Gael); no TD from the Green Party or the Social Democrats, only one from Labour and one from Sinn Féin (though he was first elected for Fianna Fáil) benefited from such a heritage. Both male and female TDs used to feature proportionately in the list of relatives, but at the last three elections this route has been almost entirely confined to men; in the 33rd Dáil only two women were aided significantly by being preceded by a relative. Of the 22 TDs in question, 16 were sons of former TDs, two were daughters, two brothers, and there was also one cousin and one nephew.

CONCLUSION

The 2011 election was dubbed Ireland's 'earthquake election', and in 2016, the tone was that the aftershocks continued to reverberate. Analysts of Irish elections are starting to run out of earthquake-related metaphors, but the seismic shifts continue. In 2020, the three mainstays of the party system that had remained fundamentally unaltered for nearly 80 years slumped to, or close to, historic low points, and the lead was taken by a party that had won only four seats in the Dáil just three elections ago. In all of this, what is happening in Ireland mirrors patterns in a number of other countries, as discussed in Chap. 14.

The election result was followed by the formation of an equally unprecedented government containing both of the two rival poles of the traditional party system, as outlined in Chap. 13. Balkanisation, or fragmentation, has now reached the government level; the incoming government became the second most fractionalised ever, its 'effective number of parties' figure of 2.78 higher than that of every previous government except the 1948–1951 inter-party coalition. That was also the only previous government in which no party held a majority of positions, but unlike its 2020 counterpart, it did have a dominant party, in that Fine Gael, with six of the 13 ministries, was far larger than the rest, no other party having more than two.

For the voters, the 'identifiability' of government options at the 2020 election was very low, as no clear alternative governments were on offer. A long-time observer of Irish elections, R. K. Carty of the University of British Columbia, observes that in the 1970s voters had a limited choice of parties, but they knew that they could choose a government, as their vote could assist in bringing about either a Fianna Fáil single-party government or a Fine Gael–Labour coalition. But now, while there is a wide choice of parties to vote for, 'elections no longer allow the electorate to choose their government and Irish democracy seems the poorer for it'.[19] In both 2016 and 2020 the fragmentation of votes and seats at the general election was similar to that at the preceding European Parliament election, and as noted in the previous volume in this series, voters are increasingly behaving at Dáil elections as if these were second-order elections (where people vote with their hearts, not having to think about government formation) rather than first-order elections (at which government formation is a central consideration in determining how individuals vote). Most of the parties do little to clarify the situation for voters, which would entail setting out realistic and viable options that they would be willing to make work.

If the Fianna Fáil–Fine Gael–Green government is able to solve the many unresolved problems that fuelled the anti-establishment vote in 2020, then perhaps at least a broad outline of the previous party system may become visible again as challenger parties fall away. If it does not, however, the incumbent parties stand to be on the receiving end of redoubled fury at the next election, and students of Irish elections will be once again reaching for their thesaurus to find new ways of summing up an outcome that would have seemed unimaginable prior to 2008.

NOTES

1. Michael Gallagher, 'The results analysed: the aftershocks continue', pp. 125–57 in Michael Gallagher and Michael Marsh (eds), *How Ireland Voted 2016: the election that nobody won* (Cham: Palgrave Macmillan, 2016), pp. 126–7.
2. David M. Farrell and Jane Suiter, 'The election in context', pp. 277–92 in Michael Gallagher and Michael Marsh (eds), *How Ireland Voted 2016: the election that nobody won* (Cham: Palgrave Macmillan, 2016), pp. 279–81.
3. For the historical pattern, see Peter Mair, 'The election in context', pp. 283–97 in Michael Gallagher and Michael Marsh (eds), *How Ireland Voted 2011: the full story of Ireland's earthquake election* (Basingstoke: Palgrave Macmillan, 2016), p. 286. As noted in Chap. 10 (see p. 250n8), the true level of vote-switching was significantly higher than this.
4. Markku Laakso and Rein Taagepera, '"Effective" number of parties: a measure with application to west Europe', *Comparative Political Studies* 12:1 (1979), pp. 3–27. The intuitive meaning of a figure such as 6.16 is that the party system is as fragmented as if there are 6.16 equal-sized parties. The calculation is based on treating each independent candidate as a separate unit, except when Independents ran under a common label such as 'Independents 4 Change'.
5. The lineage of today's Sinn Féin party, and in particular the degree of continuity between it and the party of the same name that existed early in the last century, is open to debate. John Coakley suggests that today's Sinn Féin party is most accurately seen as having been founded in 1970; see his 'Introduction: constitutional innovation and political change in twentieth-century Ireland', pp. 1–29 in John Coakley (ed.), *Changing Shades of Orange and Green: Redefining the Union and the Nation in Contemporary Ireland* (Dublin: University College Dublin Press, 2002), pp. 16–17.

6. The configuration of constituencies changed somewhat from the 2016 election on foot of the 2017 report of the Constituency Commission. The overall number of seats in the Dáil rose from 158 to 160. Eighteen constituencies were completely unchanged, while in some other cases there were minor boundary adjustments. There were only four major changes, in each cases involving significant boundary adjustments: (i) Cavan–Monaghan changed from a four-seat to a five-seat constituency; (ii) Dublin Central changed from a three-seat to a four-seat constituency; (iii) Kildare South changed from a three-seat to a four-seat constituency; (iv) the two three-seat constituencies of Laois and Offaly (re)joined together as one five-seat constituency. Because the Ceann Comhairle, who is deemed automatically re-elected, was returned from Dun Laoghaire in 2016, the number of contested seats there rose from three to four, and since in 2020 the outgoing Ceann Comhairle was a TD from Kildare South, the number of contested seats there remained at three despite the additional seat it received in the pre-election redistricting.

7. This refers to the number of Hare quotas each party's national vote total amounts to; the Hare quota is calculated by dividing the total number of votes (2,183,489) by the number of contested seats (159). Sinn Féin's votes came to 39.0 Hare quotas, Fianna Fáil's to 35.3 and Fine Gael's to 33.2, with Labour at 7.0, Social Democrats 4.6, Solidarity–PBP 4.2, Aontú 3.0, independents 19.6 and all other groups less than 1.

8. Gallagher, 'The results analysed: the aftershocks continue', pp. 137–8.

9. Neither the Green Party nor Labour nor the Social Democrats nominated more than one candidate in any constituency, so the question of internal solidarity did not arise.

10. Gallagher, 'The results analysed: the aftershocks continue', pp. 146–7.

11. Michael Gallagher, 'The election as horse race: betting and the election', pp. 148–66 in Michael Gallagher and Michael Marsh (eds), *How Ireland Voted 2007: the full story of Ireland's general election* (Basingstoke: Palgrave Macmillan, 2008).

12. All odds from www.paddypower.com. The seat figure quoted here is the break-even point, which Fine Gael was seen to have as much chance of exceeding as falling below. Thus, on 14 January, the bookmaker offered the same odds (5–6) that Fine Gael would win more than 49.5 seats as that it would win fewer than 49.5.

13. One exception was Professor Michael Marsh of Trinity College Dublin, whose prediction on 3 February was that Fianna Fáil would win 43 seats, Sinn Féin 42, Fine Gael 34 and the Greens 12; see https://www.rte.ie/news/election-2020/2020/0203/1112736-poll-of-polls/.

14. To be precise, the betting market examined here, that on www.paddypower.com, offered odds for 460 of the 531 candidates. The other 71 were presumably the object of no interest from potential punters, and

indeed they all fared poorly; only two of them qualified for reimbursement of expenses, and only six even received more than 1000 first preferences. The odds used for analysis are those on 7 February, the last day before polling day; by election day itself this market was no longer open. Probabilities are based on the raw odds offered, not adjusting for the overround, that is the amount by which the sum of probabilities of the options exceeds 1.

15. The values are those of Pearson's correlation; a value of 1 indicates a perfect relationship, while a value of zero would indicate no relationship.
16. Gallagher, 'The results analysed: the aftershocks continue', p. 150.
17. Fiona Buckley, Yvonne Galligan and Claire McGing, 'Women and the election: assessing the impact of gender quotas', pp. 185–205 in Michael Gallagher and Michael Marsh (eds), *How Ireland Voted 2016: the election that nobody won* (Cham: Palgrave Macmillan, 2016).
18. For discussion of the reasons for the under-representation of women in parliament, see Yvonne Galligan and Fiona Buckley, 'Women in politics', pp. 216–39 in John Coakley and Michael Gallagher, *Politics in the Republic of Ireland*, 6th ed (London: Routledge and PSAI Press, 2018), pp. 228–30.
19. Ken Carty, 'Another election – but not one to choose a government', www.politicalreform.ie/2020/01/17/another-election-but-not-one-to-choose-a-government/, accessed 7 February 2020.

CHAPTER 9

Geographical Factors in Constituency Voting Patterns

Adrian Kavanagh, William Durkan,
and Caoilfhionn D'Arcy

This chapter focuses on geographical influences on voting behaviour at the 2020 general election. Geography intervenes at various stages and at various levels in electoral processes, but perhaps especially in Ireland, given the high degree of localism that has been traditionally part and parcel of Irish politics. Geography shapes the candidate selection processes of political parties, as discussed in Chap. 3, and, in many cases, shapes the canvassing and vote management strategies employed by these parties, as well as independent candidates. Electoral boundaries again highlight the impact/importance of geography, as these, in part, determine the efficiency by which different political parties translate their vote levels into seats, and changes in constituency boundaries can impact on the electoral prospects of political parties and—particularly—individual candidates. Studies of voting patterns for different parties and different candidates—both at the Dáil constituency level and at the sub-constituency level—show that high

A. Kavanagh (✉) • W. Durkan • C. D'Arcy
Maynooth University, Maynooth, Ireland
e-mail: Adrian.P.Kavanagh@mu.ie

M. Gallagher et al. (eds.), *How Ireland Voted 2020*,
https://doi.org/10.1007/978-3-030-66405-3_9

support levels may be clustered in certain areas for a variety of reasons, including demographic and socio-economic factors, as well as other, more locally focused, reasons. Finally, after the votes have been counted and a new government set in place, geographical factors may be taken into consideration when ministerial and especially junior ministerial positions are being allocated, while policy and spending decisions may also be framed by geographical variables.

HOW PARTIES AND CANDIDATES MAKE USE OF GEOGRAPHY

Any account of geographical influences on voting patterns needs to take account of candidate selection (see Chap. 3 for this process in general). Reflecting what has been termed the 'local orientation of almost all political activity' in Ireland[1] and as discussed in past research by other academics,[2] Ireland is often viewed as having a highly localised style of voting when compared with other western democracies. Election candidates usually rely on a strong support base in their own local area within a given constituency. This 'friends and neighbours' voting pattern means that a candidate's support level is strongest where they reside and radiates from this point, declining with distance.[3] As well as having the advantage of being well known in their local area, or at least better known than candidates hailing from other parts of the constituency, a local candidate will be better able to take advantage of local information flows and use these to gain political advantage and secure higher support levels there. The importance of constituency work within the Irish political system also lends itself to such 'friends and neighbours voting'. People in a local area will tend to vote for the candidate whom they perceive to be most likely to 'work for' that area and gain political benefits for it, and in most cases, this candidate will be one that hails from that area. The importance of establishing a strong local base in a constituency, as well as gaining political experience at a local level, is further highlighted by the high number of former county or city councillors within the Dáil deputy ranks. In the 2020 general election, for instance, 33 of the 56 seats (59 per cent) won by non-incumbents were won by city or county councillors while five more were won by Sinn Féin candidates who were former councillors, having lost their local authority seats only a few months earlier at the May 2019 elections.

The strong degree of localism evident in Irish politics has a bearing on party candidate selection strategies. This, as tantamount to a 'which came first, the chicken or the egg' conundrum, in turn may act to further fuel the strength of strong localistic trends in support patterns for parties and individual candidates. In constituencies where political parties are selecting more than one candidate, candidate selection approaches generally take these 'friends and neighbours' voting trends into account and thus will strive to select candidates from different areas within the constituency. These geographically balanced tickets ensure that the potential party vote may be fully mobilised in different areas within the constituency, and the party does not risk losing local votes in these areas to local candidates from other political parties or groupings, which might be the case if the party opted not to select a candidate from that area. As well as pushing up the size of the party vote in that local area, the selection of a local candidate may also depress the level of local votes that might otherwise be won by other local candidates from other political parties or groupings. A geographically balanced ticket also helps in terms of party vote management strategies. This can help to ensure a relative balance between the numbers of first preference votes won by each of these candidates and help towards maximising the number of seats that party wins in that constituency, especially if an effective vote management strategy has been employed.

Parties often use geographical prompts, such as maps, as a means of implementing vote management strategies. Adverts in local newspapers, campaign leaflets and, to an increasing extent, social media may be used to ask party supporters to vote in line with these strategies. The most effective examples of maps being used in this vein at recent general elections came from the two Healy-Raes in Kerry. In 2016, days after Danny Healy-Rae had announced (minutes before the close of nominations) that he would be contesting the general election, the Healy-Raes placed adverts in local newspapers featuring a map, in which voters were asked to vote No. 1 Danny Healy-Rae and No.2 Michael Healy-Rae in the Greater Killarney area, reflecting the fact that Danny was the only high-profile candidate from that area contesting the election and was thus well placed to win large numbers of local votes there. In the rest of Kerry, voters were asked to vote Michael No. 1, given that he was the more high-profile candidate, and Danny No. 2 (see Fig. 9.1). The use of green and gold, the Kerry county colours, to highlight the two bailiwicks was a clever appeal to Kerry voters. The success of the strategy saw it being used again at the 2020 election, but with one change. The area around Killorglin—the Healy-Raes' home base—had been in Michael's area in 2016 but was established as open territory for the 2020 contest. This reflects how these vote management strategies can be tailored based on evidence from a

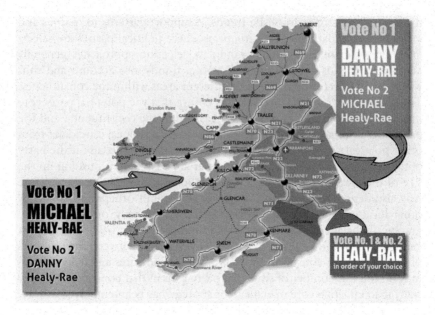

Fig. 9.1 Campaign advertisement used by Michael Healy-Rae and Danny Healy-Rae at the 2020 general election
Source: *The Kerryman*, 5 February 2020, p. 13

previous election. Given that Michael had won over ten thousand more first preference votes than Danny in 2016, the evidence suggested he could afford to cede some more territory to his brother. The purple colour assigned to this open territory may have been a nod to Kerry being known as The Kingdom.

Political parties also employed maps as part of their vote management strategies at the 2020 election. In Donegal, Sinn Féin used a map that asked party voters to give first preference votes to Pearse Doherty in the area that was formerly part of the old Donegal South-West constituency and to Pádraig Mac Lochlainn in the area that was formerly part of Donegal North-East, and to give second preference votes to the running mate. Louth was a constituency where the use of maps for vote management purposes was particularly evident (Fig. 9.2). The three main parties in the constituency—Sinn Féin, Fine Gael and Fianna Fáil—all ran two candidates in this constituency, with one candidate hailing from the

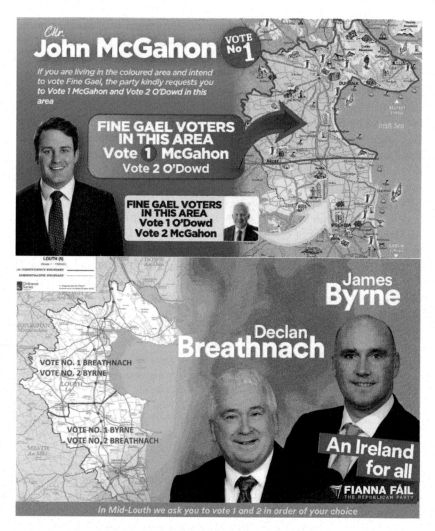

Fig. 9.2 Use of maps to promote party vote management strategies in the Louth constituency, as used by Fine Gael (top) and Fianna Fáil (bottom)
Source: Drawn from the Twitter accounts of councillors John McGahon and John Sheridan respectively

Dundalk area and the other hailing from the Drogheda area. Furthermore, an experienced, sitting TD was joined by a first-time general election candidate on all these tickets.

At the start of the campaign, these three parties all entertained prospects of winning two seats in Louth, although Fine Gael's and Fianna Fáil's ambitions became more tempered as the campaign progressed, and in the final days, the focus was on ensuring they won at least one seat. Fine Gael used a strategy that allocated the Dundalk area (including his home base) to John McGahon, but he was also allocated significant territory in the mid-Louth area, including the town of Ardee. As one local party organiser argued, 'without Ardee, it would have been difficult for John McGahon to have enough votes to stay in the race—as a new candidate he had a lower profile—so the decision was made to allocate Ardee to McGahon'. The sitting Fine Gael deputy, Fergus O'Dowd, was allocated the southern half of the constituency and encouraged to increase his efforts to win votes in the part of east Meath included in this constituency. The use of the map in local newspaper adverts was important not only in terms of applying this constituency divide but also in terms of stressing to McGahon supporters the importance of giving O'Dowd their second preference votes. As the local Fine Gael party official noted,

> First of all, it was a good graphic, so when it went into the papers people were struck by it. I think maps were actually very important during the election. They communicate a lot more than words, visually with the proper text they communicate a lot more than text on its own, I think it was extremely useful in establishing in the minds of the Fine Gael people that there was a game on here and there's rules to the game and we have to follow those rules if we are to get a result.[4]

Given that the two Fine Gael candidates won less than a quota between them (15 per cent of the first preference votes), a solid vote transfer (56 per cent of McGahon's vote on his elimination) between the candidates on the penultimate count ultimately helped secure the Fine Gael seat in Louth.

The Fianna Fáil vote management strategy was similar, with Ardee being assigned to the north Louth candidate, Declan Breathnach, while James Byrne was assigned the southern end of the constituency and Dunleer. The smaller Fianna Fáil share of the vote (14 per cent) meant, however, that there were just not enough votes to make the vote management strategy a success, and Fianna Fáil failed to win a seat here. Sinn Féin also applied a vote management strategy in Louth, with voters in towns in the north of Louth asked to support first-time general election candidate, Ruairí Ó Murchú (who replaced Gerry Adams on the party ticket), while Sinn Féin voters in the south were encouraged to give their first preference votes to incumbent deputy Imelda Munster. Such was the extent of the swing to Sinn Féin in Louth that the strategy ultimately was not required to secure two seats for the party, but it did ensure that both candidates were elected on the first count.

GEOGRAPHIES OF SUPPORT

Each candidate and each political party in Ireland has a unique geography of support and the 2020 election was no different in this regard. The impact of geography was moderated somewhat by the Sinn Féin surge in this election, with its candidates often defying the laws of geographical gravity by faring well in areas that were distant from those candidates' home bases. These geographically defined voting patterns may be attributed to the PR-STV electoral system, which facilitates the expression of localism, as well as the geography of the various socio-economic factors traditionally associated with higher support levels for different political parties. Support patterns may also illustrate an area that has been canvassed thoroughly by a given campaign, stem from a party's effective vote management strategy (as discussed earlier) or simply be shaped by the fact that people often see a local representative as an opportunity to improve services in their locality.

Various socio-economic and demographic factors have been identified by academics as influencing political voting patterns, both internationally and in the Irish context. Age, marital status, housing tenure, employment status, income level, education level and social class are factors that can shape political choices on election day. In the Republic of Ireland, a combination of these factors gives rise to specific geographies of support for the different political parties. Sinn Féin, for instance, has traditionally tended to fare strongly in working-class urban areas and less well in the more middle-class areas, as well as also faring strongly in the border region. While it is interesting to study constituency level support trends, one can only fully understand the political choices that people make through better understanding the nature of the places that they live in and the various factors that shape their lives in these places.

The rest of this chapter will focus on sub-constituency level support patterns for parties and candidates. As well as illustrating how demographic and socio-economic factors impact on political choices at the local level, such studies can also highlight the impacts that local factors, campaigns and candidates may have on political choices. The impact of localism in Ireland is well noted among academics in the field, with different studies highlighting the resultant impact, such as Sacks's study of Fianna Fáil and Fine Gael bailiwicks in Donegal North-East at the 1969 election and Parker's study of Galway West at the 1977 election.[5] This localised impact of a candidate in a given community may be further enhanced by what has been referred to as the 'neighbourhood effect', a process that outlines how political opinion and choice can be shaped by interactions among voters in a given context—effectively a process of conversion through conversation.[6] The constituencies examined in this section reflect the availability of required data (such as tally figures[7] and detailed polling scheme information) to allow for maps and graphs to be drawn up. They also highlight interesting aspects, such as the impacts of 'friends and neighbours' voting, urban–rural variations, socio-demographic influences and county identities, as well as features unique to the 2020 contest, such as the Sinn Féin surge.

Strong evidence of 'friends and neighbours' voting emerges from a study of voting patterns in the largest towns in the Louth constituency. Drogheda-based candidates tended to poll well in Drogheda, while Dundalk-based candidates fared well in that town (Fig. 9.3). What is particularly striking here is the strength of the local Sinn Féin candidates, especially Imelda Munster, in Drogheda and Dundalk, with Sinn Féin winning almost half of the valid votes (49 per cent) cast in Drogheda, for instance. The local Fine Gael and Fianna Fáil candidates did not fare as well, in large part due to the strength of Sinn Féin in both these towns but also due to strong competition from other local candidates, such as Ged Nash in Drogheda and Peter Fitzpatrick and Mark Dearey in Dundalk. The voting trends in Ardee are of interest, given that Ardee effectively lies on the border between the bailiwicks of those candidates located in Dundalk and north Louth and those located in Drogheda and south Louth. Sinn Féin's dominance is again evident here, but what is also evident here is the strength of the more experienced candidates in Ardee, given that, as incumbents, they would have had a longer political relationship with voters in this town than their running mates (all first-time general election candidates). Ardee had been allocated to Munster by Sinn

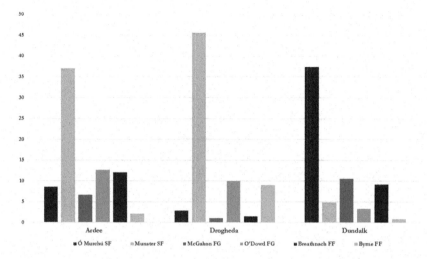

Fig. 9.3 Support levels (percentage) for Sinn Féin, Fine Gael and Fianna Fáil candidates in the three largest towns in Louth at the 2020 general election Source: Based on an analysis of tally figures for the Louth constituency for the 2020 general election, which were provided by Louth Fine Gael constituency organisation

Féin and Breathnach by Fianna Fáil for canvassing purposes, but the town fell within the area assigned to McGahon by Fine Gael. Admittedly, the margin between O'Dowd's and McGahon's vote numbers in Ardee was notably smaller than was the case with the other party candidates, and it could be argued that McGahon's Ardee vote was crucial in ensuring he remained in the race for as long as possible in order to secure one Fine Gael seat in a very competitive Louth constituency.

Turning to the Limerick County constituency, a strong geographical element can be observed in the case of Richard O'Donoghue. A large number of votes from his local area helped him to become the first independent TD to represent the Limerick County constituency (formerly Limerick West). A strong local support base can be viewed radiating from his home village of Granagh, with support levels clearly declining with distance from his home area (Fig. 9.4). O'Donoghue's local strength also made it difficult for competitors to win large numbers of votes from these areas. While the two Fianna Fáil candidates (Niall Collins and Michael

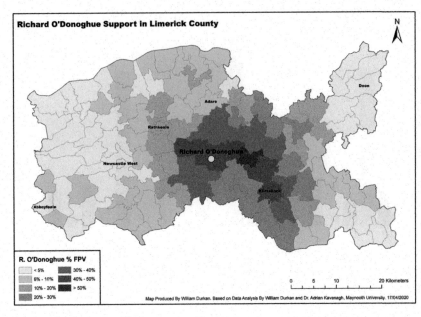

Fig. 9.4 Support levels for Richard O'Donoghue, by electoral division, in the Limerick County constituency

Source: Figures 9.4, 9.5 and 9.6 are based on an analysis of tally figures for the Limerick County constituency, as published in *Limerick Leader* 15 February 2020

Collins) also performed strongly in their local areas, they both struggled to gain a strong share of the votes in the central part of the constituency in which O'Donoghue was extremely successful (Fig. 9.5). In this case the presence of a strong independent candidate, who was formerly a Fianna Fáil councillor, appears to have significantly reduced Fianna Fáil support in central Limerick County.

It was not only Fianna Fáil that failed to appeal to supporters in central parts of Limerick County, with Sinn Féin's Séighin Ó Ceallaigh also winning his lowest levels of support in this area (Fig. 9.6). The most notable pattern for Ó Ceallaigh is the lack of a strong 'friends and neighbours' effect, with high levels of support observed in both urban and rural areas in the east and west of the constituency. This may be due to Ó Ceallaigh's established political base lying outside the constituency boundaries—he had previously served as a councillor in Limerick City—but may also suggest that factors other than local influences shaped the overall level of Sinn

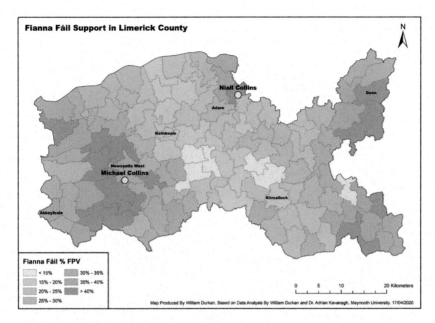

Fig. 9.5 Combined support levels for the Fianna Fáil candidates, by electoral division, in the Limerick County constituency

Féin support in Limerick County. Its low support levels in central areas of Limerick County may have been shaped by the presence of a strong candidate, O'Donoghue, who made a similar appeal to the electorate in terms of providing an 'anti-establishment' option to local voters. Ó Ceallaigh's ability to win healthy levels of support in different parts of the Limerick County constituency reflects a tendency that can be associated with a 'surge election', an ability to win strong levels of support far from your local base—a tendency exemplified by cases such as the Labour Party in 1992 and Sinn Féin in 2020, or by individual candidates, such as Mick Wallace in Wexford in 2011 and Michael Healy-Rae in Kerry in 2016.

Some candidates are consistently strong at appealing to voters from various areas across a constituency in this respect, as illustrated in the maps of support levels within the Limerick City constituency for long-time Fianna Fáil representative Willie O'Dea and his running mate James Collins (Fig. 9.7). There were few areas where O'Dea failed to win at least 10 per cent of the first preference votes, and he won over 25 per cent of the vote in a number of areas, even though the Sinn Féin surge reduced

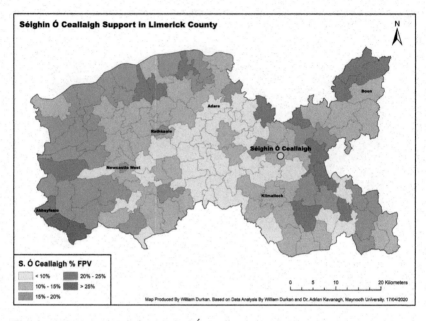

Fig. 9.6 Support levels for Séighin Ó Ceallaigh (Sinn Féin), by electoral division, in the Limerick County constituency

the overall number of first preference votes he would normally expect to win in this constituency. Being on the same ticket as a strong candidate such as O'Dea often poses challenges for party running mates, as was the case for Collins. Collins received less of a widespread distribution in his vote share, and his vote demonstrates a greater degree of localisation than his running mate. His strongest share of the vote was in the Dooradoyle region in the west of the constituency, where he is based, but his support fell to very low levels in other areas. One area where both candidates polled relatively well was the newly added area in the east of the constituency, which lies in County Tipperary. This highlights the importance of electoral boundaries, as well as county identities, but these factors will be even more evident in the next two constituencies to be studied here.

Taylor and Gudgin argue that the translation of votes into seats in any given system depends on the geography of party support within a given state and the nature in which the 'grid' of electoral boundaries is placed upon the geography of support.[8] Hence, the process of revising electoral boundaries can have a profound impact on election results. While the use

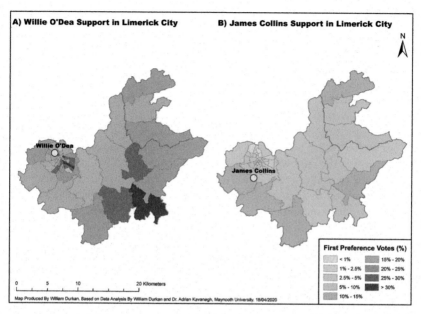

Fig. 9.7 Support levels for Willie O'Dea and James Collins (Fianna Fáil) by electoral division, in the Limerick City constituency
Source: Based on an analysis of tally figures for the Limerick City constituency, as published in *Limerick Leader* 15 February 2020

of an independent commission removes the aspect of party influence and intended bias, any boundary changes can still have unintended impacts. Revisions may impact on candidate support levels within a given constituency, as well as on party and candidate campaigning approaches. This is particularly evident in Ireland when electoral boundaries are seen to breach county boundaries. County identity is a very influential factor in shaping an individual's and a community's sense of place, and its importance is obvious when it comes to topics such as sporting allegiances, but it also has an influence on political identity. The political impact of county identity within a multi-county constituency often leads to a scenario in which candidates receive most of their support from their home county, reinforcing the observed level of 'friends and neighbours' voting. The need to maintain county boundaries 'as far as practicable' is established in the terms of reference set for the Constituency Commission. However, breaches of county boundaries are allowed in order to reduce the degree of variance from the national average representation level. John Coakley argues that 'it is confusing for voters, at best, and deeply alienating' if they 'find themselves transferred, as they see it, out of their own county and into a neighbouring one', something he views as 'a process that is potentially delegitimising'.[9] The extent of county boundary breaches was increased notably by the 2017 Constituency Commission report, even though some observers argued that these could have been limited without unduly impacting on the proportionality principle. There were a number of cases where small portions of counties were joined on to other constituencies, as was the case with the aforementioned Limerick City example.

Another example was the newly enlarged Kildare South constituency, which consisted of areas in three counties, with 9450 individuals located in County Laois and a further 2404 in County Offaly. Voting patterns differed notably between these areas and the parts of the constituency located within County Kildare. For instance, support patterns for the Labour candidate, Mark Wall, not only provide a clear example of a 'friends and neighbours' voting effect (see Fig. 9.8) but also illustrate how county boundaries may have an influence on support patterns. Wall has a high level of support in his home area of Athy, while his vote share declines the further north one travels in Kildare South. As the only Labour candidate in Kildare South, localised voting patterns appear to be the primary driver of support for him, as opposed to party policies or ideological considerations. The one area that demonstrates a notable variation from the overall Wall support patterns is the part of the constituency located within Laois and Offaly. For instance, Wall won over 17 per cent of the vote in the Quinsborough electoral division (located in Kildare), but received less than 1 per cent of the total vote in the neighbouring Portarlington North electoral division (located in Offaly), thus demonstrating the common pattern whereby a candidate's support tends to decrease when moving outside their home county.

First-time independent candidate, Cathal Berry, by contrast, won a strong level of support in the areas located in Laois and Offaly, winning over 40 per cent of the first preference votes cast in these areas. He experienced a notable drop in support immediately after crossing the Kildare County boundary, taking less than 10 per cent of the vote in the Monasterevin area. However, Berry also won over 40 per cent of the first preference votes in the Ballysax East electoral division in central Kildare, despite this being geographically removed from his home area. During his campaign, Berry, himself a former Irish Army officer, frequently appealed

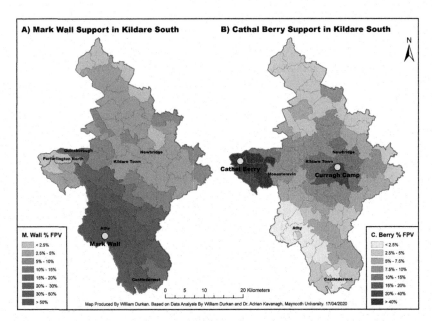

Fig. 9.8   Support levels for Mark Wall (Labour) and Cathal Berry (Independent), by electoral division, in the Kildare South constituency
Source: Based on an analysis of tally figures for the Kildare South constituency, which were provided by Cllr. Pádraig McEvoy (Independent) and the Kildare South Fine Gael constituency organisation

to members of the defence forces and outlined the need to better address concerns relevant to them, which was reflected in high level of support observed for him in the areas around the Curragh army camp. This was further highlighted when examining the postal votes in Kildare South. Berry received 583 postal votes, over two-thirds of those available.[10] Overall, Berry's strong localised support base outside of County Kildare and his appeal to members of a select demographic group within the constituency ensured a successful election campaign for him.

The 2017 Constituency Commission report resulted in some areas being joined with Dáil constituencies with which they previously had no political connection, as with the parts of Laois and Offaly that were added to the Kildare South constituency. By contrast, the (re)creation of a five-seat Laois–Offaly constituency saw the re-establishment of a two-county constituency that had been in existence from the foundation of the state up to the 2016 general election. The 2012 Constituency Commission report had recommended the creation of two new three-seat constituencies: Laois (including a portion of south-west Kildare) and Offaly (including a much larger portion of north Tipperary). The existence of these three-seaters was very short-lived, even though the recreation of a five-seat Laois–Offaly effectively resulted in the loss of a seat by a region that had one of the highest levels of population increase in the state in the 2000s. As a longer established two-county constituency, county loyalties have not traditionally been as absolute in determining political preferences in Laois–Offaly as would be the case with other two-county constituencies with shorter histories of political association. In past elections, some candidates traditionally were able to secure relatively high levels of support in areas that were located outside their home county, as was the case with Fianna Fáil's Ger Connolly, an Offaly candidate who was strong in north-east Laois—an area that was admittedly close to his Bracknagh home base—across the elections he contested between 1969 and 1992. Moreover, the Fine Gael candidates could often rely on strong support bases outside their own counties. These trends were highlighted in a study of the 1992 election in Laois–Offaly.[11]

In 2020, however, county loyalties were very much to the fore in shaping support levels for the four Fianna Fáil candidates (Fig. 9.9). The two Offaly-based candidates, Barry Cowen and Peter Ormond, fared significantly better in Offaly than in Laois, with the reverse trend observed for the Laois-based candidates (although one of Pauline Flanagan's strongest areas was in Offaly). Both Fine Gael candidates, Charlie Flanagan and Marcella Corcoran Kennedy, also failed to poll well outside their home county.

Two candidates who polled well in areas outside their home counties were incumbent TDs Brian Stanley and Carol Nolan. Stanley was the only Sinn Féin candidate in this constituency and fared very well in this election, particularly in Laois, given that his political base is in Portlaoise. Such was the extent of the Sinn Féin surge in this election that he also polled well in some parts of Offaly (Fig. 9.10). He did not fare well in areas where strong local candidates vied to win large shares of the local vote, namely south-west and north-west Offaly. Four strong local candidates in south-west Offaly were effectively competing for the last seat in Laois–Offaly—Ormond, Corcoran–Kennedy, Nolan and former Renua leader John Leahy—while Cowen polled strongly in Clara (the Cowen family base) and Tullamore (his home). Stanley won more votes than any other

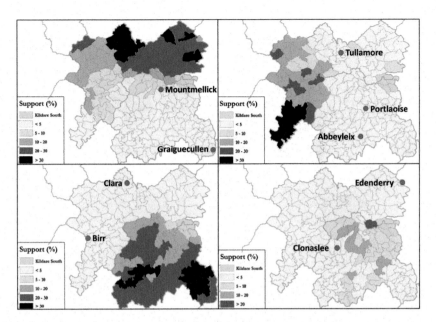

Fig. 9.9 Support levels for the Fianna Fáil candidates, by electoral division, in the Laois–Offaly constituency
Note: Maps relate to support for Barry Cowen (top left), Peter Ormond (top right), Seán Fleming (bottom left) and Pauline Flanagan (bottom right)
Source: Based on an analysis of tally figures for the Laois–Offaly constituency, which were published in a series of articles by Stephen Miller on the *Laois Today* online newspaper website between 14 and 21 February 2020

candidate in the Edenderry electoral area in north-east Offaly, however. The only strong local candidate in this area was Pippa Hackett of the Green Party, and her support levels were not particularly locally focused. Carol Nolan, who had been elected as a Sinn Féin TD in 2016 but left the party in 2018, not only fared well in her home base in west Offaly but also succeeded in winning high vote numbers in areas across the county boundary, such as the town of Clonaslee. She also tended to fare especially well in the areas where Stanley's support was lowest—a pattern that one would normally associate with party running mates, even though Nolan was no longer a member of Sinn Féin. Leahy fared strongly in west Offaly also, but his vote levels collapsed once the county boundary was crossed and his weakness in Laois ultimately prevented him from being in contention for

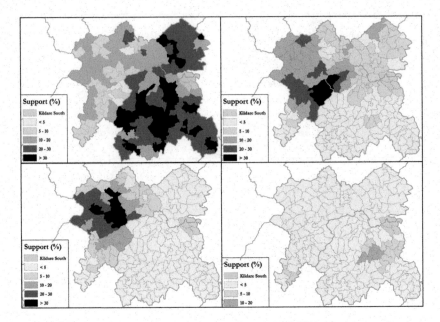

Fig. 9.10 Support levels for candidates in the Laois–Offaly constituency, by electoral division
Note: Maps relate to support for Brian Stanley (Sinn Féin) (top left), Carol Nolan (Independent) (top right), John Leahy (Independent) (bottom left) and Noel Tuohy (Labour) (bottom right)
Source: Based on an analysis of tally figures for the Laois–Offaly constituency, which were published in a series of articles by Stephen Miller on the *Laois Today* online newspaper website between 14 and 21 February 2020

the final seat here. Support patterns for Labour's Noel Tuohy saw a similar focus on his home area and home county, although he did have a pocket of support in Dunkerrin in Offaly.

Class factors were also evident in the support levels in Laois–Offaly, with Stanley winning his highest vote levels in the polling stations in Portlaoise that were associated with areas with high levels of local authority housing. Class impacts on turnout can be easier to detect, however, in the more urban areas, given that higher levels of social mix in more rural areas can limit the impact of class effects on support patterns. Higher levels of social stratification in the larger cities, especially in the Dublin

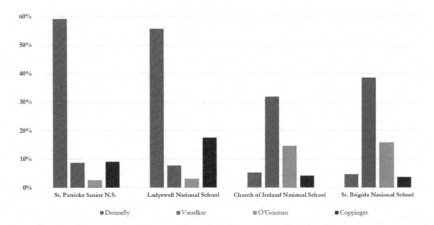

Fig. 9.11 Support levels for candidates at different polling stations in the Dublin West constituency at the 2020 general election
Source: Based on an analysis of tally figures for the Dublin West constituency, which were provided by Deputy Roderic O'Gorman

constituencies, allow for class effects on voting patterns to be easier to detect. In Dublin West, for instance, there were notable variations in candidate support levels among polling stations located in different parts of that constituency, with very different voting patterns evident in the more working-class areas in Mulhuddart and Tyrrelstown as compared with the more middle-class Castleknock area. Sinn Féin's Paul Donnelly topped the poll in Dublin West, and he fared especially well in polling stations located in the more working-class parts of the constituency, as was also the case for Solidarity's Deputy Ruth Coppinger (Fig. 9.11). In the more working-class parts of the constituency, Donnelly and Coppinger, between them, won 73 per cent of the vote in the Ladyswell National School polling station and 68 per cent of the vote in the St. Patrick's Senior National School polling station, but they won only 8 per cent of the vote in St. Brigid's National School, which was located in the more middle-class Castleknock area. Taoiseach Leo Varadkar, by contrast, tended to fare notably better in the more middle-class areas in Dublin West, so his vote share was inversely correlated with that of Donnelly, with similar support patterns also evidenced for the Green Party's Roderic O'Gorman. It would be mistaken to infer that support patterns in urban constituencies, such as Dublin West, are solely down to class effects, as 'friends and neighbours' voting is also evidenced in these. In most cases, class effects act in tandem with local candidate effects in these constituencies. In the case of Dublin West, the strength of Varadkar and O'Gorman in Castleknock may be attributed, in part, to class effects, but also reflects the fact that their political bases lie within the Castleknock area. Geography matters in Dublin too; as Fine Gael minister Richard Bruton has said, Dublin is still a 'City of Villages'.[12]

CONCLUSION

This chapter offers a brief overview of how geographical factors influenced voting at the 2020 general election. Perhaps not surprisingly, given that Irish elections are fought on the basis of geographically defined constituencies, geography has been shown to be key to various aspects of the 2020 election. Even though the Sinn Féin surge tempered this somewhat in 2020, localism again was to the fore and most candidates still tended to win their highest levels of support in and around their local areas, even though technological and societal developments might lead one to expect that the effects of localism would no longer be pronounced. The geographies of different socio-economic and demographic factors also helped to influence the geographies of support for different candidates and parties, with such influences being especially evident in the more urban constituencies. Further complicating the picture, the impacts of electoral boundary changes, especially when these involved breaches of county boundaries, also shaped the extent to which these factors impacted on support patterns and success levels, as evidenced in this chapter. Ultimately, people live, socialise and work in places, and these places will help frame the political decisions made by people, as was very much the case at the 2020 election.

NOTES

1. Michael Gallagher, 'Candidate selection in Ireland: the impact of localism and the electoral system', *British Journal of Political Science* 10:4 (1980), pp. 489–503, at p. 491.
2. J. P. O'Carroll, 'Strokes, cute hoors and sneaking regarders: the influence of local culture on Irish political style', *Irish Political Studies* 2:1 (1987), pp. 77–92.

3. Adrian Kavanagh, 'All changed, changed utterly? Irish general election boundary amendments and the 2012 Constituency Commission report', *Irish Political Studies* 29:2 (2014), pp. 215–35, at p. 224.
4. Confidential interview with a local Fine Gael party official.
5. Paul M. Sacks, 'Bailiwicks, locality and religion: three elements in an Irish Dáil constituency election', *Economic and Social Review* 1:4 (1970), pp. 531–54; A. J. Parker, 'The "friends and neighbours" voting effect in the Galway West constituency', *Political Geography Quarterly* 1: 3 (1982), pp. 243–62.
6. Ron Johnston et al., 'The neighbourhood effect and voting in England and Wales: real or imagined?', *British Elections & Parties Review* 10:1 (2009), pp. 47–63.
7. General election results in the Republic of Ireland are published officially only for the constituency level. However, as polling boxes (which relate to specific areas within a constituency) are opened at the start of the election count, party officials keep a tally of how many votes have been won by each candidate in those boxes and these tally figures give a detailed geographical breakdown of the votes won by each candidate/party at the sub-constituency level.
8. Peter Taylor and Graham Gudgin, *Seats, Votes and the Spatial Organisation of Elections* (London: ECPR Press, 2012).
9. John Coakley, 'Fixed-boundary constituencies and the principle of equal representation in Ireland', *Irish Political Studies* 30:4 (2015), pp. 531–54, at p. 550.
10. It is worth noting that members of the Irish Army posted overseas are among the few electors entitled to vote by postal ballot.
11. Michael Gallagher, 'Politics in Laois–Offaly 1922–1992', pp. 657–87 in Padraig G. Lane and William Nolan (eds), *Laois History & Society: interdisciplinary essays on the history of an Irish county* (Dublin: Geography Publications, 1999), pp. 676–8.
12. Research interview with Deputy Richard Bruton, 3 October 2019.

CHAPTER 10

Voting Behaviour: The Sinn Féin Election

Kevin Cunningham and Michael Marsh

The 2020 election was historic in that it saw a party other than Fianna Fáil and Fine Gael win the popular vote. That this party was Sinn Féin, a relatively new electoral force, and one clearly on the left rather than the centre or right of the political spectrum, made the change even more significant. The success of Sinn Féin meant that, together with other centre-left and left-wing parties, the left was on a par with the total number of votes won by Fianna Fáil and Fine Gael. This chapter explores what lies behind the rise of Sinn Féin and, by extension, the left in this election.

The decline of Fianna Fáil and Fine Gael follows a 40-year trend in Irish politics where the total vote share won by these two parties has fallen by an average of just over 8 per cent per decade. Crucially, this period is also one of significant social change in terms of educational attainment, migration, religious adherence and home ownership. The proportion of the population with a second-level education and a third-level education has increased substantially as the country has shifted from one of net

K. Cunningham
Technological University Dublin, Dublin, Ireland

M. Marsh (✉)
Department of Political Science, Trinity College Dublin, Dublin, Ireland
e-mail: MMARSH@tcd.ie

© The Author(s), under exclusive license to Springer Nature
Switzerland AG 2021
M. Gallagher et al. (eds.), *How Ireland Voted 2020*,
https://doi.org/10.1007/978-3-030-66405-3_10

emigration to net immigration, church-going has fallen sharply and home ownership has declined substantially. These significant changes yield different experiences and perspectives between generations of voters. Waves of new voters have had a profound effect on Irish politics. As a marker of this sociological change, the period is bookended by referendums which, in 1983, enshrined constitutional restrictions on abortion and then, in 2018, abolished those constitutional restrictions. Ireland's 'politics without social bases' has, in 2020, perhaps given way to an emerging left and right based on more conventional social divisions.

However, there remains a puzzle. This change in the party system was far from predictable. Firstly, the benefit from the decline of the 'big two' over ten elections has accrued to a range of different parties and groupings to varying degrees whose fortunes have waxed and waned: most notably the Progressive Democrats in 1987, Labour (1992 and 2011), independents and most recently Sinn Féin. And secondly, coming into this election Sinn Féin had performed poorly. The party declined for the first time in its recent history in the 2019 local and European elections, winning 9 and 12 per cent, respectively. Across four by-elections on 29 November 2019, 71 days before the general election, the party's vote averaged 0.5 per cent lower than its 2016 vote in the same constituencies. These are second-order elections where opposition parties are expected to overperform. Yet at some point thereafter Sinn Féin support rose dramatically.

While long-term trends influence electoral outcomes, each election also has its own dynamics driven by the context of the election. Governments are also evaluated by their performance or position on the issues that are important to voters at that time. Typically, the most prominent issue is that of the economy.[1] One issue in this election that was prominent was housing. This may have been critical as it is an issue that reflected an immediate economic grievance while also dividing the country along the aforementioned sociological divisions.

In this chapter we explore the key drivers of voting behaviour at this election. We will look at how long-run sociological changes and short-run economic grievances provide clues to our understanding of why and how Sinn Féin performed so well. One of the first features we explore is party identification, the long-run loyalty voters have to their chosen party. We evaluate whether this has continued to decline and how it may have influenced volatility in the run-up to the election. We then explore the role of social bases: whether generational and economic divisions of age, education, class, income, religious adherence and home ownership reflect emerging divisions in the political system. Then we look to features unique to this election. Firstly, how perceptions of the economy influenced vote choice, support for or opposition to the government. And secondly, we explore the issues that were prominent in the election—the role of housing and the decline in significance of Brexit and the consequences of that. We then look at ideology, the role of left and right and also briefly the influence of populism. Finally, we explore evidence on the impact of party leaders and candidates. First, we explore the timing of the election decision.

This chapter makes use of evidence from the series of polls for various newspapers, as well as special polls funded wholly or in part by academic sources to enable us to maintain the sort of analyses started by the Irish National Election Study, which since 2007 has regrettably no longer been funded by the Irish Research Council. These comprise the MRBI exit poll, funded by the *Irish Times*, RTÉ, TG4 and UCD; an Ireland Thinks online exit poll, part-funded by UCD, completed on the day of the election; and an online poll carried out after the election in the first half of March, by RED C with funding from TCD and UCC. These are referred to below as the MRBI exit poll, the Ireland Thinks online poll and the RED C post-election poll.[2]

LATE DECIDERS

It is clear that Sinn Féin did not expect electoral success in 2020. Had it done so, it would have nominated more candidates and finished as the largest party in the Dáil (by up to 14 seats, as discussed in Chap. 8). The first poll published in the campaign (though taken by B&A before it started) featured a very strong showing for Fianna Fáil (at 32, up 5) and a collapse in the vote of Fine Gael (20, down 7). While Sinn Féin polled relatively well (at 19), this was not out of the ordinary for this firm, which had recorded similar figures previously. Three more firms released start-of-campaign polls within a week, all showing the Sinn Féin vote up between 5 and 8 per cent compared to the end of 2019 (see Fig. 1.1 on p. 9).

Figure 10.1 shows this and later campaign polls as well as the final result, set against where the polls stood at the close of the year. The trend during the campaign is also clear: Sinn Féin rose and Fianna Fáil declined sharply on the B&A poll. The dashed lines in Fig. 10.1 show respective poll standings in December (when there was just one poll, also by B&A), based on smoothed trends to that point.[3] This emphasises how far up was support for Sinn Féin by January, and how far down was that for Fine

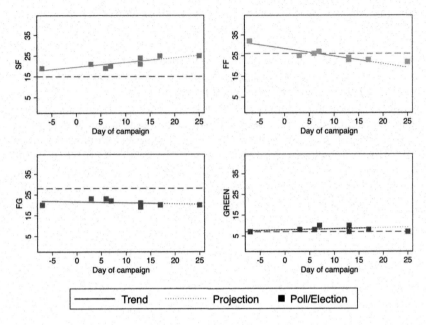

Fig. 10.1 Campaign polls in 2020, linear trend line projected to election result, and average poll support at end of 2019
Note: Dashed line indicates average poll standings at the end of 2019

Gael. Sinn Féin support had been around 20 per cent early in 2019, but its poor showing in the May elections was followed by much lower ratings in the second part of the year.

For Fianna Fáil, this first poll enabled the party to dream, only for later ones, and the count, to provide a very rude awakening. As Fig. 10.1 shows, the campaign polls were consistent in showing Sinn Féin support continuing to go upwards and Fianna Fáil dropping back. Sinn Féin's rise did in part pre-date the campaign, but January saw the party build on that increase very effectively. Its final result was up six points on the initial B&A poll, whereas Fianna Fáil dropped even more sharply.

The initial January poll may have exaggerated support for Fianna Fáil, but it is clear that this election gave us a result that was not what might have been expected in the autumn of 2019. The difference cannot be down simply to the campaign, since a significant part of the rise in Sinn Féin support, and fall in support for Fianna Fáil and Fine Gael, pre-dated any real campaign activity, let alone the publication of manifestos and TV debates. Arguably, voters in the last few weeks of the old government were thinking more seriously about the next election than they might have been a month or so earlier, but there was never much doubt that there would be an election in the spring of 2020.

Clearly, many voters decided to vote Sinn Féin between December 2019 and February 2020; some during the campaign, and some before. Asked by the MRBI exit poll (see Table 10.1) when they made up their mind, voters split evenly between pre-campaign and campaign deciders. However, the split is more akin to that seen 20 years ago than was the case in 2011 and 2016, with almost half of all voters claiming that they made up their mind before the election was called. Those deciding during the campaign were relatively unlikely to support Fianna Fáil: 42 per cent of its voters did so, compared with 50 per cent of those opting for Sinn Féin and 53 per cent of those choosing Fine Gael. It was a poor campaign for Fianna Fáil. These voting for the smaller parties and independents also decided late, a typical enough pattern.

Among those who decided before the campaign, 62 per cent had a poor evaluation of the government in contrast to 49 per cent among those who decided during the campaign and 44 per cent among those who decided on polling day or the eve of the poll. In Fig. 10.2 we can see more details on the party choice by the timing of decision. Of those voters who decided before the election was called (but who did not always vote that way), Sinn Féin won a substantial proportion and also did relatively well among those deciding in the early phases of the campaign. Of course, this is based on retrospective evaluations of voters about when they decided to vote for their chosen party, but it does provide further indications of a significant shift occurring prior to the campaign.[4]

Table 10.1   Reported time of decision 1997–2020

	1997	2002	2007	2011	2016	2020
Day of the election, or day before	12	10	13	20	15	8
Week of election	15	14	17	21	21	16
2–3 weeks before	25	30	22	23	23	28
Before election called	48	46	48	36	41	48
Total	100	100	100	100	100	100

Source: RTÉ exit polls 1997–2020

Note: The 2020 question used the terms 'during campaign', 'in the last couple of days' and 'today/when casting my vote' for the three campaign timings

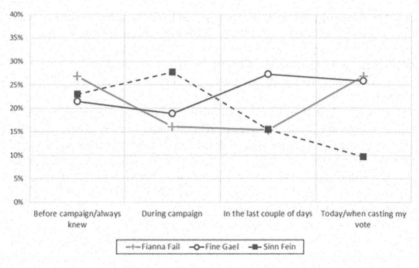

Fig. 10.2   Party support by timing of voting intention
Source: MRBI exit poll

PARTY LOYALTY AND CHANGE

The volatility we observe in the campaign is understandable when we look at party loyalty. How susceptible was the system to change and who exactly changed their vote? Was there an unusual level of volatility in this election? How does this election differ from previous elections?

Partisanship, where it exists, ensures some level of stability. Without that loyalty, unpopular parties have less of a cushion. Those who are 'close' to their party have been shown to be far more likely to vote the same way in successive elections,[5] and indeed, the habit of voting the same way also builds up closeness. Partisanship has declined substantially in the last half-century. In the 1970s, more than half of all voters felt 'close' to a particular party, typically Fianna Fáil or Fine Gael. Thus, throughout more turbulent economic periods in the 1980s, party support remained relatively stable. By 2007 less than a third felt close, and since the economic crisis that figure has fallen further: 22 per cent in 2011 and 27 per cent in 2016.[6]

In 2020 the number for those who felt close to a party was just 24 per cent (Ireland Thinks online poll).[7] Fine Gael and Fianna Fáil supporters constituted most of these, 8 per cent each, with Sinn Féin 4 per cent. Not all those close to a party give it their first preference, but such supporters contributed a quarter of the Fianna Fáil vote and closer to a third of that for Fine Gael. In contrast, those close to Sinn Féin accounted for just 15 per cent of its support. Having lost support, Fianna Fáil and Fine Gael might be somewhat closer to what one might consider to be their 'core vote', while the Sinn Féin tally in 2020 invariably consists of a substantial number of people who voted for the party for the first time and who do not (yet perhaps) feel close to it.

Table 10.2 shows the turnover of voters, based on respondents' recall of how they voted in 2016.[8] Only the largest four parties hung on to at least half their supporters, with Sinn Féin having the highest retention rate. Sinn Féin picked up support from everywhere. While the party picked up a higher share of the vote from smaller left-wing parties, in aggregate it collected more votes from Fianna Fáil and Fine Gael together, because that pool of votes was much larger. The number of cases here for the minor parties is generally small, but the data suggest that Fianna Fáil and Fine Gael won very few votes from them; Sinn Féin was generally the major beneficiary when voters moved, including those who moved from Fianna Fáil. As we have seen before, though, voters do move in all directions.

Table 10.2   Party support in 2020 by recalled vote in 2016

| | *Recalled vote choice in 2016* | | | | | | | | | |
	SF	*FF*	*FG*	*Grn*	*Lab*	*SD*	*A–PBP*	*Ind*	*Oth*	*Total*
Sinn Féin	77	13	8	6	18	29	39	28	27	25
Fianna Fáil	4	64	12	0	3	4	3	11	14	22
Fine Gael	3	7	60	10	14	9	0	6	32	21
Green	4	2	6	66	15	23	4	7	0	7
Labour	1	1	2	0	36	0	0	4	0	4
Soc Dems	1	1	1	12	6	25	2	4	0	3
Sol–PBP	2	1	0	2	3	7	35	1	0	3
Independent	5	7	9	2	2	4	17	35	15	12
Other	3	4	2	1	2	0	0	4	12	3
Total	100	100	100	100	100	100	100	100	100	100

Source: Ireland Thinks exit poll

Note: Cell entries are percentages. Data is adjusted to conform to actual results in 2020. Excludes those who could not remember or did not vote in 2016. 'A–PBP' refers to the AAA–PBP alliance; the AAA (Anti-Austerity Alliance) changed its name to Solidarity in March 2017

If we group the parties roughly into those that tend to lean towards the right (Fine Gael and Fianna Fáil) and parties that tend to lean towards the left (Sinn Féin, Green, Labour, Social Democrats and Solidarity–PBP), then the left kept 83 per cent of its 2016 vote while the right kept 71 per cent. Those leaving one of the two centre-right parties split 17–11 in favour of the left as against independents and others, while left voters divided evenly between the other two options. Those leaving independents and others split 42–20 for the left.

The Ireland Thinks online, MRBI exit and final RED C polls indicate that between 40 and 45 per cent of voters changed their vote from the last election. (The small group of others, and independents, are each treated as single parties for this exercise, almost certainly exaggerating stability.) The figure is similar to that in 2016, when the RTÉ exit poll indicated a figure of 42 per cent, suggesting less mobility than in 2011 (48 per cent), but much more than in 2002 and 2007, when it was closer to 30 per cent.[9]

Table 10.2 does not include those who said they did not vote in 2016, who comprised 8 per cent of the sample. These favoured leftist parties in 2020, with only 12 per cent opting for Fianna Fáil and 18 per cent for Fine Gael. The Greens did particularly well here, both among those too young in 2016 and those who simply did not previously vote, winning 18 per cent. Sinn Féin won 27 per cent, only just above its success rate among those who did vote last time.[10]

As we might expect with declining partisanship, voters have become more volatile and less loyal. However, although Sinn Féin has fewer partisan supporters, its success is not solely a result of rudderless volatility. While we might expect younger voters to have the weakest affiliations, it is in fact those under 35 that are most likely to say they feel close to their party of choice: 34 per cent do so as against 22 per cent of those aged 35–54 and 26 per cent of those 55 and over. In that younger group, Sinn Féin affiliation is on a par with Fine Gael and slightly ahead of that for Fianna Fáil.

POLITICS WITH SOCIAL BASES

If the rise of Sinn Féin has been consistent with social change, we might expect the party's rise to be concentrated among those aged under 50, or linked to low religiosity. If economic, we might expect social class, income or, indeed, housing status to be more relevant. In 2016, we saw Sinn Féin perform very well among younger voters, being the most popular party in the 18–30 age group.[11] While this may have indicated future promise, that group is only a small part of the electorate and typically an even smaller one in terms of those voting. While Sinn Féin continued to make big gains among the newer generations of voters, it also increased support substantially among older age groups (see Table 10.3). Sinn Féin rose in all age groups bar the oldest one by between 11 and 15 points, and even among those over 65 support was up by 6 points. Age is no longer an important defining feature of Sinn Féin support. The Sinn Féin voter is now, on average, older than we have seen in previous elections. A rough estimate is that the average Sinn Féin voter is 42, continuing a trend up from 35 years old in 2002. It was the largest party in all age groups bar those 65 and over, and the largest by some margin among those 18–35.

Age is more clearly linked to the Fianna Fáil vote, and only among those 65 and over does the combined vote of Fianna Fáil and Fine Gael exceed 50 per cent: even then they win under 60 per cent. Among those under 35 the combined vote for the two parties amounts to less than one-third of all voters. The Green Party did best among younger voters (13 per cent) but is far from being confined to that age cohort. The left group of parties as defined earlier is dominant among those under 35 and has parity with Fianna Fáil/Fine Gael in the 35–64 age group. This may be a pointer to the future, but the support of younger voters is more fragile. In general, change in support relative to 2016 was associated with age: 54 per cent of those under 30 changed their party preference from 2016 as opposed to

Table 10.3   Age and vote in 2020

	18–24	24–34	35–49	50–64	65+
Sinn Féin	35	35	25	26	14
Fianna Fáil	13	15	22	22	30
Fine Gael	14	16	20	21	29
Green	13	8	8	6	4
Labour	2	4	4	4	4
Social Democrats	4	4	3	3	2
Sol–PBP	7	4	3	2	2
Independent	9	11	12	13	12
Other	3	3	3	3	3
Total	100	100	100	100	100
Combined left	61	55	43	41	26
Share of total	7	15	28	29	21

Source: MRBI exit poll (weighting to actual results)

just 39 per cent of those over 65. Overall, given the rise of Sinn Féin and the party's (albeit less defined) age profile, it is clear that age does define the party system more than it has typically done in the past.

Religious practice is also linked clearly to party support. The largest group (45 per cent) here say they never attend church, with only 19 per cent attending at least weekly. In the 1980s, weekly attendance was the practice of a sizeable majority, and only a very small number never went. Sinn Féin is almost three times as popular among those who never go to church as it is among those who attend at least weekly; Fianna Fáil is very much a mirror image of Sinn Féin (Table 10.4). The left as a whole gets 21 per cent of the votes of weekly attenders as against 56 per cent of the vote from those who say they never go. Interestingly, Fine Gael support varies little between weekly and occasional, though drops off a little more sharply among those who never attend church.

Support for Sinn Féin has always been stronger amongst the less well off. Did this election see a weakening of its class basis, with broader support across all groups, or did it perhaps strengthen that base still further? There was no class variable in the MRBI exit poll in 2020, and the sample size in the campaign polls is rather small for detailed analysis, so we use the RED C online poll here. It is clear from Table 10.5 that Sinn Féin was much more successful in the working-class C2DE group than the middle-class ABC1 and that Fine Gael was more successful among middle-class voters. Fianna Fáil, by contrast, is a cross-class party. The left in general

Table 10.4 Religious attendance and vote in 2020

	Weekly	Monthly	Occasional	Never
Sinn Féin	12	20	22	32
Fianna Fáil	36	29	23	14
Fine Gael	27	23	24	18
Green	3	3	7	10
Labour	3	5	4	4
Social Democrats	2	1	2	5
Sol–PBP	1	1	1	5
Independent	11	14	13	11
Other	6	4	4	1
Total	100	100	100	100
Combined left	21	30	38	56
Share of total	19	13	23	45

Source: Ireland Thinks exit poll (adjusted to actual party choice and age of voter)

Table 10.5   Class and vote in 2020

Party	Social class		
	ABC1	C2DE	Farmers
Sinn Féin	16	33	8
Fianna Fáil	22	23	33
Fine Gael	27	14	41
Green	10	4	3
Labour	5	5	0
Soc Dems	4	1	1
Sol–PBP	3	3	1
Independents	12	14	11
Others	2	3	1
Total	100	100	100
Share of sample	44	50	6

Source: RED C post-election poll (adjusted to actual party choice and age of voter)

seems to have no strong class basis, and not just because the Green vote is more middle class: Labour and perhaps surprisingly Solidarity–PBP also seem to be cross class, but the Ns are small for these minor parties. Since 2016, Sinn Féin has increased its support among middle-class voters by 7 percentage points and among working-class voters by 13. The party has maintained a ratio of 2 to 1 working-class to middle-class voters. Fine Gael has lost 3 and 4 per cent of its middle- and working-class voters. In losing a larger proportion of its working-class vote, the party edged much closer to an equivalent 2 to 1 ratio of middle-class to working-class vote. This can be compared with the last pre-election MRBI poll in February 2020 that suggested that relative to the 2016 exit poll, Sinn Féin was up 9 points among ABC1s and 14 points among C2DEs. This suggests that the Sinn Féin vote is a little more class defined than it was. Three quarters of all farmers still vote for Fine Gael or Fianna Fáil: not much change there, although almost 90 per cent did so in 2007.

In 2016, there was a contrast in the degree of class voting between Dublin and the rest of the country, with Sinn Féin 19 points more successful among working-class Dubliners than middle-class ones, and Fine Gael 13 points more successful among the middle class than it was among working-class Dubliners. These differences were much more stark than those outside the capital in 2016.[12] Yet, this time there is no such difference. The working-class bias towards Sinn Fein is +17 in Dublin and +17 elsewhere. However, the middle-class Fine Gael bias is −5 and −15, suggesting that it is pronounced only outside Dublin this time. (Overall, the two major class groups are much the same size, but the middle class is larger in Dublin and the working class predominates elsewhere.)

Arguably though, it is increasingly difficult to measure social grade due to changes in the structure of work, management and job titles. Many on lower social grades have higher incomes and job security than those on higher social grades. For a more extensive understanding, we can look at the relationship between self-reported income and vote. While support for Fianna Fáil is uncorrelated with income, it is notable that there is a strong relationship between income and vote choice for both Sinn Féin and Fine Gael voters.

Sinn Féin has a lead among those earning under €20,000 with 33 per cent of the vote from this low-income group. Support is just 16 per cent among those earning over €40,000. Support for Fine Gael increases substantially with income, from 14 per cent in the lowest group to 29 per cent in the most affluent one, while Fianna Fáil support is relatively flat. Votes for the left as a whole range from 50 per cent in the lowest-income group to just 35 per cent in the highest, but most of this difference is accounted for by Sinn Féin voters. In other words, the left that does not include Sinn Féin wins 17 per cent in the poorest group and 18 per cent in the most affluent one. We can see a similar division in the left vote in terms of educational attainment.

In many countries educational attainment is an emerging cleavage in party systems and particularly associated with support for populism.[13] In Ireland, this is complicated by substantial changes in access to education over 40 years. The 2016 census indicates that 58 per cent of those aged over 50 had no education beyond secondary school, as against just 23 per cent among those under 50. It makes sense therefore to separate educational attainment by age group, as we do in Table 10.6. Age is a significant factor, as we saw in Table 10.3, but education matters: in each of the four

Table 10.6   Vote in 2020 by age and level of educational attainment

Demographic	FF	FG	SF	Other left	Other	Total
Over 50 and no third level	29	24	19	15	13	100
Over 50 and has third level	24	37	16	17	6	100
Under 50 and no third level	19	13	33	21	14	100
Under 50 and has third level	18	20	24	28	10	100

Note: 'Other left' includes Green Party, Labour, Social Democrats, Solidarity–PBP. The strongest bloc within each demographic category is indicated in bold.

Source: MRBI exit poll

sections of the electorate a different party or grouping leads. Fianna Fáil leads with older voters without a third-level degree, Fine Gael among older voters with a third-level degree, Sinn Féin with younger voters without third level and the smaller left-wing parties among younger voters with a third-level qualification.

Thus, we can see how the Sinn Féin vote has reflected social change, winning more from (relatively) younger voters, from those no longer (or never) under church influence, but also those missing out on higher education. But this hardly explains its support: we need to explore issues that might underpin that vote.

These social differences observed are also reflected in housing status. According to the RED C post-election survey, Sinn Féin won 35 per cent of the vote among those that rent privately, more than Fianna Fáil (14 per cent) and Fine Gael (17 per cent) together. This is a particularly significant part of the electorate as it has increased substantially as a share of the population from 8 per cent in 1991 to 20 per cent in 2016, and further in the years since the most recent census. Developments in the housing market have a profound effect on society. And as we will see, as an issue housing was the most salient one for the three years leading up to the election.

Support for Fianna Fáil and Fine Gael is less well defined, but where it is, each appears as the mirror of Sinn Féin. Fianna Fáil exceeds 30 per cent only among those that attend church on a weekly basis and among those aged over 65. The party has 29 per cent of the vote among those both over 50 and without a third-level education. Support for Fine Gael is larger among those that are more affluent; it exceeds 30 per cent only among those over 50 with a third-level education while it wins 29 per cent of the vote among those earning over €40,000.

It is also worth bearing in mind that Sinn Féin does not win *more* than 35 per cent of the vote in *any* of these categories that we have analysed thus far, such are the limits of demography in explaining vote choice. We will next seek to explain the vote in terms of economic perspectives, salient issues, attitudes and ideology.

ECONOMIC GRIEVANCES

As in 2016, the government may have hoped to benefit from the return to economic growth and full employment. However, the failure of Fine Gael's 'keep the recovery going' in that campaign was a warning that elections are about more than the macro economy, and that growth and rising employment alone is not sufficient. In January 2020, unemployment was below 5 per cent for the first time since early 2008. The consumer confidence survey run by B&A shows that positive feelings about the economy over the previous year outweighed negative ones early in 2016. They became more positive over the next couple of years, but started to decline late in 2018, and were below 2016 levels throughout 2019. By January 2020 positive and negative evaluations were the same, while confidence looking forward had not been positive since May 2019, not least probably because of real concerns about the likely impact of Brexit.[14] Confidence started to ebb in late 2018 and was much lower by the end of 2019 than it had been four years earlier. As Fig. 10.3 shows, this pattern coincides with Fine Gael fortunes to some degree, most notably the decline from a peak early in 2018, although Fine Gael's strong showing in the autumn 2019 polls was a departure from this trend.

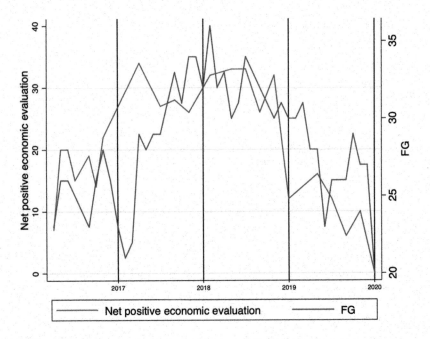

Fig. 10.3   Consumer sentiment trends and Fine Gael support in B&A polls 2017–2020

Asked in the Ireland Thinks online poll 'Thinking about the economy as a whole, do you think that the country is better off, worse off, or about the same as last year?', negative assessments outweighed positive ones with 36 per cent saying things were worse, as against 29 per cent who thought they were better and 35 per cent who thought they were about the same. (This is much the same result as that recorded by B&A using much the same question in January 2020.) It gives a positive–negative score of minus six. This compares with a score of +27 last time recorded in the 2016 exit poll.[15]

How do these evaluations tie in with party support? Sinn Féin won 45 per cent among those who thought the economy was getting worse, Fianna Fáil 30 per cent among those who thought it was the same and Fine Gael 51 per cent of those who thought it was getting better. Better–worse comparisons show Sinn Féin voters at -39, Fine Gael +47 and Fianna Fáil -2. There seems little doubt that worsening evaluations benefited Sinn Féin by February 2020, but it is not clear why they did not do so earlier. In general, parties of the left did better where feelings were negative rather than positive (57 per cent as against 22 per cent), although both Labour and Greens did better among those with more positive evaluations. Broadly speaking, it seems that evaluations were connected strongly to support for Sinn Féin and Fine Gael, but weakly enough otherwise.

There is certainly room for doubt about causality in this relationship, and there is a very substantial set of research on this point. All of this research admits to some influence of party on evaluations, though there is disagreement about how much. Most of the research also finds some influence of evaluations on party choice.[16] One way to deal with this is to control for underlying party attachment and see whether there is still a strong link between evaluation and party choice. If we look just at those voters who do not feel close, or we look just at those who changed their vote since 2016, we still see a similar pattern: that negative evaluations are linked to voting for Sinn Féin and positive ones to voting for Fine Gael.

We might expect that evaluations would be linked to those social factors explored earlier, with younger people and working-class groups feeling more pessimistic. In fact, the most negative responses were from those aged 35–54: younger groups were marginally positive, as were those over 65. No data is available on social class, but those who left school without finishing their leaving certificate were particularly negative, and only those with a third-level qualification showed similar numbers in the positive and negative groups.

There was some evidence in 2016 that while people did see improvement in the wider economy, they felt that they had seen no personal benefit and in consequence did not reward the government. These two types of evaluations, usually called sociotropic and pocketbook, are typically connected, being at similar levels, but in post-crash Ireland, they have not been so. Positive sociotropic evaluations were offset by negative pocketbook ones in 2016. This time both sets of evaluations were, on balance, negative: 39 per cent said things were worse for them personally and only 17 per cent better. As in 2016, then, personal evaluations were more negative than sociotropic ones. Looking at these two sets of evaluations together, in Table 10.7, 24 per cent saw both the economy and their personal fortunes as getting worse and only 13 per cent saw both as getting better. In 2016, the corresponding figures were 14 and 23: a change for the worse.[17]

Sinn Féin won almost 50 per cent of the votes of the first group (this was half of the Sinn Féin vote), while Fine Gael won 60 per cent of the votes of the second one. Sociotropic evaluations seem to have mattered more, as is found by most studies. More positive pocketbook evaluations are associated at -33 with voting for Sinn Féin and +42 with Fine Gael voting, slightly smaller impacts than those above for sociotropic voting, although the Fianna Fáil figure of -8 is a little higher. Combining the two also suggests that the impact of sociotropic voting is higher. The Sinn Féin vote is relatively high when sociotropic evaluations are negative regardless of pocketbook ones, and the same is true for Fine Gael when sociotropic evaluations are positive. When sociotropic evaluations are 'the same', pocketbook evaluations make a difference to the Sinn Féin vote of 19 points and to the Fine Gael vote of 18 points; but when pocketbook evaluations are 'the same', sociotropic evaluations can push the Sinn Féin vote up or down 30 points, and the Fine Gael vote by 44 points.

Table 10.7 Pocketbook and sociotropic economy evaluations

| | Personal | | | |
Economy	Worse	Same	Better	Total
Worse	24	10	1	34
Same	11	21	4	35
Better	4	14	13	31
Total	38	44	17	100

Source: Ireland Thinks exit poll (adjusted to party choice and age of voter)

OTHER ISSUES

It is clear that economic differences and evaluations were important in driving support for Sinn Féin. At the start of 2020, the macro economy was certainly healthy, with unemployment low and economic growth strong, while wages were also increasing after a long period of stagnation following the decline post-crash. However, there was a severe shortage of housing, with too few properties to buy, particularly at the lower end of the market, and strong upward pressures in the rental sector (see Chap. 1 for the record on these issues). According to the Residential Tenancies Board's rent price index, between Quarter 1 of 2016 and Quarter 3 of 2019 private rents increased by 32 per cent, without anything like the same level of increase in incomes over that period. This made Dublin one of the most expensive cities in the world to live in and put pressure on housing in the much wider commuter belt. Healthcare has long been a serious issue. Despite increased spending, there are long waiting lists for non-emergency care and a shortage of beds. A new children's hospital that had been on the drawing board for at least 20 years was finally being built, but at a cost two to three times as high as earlier estimates. Brexit was an important issue for the Irish government to deal with in particular from 2017 to 2019, but victory for Boris Johnson's government under the slogan 'Get Brexit Done' in the UK general election of 12 December 2019, and the approval of the withdrawal agreement by the House of Commons eight days later, may have persuaded many Irish voters that the issue was 'done' (see Chap. 5 for fuller discussion).

Figure 10.4 shows coded responses to the open-ended question about the most important issue asked in the Ireland Thinks poll series. Housing (including homelessness) appears to dominate over the period, particularly since late 2017. Health and Brexit were also significant issues until the end of the series in December, when health rose sharply and Brexit dropped in significance. In 2016, housing had been the most important issue for just 4 per cent, while Brexit was a distant cloud.

The MRBI exit poll asked voters to select the most important issue influencing their vote. From a given list, 32 per cent selected health, 26 per cent housing and homelessness, just 6 per cent selected climate change and 1 per cent selected Brexit. It reflects the trend that emerged in the run-up to the election (see Chaps. 4 and 6). No other issue featured much: the pension age, an issue that emerged during the campaign, was identified by 8 per cent, jobs 6 per cent, taxation 4 per cent, childcare and crime 3 per cent each.

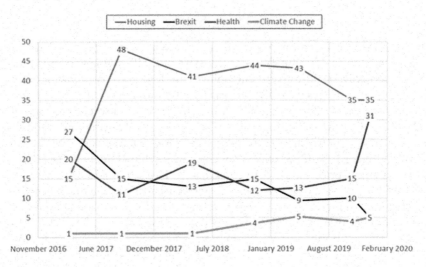

Fig. 10.4 Issue salience 2017–2020
Source: Ireland Thinks poll series
Note: The question is 'What, do you think, is the most important issue facing the country?' It is open-ended

Immigration, an issue very prominent in many other European countries, was selected by only 1 per cent. Notably the list did not include economic management, which featured somewhat in open-ended surveys (see below). The re-emergence of healthcare as such an important issue reflected the looming vote of no confidence in Minister for Health Simon Harris, the annual winter hospital trolley crisis and the space vacated by the considerable decline in the relative importance of Brexit as an issue.

Housing and health were the two most important issues for supporters of all parties except the Greens, which might raise questions about exactly how these issues impact on vote choice (see Table 10.8). Beyond the big two issues, numbers in the poll are too small in general to draw any conclusions about relative party support. However, among those who mentioned housing and homelessness, Sinn Féin was most popular, winning as much support as Fianna Fáil and Fine Gael combined, with Fine Gael support notably low. Party choice was less obvious in relation to health, but Fianna Fáil did best. However, neither healthcare nor housing is 'owned' by any one party as an issue. In contrast, of those that mentioned climate change, 57 per cent voted for the Green Party. And of the 1 per cent that identified Brexit as the most important issue, 85 per cent voted for Fine Gael.

Table 10.8 Issue priorities and the vote in 2020

Issue	Sinn Féin	Fianna Fáil	Fine Gael	Green	Others	Total	Overall
Health	19	28	22	3	27	100	34
Housing/homelessness	32	20	11	7	30	100	27
Pension age	26	28	21	4	21	100	9
Jobs	26	26	21	4	24	100	6
Climate change	7	7	13	57	16	100	6
Taxation	21	18	41	3	17	100	5
Childcare	11	18	45	11	15	100	3
Crime	18	25	44	6	7	100	3
Brexit	8	0	85	0	7	100	1
Immigration	38	11	22	0	29	100	1
Something else	14	15	25	5	41	100	6

Source: MRBI exit poll

There are differences in priorities dividing the generations. Among those under 35, housing and homelessness is the dominant issue for 36 per cent. Healthcare is the more important issue for 40 per cent of those aged over 55. Similarly, the pension age is an issue for those over 50, whereas jobs, climate change and childcare are especially issues for those under 50.

One might argue that the link between social bases and party choice is because social location influences the issues voters perceive as important: younger voters identifying housing as an important issue and therefore being led to the party that is prominent in raising this issue. The left-wing parties, including Sinn Féin, have made more noise about housing but also emphasised a more state-centred approach to the issue, promising substantially more investment than their rivals and also promising to control rents. At the same time, parties can also influence their supporters; Fine Gael has emphasised the importance of issues such as Brexit and perhaps its supporters will have responded.

This is further underlined by a RED C campaign survey[18] that asked voters which party was most *suited* to address each of the big issues. This is a more direct way of finding out which issues benefit which parties than making inferences from the link between issue salience and party support. In relation to resolving the housing crisis, Sinn Féin was identified as the best equipped by 33 per cent of voters, more than Fianna Fáil and Fine Gael together, at 28 per cent, and in relation to healthcare, Sinn Féin scored 27 per cent, again more than the other two together, 25 per cent, suggesting a dominance on the two main issues in contrast to what might be inferred from the MRBI exit poll. Fine Gael led on safeguarding the economy and on Brexit with 34 per cent and 40 per cent, again more than the other two parties, Sinn Féin and Fianna Fáil, together, but it would appear relatively few people were motivated by these concerns.

IDEOLOGY

While issues may explain some of the variance in party support, a voter's response to the salience of those issues is likely to vary according not just to their economic position but also to their attitudes and ideological perspective more generally. To understand more about the way in which political attitudes underpin party support, we can compare the vote choices of people with a range of different attitudes. Four scales were presented to voters in the Ireland Thinks online poll. These were from abandoning the aim of a united Ireland [0] to insisting on a united Ireland now [10]; between whether they believed that we should protect the environment even if this damages economic growth [0] to whether we should encourage economic growth even if this damages the environment [10]; from [0] believing that government should act to reduce differences in income and wealth to [10] believing that the government should not act to do so; and from believing the government should cut taxes a lot and spend much less on health and social services [0] and believing the government should increase taxes a lot and spend much more on health and social services [10]. The average position of the supporters of each party is presented in Fig. 10.5. We can observe how on each issue the parties line up, from Fine Gael and Fianna Fáil voters indistinguishable from one another on one end and Sinn Féin and Solidarity–PBP typically on the other. Clearly, Sinn Féin and Green Party voters are most clearly identified by issues that their parties promote: a 'united Ireland' and protection of the environment respectively. It is notable that the left–right economic differences are clearer with respect to economic redistribution as opposed to tax-and-spend economics.

Voters have also been asked to place themselves on a general 'left–right' scale, from zero (left) to ten (right). This question has always found voters grouped around the mid-point, but there are some signs that the distribution has shifted a little to the left, particularly since the economic crash. Taking all Irish National Election Study (INES) surveys to date, the median point was 6 in 2002–2011, but 5 in 2016 and 5 again in 2020.[19]

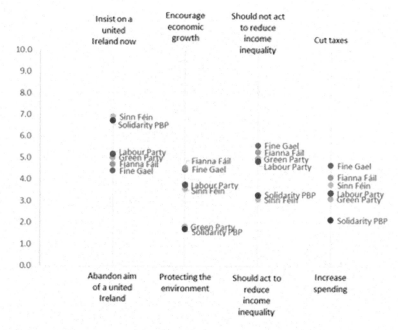

Fig. 10.5 Attitudes of each party's voters on several scales
Source: Ireland Thinks Exit Poll

(The average in 2002 and 2007 was 5.7; it went up to 6.0 in 2011, then fell to 5.0 in 2016 and 4.9 in 2020.) More importantly, perhaps, while half of all voters placed themselves between 5 and 7 in 2002–2011, that has shifted to between 4 and 6 in 2016 and between 3 and 6 in 2020. These are not huge shifts, and it should be said that no such movement is evident in the series of European Social Survey (ESS) polls, conducted every two years, the most recent prior to the election taken in 2019. We will have to wait for more evidence to be sure.

Nevertheless, in Fig. 10.6, we explore how this relates to vote choice, showing a series of plots giving the distribution of each party's support on the left–right scale. The means are also provided. Voters of each of Solidarity–PBP, Sinn Féin, Labour, Social Democrats and the Green Party tend to place themselves on the left of the political spectrum, whereas supporters of Fianna Fáil and Fine Gael tend to be towards the right. Much of Fine Gael and Fianna Fáil support is placed between 5 and 8; Labour and the Greens between 3 and 5, and Social Democrats and Sinn Féin

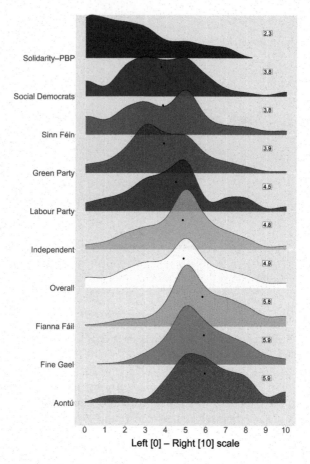

Fig. 10.6 Left–right placement of each party's voters in 2020
Source: RED C Post election poll
Note: Mean values are shown in labels; each black dot identifies where this mean value is on the horizontal axis

between 2 and 5, with half of Solidarity–PBP voters in the range between 1 and 3. This picture is not very different to the one we would have seen in the past, though in 2002 Labour voters were a little more centrist. It is still worth pointing out that almost one-fifth of Sinn Féin voters place themselves to the right of centre, as do a similar portion of Labour, Green and Social Democrat voters. Of course, there may be confusion here about what the terms left and right mean, not least because Irish party competition has served to obscure rather than highlight this dimension. A similar graph on UK data on the UK 2015 election shows that the Labour party spread around a median score of 3 and the Conservative Party more tightly packed around a median score of 8.[20]

To some degree, this dimension acts as a summary of many attitudes, although we have seen in the past that the links between this dimension and social and economic issues are far from exact.[21] Left and right can mean different things to different voters, and in the past in Ireland, this dimension mapped more closely onto issues such as abortion than to matters like the balance between taxation and public spending, or public versus private enterprise. Looking again at the variables we observed in Fig. 10.5, left–right self-placement is correlated most strongly with attitudes towards income redistribution (correlation is 0.40). That is not a strong link, but it is stronger than links to a variety of questions about equality asked in the past. The ties to the environment issues (0.31) are weaker again, as are those with tax and spend (0.28) and a united Ireland (0.25); the last of these is not typically considered an issue that divides right and left. The relationship with attitudes to abortion is correlated only at 0.20.[22] This is higher than the correlation of 0.13 in 2002, but in that year the tax and spend correlation was just 0.04. It seems there may now be more agreement among the public about what the terms left and right mean.

One other factor that does not fit onto left and right labels is whether the rise of Sinn Féin reflects a rise in populism—which may be defined as an ideology that considers society to be ultimately separated into two homogenous and antagonistic camps, 'the pure people' versus 'the corrupt elite', and which argues that politics should be an expression of the general will of the people.[23] The narrative is that the two 'established' parties could be merged together for voters as representing the establishment. The RED C post-election survey asks voters whether they agreed or disagreed with some statements that have been widely employed to identify populist voters: including 'Most politicians do not care about the people', 'Most politicians are trustworthy' and 'Most politicians only care about the interests of the rich and powerful'.[24]

This is what is known as an 'agreement bias' in the phraseology of these questions (the second of which we expect populists to disagree with), but the point is less to know how people as a whole answer the question and more to contrast the answers of different groups. Figure 10.7 shows how supporters of Sinn Féin have quite different perspective on these statements, reflecting a more populist stance in contrast to supporters of other

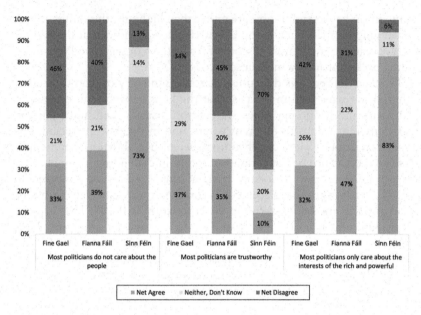

Fig. 10.7 Populist attitudes, by party supported
Source: RED C post-election poll

parties. The magnitude of the differences here is stark compared to other variables we have looked at.

Finally, on this note, two pre-election polls, one conducted by RED C[25] and a second conducted by Ireland Thinks, asked voters the simple open-ended question of 'why' voters chose their party. After coding the data, both firms independently identified two dominant and consistent responses for the Sinn Féin voter. One was that voters wanted 'change'—perhaps this reflects economic and other grievances these voters had with the incumbent government—and the second was that voters stated a position most commonly articulated as 'Anti-FFFG', opposed collectively to Fianna Fáil and Fine Gael, notable as Fianna Fáil had technically been in opposition (see Chap. 1).

LEADERS

It is now very many years since people started to say that leaders were becoming at least as important as their parties in determining voters' choice, as television dominated campaigns and brought each leader before the public much more directly. The ability of parties to mobilise a large set of committed supporters is certainly less evident these days, but that is not to say that parties are not central to elections. The academic evidence on the importance of leaders is mixed, but with the stronger view being that while leaders do help and hinder their parties, it is typically by small margins.[26] The MRBI exit poll reported just over 50 per cent of voters saying that the party leader was an important factor in their choice, as opposed to 27 per cent who said it was somewhat important and 21 per cent not important at all. There was generally little difference between the parties on this, but among those who said it was very important, 30 per cent voted Sinn Féin, as opposed to 24 and 22 per cent for Fianna Fáil and Fine Gael, respectively.

Some polling companies try to measure the popularity of different leaders. However, the question typically used is ambiguous as respondents are asked if they are satisfied with the way a particular leader is doing his or her job as leader of their party. If you like a party, this makes some sense, but if you do not, the meaning of 'satisfied' is far from obvious. Figure 10.8 shows the satisfaction with different leaders since the start of 2017. This was an odd time in Fine Gael as Enda Kenny had already indicated that he would be standing down, but it was not until June that Leo Varadkar took over. By late summer, his ratings were on a par with those of the Fianna Fáil leader Micheál Martin, and far ahead of those for the then Sinn Féin leader Gerry Adams. Adams was replaced by Mary Lou McDonald in 2018, and it was not long before she joined Martin and Varadkar, with close to half of all respondents expressing satisfaction, and McDonald actually doing little better than the Fianna Fáil leader. Yet, the surge was quite short-lived, as all leaders started to record lower ratings after the middle of the year. To have a significant impact, a leader should be expected to have higher ratings than their rivals, but in the run-up to the election, Martin seemed to be striking the most positive chord with voters, with McDonald well behind.

Of course, it could be that leaders can help by running ahead of their parties, but this is difficult to assess as party and leader popularity are not measured on the same scales. Leader satisfaction scores are ratings, while

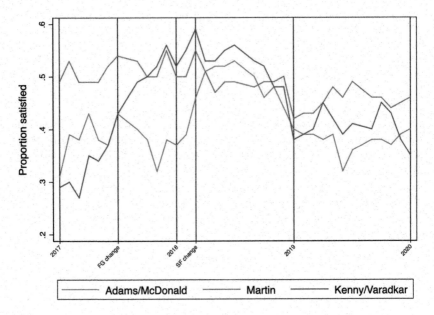

Fig. 10.8 Satisfaction with the way leader doing their job, 2017–2020
Source: Based on Behaviour & Attitudes poll series

parties are assessed by the percentage who would make them their first choice. We can match these two by indicating the variation over time in a leader's popularity and the popularity of their party, but what this tells us is simply whether high and low points coincide. This is done in Fig. 10.9. To a substantial degree, this shows us that leaders go up and down with their parties. As one early analysis of the impact of leaders observed, they float up and down on the same waves.[27] Varadkar did seem to push up Fine Gael support when he took over, but as his ratings fell so did his party's popularity from late 2018; Mary Lou McDonald was more 'popular' than Adams, and her term as leader also seemed to coincide with a rise in support. Again, leader and party fell together, although Sinn Féin's poll ratings did not fall to the degree that McDonald's did in 2019.

In general, there is nothing here to suggest that any leader would have a particular impact in the campaign, but of course, these figures pre-date that campaign. The two MRBI polls for the *Irish Times* in the course of the campaign showed McDonald's ratings going up seven points to 41 per cent satisfied, against Varadkar's 30 per cent, down five points and Martin's

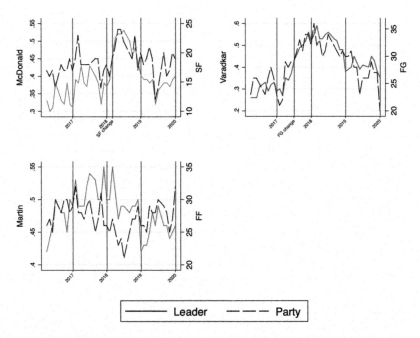

Fig. 10.9 Leader satisfaction rating and party support, 2016–2020
Source: Based on Behaviour & Attitudes poll series

30 per cent, down three points, again arguably simply in line with party trends. However, another poll by Amárach asked respondents who was the best communicator, and McDonald easily topped that poll with 32 per cent as against Varadkar's 15 per cent and Martin's 14 per cent.[28] This later evidence gives more support to the view that McDonald was a positive factor for the party in the last few weeks.[29]

THE CANDIDATE FACTOR

This discussion so far has been about parties, but Irish elections are also about candidates, and a good candidate is generally expected to be able to pull in a personal vote beyond any party one. In addition, around a quarter of candidates are independents. Asked about the importance of parties and candidates, voters tell survey researchers that candidates are very important. In fact, between 40 and 50 per cent have given as the main reason for their choice picking a candidate to serve the needs of the constituency, as opposed to the leaders, policies or set of ministers presented. Voters have also been asked about the respective importance of the party or the candidate in their choice. The majority opted for the candidate in 2002 and 2007; party was dominant in 2011, but candidate just edged it in 2016. However, there were changes in the wording, with independent voters asked a different question in 2011 and 2016: was it the candidate or the fact that the candidate was independent? These were merged in one survey in 2020, with voters asked to pick between candidate and party (or the fact that the candidate was independent/nonparty). The dominant factor was party, by 53–47 per cent. A slightly different question was included in the exit poll: 'Which was more important to you when voting today—the CANDIDATE or the PARTY?' Candidate won this one, 54–46. These differences are small enough. What this suggests is that voters were a little more party-centred than in 2002 and 2007 when candidate was the choice of 60 per cent.

This seems surprising given that in 2020 the independent vote was stronger and the party system more fragmented. Party seems to matter more to those voting Sinn Féin and Green, a pattern found in both surveys. Both also found party mattered more to Fine Gael voters than to Fianna Fáil ones. This has been true since 2011, but the reverse was true in 2002–2007. This may be a consequence of being in government as far as those two are concerned. Left parties as a whole also seem to be more dependent on a 'party' vote, getting close to 50 per cent among 'party' voters as opposed to 30 per cent among 'candidate' voters according to both polls. A second question has also been asked in election studies since 2002: 'Would you still have voted for the same candidate if they had run for a different party?', with response options being yes, no and it depends on the party. Those who say party was most important, and who would not follow the candidate to another party, can be seen as strong party voters, and those who emphasise the candidate and would follow that candidate if they switched can be called strong candidate voters, with the rest being mixed in motivations. In 2020, almost half of all voters could be said to have mixed motivations, but of the rest, 30 per cent were party and just 15 per cent candidate voters.

This is by far the lowest level of candidate motivation and the highest mixed level since the series was started in 2002. Sinn Féin voters are least candidate-centred at just 6 per cent as against 45 per cent party; only 12 per cent of Fine Gael voters are totally focussed on candidate and 38 per cent of them can be labelled party; while those supporting Fianna Fáil are

Table 10.9   Candidate versus party focus 2002–2020

	2002	2007	2011	2016	2020
Candidate	39	32	33	39	15
Mixed	33	36	39	43	55
Party	28	32	28	28	30

Note: Independent voters excluded here

Source: 2002–2016 from Michael Courtney and Liam Weeks, 'Party or candidate?' in Marsh, Farrell and Reidy, *Post-Crisis Irish Voter*, p. 133; RED C post-election poll

34 per cent candidate and only 23 per cent party. (Most independent voters can be labelled as mixed, but this probably means they value the non-party nature of their candidate and would not follow them into a party. They are not included in Table 10.9.) It is reasonable to ask what it means when voters say 'party' or 'candidate'? We have seen in the past that candidate voters are less influenced by national issues and have weaker ideological ties to the party they support[30]; in addition, 'party' voters are more likely to go on and support other candidates nominated by that party with their lower preferences (see Appendix D for an explanation of the electoral system).[31] The data is not available this time to explore the question of issues to any great extent, but we can look at the importance of economic evaluations in the two groups of voters. As we have seen earlier, economic evaluations did seem to play a part in voting for Sinn Féin and Fine Gael in particular. Is this factor as strong for 'candidate' as it is for 'party' voters? The answer is that there is a significant difference: the more they emphasis party, the more negative judgements of the economy make a person likely to support Sinn Féin, and the same is true for positive economic evaluations and the Fine Gael vote. Party voters who see the economy as getting worse are 48 points more likely to vote Sinn Féin than are candidate voters who see the economy the same way. Party voters who see the economy as doing well are 17 points more likely to vote for Fine Gael than candidate voters.

If Irish electoral politics is often said to be candidate-centred, it is equally often described as being localistic, with a focus on the constituency, or a part of it, rather than national politics. The MRBI exit poll asked people: 'To what extent should TDs focus on the needs of their local constituency versus national issues?' A small majority said national issues were more important, but the difference is small. Locally focussed voters were three times more likely to vote independent than nationally focussed ones, as we might expect. More generally, Sinn Féin, Fine Gael and Greens did best among nationally focussed voters and Fianna Fáil among localistic ones, but the differences are generally quite small compared to those between the candidate and party voters as defined by that exit poll. The two things are correlated: candidate voters are more likely to be local in emphasis, and party voters national. However, the exit poll does not have other questions that would allow us to explore ways in which these groups might differ in terms of factors in their decision.

CONCLUSIONS

This chapter has explored the factors behind the rise of Sinn Féin in particular and the left in general in this election. We should now consider whether the behaviour of voters was something that will remain unique to 2020 or whether it represents a long-running trend. Did this election mark a distinctive break from the past or did a particular combination of events and problems give us a result that is more likely to serve as an outlier rather than an indicator of the future?

Perhaps the most obvious factor in this election was the failure of the two larger parties to assure the voters that they could handle the issues on the minds of most voters. Fine Gael placed its faith in Brexit and the economy, but neither seemed to matter to enough people when they came to vote. In any case, dissatisfaction with economic progress outweighed satisfaction. Fianna Fáil's lead on health and even more on housing vanished as the campaign progressed. These were the two big issues. On the first of these, housing, Sinn Féin was simply more convincing, as both the MRBI exit poll and earlier the RED C campaign poll showed in their different ways. Health concerns seem to have been linked more closely to Fianna Fáil support than that for Sinn Fein, but voters also trusted Sinn Fein more to fix the problem. Fine Gael, like all government parties, got the blame for whatever was wrong, and Fianna Fáil seems to have been seen as complicit. The other opposition parties all grouped Fianna Fáil in with Fine Gael, fairly or unfairly, because of the confidence and supply agreement. The economy, with full employment, should have helped Fine Gael, but whether due to Brexit uncertainties or housing problems or more general concerns about the cost of living, most people did not perceive that the national economy was improving, and very few saw improvements in their own circumstances. This hurt Fine Gael and, significantly, did not help Fianna Fáil in the way we might expect an opposition party to benefit, as it had in 2016. Concerns that a Fianna Fáil–Fine Gael grand coalition would open the door to Sinn Féin and the left were expressed in 2016, and Fianna Fáil thought, or hoped, its confidence and supply arrangement would avoid that problem, but it seems that it did not. In retrospect, Fianna Fáil got the responsibility, but without the power to go with it (see also Chap. 2 on how far Fianna Fáil secured implementation of its policies during this period).

Who could benefit? Evaluations of Labour are still linked to its perceived inadequacies in government from 2011 to 2016; so advantage accrued to a revived Green Party, encouraged by wider concerns about climate change, and Sinn Féin was also well placed. Its impact was slow in coming, but perhaps, this left less time for second thoughts. The fact that the party had a new leader without the baggage of the previous one was almost certainly not a disadvantage, but the data we have is simply not suitable to indicate what impact she did have.

Sinn Féin gains were across the board. Unlike the wider left as a whole, it is still clearly a party of the less well off and is particularly strong in the youngest age groups, but now has significant support in almost all social groups. Did the more general attitudinal shifts benefit leftist parties? We have not been able to explore much beyond general left–right placement here, but as with declining party attachment, the more secular, more urban and younger electorate is more open to a wider set of political choices. The evidence that there is a more left-inclined electorate is more mixed. High-quality long-term polls say not, but recent polls close to elections suggest there is some leftward movement. Even so, most voters are still centrist, and centrist voters spread their favours very widely. Whether the distribution of left and right has changed or otherwise, it is more closely aligned with party preferences, particularly for Sinn Féin. While Sinn Féin may have previously been viewed as a party strongly associated with an ethno-nationalist conflict, its presence in Irish politics today more closely reflects a typical left-wing party with a base of support that tends to be working class, on low incomes and somewhat populist.

As it turned out, the government that was formed was one that excluded Sinn Féin, leaving it as the largest opposition party by some margin. For this reason, the election may change how people view the party system. More than any previous pattern of government and opposition, this provides an opportunity for a clearer left–right divide in Irish politics although, with a programme for government that has been seen as broadly social democratic, we should not bet too much money on Irish politics providing us with simple alternatives at the next election.

NOTES

1. Michael S. Lewis-Beck, *Economics and Elections: the major western democracies* (Ann Arbor: University of Michigan Press, 1988).
2. The MRBI exit poll was based on 5376 interviews, but for most questions, the N is around 1000 as there were different versions of the questionnaire administered to five subsamples. The Ireland Thinks online poll gathered 1546 responses, and the RED C post-election online poll included 3099 respondents. However, there were only 1500 for some questions, as two slightly different versions of the questionnaire were employed.
3. The poll standings here are based on a moving average calculated over all polls since the last election (see Chap. 1, Fig. 1.1), but simply averaging the polls in the last three months of 2019 gives the same result.
4. The distribution of recalled timings in the Ireland Thinks online poll and the MRBI exit poll shown in Table 10.1 differ, even allowing for differences in the categories given to the respondent, with Ireland Thinks finding people made up their mind earlier than was found in the MRBI exit poll. However, in both polls Sinn Féin voters, on average, did decide earlier.
5. Rory Costello, 'Party identification in the wake of the crisis: a nascent realignment', pp. 82–98 in Michael Marsh, David M. Farrell and Theresa Reidy (eds), *The Post-Crisis Irish Voter: voting behaviour in the Irish 2016 general election* (Manchester: Manchester University Press, 2018).
6. Our analysis of Irish National Election Study Data 2002, 2011 and 2016 (INES3). On these studies see Michael Marsh, Richard Sinnott, Fiachra Kennedy and John Garry, *The Irish Voter: the nature of electoral competition in the Republic of Ireland* (Manchester: Manchester University Press, 2008); Michael Marsh, David M. Farrell and Gail McElroy (eds), *A Conservative Revolution? Electoral change in twenty-first-century Ireland* (Oxford: Oxford University Press, 2016); and Marsh, Farrell and Reidy, *Post-Crisis Irish Voter.*
7. A problem with this question is that responses are quite closely related to interest in politics, and most polls include far more people with strong interest than are found in the population. We have adjusted the data on 2016 and 2020 to ensure that interest is on a par with what is found in the high-quality European Social Survey (ESS) polls, taken every two years since 2002.
8. The Ireland Thinks poll is used here because N is larger than the exit poll or final RED C poll of the campaign. However, patterns in all three are similar. It is well known that the true level of change tends to be underestimated as voters are likely to associate their current support with their past support. A further problem in this election is that all polls in 2020 seem to have shown over-reporting of Fine Gael voting in 2016. The analysis here adjusts for that.

9. See Michael Marsh and Gail McElroy, 'Voting behaviour: continuing de-alignment', pp. 159–84 in Michael Gallagher and Michael Marsh (eds), *How Ireland Voted 2016: the election that nobody won* (Cham: Palgrave Macmillan, 2016), p. 160.
10. The MRBI exit poll contained only 73 cases of individuals reporting non-voting in 2016.
11. Marsh and McElroy, 'Voting behaviour', p. 164.
12. Marsh and McElroy, 'Voting behaviour', p. 167.
13. Sara Hobolt, 'The Brexit vote: a divided nation, a divided continent', *Journal of European Public Policy* 23:9 (2016), pp. 1259–77; Hanspeter Kriesi, 'Restructuration of partisan politics and the emergence of a new cleavage based on values', *West European Politics* 33:3 (2010), pp. 673–85.
14. B&A Consumer Confidence Tracker, Jan 2020 (https://banda.ie/wp-content/uploads/J.1611-Banda-Consumer-Confidence-Tracker-FINAL.pdf). Much the same pattern is evident in the more broadly based ESRI/KBC Consumer Sentiment Index (https://www.kbc.ie/blog/consumer-sentiment-surveys/irish-consumer-concerns-ease-further-in-december).
15. Marsh and McElroy, 'Voting behaviour', pp. 168–71.
16. A good review is Christopher J. Anderson, 'The end of economic voting? Contingency dilemmas and the limits of democratic accountability', *Annual Review of Political Science* 10 (2007), pp. 271–96; see Michael Marsh 'Why did the "recovery" fail to return the government?', pp. 99–125 in Marsh, Farrell and Reidy, *Post-Crisis Irish Voter.*
17. Marsh and McElroy, 'Voting behaviour', p. 169.
18. Red C Opinion Poll, Jan 2020. (https://www.redcresearch.com/wp-content/uploads/2020/01/SBP-January-2020-Poll-Report.pdf).
19. See note 6.
20. Kevin Cunningham and Johan A. Elkink, 'Ideological dimensions in the 2016 elections', pp. 32–62 in Marsh, Farrell and Reidy, *Post-Crisis Irish Voter*, p. 47.
21. A comprehensive analysis from 2002 showed left–right self-placement was much more closely related to religious/moral attitudes than to those on the economy: Marsh et al., *Irish Voter*, pp. 39–42. Cunningham and Elkink, 'Ideological dimensions in the 2016 elections', find stronger links with social and economic attitudes than in the past (pp. 39–46), but Gail McElroy explores the pattern among candidates and voters, and while the position of candidates could be predicted from their views on tax versus spending, the dimension is still only weakly related to socio-economic issues amongst voters: 'Party competition in Ireland: the emergence of a left–right dimension?', pp. 61–82 in Marsh, Farrell and McElroy, *Conservative Revolution*, particularly pp. 69–75.

22. The moral agenda is associated with party support but not to any great extent. The RED C post-election online poll addressed this question. An 11-point scale on abortion with the range between a total ban (0) and unlimited access (10) finds some differences between parties. Forty-two per cent of Sinn Féin voters are at 10, compared with 36 per cent of Fine Gael voters and 24 per cent of Fianna Fáil voters. Mean positions are not so different though: 8.4 for Sinn Féin, 8.3 for Gael and 7.2 for Fianna Fáil voters, who are also spread more widely. The average Aontú voter is at 3.4, while all the left-wing parties are more liberal than Sinn Féin. See Chap. 11 for candidates' views on this issue.

23. Cas Mudde and Cristóbal Kaltwasser, *Populism: a very short introduction* (Oxford: Oxford University Press, 2017).

24. These questions come from the CSES Wave 5 questionnaire (see Sara Hobolt, Eva Anduiza, Ali Carkoglu, Georg Lutz, and Nicolas Sauger, *CSES Module 5—Democracy Divided? People, Politicians and the Politics of Populism*. CSES Planning Committee Module 5 Final Report, 2016 (http://www.cses.org/plancom/module5/CSES5_ContentSubcommittee_FinalReport.pdf) and reflect the anti-elitism aspect of populism. For Irish analyses of the same questions in 2016, see David M. Farrell, Michael Gallagher and David Barrett, 'What do Irish voters want from and think of their politicians?', pp. 190–208 in Marsh, Farrell and Reidy, *Post-Crisis Irish Voter*, pp. 202–5; Theresa Reidy and Jane Suiter, 'Who is the populist Irish voter?', *Journal of the Statistical and Social Inquiry Society of Ireland* XLVI (2016–2017), pp. 117–31. For comprehensive analysis of populism measures, see Alexander Wuttke, Christian Schimpf and Harald Schoen, 'When the whole is greater than the sum of its parts: on the conceptualization and measurement of populist attitudes and other multi-dimensional constructs', *American Political Science Review* 114:2 (2020), pp. 326–41.

25. https://www.redcresearch.ie/general-election-2020-momentum-with-sinn-fein/.

26. See Stephen Quinlan and Eoin O'Malley, 'Popularity and performance? Leader effects in the 2016 election', pp. 209–32 in Marsh, Farrell and Reidy, *Post-Crisis Irish Voter*, at pp. 209–10.

27. The analogy is from Charles A. Goodhart and R. J. Bhansali, 'Political economy', *Political Studies* 18:1 (1970), p. 69; quoted in M. J. Harrison and Michael Marsh, 'What can he do for us? Leader effects on party fortunes in Ireland', *Electoral Studies* 13:4 (1994), pp. 289–317, at p. 292.

28. https://www.breakingnews.ie/ireland/sinn-fein-leads-poll-as-new-survey-lists-mcdonald-as-most-effective-communicator-among-leaders-979642.html.

29. Unlike at some previous elections, there was no significant gender gap in
    Sinn Féin's vote this time. It is possible that McDonald, rather than Adams,
    as leader had some impact on this, but the gap was also small in 2016
    according to the RTE exit poll.
30. See Marsh et al., *Irish voter*, pp. 181–3.
31. Michael Courtney and Liam Weeks, 'Party or candidate?', pp. 126–45 in
    Marsh, Farrell and Reidy, *Post-Crisis Irish Voter*, at pp. 135–7.

CHAPTER 11

The Evolving Nature of the Irish Policy Space

Lisa Keenan and Gail McElroy

If there was a leitmotif of the 2020 campaign, it was the repeated reference to a need and widespread desire for change. Indeed, 'time for change' was the introductory heading of Sinn Féin's manifesto.[1] Similarly, the Social Democrats wanted to 'help move Ireland in a new direction' away from 'the same old ways of doing politics',[2] while Solidarity–People Before Profit pitched itself as the alternative to 'the same establishment parties that have run this country for nearly a century'.[3] Overall, parties of the left went to great lengths to sell themselves as vehicles of transformation, with claims that they offered very distinct alternatives to Fianna Fáil and Fine Gael.

In this chapter we explore the nature and extent of these differences for the main parties competing in the 2020 election. We begin by exploring parties' left–right positions over time, as revealed through their candidates' political preferences. Next, we proceed to compare the parties' own views on their left–right placement with their placement by their competitors. Finally, we explore differences between the parties across

L. Keenan (✉) • G. McElroy
Trinity College Dublin, Dublin, Ireland
e-mail: LIKEENAN@tcd.ie

© The Author(s), under exclusive license to Springer Nature
Switzerland AG 2021
M. Gallagher et al. (eds.), *How Ireland Voted 2020*,
https://doi.org/10.1007/978-3-030-66405-3_11

255

specific policy areas in 2020. In the process, we aim to answer the following questions: Where do Irish political parties fall along the left–right spectrum? Has their placement changed substantially over time? On what issues are the parties most similar and different? How distinct are Irish parties from each other on issues such as climate change and economic redistribution, for example? Are Fianna Fáil and Fine Gael really flip sides of the same coin? And is Sinn Féin really the far left alternative that it is sometimes seen as being? In order to explore these policy issues, we draw on a unique database of candidate surveys covering general elections between 2007 and 2020.

THE IRISH COMPARATIVE CANDIDATE SURVEY

Run in the immediate aftermath of each general election since 2007, the Irish *Comparative Candidate Survey (CCS)* is part of a cross-national project that aims to collect comparable data covering the views and campaign experiences of candidates running in elections to national parliaments around the world. In Ireland, the *CCS* consists of a hardcopy questionnaire that is sent to every single individual whose name appeared on a constituency ballot paper. In 2020, for instance, 531 names in total appeared on these constituency ballots, representing 520 individual candidates.[4] A packet containing a 12-page survey was mailed to 519 of these candidates[5] on 8 February 2020, the day of the general election, along with a freepost envelope to return the booklet to the research team. Surveys take between 20 and 25 minutes to complete. A reminder postcard was sent to all candidates two weeks after the initial mailing. Data collection continued throughout the spring. As of mid-May 2020, 111 booklets had been returned to the research team, representing a response rate of 21 per cent.[6]

The overall response rate for the surveys conducted in 2007, 2011, 2016 and 2020 is provided in Table 11.1. This has varied by election, with nearly half of respondents replying in 2011 but just over a third in 2016 and only a fifth in 2020. The response rate was highest among Labour and Green Party candidates. It is also worth mentioning that the overall response rates for the Irish *CCS* have been at or above international averages for similar studies. For instance, in the 2017 German election survey, where only a representative sample of all candidates were surveyed, the final response rate was 32 per cent. In the UK in 2017, the final response

Table 11.1 Response rates for Irish *CCS* by party, in per cent

	2007	*2011*	*2016*	*2020*
Fianna Fáil	40.6	62.7	33.8	20.2
Fine Gael	40.7	40.4	23.9	14.6
Labour	60.0	47.0	44.4	16.1
Sinn Féin	29.3	36.6	34.0	28.6
Green Party	45.5	62.8	55.0	28.2
Independents/others	23.9	39.6	35.6	22.4
Total	37.2	45.2	35.3	21.4

rate (in a two-wave study) was 25 per cent, while in Italy in 2013 it was just 23 per cent.

The survey contains six different modules, covering issues such as the candidate's experience on the campaign trail, their ideological beliefs, their views on democracy and (more recently) their outlook on life. These surveys are completely anonymous (meaning that respondents cannot be identified by the research team).

There are several other ways of exploring parties' policy positions. We could, for instance, compare the election manifestos of the parties, we could examine the leadership debates or we could ask experts, such as journalists and academics, to estimate the parties' positions. Each method has its own advantages and drawbacks. In what follows, we use candidates' answers to questions about their own ideological positions and beliefs, as well as their placement of the parties along a general left–right political spectrum. We then aggregate these responses by party to produce overall party positions that are reflective of the views of their general election candidates.[7] We compare these overall party positions below.

PARTY MOVEMENT OVER TIME

This section compares the main Irish political parties with one another using a general left–right measure to capture the parties' positions. We do this by exploring where candidates choose to place their own parties in response to the following question: 'In politics, people sometimes talk about the "left" and the "right". Where would you place your own views and the views of some Irish parties on a scale of 0 to 10? Where 0 represents Left and 10 represents Right.'[8] Responses can take any value between 0 and 10. These items are presented to respondents in a single graphical matrix, enabling them to position the parties in relation to one another across the spectrum with ease prior to making their choice. This means that we can be confident that when respondents are making their selection they are thinking about how close the parties are to one another (e.g. is Fianna Fáil closer to Fine Gael or to the Labour Party?) rather than placing each party on the 11-point scale independently of one another.

In addition to party placement by candidates for each general election at which a candidate study was carried out (2007, 2011, 2016 and 2020), we include in our analysis the same data from the *Local Election Candidate Study (LECS)* in 2014 and 2019. The *LECS* is an equivalent candidate study that has been carried out at local elections in Ireland since 2014. Modelled on the *CCS*, it aims to gather data on the demographics and views of candidates in Ireland's local elections. The response rate for this candidate study has thus far been in line with, or higher than, that of the *CCS* (at 40 per cent in 2014 and 31 per cent in 2019).

Figure 11.1 presents the mean scores over time for the positions of the main political parties. These means are computed from the scores

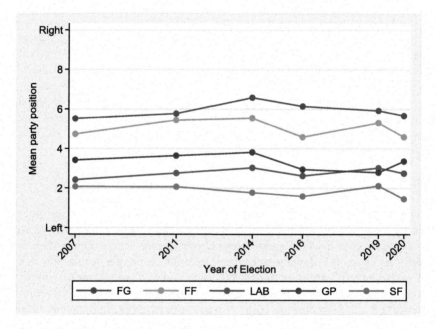

Fig. 11.1   Irish political party left–right placement, 2007–2020

provided by candidates running for that political party only (i.e. the score for Fine Gael is provided by Fine Gael candidates only, etc.). The first thing to note is the high degree of consistency of the mean party positions across the left–right political spectrum over time. None of the parties substantially changes position across the six elections for which we have data. Second, while the candidates do not make use of the full left–right spectrum when positioning the main parties in the Irish political system, it is clear that they do still make important distinctions between themselves (recall that higher values on this scale indicate a position that is farther to the right of the political spectrum). Third, there are no parties on the far right of the spectrum or even close to this position, unlike the case with many other European nations. None of the main political parties in Ireland self-defines as clearly right-wing.

Overall, Fine Gael is consistently positioned farthest to the right, with Fianna Fáil falling relatively close to it. These two parties have staked out the centre/centre-right ideological space, with the remaining three parties (Labour, the Greens and Sinn Féin) fanning out across the left of the political spectrum. Labour and the Greens start the period with a full point between their mean scores, but this difference narrows progressively over time so that by the 2016 election the parties' positions are indistinguishable from one another. We see a little separation in 2020, with Labour positioned very slightly to the left of the Greens. By contrast, Sinn Féin consistently finds itself the farthest to the left across the period, with the party's position pulling away from its nearest neighbour (Labour) in 2007, and moving slightly towards the left by 2020, at the end of the period.

With relatively small movements in the positions on the left–right spectrum, the most striking conclusion that we can draw from this initial analysis is the extent to which party positions remain largely consistent between 2007 and 2020. Fine Gael begins and ends the period in the same position. The same can be said of Fianna Fáil, Labour and the Green Party, with their 2020 mean scores representing only tiny differences. Only candidates running for Sinn Féin in 2020 are inclined to place their party identifiably to the left of its position in 2007, though this difference is only two-thirds of a point and does not represent a large jump on the scale. Taken together, these results suggest that, in the aggregate, the Irish electorate has been presented with a relatively consistent choice between parties that continue to occupy the same political space that they have long ago staked out.

To highlight this last point, Fig. 11.2 graphically illustrates party placement in 2020. Each point represents a party's left–right mean position (as revealed by its candidates' responses) with the bars representing the 95 per cent confidence intervals. These confidence intervals indicate the degree of uncertainty around the true value of the mean party position; the narrower the confidence interval the greater the degree of certainty.[9] Three things are particularly noteworthy in this figure. First, we can see clearly that in 2020 none of the five main political parties is occupying the right of the political spectrum. Indeed, only one party (Fine Gael) has a mean response that places it to the right of the centre position (5), and then only barely so (with a mean response of 5.7). Somewhat surprisingly, almost all party candidates consider their own parties to be left-wing. Second, the confidence intervals for some parties (notably Labour) are very wide, suggesting party members are not in agreement about the party's position or that the party represents quite a broad church.[10] The confidence intervals for Fianna Fáil and Sinn Féin are not as wide as that of Labour, but they do still indicate a lack of agreement within the parties. On the other hand,

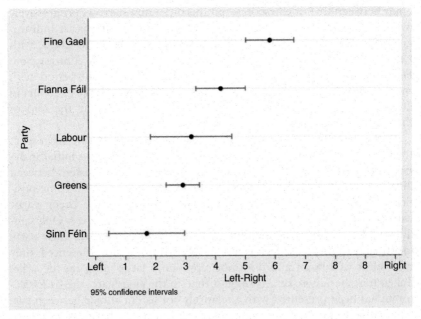

Fig. 11.2   Placement of parties on a general left–right scale, 2020
Source: CCS 2020

the Green Party's candidates are in agreement on the party's position. Third, there is overlap in the party positions of all parties. For instance, some members of Fianna Fáil consider themselves as left-wing as members of the Labour Party. It is also interesting to note that despite the efforts of Fine Gael and Fianna Fáil to differentiate themselves from one another in the minds of the electorate over the course of the 2020 campaign, even some of their own candidates fail to make an important distinction between their own party's left–right position and that of their main rival.

How Do Parties View One Another?

Having examined where candidates running for each of the five main political parties in Ireland have positioned their own parties along the left–right spectrum, we next investigate whether the party positions assigned by partisans are shared by their opponents. That is, do candidates running for a particular political party place their own party in the same position as do candidates running for other parties in the general election?

For each of the main political parties, we computed two left–right spectrum mean scores, one computed using responses from partisans only (these scores were presented in Fig. 11.2) and a second score computed using the responses from all other candidates who completed that item in the *CCS*.[11] Figure 11.3 presents the party positions for both the partisans (on the X-axis) and their opponents (on the Y-axis). The results are striking. Partisans and their opponents are broadly in agreement about whether a party is on the left or the right of the ideological spectrum. However, the two groups display significant disagreements about where *exactly* they should be positioned. Overall, partisans disagree with their opponents about how left-wing their party is; they consistently position their parties farther left than where their opponents place them.[12] If there was agreement on placement, we would expect the parties to line up along a 45-degree line; instead, they are consistently placed above it.

We can see that Fine Gael and Fianna Fáil exhibit the largest gaps between the views of its candidates and the views of its opponents. Fine Gael agrees that it is on the right of the political spectrum, but it views itself as a party that is only very slightly right-of-centre (with a placement score of 5.7). Its opponents, by contrast, assign it a position much farther to the right (with a score of 7.6). Fianna Fáil's ratings demonstrate a similar gap between its perception of itself as a party and its opponents' evaluations. Fianna Fáil partisans position the party on the centre-left, while its

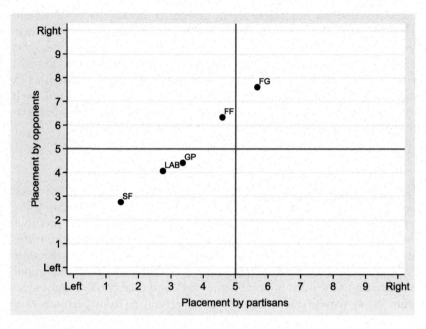

Fig. 11.3   Party positions as judged by partisans and by opponents, 2020
Source: CCS 2020

opponents view it as a centre-right party. The disagreements with respect to the three other parties are smaller in magnitude but display the same pattern: Labour, Sinn Féin and the Greens all believe they are farther to the left than their opponents do. This gap is the least pronounced for the Green Party.

It is interesting to note that whether we look at the partisan or opponent score, the ranking of the parties from left to right is consistent (Sinn Féin, Labour, the Greens, Fianna Fáil and Fine Gael). This suggests that there is broad agreement about the order in which political parties fall across the ideological spectrum. However, the consistency with which parties present themselves as being farther to the left than their opponents believe them to be is worth further consideration.

It is possible that the discrepancy may arise because opponents and partisans have different levels of knowledge with respect to the policy positions of each of the parties. This interpretation suggests that partisan positions are 'correct' in the sense that the candidates' greater familiarity allows them to more successfully evaluate the true position of the party. Placing such an interpretation on this finding is, however, potentially problematic. In the context of a hotly contested general election campaign, we can expect knowledge of policy positions of political parties to be high amongst all candidates, regardless of their party identification. An alternative variant on this interpretation is that opponents focus on a subset of salient policy positions when making their evaluations, while partisans take into account more information.

Whatever the cause, it is clear that partisans are consistently presenting their parties as farther to the left than their opponents' placement of them. This suggests that with respect to Irish party competition, it is desirable to be located more towards the left than the right of the political spectrum.[13]

Party Placement in 2020

In this section we explore in more detail the parties' positions on specific policy dimensions in the 2020 general election, as revealed by the candidates running for each party. In the previous sections, we looked at the general left–right placement of parties, but this is a rather broad conceptualisation of party positions; it reduces economic and social issues to one dimension and respondents may not understand the scale in the same way. For one candidate the concept of left may mostly refer to his or her attitudes to social issues such as abortion and marriage equality, whilst for another it may primarily reference attitudes to taxation and income redistribution. And while both issues probably go together for many candidates, it is, for instance, possible to be socially very liberal but fiscally quite conservative. In this section, we are particularly interested in exploring the degree to which the parties occupy distinct policy positions on some of the issues that mattered most in the 2020 election.

Figure 11.4 represents, in two dimensions, the Irish policy space in terms of a classic economic and social issue, income inequality and abortion rights. In both cases, the candidates were presented with a differential scale, with two opposing items at either end, and asked to place themselves along this continuum. With respect to the inequality item, respondents were asked to place themselves between the two opposing statements: 'the government should act to reduce differences in income and wealth' and 'the government should not act to reduce differences in income and wealth', anchored at zero and ten, respectively. For the abortion issue, the two end points were 'by law, abortion should never be permitted' (0)

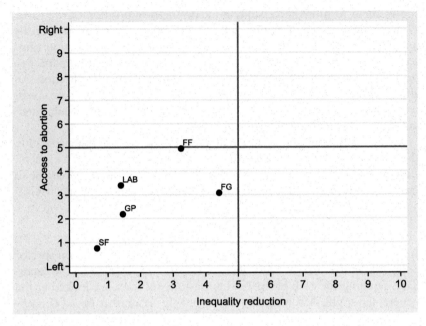

Fig. 11.4 Party placement on issues of abortion and income inequality, 2020
Source: CCS 2020

and 'by law, women should always be able to obtain an abortion as a matter of choice' (10). As we can see from Fig. 11.4, there is surprisingly little differentiation between the parties on either of these issues. All of the parties are more in favour of inequality reduction than not, being located to the left on the X-axis. While Fine Gael is to the right of the other four parties on this dimension, it is still more supportive of than opposed to government intervention to reduce income and wealth disparities. The Greens and Labour are barely distinguishable from each other on this dimension, while Sinn Féin is furthest left.

When it comes to the free availability of abortion (Y-axis), only Fianna Fáil finds itself nudging the upper-left quadrant of the graph, indicating lower levels of support for unrestricted access to abortion, but even so this position is at the centre. This is one policy dimension where Fine Gael and Fianna Fáil exhibit a marked difference which, given the history of the recent campaign to liberalise access to abortion in Ireland through the repeal of the eighth amendment to the constitution, is not surprising.[14]

Sinn Féin candidates have by far the most liberal views on access to abortion. Overall, the lack of variation between the parties, on both of these key dimensions, is striking. With the exception of Fianna Fáil's comparatively less liberal view regarding abortion restrictions, all of the parties position themselves in the bottom left-hand quadrant, indicating a left-wing position on both the economic and the social dimensions.

Given the centrality of housing as an issue in the 2020 campaign, we next explore party differences on this topic. The housing crisis had intensified significantly between the 2016 and 2020 general elections, marked by high levels of homelessness and spiralling rents (see Chaps. 1 and 10). The failure to adequately address the issue was seen as a significant weakness on the part of the incumbent Fine Gael government. As one of the key issues of the campaign, significant portions of all parties' manifestos were dedicated to policy solutions for the problem.

Fianna Fáil adopted a three-pronged approach, which included expanding social housing, bolstering tenants' rights and also offering incentives to the construction sector. In addition, the party's proposed Special Savings Incentive Allowance (SSIA)-type scheme for first-time buyers would give those saving for a deposit €1 for every €3 saved up a maximum of €10,000.[15] Fine Gael, meanwhile, proposed the expansion of its existing Help to Buy scheme (a tax cut for first-time buyers), alongside an increase in the stock of new-build housing. Sinn Féin resolutely set itself up in opposition to these kinds of market-based solutions, with its leader Mary Lou McDonald stating during one of the earlier televised debates that '[i]f Fianna Fáil were the party of the developers, Fine Gael are the party of the landlords'.[16] Instead, Sinn Féin proposed that 100,000 public homes be built on public land over the next five years, 10,000 of which would be affordable rental accommodation. In addition, its proposal to freeze rents for the first three years of the next government, along with a tax credit for renters worth up to €15,000, positioned the party as a champion of renters rather than homeowners.[17]

In Fig. 11.5 we plot the parties' positions on the issue, by examining whether the parties have a preference for providing subsidies to renters or home buyers. Again, candidates were presented with opposing statements and asked where their view would fall between the two. With respect to housing subsidies (the X-axis on the graph), the farthest left position is captured by the statement: 'the government should prioritise initiatives that subsidise renters to lower the cost of their monthly rental payments', while the farthest right position is captured by the statement 'the

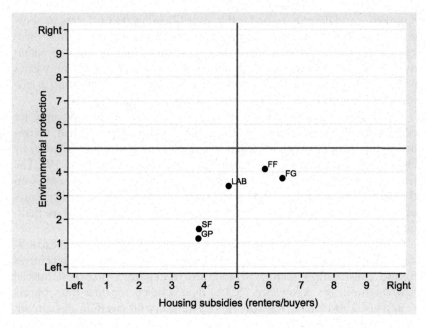

Fig. 11.5 Party placement on issues of environment and housing subsidies, 2020
Source: CCS 2020

government should prioritise initiatives that subsidise those seeking to buy a home'. The question wording is not unproblematic—it is difficult to capture the complexity of housing policy in one simple issue item. However, the question is designed to capture a preference for prioritising affordable rents over private property ownership. We would expect a left-wing partisan, when faced with this choice and forced to make a decision, to favour affordable rents over private ownership.

The Y-axis places the parties in terms of their attitudes to environmental protection, another issue that received a lot of media coverage in 2020, although, as it turned out, it was not a top issue for Irish voters when it came to casting their ballot (see Chap. 10 for a discussion). The anchor points of the Y-axis represent the following positions: 'we should protect the environment even if this damages economic growth' (0), and 'we should encourage economic growth even if this damages the environment' (10).

As we can see from the figure, there is some variation on the housing issue, with both Fianna Fáil and Fine Gael candidates having a preference for subsidising home ownership over renters. Labour is neutral on the issue, while the Greens and Sinn Féin have a slight preference for rental subsidies. On the environment, all parties favour its protection over economic growth with, unsurprisingly, the Green Party taking the strongest position on the issue. But again, on these two dimensions, there is surprisingly little variation amongst the parties; they all cluster around the centre of the bottom half of the graph. This result is interesting given that the parties did exhibit significant variation during the campaign with respect to their proposed policies addressing climate change. Only the Greens' manifesto put forward very significant commitments—such as the 7 per cent annual reduction in CO_2 emissions—that could prove to be very economically costly.[18] It is likely then that the clustering that we observe across parties on this item results either from respondents' exhibiting social desirability bias or from a rejection of the premise of the item (i.e. that there is a trade-off between environmental protection and economic growth).

To see if there were any greater differences than those found above between the parties on policy, we further investigated variation in party positions across four other policy areas included in the candidate study. Two of these ('right to privacy' and 'legalisation of recreational drugs') capture social issues and relate to parties' positions to issues of crime. Discussion of whether parties were 'soft' on crime did emerge over the course of the general election campaign, in part due to a number of murders that took place in the opening week of the campaign, leading Fine Gael's opponents to question its record in that area and threatening its historical position as the party of law and order.[19] Fianna Fáil and Fine Gael also sought to portray Sinn Féin as soft on crime as support for that party jumped sharply in the polls. They used the three-way leaders' debate to press Sinn Féin leader Mary Lou McDonald on the issue of her party's lack of support for the Special Criminal Court, which is used to prosecute the most serious criminal offences.[20] And the issue of the parties' stance on the use of recreational drugs was very briefly covered in the wake of Virgin Media's two-way leaders' debate between Micheál Martin and Leo Varadkar at the outset of the campaign, where the Taoiseach was taken by surprise after being pressed on his personal drug use.[21] The two other policy areas ('regulation' and 'increasing spending and taxation') are

Table 11.2   Party policy positions (economic and social dimensions)

		Fianna Fáil	Fine Gael	Greens	Labour	Sinn Féin
Social issues	Privacy rights (0) versus combat crime (10)	6.40	6.58	5.64	6.40	5.92
	Drug legalisation: Anti (0) versus pro (10)	7.19	5.33	2.36	4.40	5.18
Economic issues	Tax/spend: Increase spending (0) versus cut taxes (10)	4.00	4.58	2.18	2.40	1.75
	Regulation of business: Strict (0) versus none (10)	5.00	4.75	3.18	3.80	2.42

Note: See Appendix for full details of questions

standard items used cross-nationally capturing economic issues. The wording of these items can be found in the Appendix to this chapter.

As we can see in Table 11.2, some interesting differences between the parties emerge across these issues. With respect to the two items capturing social issues, we can see that it is only for the issue of drug legalisation that the parties display significant disagreement. When it comes to protecting privacy rights even if this were to hinder efforts to combat crime, the parties cluster together, with the positions of Fianna Fáil, Fine Gael and the Labour Party being indistinguishable on the issue. There is a slight separation between this group and Sinn Féin, with the Green Party finding itself closest to the centre. On the whole, though, we can see little variation across parties with respect to their willingness to trade off the privacy rights of the individual if this will help to combat crime.

With respect to support for the legalisation of recreational drugs, we do see the parties fanning out across the left and right to a significant degree. The Greens and Labour occupy the left of the spectrum here, with the position of the Green Party farthest to the left, while Fine Gael and Sinn Féin's positions are in the centre, just barely to the right. But it is Fianna Fáil that finds itself substantially to the right, expressing the greatest degree of opposition to legalisation. This represents an important area of separation between Fine Gael and Fianna Fáil, and something that emerged during the RTÉ leaders' debate, moderated by Claire Byrne: Leo Varadkar advocated a public-health-based approach, while Micheál Martin adopted the position that drug use was a criminal justice issue.[22]

With respect to the two items capturing two economic issues, we again largely observe the same pattern of clustering of parties on the left of the political spectrum. Sinn Féin is farthest to the left with respect to its support for strict regulation on business and industry, and support for increasing taxation and expenditure on health and social services. The party is followed by the Greens, then Labour. We see some very slight separation between Fianna Fáil and Fine Gael here. Fine Gael candidates place their party to the left both with respect to attitudes towards regulation and tax/spend. Fianna Fáil however finds itself to the left of its closest rival on the tax/spend item, but very slightly to its right with respect to regulation of business and industry (though still in the centre of the left–right spectrum).

Across the four issues explored in this section, we found the parties to be surprisingly similar. The only issue on which we found significant variation was the issue of drug legalisation which, though it was raised briefly, was notably not an issue in the campaign. And it is worth noting the separation of Fianna Fáil with respect to its attitude towards liberalisation of abortion. Overall, though, when we dig into representative issues, we can conclude that the main Irish political parties compete with one another around the left and centre of the political spectrum.

CONCLUSION

Historically, Ireland has been the 'odd man out' in European politics, in that party competition has been a battle 'between two centre-right parties that were ideologically indistinct' from each other.[23] But in 2020 the campaign narrative revolved around the emergence, for the first time, of a credible alternative left-wing led government. In this chapter, we explored to what extent this account of left- versus right-wing holds.

Overall, it is clear that the parties self-identify as occupying distinct positions on a general left–right scale, neatly lining up with Sinn Féin and Fine Gael as bookends. And these positions are maintained over time, with very little variation in the period 2007–20. However, it is also clear that Irish parties consider themselves to be quite left-wing, with no parties occupying the right to far right of the political spectrum. Even Fine Gael considers itself to be essentially a centrist party—though other parties view it as more to the right.

However, when one decomposes the super-dimension of left–right into its component parts, the degree to which the parties are offering distinct policy platforms is less clear. There is surprisingly little variation (as revealed by the preferences of party candidates) on issues such as inequality, environmental protection, housing and even once divisive moral issues such as abortion.

It should be noted that the analysis in this chapter focussed on the views and preferences of the candidates running for election for the five main parties, rather than on official party policy, as revealed in, for instance, party manifestos. We have taken an average of the candidates' responses to represent the party positions, but averages can hide a lot of information. As we saw in Fig. 11.2, candidates from the same party can have quite varied views on issues and their own party's position.

The question of whether parties are chasing voters or whether there are large swathes of voters whose views are not represented has not been directly addressed in this chapter, but it is notable that the right of the political spectrum is a space that is not currently occupied by a viable political party. It does suggest, though, that the framing of the 2020 election as a 'change election' with a clear left alternative being offered to voters has perhaps been overstated. In fact, there is a high degree of policy agreement between the main political parties and, in the aggregate, there has been little movement in party positions since 2007.

Appendix: Question Wording

Abortion rights: 'Opposing statements are listed. Where would you place yourself on this scale?
0 = by law, abortion should never be permitted
...
10 = by law, women should always be able to obtain an abortion as a matter of choice'

Drug legalisation: 'Opposing statements are listed. Where would you place yourself on this scale?
0 = the use of recreational drugs should be legalised in Ireland
...
10 = all recreational drugs should remain illegal in Ireland'

Environment: 'Opposing statements are listed. Where would you place yourself on this scale?
0 = we should protect the environment even if this damages economic growth
...
10 = we should encourage economic growth even if this damages the environment'

Housing subsidies—renters/homeowners: 'Opposing statements are listed. Where would you place yourself on this scale?

0 = the government should prioritise initiatives that subsidise renters to lower the cost of their monthly rental payments

…

10 = the government should prioritise initiatives that subsidise those seeking to buy a home'

Inequality: 'Opposing statements are listed. Where would you place yourself on this scale?

0 = the government should act to reduce differences in income and wealth

…

10 = the government should not act to reduce differences in income and wealth'

Left–right party position: 'In politics, people sometimes talk about the "left" and "right". Where would you place [PARTY]?'

0 = Left

…

10 = Right

Privacy rights: 'Opposing statements are listed. Where would you place yourself on this scale?

0 = privacy rights should be supported even if they hinder efforts to combat crime

…

10 = privacy rights should be restricted in order to combat crime'

Regulation: 'Opposing statements are listed. Where would you place yourself on this scale?

0 = business and industry should be strictly regulated by the state

…

10 = business and industry should be entirely free from regulation by the state'

Tax/spend: 'Opposing statements are listed. Where would you place yourself on this scale?

0 = government should increase taxes a lot and spend more on health and social services

…

10 = government should cut taxes a lot and spend much less on health and social services'

NOTES

1. *Giving workers & families a break: a Manifesto for Change*, January 2020, p. 3, available at: https://www.sinnfein.ie/files/2020/SF_GE2020_Manifesto.pdf.

2. *Invest in better: general election manifesto 2020*, January 2020, p. 5, available at: https://www.socialdemocrats.ie/wp-content/uploads/2018/06/Invest-in-Better-GE2020-1st-Feb.pdf.

3. *People Before Profit: election manifesto 2020*, January 2020, p. 6, available at: https://manifesto.pbp.ie/wp-content/uploads/2020/01/People-Before-Profit-General-Election-Manifesto-2020.pdf.

4. Independent candidate Peter Casey contested the election in two constituencies, Donegal and the Taoiseach's constituency of Dublin West, while Seán O'Leary's name appeared on the ballot in 11 separate constituencies.

5. One candidate, Marese Skehan, passed away on 3 February, five days before the election, but her name remained on the ballot in Tipperary.

6. The 2020 survey response rate was affected by the Covid-19 pandemic in Ireland. Universities closed on 12 March, interrupting the data collection process.

7. Other research in the Irish context has been concerned with exploring intra-party variation in these attitudes using survey data. See, for example, Michael Courtney, 'Social background and intra-party attitudes in Ireland', *Irish Political Studies* 30:2 (2015), pp. 178–98.

8. Respondents were asked to provide left–right positions for all of the main political parties discussed here (Fine Gael, Fianna Fáil, Labour, the Greens and Sinn Féin), as well as Solidarity–People Before Profit. In addition, we asked them to indicate where they would position their own views.

9. Where confidence intervals overlap with one another, it is not possible to conclude that the mean party positions are different from one another. So, while we can conclude that Fine Gael and Sinn Féin's positions on the left–right spectrum are different from one another, we cannot say the same for those of the Greens and Labour.

10. This is also probably a function of the number of responses that were received from Labour Party candidates before the pandemic lockdown put an end to data gathering. We would expect this confidence interval to narrow with a higher response rate.

11. Although the analysis for this chapter is concerned with the five main political parties, the mean non-partisan ideological placement score contains responses from candidates from all other parties, as well as from independent candidates.

12. The differences between the mean partisan and mean opponent scores are statistically significant for all parties except for Labour. This is probably a function of the low number of responses from that party.
13. Certainly, there does seem to be a political calculation around placement of the political parties. When we consult the placement of Irish political parties by contributors to the *Chapel Hill Expert Survey*, we find that the experts give a score that falls between those of partisans and opponents. In 2019, the most recent year for which this data is available, the experts assigned the parties the following positions on a 0–10 scale: Fine Gael (5.9), Fianna Fáil (5.4), Labour (3.6), Green Party (3.1), and Sinn Féin (2.6). This ordering of the parties from right to left is consistent with the order from the 2019 LECS responses (see Fig. 11.1). Data from Ryan Bakker et al., 1999–2019 Chapel Hill Expert Survey Trend File, version 1.2 (2020). Available on chesdata.eu.
14. Luke Field, 'The abortion referendum of 2018 and a timeline of abortion politics in Ireland to date', *Irish Political Studies* 33:4 (2018), pp. 608–28.
15. *An Ireland for all Éire do Chách*, January 2020, p. 57.
16. Pat Leahy, 'Leaders' debate: Fine Gael, Fianna Fáil target Sinn Féin's economic policies', *Irish Times* 5 February 2020.
17. *Giving workers & families a break: a Manifesto for Change*, January 2020, p. 3, available at: https://www.sinnfein.ie/files/2020/SF_GE2020_Manifesto.pdf.
18. *Towards 2030: a decade of change*, January 2020, available at: https://www.greenparty.ie/wp-content/uploads/2020/01/GREEN_PARTY_TOWARDS_2030-WEB-VERSION.pdf.
19. Conor Lally, 'Election 2020: Is Leo Varadkar right when he says Ireland's crime rate is low?', *Irish Times* 20 January 2020.
20. Philip Ryan, Cormac McQuinn and Hugh O'Connell, 'General election 2020 Prime Time debate: leaders clash over housing and Special Criminal Court', *Irish Independent* 4 February 2020.
21. Fiach Kelly, '"I'm not going to go into any more detail"—Varadkar faces drugs question again', *Irish Times* 23 January 2020.
22. Patrick Freyne, 'Election 2020 TV debate: the best debater is, unexpectedly, Richard Boyd Barrett', *Irish Times*, 28 January 2020.
23. Gail McElroy, 'Party competition in Ireland', pp. 61–82 in Michael Marsh, David M. Farrell and Gail McElroy (eds), *A Conservative Revolution? Electoral change in twenty-first-century Ireland* (Oxford: Oxford University Press, 2017), p. 61.

CHAPTER 12

The Seanad Election: Voting in Unprecedented Times

Claire McGing

The 2020 general election to Seanad Éireann, the upper of the two Houses of the Oireachtas (parliament), was very unusual. Regulations introduced by the government in an attempt to slow the spread of the coronavirus (Covid-19) necessitated changes to the conduct of the campaign and the counting of votes. In addition, the absence of a new government meant that the Seanad membership was not fully constituted for another 12 weeks after the counting of the votes. As a result, the 2020 Seanad elections seemed to have more public visibility than previous elections to the house.

I am very grateful to the candidates, electors and party strategists who agreed to be interviewed for this chapter. Thank you to Dr Adrian Kavanagh (Maynooth University), who provided me with access to his database of candidates in the 2020 Seanad elections. For a full list of candidates per panel, see his blog: https://adriankavanaghelections.org/2020/02/17/elections-to-26th-seanad-2020-lists-of-nominated-declared-candidates/.

C. McGing (✉)
Institute of Art, Design and Technology (IADT), Dún Laoghaire, Ireland
e-mail: Claire.McGing@iadt.ie

© The Author(s), under exclusive license to Springer Nature Switzerland AG 2021
M. Gallagher et al. (eds.), *How Ireland Voted 2020*,
https://doi.org/10.1007/978-3-030-66405-3_12

The chapter first summarises the history of Seanad Éireann and outlines the chamber's role in the legislative process, its composition and voting system. It examines the election of the 43 vocational panel members in detail—their nomination, the electorate, the particular dynamics of a Seanad campaign and the results. It then considers the election of the six university seats and the appointment of 11 senators by the Taoiseach. To conclude, the chapter speculates on the role that the 26th Seanad might play in the Fianna Fáil, Fine Gael and Green Party coalition government. The prospect of long-overdue Seanad reform occurring over the lifetime of this government is also assessed.

SEANAD ÉIREANN

The Republic of Ireland has a bicameral system of government; that is, a legislature comprising two chambers. As of 31 December 2019, 59 per cent (113) of parliaments around the world were unicameral and 41 per cent (79) bicameral.[1] The current Seanad dates from 1937, but the island of Ireland has experienced various forms of bicameralism since the fourteenth century.[2] The Irish Free State Seanad was initially not organised along party lines, and it played an active legislative role before being abolished by the Fianna Fáil government in 1936.[3] The 60-seat Seanad was established by the 1937 constitution. In the area of legislation, Dáil Éireann is by far the more powerful of the two houses, and the constitution gives the Seanad delaying powers only.[4]

What makes Seanad Éireann particularly unusual in comparison to other upper chambers is that it formally emphasises the representation of vocational and technical interests as opposed to the representation of territories or populations. The drafters of the 1937 constitution were heavily influenced by Roman Catholic ideals, and vocationalism was a popular concept in Catholic social theory in the 1930s.[5] The chamber combines indirectly elected members and appointees, being composed of:

- Forty-three members indirectly elected from five 'vocational' panels
- Six members elected by university graduates (three seats allocated to the University of Dublin (Trinity College) constituency and three to the National University of Ireland (NUI) constituency)
- Eleven members nominated by the Taoiseach

In reality the chamber has been dominated by party politicians, particularly on the vocational panels and also among the Taoiseach's nominees, although the latter were less partisan in 2011 and 2016 (the Taoiseach's nominees are essentially intended as a safeguard to ensure government control of the house).[6] The Seanad has been criticised as being a 'crèche' for aspiring TDs attempting to build up their political capital or a 'retirement home' for former TDs.[7] In 2013, a referendum to abolish it was rejected by a 52–48 margin, with a turnout of just 39 per cent. Numerous recommendations for reform have been published over the years, but so far governments have not had the political interest to implement many.

The constitution links the timing of Seanad elections to the Dáil electoral process. The specifics of Seanad elections are dealt with by legislation. A general election to the Seanad must take place not later than 90 days after the dissolution of the Dáil. The dates for the various stages of the election (candidate nominations, issuing of ballot papers and closing of polls) are set by order of the Minister for Housing, Planning and Local Government. In 2020, polling for the vocational panels closed at 11 am on 30 March, and votes were counted between 30 March and 3 April. For the university seats, polling closed at 11 am on 31 March, and counting was completed the following day. A series of contingency measures were put in place at the count centres to deal with the Covid-19 pandemic, including severely restricting access.

THE PANEL SEATS

The five vocational panels elect between 5 and 11 Senators each (see Table 12.1). Article 18.7 of the constitution lists the various panels:

- National Language and Culture, Literature, Art, Education and such professional interests as may be defined by law for the purpose of this panel
- Agriculture and allied interests, and Fisheries
- Labour, whether organised or unorganised
- Industry and Commerce, including banking, finance, accountancy, engineering and architecture
- Public Administration and social services, including voluntary social activities

Table 12.1   Seanad vocational panels and nominating bodies, 2020

Panel	Senators		Nominating bodies (2020)	
	Total seats	Minimum seats per sub-panel	No. of bodies	Maximum nominees per body
Administrative	7	3	20	1
Agricultural	11	4	10	2
Cultural and Educational	5	2	34	1
Industrial and Commercial	9	3	47	1
Labour	11	4	2	7
Total	43	–	113	–

The Panel Nominations

The nomination process for candidates is considerably more complex than it is for Dáil elections. There are two sub-panels for each panel: the nominating bodies sub-panel (known as the 'outside' panel) and the Oireachtas sub-panel (known as the 'inside' panel). The law specifies a minimum number of candidates who must be elected from each sub-panel. Candidates running for the outside panel require nomination by a recognised nominating body. The Seanad returning officer (the Clerk of the Seanad) maintains a register of bodies entitled to nominate candidates, which is revised annually. They must meet minimum requirements, and profit-making bodies are not eligible for registration. A body cannot be registered in respect of more than one panel. Additionally, any four members of the newly elected Dáil or outgoing Seanad may nominate one candidate for any panel, but each member may join in only one nomination. Proposals for outside nominations close earlier than proposals for inside nominations (in 2020, the former closed on 24 February and the latter on 2 March). Parties wait to see which of their candidates have secured outside nominations before finalising their inside candidates. Some candidates may feel confident about their prospects of attaining an inside nomination. Those, often including some former TDs, who are not confident of their standing with the party leadership will usually seek an outside nomination. Many aspirants regard an inside nomination as a stronger route to election, though not all candidates share this view. Electoral success is largely determined by the individual's public profile, the ability to attain votes across the political system, support provided by the political party and having the resources to conduct a large campaign.[8]

Nominating Bodies Sub-panel

The number of nominations each body can make depends on the number of bodies registered for the panel and the number of senators to be elected from it. Overall, the higher the number of bodies eligible to propose candidates, the lower the number of candidates each one can put forward (see Table 12.1). Candidates can be nominated by more than one nominating body on the same panel. Individuals with multiple nominations are often high-profile candidates and/or strongly associated with a particular cause or issue. In 2020, for example, former Fianna Fáil TD Timmy Dooley was nominated to the Industrial and Commercial panel by a diverse group of five bodies including the Restaurants Association of Ireland and the Irish Postmasters' Union. Seanad incumbent and disability campaigner, John Dolan, was nominated to the Administrative panel by six different bodies concerned with various aspects of disability supports. Of course, another motivation for party members to secure multiple nominations is that it blocks the opportunity for a rival to get one of these nominations.[9]

Reflecting the nominally vocational nature of the panels, the constitution states that members must have 'knowledge and practical experience' of the 'interests and services' of the relevant panel (Article 18.7). In reality, there is no statutory definition for the level of qualification a candidate must possess.[10] The level of connection that candidates have to the vocational theme of the panel they are running on is, at times, vague or even questionable—this is further illustrated by the influence of political parties. It is rare for nominees to be deemed ineligible to run, and it happened to only one in 2020. Paul Hayes, a Sinn Féin councillor, was nominated by the Irish South and West Fish Producers Organisation (ISWFPO) to contest the Agricultural panel. However, an assessment process by a panel including the returning officer and a high court judge concluded that although he had knowledge of issues regarding fishing and farming, he did not have the practical experience to contest the panel and he was excluded.[11] Advocates of Seanad reform have argued that the qualifications of eligible candidates should be defined by legislation.[12] The Clerk of the Seanad, Martin Groves, is also on record as supporting such a change.[13]

The profiles of candidates in 2020 show the dominance of political parties on the outside sub-panels (see Table 12.2). Of the 74 candidates, 53 were linked to parties. Fifty seven were elected representatives at national

Table 12.2   Candidates on sub-panels by party affiliation, 2020

	Fianna Fáil	Fine Gael	Sinn Féin	Labour Party	Green Party	Social Democrats	Independent/ Other	Total
Nominating body	27	22	2	2	0	0	21	74
Oireachtas	9	14	5	3	3	1	9	44
Total	36	36	7	5	3	1	30	118

Note: The Independent/Other column includes Aontú

or local level, and seventeen were unsuccessful candidates in the recent general election. Nominating bodies may feel that party affiliation equates with electability for candidates and therefore gives them better access to Oireachtas members for lobbying and advocacy purposes.[14] Parties flex their muscles on all sub-panels, from 79 per cent of Industry and Commerce panel nominees to 50 per cent of the Administrative panel nominees. However, the increasing number of independents and candidates attached to particular causes illustrates some movement towards a less partisan system. In 2020, 21 independents contested on an outside sub-panel; the corresponding figure in 2016 was 15. Between three and five independents contested each panel. Notably, five of the 10 candidates on the Administrative panel (where bodies could nominate a single candidate each) were independents, all closely linked to civil society. Among these, Salome Mbugua Henry (nominated by the Immigrant Council of Ireland) was the first woman of colour in history to contest for a seat in the Seanad.

Oireachtas Sub-panel

Oireachtas sub-panel nominations are also dominated by political parties. There are usually fewer inside nominations than outside, and each party, able to calculate the number of electoral quotas available to it on each panel, tightly manages the selection process (see Table 12.2). Parties employ different candidate selection methods for the Seanad. In Fianna Fáil, the party leadership decided on candidates and prioritised the selection of candidates who had been unsuccessful at the Dáil general election. In 2011 and (unofficially) in 2016 the leadership encouraged Fianna Fáil electors to give higher levels of support to candidates on a preferred list, but this was not practised in 2020. In Fine Gael a selection commission (appointed by the executive council) chose candidates from a panel submitted by various organs of the party. Party strategy focused on candidates in constituencies where Fine Gael could make gains in the next general election and on gender balance. Following the party's failure to progress women's representation in the general election, many were surprised when former deputy Kate O'Connell, a prominent figure in the campaign for abortion rights, failed to receive an inside nomination from Fine Gael.[15] In Labour the central council and parliamentary party choose candidates through a vote (see account of Labour senator Marie Sherlock in Chap. 7). Labour had not returned any women TDs in the general election and selectors were encouraged to consider gender balance. The Sinn Féin ard chomhairle (executive committee) decided its nominees. The Social Democrats' national executive chose its candidate following nominations by branches (two or more branches needed to nominate). Finally, aspirants in the Green Party had to obtain endorsement from a member of the executive committee and submit an application form, with shortlisted candidates invited to interview. There were reports of disquiet within the party after some high-profile candidates failed to get selected.[16]

As with the nominating bodies sub-panel, independents have become more prominent on Oireachtas sub-panels, and nine ran in 2020 (an increase of one since 2016). With the exception of Culture and Education, between one and three independents contested each Oireachtas sub-panel. Across the panels, the increasing number of independent candidates in 2020 reflects wider shifts in the electoral landscape. Non-partisan representatives were highly visible in Irish politics between 2016 and 2020, including presence at the cabinet table and the formation of technical groups by independent members in the Dáil and Seanad. Gerard Craughwell was a particularly high-profile independent in the 25th Seanad. In the 2016 Seanad election, Craughwell played a key role in actively engaging independent councillors to vote for independents and building an informal alliance between independent politicians.[17] A number of independent candidates strategically engaged with independent voters in 2020, one of the most prominent being Sharon Keogan, who contested the Industry and Commerce Oireachtas sub-panel (Craughwell was one of her nominators). All of these factors contributed to the overall increase in the number of non-partisan candidates in 2020.

The Panel Electorate

The composition of the electorate for the five vocational panels is determined by legislation. In 2020, the electorate numbered 1161: 949 city and county councillors, 160 incoming TDs and 52 outgoing senators (see Table 12.3). Separate ballot papers are issued for each of the five panels (electors have a vote on each panel), and they show the names of the candidates in alphabetical order, their addresses and descriptions, photographs, if any, and the sub-panel for which each is nominated. Political affiliations are not listed. The electoral system is proportional representation by the single transferable vote (PR-STV).[18] In previous elections, political parties, including Fine Gael and Sinn Féin, have brought their members together in Leinster House or at local authority level to vote. This was not possible in 2020 because of social distancing regulations.[19] Electors had to make one-on-one appointments with a local authority official or Garda superintendent to have their declaration of identity form signed. The number of people in social isolation during the polling period, including members of the electorate and officials, and the fact that council officials had other work pressures (e.g. housing issues) created difficulties for electors trying to cast their votes. All votes are cast by registered post. Party organisers remind their representatives to vote.

The Seanad electorate has changed considerably from earlier elections. Notable has been the decline in the combined strength of what were formerly Ireland's major political parties, Fianna Fáil, Fine Gael and Labour, and an increase in support for independent and other party representatives, which is further reflected in the diversifying membership of the upper house. The three parties comprised 84 per cent of the electorate in 2002,[20] but by 2020 this figure had fallen to 60 per cent (see Table 12.3). One of the main changes is the increased presence of Green Party and Social Democrat voters. Independent and other councillors made up a fifth of the electorate in 2020, and they are canvassed by candidates across the party spectrum as floating voters. Importantly, a number of independent councillors have previous links to Fianna Fáil, Fine Gael and increasingly Sinn Féin. These 'gene pool' candidates are potential sources of support for former party colleagues and are strategically targeted by them.

Seanad election campaigns have been described as the 'Discover Ireland' route to the Oireachtas.[21] Campaigns are considerably more onerous than Dáil elections, and personal interaction with local councillors and Oireachtas representatives is key. Traditionally, candidates travel across the country to

Table 12.3 Composition of the Seanad electorate, 2020

Component	Fianna Fáil	Fine Gael	Sinn Féin	Labour Party	Green Party	Social Democrats	Independent/Other	Total
Councillors	279	255	81	57	49	19	209	949 (82%)
TDs	38	35	37	6	12	6	26	160 (14%)
Senators	12	17	4	2	1	0	16	52 (4%)
Total	329	307	122	65	62	25	251	1161
	(28.3%)	(26.4%)	(10.5%)	(5.6%)	(5.3%)	(2.1%)	(21.6%)	(100%)

Note: The Independent/Other column includes Solidarity–PBP (which had 11 councillors and five TDs), Aontú and all other minor parties meet electors in their homes, at workplaces or at council meetings, and any other forms of campaigning were supplementary. However, the outbreak of Covid-19 fundamentally changed the dynamics of the campaign for the 2020 election. Candidates were forced to cease physical canvassing when social distancing regulations were introduced just three days into the official campaign on 12 March, and instead they communicated with electors by email, video-conferencing software, letter or over the phone. Candidates often report that it is difficult to gauge how successful a Seanad campaign has been in garnering enough votes to be elected.

One of the most hidden elements of a Seanad election is the degree of brokering between individual candidates and parties for votes, essentially 'politicians doing politics'.[22] These 'gentlemen's agreements' see smaller parties agree to support each other on panels where they are not running a candidate or they target transfer votes. Independents may engage in similar agreements with other independents or parties.[23] In larger parties, pacts are usually negotiated at a local level or on specific panels. To ensure that promised votes are 'delivered', party organisers contact electors with strong guidance on how to vote on specific panels.[24] As we shall see later, a number of vote pacts appear to have existed in the 2020 election.

The Panel Results

The shutdown placed the 2020 Seanad election in unprecedented territory. Strict social distancing guidelines were introduced at the count centres, and access to these spaces was severely limited. All bar two electors (1159) returned the covering envelopes, but 16 were rejected because of issues with the covering envelope (compared to 12 in 2016), and 6 were rejected because the declarations of identity were not completed (4 in 2016).

Since the political composition of the electorate is known and party discipline is strong, the outcome of Seanad elections can be predicted with a high degree of confidence. Fianna Fáil gained two seats on the vocational panels (see Table 12.4). Fine Gael lost a seat on the Industrial and Commercial panel due to errors in electoral strategy. Sinn Féin attained a seat on each panel but lost two seats overall after local election losses in 2019, and the party performed poorly on transfers, as discussed below. The Labour Party figure registered no change from 2016, while the Green Party gained one seat. Following a breakthrough in 2016, the number of independent/other senators remained unchanged. In 2020, 24 senators were

Table 12.4 Party affiliation of 49 elected senators (panel and university seats)

Party	No. of senators	Change since 2016
Fianna Fáil	16	+2
Fine Gael	12	-1
Sinn Féin	5	-2
Labour	5	0
Green party	2	+1
Independent/other	9	0
Total	49	0

nominated by Oireachtas members and 19 by nominating bodies. This contrasts with most elections over the period 1987–2016, where a higher number of elected senators came from the nominating bodies panel.[25] Inside candidates won an average 65 votes, compared to 37 votes for outside candidates. This trend has been well established in previous elections and gives some weight to the suggestion that an Oireachtas nomination is a better route to election. However, this crude analysis does not consider the different level of competitiveness across the sub-panels and the fact that outside candidates are less likely to have a strong public profile.[26]

The results illustrate high levels of partisanship among Fianna Fáil electors, and the party did considerably better than its electoral profile. It exceeded its 'core' vote across all panels, by 113 votes on Administration down to 12 votes on Industry and Commerce (see Table 12.5), and attracted transfers from across the party system and independents. It gained a seat on the Administration and Agricultural panels. On Administration, incumbent Mark Daly's tally of 167 votes was the highest vote won by any vocational candidate in 2020. Significantly, Fianna Fáil received over four electoral quotas on the Labour panel with seven candidates. Lisa Chambers and Malcolm Byrne were among the most high-profile losses in the Dáil election, and both secured seats on the Culture and Education panel. Timmy Dooley, another high-profile TD to lose his seat in 2020, was not successful on the Industry and Commerce panel.

An analysis of the outcome shows that partisanship was strong among Fine Gael voters, although there was some slippage on Agriculture and Administration (see Table 12.5). The party gained 58 votes from unaffiliated electors on Culture and Education and 38 on Industry and Commerce. Fine Gael secured three electoral quotas on the Industrial and Commercial panel, but it had too many candidates on this panel: 16 candidates (13 outside and 3 inside)—a number of whom were low profile—contesting

Table 12.5   Results of Seanad panel elections by party, 2020

Group	Fianna Fáil	Fine Gael	Sinn Féin	Labour Party	Green Party	Social Democrats	Independent/ Other	Total
Culture and education	377	365	151	0	114	0	126	1133
(candidates–seats)	(7–2)	(6–2)	(1–1)	(0–0)	(1–0)	(0–0)	(5–0)	(20–5)
Agriculture	364	296	147	72	76	0	175	1130
(candidates–seats)	(8–4)	(6–3)	(2–1)	(2–1)	(1–1)	(0–0)	(6–1)	(25–11)
Labour	408	311	92	79	80	0	163	1133
(candidates–seats)	(8–4)	(4–3)	(2–1)	(1–1)	(1–1)	(0–0)	(4–1)	(20–11)
Industry and commerce	341	345	95	84	0	88	182	1135
(candidates–seats)	(7–3)	(16–2)	(1–1)	(1–1)	(0–0)	(1–0)	(8–2)	(34–9)
Administration	442	288	120	104	0	0	180	1134
(candidates–seats)	(6–3)	(4–2)	(1–1)	(1–1)	(0–0)	(0–0)	(7–0)	(19–7)
Electorate	329	307	122	65	62	25	251	1161
(total candidates–seats)	(36–16)	(36–12)	(7–5)	(5–4)	(3–2)	(1–0)	(30–4)	(118–43)

Source: Collated from seanadcount.ie

Note: The Independent/Other column includes Solidarity–PBP, Aontú and all other minor parties

for nine seats, and a leakage of transfers, cost it one of the three seats it had won in 2016. This speaks to a difficulty with vote management for larger parties more broadly on the outside sub-panel, as the leadership has little control over who gets an outside nomination.[27] Fine Gael won its highest number of votes on Culture and Education and received approximately 58 votes from unaffiliated electors. Incumbent Seán Kyne (who was previously a Galway West TD and junior minister and had been nominated to the Seanad by the Taoiseach in February 2020 to fill a vacancy) was the first candidate deemed elected on the panel. The Fine Gael results were marked by a gender problem, with the party returning no female senators despite the leadership appealing to electors to rank female candidates highly. As a result, the Taoiseach pledged that gender balance would be prioritised among Fine Gael's share of Seanad nominees.[28]

As expected, Sinn Féin elected five senators with one on each panel, but seat losses in the 2019 local elections saw the party's vote fall relative to 2016. Sinn Féin also supported a number of non-party candidates, including outgoing senator Frances Black (Industry and Commerce) and John Bosco Conama (Administration), who is a campaigner for the deaf community and has worked closely with former Sinn Féin TD Caoimhghín Ó Caoláin.[29] Its candidates polled well on first preferences, but performed poorly on transfer votes across the board. It appears that even though Sinn Féin's transfer profile has been slowly improving among the voting public, it remains transfer-toxic with public representatives outside of the party fold. This was especially marked in the case of former MP and MLA Elisha McCallion, who topped the Industry and Commerce poll with 95 votes and remained at this figure until the 30th count. The party exceeded its core vote on Culture and Education and on Agriculture and held it on Administration, but fell below it considerably on the other two—a margin of 30 votes on Labour and 27 on Industry and Commerce. The figures suggest that Sinn Féin may have traded a proportion of votes on these panels for support elsewhere.

Sources interviewed for this research advised that the Green Party and the Social Democrats had a vote pact across every panel, with 87 electors available between them. The Social Democrats' Niall Ó Tuathail, a Galway councillor, lost out in a five-horse race for the final four seats on Industry and Commerce. The result was a huge disappointment to the party after its gains in the general election (see Chap. 8). The Green Party elected two senators. One unsuccessful candidate was Saoirse McHugh, a former Green European and general election candidate with a significant public profile, who won the second highest number of first preferences on the Culture and Education panel, on which the Greens had negotiated a partial pact with Labour, which did not nominate a candidate. However, she did not pick up enough transfers and was not elected. The Labour Party won a considerably higher percentage of seats than its share of the electorate (see Table 12.5). All of Labour's four elected senators were sitting councillors, and they proved to be very transfer-friendly (the party had a pact with Fine Gael for a handful of second preferences on two panels).

Three of the four outgoing independents on the vocational panels retained their seats. Traveller rights activist Eileen Flynn missed out in a tight four-way contest on the Labour panel by just two votes, but she was later appointed to the Seanad by the Taoiseach (see below). Two women independents were elected to the highly competitive Industry and Commerce panel: incumbent senator Frances Black was joined by Meath councillor Sharon Keogan. The results show that independent electors are key sources of support for independent candidates. Independent votes were relatively stable across all panels apart from Culture and Education. Aontú (which has four electors) contested this panel, and the party won 29 votes; one can speculate that the party's anti-abortion stance won support from a number of independents for whom this is an important issue.

THE UNIVERSITY SEATS

A further six seats are elected by graduates of the University of Dublin (Trinity College) and the National University of Ireland (NUI).[30] The concept of university representation in Ireland pre-dates the 1937 constitution.[31] The electorate is confined to graduates of the university who are Irish citizens.[32] In 1979 a referendum to allow for legislative change to extend the Seanad franchise to graduates of other higher education institutions was approved by 92 per cent of voters, but the result was never implemented.[33] Political parties are not listed on the ballot paper. Candidates do not have to be alumni to contest a university seat. Ten graduates of the institution need to sign their nomination form, and all nominators must be registered to vote.

Of all components of the Seanad, the university seats have been most widely characterised as elitist and undemocratic.[34] However, the electorate is considerably larger than the vocational panels. University senators come from different backgrounds, predominately professional, and some are, or have been, close to political parties. Many have given particular representation to social issues.[35]

Ballot papers are distributed to voters by registered post. Voter turnout for the university seats has been notoriously low over the years. In 2020, 34 per cent of NUI graduates and 23 per cent of Trinity College graduates cast their vote[36]; the equivalent figures in 2016 were 35 per cent and 28 per cent respectively.[37] The distribution of ballot papers was somewhat staggered in 2020.[38] Given the hundreds of registered post ballot papers that are returned because of incorrect postal addresses, questions have been raised about the reliability of the electoral registers.[39] Universities report difficulties with getting graduates to register to vote,[40] but they do not appear to actively encourage them to do so.

Campaigning for the university constituencies is challenging given the large and geographically dispersed nature of the electorate. All candidates can avail of one free mailing to electors. Other forms of campaigning are mostly done online. A number of candidates in 2020 were active across various social media platforms. Some initially organised public events, distributed leaflets in public places or engaged in door-to-door canvassing in urban areas with high numbers of graduates. These activities had to cease after the introduction of social distancing regulations.

There was no turnover of seats in the 2020 university elections.[41] Ten candidates contested the University of Dublin constituency. David Norris, Ivana Bacik and Lynn Ruane were re-elected, with Ruane doubling her share of the first preference vote since 2016. Former Ireland international rugby player Hugo MacNeill, whose wife had been elected as a Fine Gael TD in February, was a first-time Seanad candidate and placed fourth in the contest. The NUI constituency was more widely contested with 19 candidates. The three re-elected incumbents, Rónán Mullen, Michael McDowell and Alice-Mary Higgins, all increased their vote relative to 2016, and Higgins's first preferences doubled. As in 2016 a notable feature of the NUI election was the number of candidates, mostly female, with equality and social justice platforms. These included Ruth Coppinger (a former Solidarity TD), Laura Harmon, Michelle Healy, Rory Hearne and Eva Dowling. Transfers between these candidates were strong.

The Taoiseach's Nominees

The lack of a new government (see Chap. 13) delayed the 26th Seanad from being fully populated for nearly three months after the election. The government's legal advice was that the chamber was not validly constituted without the 11 Taoiseach's nominees (these must be nominated by the Taoiseach elected by the new Dáil, not by the outgoing Taoiseach) and therefore could not pass legislation.[42] With the possibility of important security legislation lapsing, ten senators took a case to the High Court on 24 June to clarify whether or not the constitution enabled the Seanad to sit and pass legislation before the 11 appointments were made. In their view, the legislative stalemate had 'startling consequences' for the governance of the country.[43] The High Court rejected their case on 29 June, by which time the new government was in place and full membership of the Seanad had been completed.[44]

The Taoiseach's nominees were announced on 27 June, a few hours after Micheál Martin was appointed Taoiseach by the President. Although a number of Seanad nominees in 2011 and 2016 were nonpartisan and linked to particular causes, in 2020 all nominees bar one had political affiliation to one of the three government parties. To counterbalance the under-representation of women in the new cabinet and lower house, a large emphasis was placed on gender.[45] Of the 11 appointments 9 were women. Geography was also an important factor,

aim to secure representation in the next general election. Eight of the
partisan nominees had contested the 2020 general election. The four
Fianna Fáil nominees were councillors Mary Fitzpatrick and Erin
McGreehan, former senator Lorraine Clifford-Lee and former Clare
TD Timmy Dooley. Fitzpatrick (Dublin) and McGreehan (Louth) are
both based in constituencies where Fianna Fáil currently has no seats.
Fine Gael leader Leo Varadkar selected three councillors, Aisling Dolan,
Emer Currie and Mary Seery Kearney (whom the Taoiseach had added
to contest the Labour panel in the election because there was an insuf-
ficient number of sub-panel candidates). Dolan contested the general
election as the sole Fine Gael candidate in Roscommon–Galway, where
the party has no representation. The fourth Fine Gael nominee was
outgoing Minister for Social Protection Regina Doherty. After losing
her Meath East seat in the general election, Doherty had played a key
role in the government's response to the Covid-19 pandemic. She was
appointed Leader of the Seanad as part of a deal struck between Fianna
Fáil and Fine Gael. The Green Party nominees were councillors Vincent
P. Martin and Róisín Garvey, who were the party's next two best performing candidates in the general election based on their percentage
share of first preference votes.

Significantly, Traveller rights activist Eileen Flynn was the only non-
partisan nominee, and this was supported by the three government parties. As discussed above, Flynn narrowly missed out on a seat for the
Labour panel in the 2020 election. She is the first Traveller woman to sit
in the Oireachtas, and her appointment was widely welcomed.[46] Flynn
stated that she wanted to represent people at the 'very end of Irish society'
and to be a role model for young Traveller women.[47]

After independent Unionist and anti-Brexit campaigner Ian Marshall
failed to retain his seat on the Agricultural panel, the three parties had
been widely expected to agree a nominee to represent Northern
Ireland's political interests, thus reviving a tradition practised over the
period from 1982 to 2002,[48] but this did not materialise. The lack of
representation from the Unionist tradition was notably criticised by
Marshall himself, in addition to the Sinn Féin leadership and a number
of sitting senators.[49]

The New Seanad

Table 12.6 outlines the overall result of the 2020 Seanad election.[50] Fianna Fáil gained six seats and replaced Fine Gael, which lost three seats, as the largest party in the chamber. The Green Party advanced from one to four, and one of its senators, Pippa Hackett, was appointed as a 'super junior' minister at the Department of Agriculture (see Chap. 13). In contrast to its record performance in the general election, Sinn Féin lost two Seanad seats due to changes in its electoral profile. Independents have ten seats, a decrease of four that reflects the partisan nature of the Taoiseach's nominees in contrast to 2016. The number of Labour Party members remained unchanged.

In terms of gender representation, 24 women senators were returned compared to just 18 in 2016 (see Table 12.6). Women now comprise 40 per cent of the chamber, and this represents a record high for a Seanad election, largely due to the high number of women appointed by the Taoiseach. This stands in contrast with the outcome of the Dáil election, where the number of women TDs rose by only one seat, and they comprise 23 per cent of the house (see Chap. 8).

Table 12.6 Overall result of Seanad election 2020

Group	Fianna Fáil	Fine Gael	Sinn Féin	Labour	Green Party	Independent/ Other	Total (women)
Panels							
Culture and education	2	2	1	0	0	0	5 (1)
Agriculture	4	3	1	1	1	1	11 (3)
Labour	4	3	1	1	1	1	11 (2)
Industry and commerce	3	2	1	1	0	2	9 (4)
Administration	3	2	1	1	0	0	7 (2)
Universities							
Nat Univ of Ireland	0	0	0	0	0	3	3 (1)
University of Dublin	0	0	0	1	0	2	3 (2)
Taoiseach's nominees	4	4	0	0	2	1	11 (9)
Total	20	16	5	5	4	10	60 (24)

CONCLUSION

The 2020 Seanad general election campaign was held in very strange circumstances. It was one of numerous elections around the globe that proceeded as scheduled during the pandemic, while others were postponed or procedures were amended.[51] The lockdown introduced by the government only days into the national campaign impacted on the campaign and counting. Due to the long negotiations on agreeing a programme for government, the full membership of the 26th Seanad was not completed until three months after the vocational and university panel elections. With 40 seats between them, the government parties have a strong upper hand in the 26th Seanad. The opposition is unlikely to have as much of a legislative impact as it did in the previous Seanad, where the government party Fine Gael was in a minority and the institution had a more independent oriented institutional character.[52] The 26th Seanad is a slightly more diverse chamber with 40 per cent female representation, which is a record high at a Seanad election, and the chamber has a female representative from the Traveller community for the first time.

A common theme of the Seanad chapter in previous editions of *How Ireland Voted* has been to consider whether the upper chamber will finally be reformed within the lifetime of the new government. In 2020, neither the Fianna Fáil nor Fine Gael general election manifestos committed to Seanad reform (although the Green Party's did), and the Programme for Government makes no reference to it, at Fine Gael's insistence (see Chap. 13, p. 309). There does not appear to be the political interest to implement the reform recommendations made by the Manning Report (2015)[53] and the Report of the Seanad Reform Implementation Group (2018).[54] Following the publication of the programme for government, Fianna Fáil senator Malcolm Byrne announced his plans to introduce legislation to extend Seanad voting rights to graduates of all third-level institutions, 41 years after the referendum on this issue.[55] However, we could still be talking about more fundamental Seanad reform for some time to come.

NOTES

1. Interparliamentary Union (IPU), IPU Parline: Global data on national parliaments, https://data.ipu.org/.
2. Muiris MacCarthaigh and Shane Martin, 'Precarious bicameralism? Senates in Ireland from the late middle ages to the present', in Nikolaj Bijleveld et al. (eds), *Reforming Senates: Upper Legislative Houses in North Atlantic Small Powers 1800–Present* (London: Routledge, 2019), p. 240.

3. Mel Farrell, *Party Politics in a New Democracy: the Irish Free State, 1922–37* (Basingstoke: Palgrave, 2017), p. 103.
4. Michael Gallagher, 'The Oireachtas: president and parliament', pp. 164–90 in John Coakley and Michael Gallagher (eds), *Politics in the Republic of Ireland*, 6th edition (London: Routledge and PSAI Press, 2018), pp. 183–4.
5. Farrell, *Party Politics in a New Democracy*, p. 288.
6. Martin O'Donoghue, 'Vocational voices or puppets of the lower house? Irish senators, 1938–1948', pp. 202–13 in Bijleveld et al. (eds), *Reforming Senates*.
7. MacCarthaigh and Martin, 'Precarious bicameralism?', p. 244.
8. Mary C. Murphy, 'The Seanad election: second chamber, second chance', pp. 227–53 in Michael Gallagher and Michael Marsh (eds), *How Ireland Voted 2016: the election that nobody won* (Cham: Palgrave Macmillan, 2016), p. 234.
9. Michael Gallagher and Liam Weeks, 'The subterranean election of the Seanad', pp. 197–213 in Michael Gallagher, Michael Marsh and Paul Mitchell (eds), *How Ireland Voted 2002* (Basingstoke: Palgrave, 2002), p. 199.
10. Murphy, 'The Seanad election', p. 232.
11. Kieran O'Mahony, 'Hayes disappointed as Seanad nomination bids fail', *The Southern Star* 25 March 2020.
12. This is a recommendation of the *Report on the Seanad Reform Working Group 2015*.
13. Seanad Reform Implementation Group—Third Meeting, 12 June 2018, available at: https://assets.gov.ie/3593/301118151408-17c7dc50bc56471da257862ca08cdf67.pdf#page=5.
14. This point was made by a successful outside candidate in an interview for this chapter.
15. Juno McEnroe, 'FG's Kate O'Connell not selected to contest Seanad elections', *Irish Examiner*, 28 February 2020.
16. Justine McCarthy, 'Big names in Green Party fail to secure nominations', *The Times*, 1 March 2020.
17. Murphy, 'The Seanad election', p. 237.
18. To facilitate counting each vote is given a value of 1000. See Appendix D for a full explanation of PR-STV.
19. The Clerk and clerk assistant of the Seanad and Clerk and clerk assistant of the Dáil are authorised to witness the votes of TDs and Senators, but they did not do so in 2020 because of the pandemic. See Marie O'Halloran, 'Coronavirus: Seanad election procedures changed over concerns', *Irish Times*, 19 March 2020.

20. John Coakley, 'The final Seanad election?', pp. 240–63 in Michael Gallagher and Michael Marsh (eds), *How Ireland Voted 2011: the full story of Ireland's earthquake election* (Basingstoke: Palgrave Macmillan, 2011), pp. 247–8.

21. Averil Power, 'On the campaign trail', pp. 134–8 in Gallagher and Marsh (eds), *How Ireland Voted 2011*.

22. This is how it was described by an interviewee who was elected to a vocational seat in 2020.

23. Murphy, 'The Seanad election', p. 237.

24. This practice was discussed by party strategists who were interviewed for this research.

25. For the distribution of seats between nominating bodies and Oireachtas sub-panels in Seanad elections from 1987 to 2016, see Houses of the Oireachtas (2016), *Seanad General Election, April 2016 and Bye-Elections to 2011–16 Seanad*, p. 49. Available at: https://data.oireachtas.ie/ie/oireachtas/electoralProcess/electionResults/seanad/2017/2017-07-19_seanad-general-election-april-2016-and-bye-elections-to-2011-16_en.pdf.

26. Coakley, 'The final Seanad election?', p. 253.

27. This issue was raised by candidates and strategists in a number of parties.

28. Marie O'Halloran, 'Poor showing for women in Seanad elections as Varadkar's plea ignored', *Irish Times*, 2 April 2020.

29. Marie O'Halloran, 'Dramatic climax to Seanad count as five contenders compete for four seats', *Irish Times*, 3 April 2020.

30. The NUI constituency consists of University College Dublin (UCD), University College Cork (UCC), Maynooth University and NUI Galway.

31. Maurice Manning, 'The Senate', available at: http://www.nui.ie/elections/referendum/docs/The_Senate_Maurice_Manning.pdf.

32. The Trinity electorate also includes foundation scholarship students who are Irish citizens and at least 21 years of age.

33. Laura Cahillane, 'Why reform of Seanad Éireann should start with the electorate', *RTE Brainstorm*, available at: https://www.rte.ie/brainstorm/2018/0529/966821-why-reform-of-seanad-eireann-should-start-with-the-electorate/.

34. Ibid and Coakley, 'The final Seanad election?', p. 253.

35. Manning, 'The Senate'.

36. The NUI electorate in 2020 was 112,216 (available at: http://www.nui.ie/news/2020/SE2020Live.asp). The Trinity College electorate is approximately 65,000 (available at: https://data.oireachtas.ie/ie/oireachtas/libraryResearch/2020/2020-02-26_l-rs-infographic-seanad-eireann-electoral-process_en.pdf).

37. Murphy, 'The Seanad election', p. 243.

38. Anecdotally, some candidates expressed concerns that voters abroad might not have had sufficient time to return their vote. Freepost is available only to electors living within the state, and this may also negatively impact on the propensity of overseas graduates to vote.
39. Marie O'Halloran, 'Seanad election turnout of NUI graduates tops Trinity', *The Irish Times* 25 March 2020.
40. Coakley, 'The final Seanad election?', pp. 254–5.
41. Results for the university seats are produced by the universities themselves. The NUI count is available at: http://www.nui.ie/news/2020/SE2020Live.asp. The University of Dublin count is available at: https://www.tcd.ie/seanad/results/.
42. Pat Leahy, 'Coalition talks reach "do-or-die" stage as parties struggle to make progress', *Irish Times*, 8 June 2020.
43. Marie O'Halloran, 'Senators to go ahead with High Court case over Seanad sittings', *Irish Times*, 12 June 2020.
44. Ann O'Loughlin, 'High Court rules first lawful meeting of Seanad must have 60 members', *Irish Examiner*, 29 June 2020.
45. Kitty Holland, 'Seanad nominees welcomed by National Women's Council', *Irish Times*, 28 June 2020.
46. Ibid.
47. Maggie Doyle, '"Phenomenal" to be nominated as senator, says Travellers' rights campaigner', *RTE.ie*, 28 June 2020.
48. Coakley, 'The final Seanad election?', p. 257.
49. Vivienne Clarke, '"Huge insult" not to be told about Seanad snub, says Marshall', *Irish Times* 30 June 2020.
50. The Oireachtas Library and Research Service produced an infographic of the 2020 Seanad election results, which can be accessed here: https://data.oireachtas.ie/ie/oireachtas/libraryResearch/2020/2020-07-02_l-rs-infographic-seanad-election-2020-a-statistical-profile_en.pdf.
51. Interparliamentary Union (IPU), Global overview of COVID-19: Impact on elections, https://www.idea.int/news-media/multimedia-reports/global-overview-covid-19-impact-elections.
52. Murphy, 'The Seanad election', p. 246.
53. The report can be accessed at: https://static.rasset.ie/documents/news/final-seanad-reform-web-version.pdf.
54. The report can be accessed at: https://assets.gov.ie/5245/211218143426-25949b1b57ce47d5aff3eb83402fb99e.pdf.
55. Marie O'Halloran, 'Referendum result on extending Seanad vote may be put into effect after 41 years', *Irish Times*, 22 June 2020.

CHAPTER 13

The Slow Formation of the Government

Eoin O'Malley

Ireland appears to be following an increasing trend among some western parliamentary democracies: that of fragmentation of the party system that brings with it an increased difficulty in forming governments. Perhaps the increased difficulty in forming governments is why the campaigns feature so much discussion of government formation. More than in many past Irish general elections, 'Coalitionology'—that is, which parties might be open to a coalition with which other parties—featured heavily in the 2020 election campaign (see Chap. 4). Polls during the campaign suggested (and the result confirmed) that Sinn Féin would figure in many of the numerically viable options. Reacting to this, the leaders of the mainstream parties, Fianna Fáil, Fine Gael, and Labour, ruled out working with Sinn Féin, on the ground that it was not a 'normal' political party, in reference to its association with the Provisional IRA, but also saying this position

This chapter is based partly on non-attributable interviews with six people who were close to the government formation process. Unsourced quotes in the chapter derive from these interviews.

E. O'Malley (✉)
Dublin City University, Dublin, Ireland
e-mail: eoin.omalley@dcu.ie

© The Author(s), under exclusive license to Springer Nature Switzerland AG 2021
M. Gallagher et al. (eds.), *How Ireland Voted 2020*,
https://doi.org/10.1007/978-3-030-66405-3_13

297

was because of deep policy differences (see Chap. 14 for fuller discussion).[1] Fianna Fáil also ruled out coalition with Fine Gael. When the results revealed the scale of Sinn Féin's success, the real prospect of a Sinn Féin-led government emerged, if briefly. Fianna Fáil and Fine Gael reacted negatively, and both reiterated objections to working with Sinn Féin. Fine Gael declared its intention to go into opposition. Sinn Féin tried to form a left-wing coalition government, but when the Dáil met on 20 February, none of the candidates for Taoiseach came close to getting sufficient support. Taoiseach and Fine Gael leader, Leo Varadkar, and Fianna Fáil leader, Micheál Martin, later met to explore the possibility of government formation, but very little happened, and there appeared no urgency on government formation in advance of the expected St Patrick's Day exodus.[2] The emergence of the Covid-19 crisis changed that somewhat. Fine Gael once again seemed interested in governing, especially after Varadkar was seen to have performed well in his role as crisis leader.

Parties' reactions to the results were often guided by where their respective leaders saw their party going. Some played a longer game, considering either going into opposition for rebuilding or working for a fresh election in the expectation that it could deliver an improved performance. The idea that smaller parties are always damaged by government is so strong in Ireland that few are willing to take the risk, except after a good election for a party. As good elections tend to be followed by bad elections, the idea becomes a self-fulfilling prophecy.[3] Only Martin, in part guided by the need to save his own political life, was anxious to form a government.

In May talks between Fianna Fáil, Fine Gael, and the Green Party got under way, and it took over six weeks for them to agree a programme for government (PfG), *Our Shared Future*. That programme could be seen to have strong Green Party influence on it, with a significant reorientation of transport policy, and an ambitious plan to halve Irish carbon emissions by 2030, though opponents within the party emphasised elements the PfG did not contain. The programme was passed by all three parties, and Micheál Martin was elected Taoiseach on 27 June, 140 days after the election day. What might have been a historic coalition of the two 'civil war parties' appears less seismic following the 2016–20 confidence and supply arrangement. Still, Sinn Féin's new role as the main opposition party could shift the Irish party system to one with a clearer left–right divide.

THE ELECTION DEBATE ON GOVERNMENT FORMATION

There had always been the risk for Fianna Fáil that the confidence and supply arrangement would not allow it to make a distinct pitch in the subsequent election. Throughout the campaign, and indeed in the year before the election, Sinn Féin developed a consistent message that Fianna Fáil and Fine Gael were indistinguishable. During the campaign and especially in the final election debate, the Sinn Féin leader, Mary Lou McDonald, continually referred to Fianna Fáil as a government party, or associated the names Fianna Fáil and Fine Gael. This was part of the party's strategy to deny Fianna Fáil the ability to be seen as a party of change. Sinn Féin said it wanted to end the stranglehold of Fine Gael and Fianna Fáil on government formation and so would prefer not to be part of a government with either of those two parties, but was willing to talk to anyone.[4]

While Fine Gael would struggle to find potential coalition partners, Micheál Martin's route to government seemed clearer. His stated preference was for a government led by Fianna Fáil that included the Greens, Labour, and perhaps the Social Democrats.[5] Fine Gael too suggested that it and those smaller centre-left parties could form a government, but most of these parties were campaigning on the basis of removing the Fine Gael-led government and if forced to were unlikely to choose Fine Gael over Fianna Fáil. During the campaign Leo Varadkar indicated that he would be willing to engage with Fianna Fáil, and on 22 January, in the Virgin Media TV debate, he said that he would not rule out a coalition between the parties:

if it's the case that the people vote in a certain way, and the only way to form a stable government is for Fianna Fáil and Fine Gael to work together, well I'm willing to do that…whether that means a confidence and supply arrangement or it means coalition, but it's not my preference, I'd prefer to form a coalition with old allies like Labour, and independents, and perhaps new allies like the Greens.

The following day in a doorstep interview Micheál Martin ruled out a grand coalition or even another confidence and supply agreement on the basis that 'people want change in this country, they want Fine Gael out of office.'[6]

Fine Gael made a series of attacks on the Green Party. The thinking was that the Greens represented a threat to Fine Gael seats, as the party had a sense that some discontented Fine Gael supporters had voted Green in the European elections in 2019. However, it had another effect: it soured relations with the Greens and made them more hostile to Fine Gael in the post-election period.

Early opinion polling and the Sinn Féin candidate strategy suggested that Fine Gael and Fianna Fáil were the only two parties likely to be able to lead a government and so provide a Taoiseach. It was clear that each would need another party, and so polling asked samples of potential voters their preference for government. Most showed that they wanted a government led by Fianna Fáil (see Table 13.1), and while Sinn Féin emerged as a more popular party, it was also the party that a plurality of voters did not want in government.[7]

Both Fianna Fáil and Fine Gael leaders vociferously, consistently, and clearly set out their objections to working with Sinn Féin. Micheál Martin said 'I could never be sure with Sinn Féin in terms of who you are dealing with. Is it unelected officials in Belfast who rule the roost, who control the levers of power within that party?' He said he believed Sinn Féin's

Table 13.1 Stated coalition preferences in opinion polls

Coalition	2 February	3 February	16 February	6 June
	Red C	IpsosMRBI	Red C	IpsosMRBI
FF, Greens, Labour, SocDems, and others	22	17	28	–
SF, Greens, Labour, SocDems, and others	21	–	–	–
FF and FG (col 3: with another party; col. 4: with Greens)	17	14	28	36
FG, Greens, Labour, SocDems, and others	17	14	–	–
FF, SF (plus)	9	15	21	–
FG, SF	3	7	–	–
Another combination	–	23	–	27
Don't know/refused	11	10	6	4
New election	–	–	16	33

Note: an online Red C poll in March (see Chap. 10 for details) found that, among five options offered, the most popular was the eventual FF + FG + Green government (35 per cent), followed by an SF-led left-wing government (33 per cent), FF and SF plus others (14 per cent), a coalition of FF + FG + SF (10 per cent), and an FF minority government (9 per cent) representatives were not in control of the party and that decisions were being made by 'shadowy figures' and 'unelected officials'.

There was some dissent within Fianna Fáil, as a Donegal TD said he did not think it was right to exclude Sinn Féin, and others, such as Éamon Ó Cuív, a former deputy party leader, were known to prefer it to Fine Gael as a potential coalition partner. Many other TDs, particularly in Dublin, were much more supportive of the strong line Micheál Martin took. That apparent division in Fianna Fáil featured as a Fine Gael campaign tactic. One social media video for Fine Gael featured the Taoiseach Leo Varadkar asking leading members of his party whether they would countenance government with Sinn Féin, all delivering an emphatic 'No'.

Some parties, led by Sinn Féin, but including the more clearly left-wing parties such as Solidarity–PBP, emphasised that a left-led government was possible and used the slogan 'Vote Left, Transfer Left' (see Fig. 6.4 on p. 127 above) to attempt to deliver that. The Labour leader, Brendan Howlin, hoped to build a 'progressive alliance' and to negotiate a common platform of centre-left parties to form the basis for government formation, but ruled out working with Sinn Féin.[8] 'Government identifiability' was low: by election day there were no clear alternative governments presenting themselves to voters, just a series of 'red lines' that made government formation look very uncertain unless the results produced a substantial increase in seats for Fianna Fáil.

RESULTS AND COALITION OPTIONS

Despite the surge in Sinn Féin support, the actual results (see Table 13.2) did not suggest an obvious government that could be formed. The constitution stipulates that the Dáil must nominate a Taoiseach, who is then appointed by the president. The Taoiseach then nominates ministers, who must collectively get the approval of the Dáil before they can be formally appointed by the president.[9] There is no requirement for an absolute majority in the Dáil, and sometimes, as in 2016, the elected Taoiseach does not achieve this. While it is always theoretically possible to form a majority coalition, the level of fragmentation in the party system in 2020—the effective number of parliamentary parties was 5.98—was at a record high (see Chap. 8). For the first time ever, no two parties could form a majority in Dáil Éireann.

An 'Index of Coalition Difficulty' (ICD) attempts to estimate how difficult government formation could be given the level of fragmentation

Table 13.2   Dáil strengths after the 2020 election

Party	Seats	
Fianna Fáil	37[a]	
Sinn Féin	37	
Fine Gael	35	
Green Party	12	
Labour	6	
Social Democrats	6	
Solidarity–PBP	5	
Aontú	1	
Independents	20	*Who formed themselves into three technical groups:*
Rural group		6
Regional group		8[b]
Independent group		6[c]
Total	159	

[a]Fianna Fáil won 38 seats, including the automatically returned Ceann Comhairle, Seán Ó Fearghaíl. He was re-elected as Ceann Comhairle on 20 February, thus reducing Fianna Fáil's voting numbers

[b]The 'Regional' technical group also includes the Aontú TD, so it has nine members

[c]The Independent technical group includes the TD elected under the 'Independents 4 Change' label

(measured as the effective number of parliamentary parties) and the size of the largest party: $ENPP * sqrt(50 - largest\ party)$. Higher values indicate likely greater difficulty in government formation.[10] In 2020 the index stood at 29, up from 21 in 2016 and 7.3 in 2011, suggesting that coalition formation would be a lengthy affair.

This appears to be a trend in several countries, such as Belgium and the Netherlands, where the government formation process is getting longer and longer. The May 2019 election in Belgium (ICD = 56) saw the previous parliament's caretaker government remain in office, and its incumbency was reaffirmed by parliament in March 2020 to allow it to deal with the Covid-19 crisis. Over a year after its election the country was still without a new government commanding a majority. In the Netherlands (ICD = 43) government formation after the 2017 election took 225 days. Spain (ICD = 26) and Israel (ICD = 19) had seen similar difficulties in forming a government in 2019 and 2020, though their constitutions stipulate time limits that meant new elections had to be called.

As the largest party in terms of first preference votes, if not seats, Sinn Féin declared that it would seek to put together a left-led government.

Even before the final results were in Mary Lou McDonald contacted the leaders of the Green Party and Social Democrats. Its finance spokesperson Pearse Doherty was appointed to lead its team in any talks. It met with Martin Fraser, the Secretary General of the Department of the Taoiseach, as it claimed to be 'stepping up its preparations' for entering government. This approach was quickly rebuffed by smaller parties who pointed out that the 'the numbers just aren't there.'[11] Brendan Howlin indicated that Labour did not want to enter a coalition government. By the end of the week Sinn Féin TD Eoin Ó Broin admitted that it was not going to be possible to form a government without either Fianna Fáil or Fine Gael.[12]

Fine Gael's poor performance led its leaders to indicate that they saw the party going into opposition. No government was possible unless Fianna Fáil broke at least one of its red lines but, given the fragmentation of the results, even that would not make government formation easy. Observers looked closely at noises from Fianna Fáil as to whether it would signal a change in its approach to Sinn Féin. Micheál Martin felt that as the leader of the largest party he had a duty to attempt to form a government. He appeared to be less categorical about Sinn Féin in the immediate aftermath of the election. On 9 February he told reporters outside a count centre in Cork city, 'The election result has happened, we will listen to people, we have listened to the people, they have voted in the main for three main parties... I think there is an onus and an obligation on all to ensure that such a functioning government is formed after this.' This was interpreted as a shift in his position. While some indicated they supported such a shift (if it was real), Martin was put under pressure from within his party: Justice spokesperson Jim O'Callaghan said he would refuse to serve in a government with Sinn Féin.[13] The Fianna Fáil parliamentary party met and was overwhelmingly opposed to coalition with Sinn Féin, but gave the party leadership a mandate to talk to 'like-minded parties'. Martin indicated he would 'reach out' to Fine Gael.

There was a lot of reaching out but no touching in the days before the first meeting of the Dáil on 20 February. Fine Gael was reticent. The chairman of the parliamentary party, Martin Heydon, told an interviewer 'as a last resort, we will consider [going into government], if that's what needed', but that Fianna Fáil and Sinn Féin 'have a responsibility' to seek to form a government.[14]

The debate on the nominations for Taoiseach on 20 February was lengthy and vitriolic and yielded no positive results. The Dáil re-elected Fianna Fáil TD Seán Ó Fearghaíl as Ceann Comhairle (speaker), bringing

Fianna Fáil's voting strength down to 37, the same as Sinn Féin's. The tone of the attack on Sinn Féin showed that any chance there was of Micheál Martin changing his mind about coalition with that party was over. All four nominees—Leo Varadkar, Micheál Martin, Mary Lou McDonald, and Éamon Ryan—were decisively rejected. McDonald received the most votes in favour, 45, compared to 41 for Martin, 36 for Varadkar, and 12 for Ryan. The Sinn Féin nominee was supported by a number of independents and the five Solidarity–PBP TDs. Varadkar submitted his resignation to the president, though this means little as a Taoiseach and his or her ministers (even those who have lost their Dáil seats) continue in office until replacements are appointed. There is a tacit convention that a government that has lost the confidence of the Dáil will not take major policy decision, though the Covid-19 crisis would make this impossible to maintain.

The Dáil was adjourned until 5 March. That evening Varadkar and Martin spoke on the phone and agreed to hold exploratory talks about a coalition, though Fine Gael still insisted publicly that it foresaw itself going into opposition. Privately, however, some in the party thought a centrist government with Fianna Fáil could deal with many of the issues raised in the election, dampening Sinn Féin's appeal at a future election.

Though Sinn Féin had accepted it did not have the numbers, it seized on McDonald's vote being the highest, starting a campaign based on delivering a 'Government of Change', and against a 'carve up of power by Fianna Fáil and Fine Gael'.[15] The party had a point; a Fianna Fáil–Fine Gael coalition, though 'historic' in some terms, hardly represented change. The campaign involved public meetings around the country. The meetings seemed more like election rallies, suggesting Sinn Féin was preparing for a new election. Those rallies soon had to be cancelled because of the emerging Covid-19 crisis. The 5 March Dáil meeting came and went with no formal movement on government formation. However, Micheál Martin told RTÉ radio that he was 'open to coalition with Fine Gael'.[16]

NEGOTIATIONS 1: CHOOSING PARTNERS

The question of which coalition government emerges after an election is often thought to depend on three things: office, policy, and votes.[17] Oversized coalitions (i.e., those containing a party that is not necessary to give the government a majority) are thought unlikely because inclusion of the surplus party unnecessarily dilutes the office rewards of each of the other participants. So we expect any government to be a 'minimal-winning' coalition: that is one in which every participant is needed to ensure that the government has a majority. This expectation on its own is not very useful and cannot predict any Irish government formed since 2002. As no two parties could form a majority government in 2020 any likely government would need two of the three bigger parties, plus at least one other party. With Fianna Fáil and Fine Gael ruling out working with Sinn Féin, it followed that a coalition based on those two parties was the only feasible government.

On 10 March they issued a joint statement indicating that they would enter talks as 'equal partners'. No talks followed immediately as much of the Irish political elite decamped to Washington DC for the annual St Patrick's Day celebrations. It then became apparent that Covid-19 was a much more serious problem than initially hoped, with the Taoiseach addressing the nation from Washington and returning early to introduce emergency legislation to deal with the outbreak. Varadkar had consider-able power in setting the Irish response, as the Dáil met less frequently and the government suspended answering parliamentary questions. The coro-navirus crisis slowed the process of producing a document that the parties hoped would attract a third party into the government. In a very unusual move Martin Fraser, the country's most senior civil servant, warned politi-cal leaders that his legal advice was that the Seanad would not be properly constituted until a new Taoiseach was appointed, and his or her 11 nomi-nees appointed (see Chap. 12 for the Seanad). The (as then untested) view was that no new legislation could be passed by the Oireachtas without a fully constituted Seanad.[18] His intervention was an attempt to inject some urgency into the government formation process.

The Green Party leader, Éamon Ryan, called for a government of national unity, but both Fianna Fáil and Fine Gael rejected that, reiterating that they would not work with Sinn Féin. They started to negotiate a document that would not be a programme for government per se. With a combined Dáil vote of 72, the parties were still eight short of a majority. Fine Gael was thought to be anxious that a third party was needed, whereas Fianna Fáil was of the view that, while it would be ideal to have a third party, a viable government could emerge with the support of some inde-pendents, to whom Fianna Fáil was speaking. Nor was either party assured of the other's support because both had special arrangements for seeking the approval of their members and parliamentary parties (see below).

Policy considerations also affect the choice of whether to participate in a proposed coalition. A party that could significantly advance its policy agenda might be willing to sign up if the other parties are compatible in policy terms. This would also depend on the bargaining power in programme for government negotiations. Fianna Fáil and Fine Gael appeared to be relatively open to policy compromise. On 14 April the two leaders signed off on the 'draft document'. The document was more aspirational in nature than a programme for government, with many rhetorical flourishes. Though Fine Gael was defensive of its record in government, and had to be pushed to accept a 'change' narrative in the document, it was relatively easy for the two parties to agree this because there were few specifics. The document was not intended to encapsulate these parties' vision; instead, it was an invitation to other parties to make a viable government. Rather than providing detailed policies, though some were there, it set out ten areas that it would seek to prioritise, described as 'new missions for a new government': Reigniting and Renewing the Economy, Universal Healthcare, Housing for All, A New Social Contract, A New Green Deal, A Better Quality of Life for All, Supporting Young Ireland, Opportunities Through Education and Research, A Shared Island, At the Heart of Europe: Global Citizenship. It signalled a leftward shift by the two parties, with commitments to removing the two-tier health system and an investment in public housing, though it also committed not to raise income taxes.

The document's intended target was the Green Party, because it was known that its leader Éamon Ryan was keener on entering government than any of the other party leaders. But the party was also known to be split on the matter. On 23 April the Greens produced a six-page response document that had 17 questions, including 'Will you commit to an average annual reduction in greenhouse gas emissions of at least 7%?' These 17 questions were not a statement of 'red lines' but were designed 'to establish a better understanding of what these parties would be willing to do in government'.[19] The Labour Party also produced a response letter setting out 21 party principles and posing five questions centred on whether the government would raise taxes to pay for the economic fall-out of Covid-19, but its new leader, Alan Kelly, did not shift the party's position on its preference for opposition. The Social Democrats also had queries but declined the invitation to negotiate. Fine Gael and Fianna Fáil responded to the Greens' questions on 28 April in a non-committal though amenable manner, for instance seeking further discussions to tease out how greenhouse gas emissions could be reduced, and the Greens embarked on a close consideration of the proposals.

The third consideration is votes. When parties coalesce they send signals to their voters about what type of party they are. Most of the parties on the left and centre-left had categorised Fine Gael and Fianna Fáil as anathema to 'change'. Many of the smaller parties would not go into government because of the impact they thought association with the two establishment parties might have on their votes in a subsequent election. Government is known to have a negative electoral impact on parties, and this effect is stronger for junior coalition partners, in part because of the need to make policy compromises.[20]

The mood music was not good by the May Day weekend, as Tánaiste and Fine Gael deputy leader Simon Coveney told an *Irish Examiner* interview that the 7 per cent carbon emissions reduction target was negotiable only insofar as it did not damage farmers: 'we are not going to sign up to a programme for government that decimates rural Ireland. That'll never happen, even if that means another election.'[21] The Green Party deputy leader, Catherine Martin, then told a radio show that she found those comments 'shocking' and 'disturbing'.[22] Despite this the Green TDs met a few days later and voted by eight votes to four to agree to enter government negotiations. They may have also been conscious that there could be an electoral cost of *not* going into government if a new election were called.

The choice of a Fianna Fáil, Fine Gael, and Green government is one that satisfies the minimal-winning coalition expectation, in that no party is surplus to requirements, though it is not the smallest winning coalition, as a combination of Sinn Féin and Fianna Fáil with either Labour or the Social Democrats would have had 80 seats as against 79 for the opposition, the barest possible majority. Fianna Fáil and Fine Gael continued to speak to Labour and independents even after the formal negotiations with the Greens had begun.

Negotiations 2: Agreeing a Deal

The party leaders met on 5 May to set out the process of negotiations, with formal negotiations starting on 7 May with the meeting of the three lead negotiators for each party, in each case the deputy leaders: Simon Coveney of Fine Gael, Dara Calleary of Fianna Fáil, and Catherine Martin of the Green Party. They were supported by the three leaders' advisers: the Taoiseach's adviser John Carroll, Micheál Martin's chief of staff Deirdre

Gillane, and the parliamentary political manager of the Green Party, Anna Conlon. These met to set the agenda for the week and discuss likely problems, and to set the pace.

There was an expectation that negotiations would conclude by the end of May. However, the management of negotiations was made more difficult by Covid-19 rules that stipulated that the full plenary of the three parties' negotiating teams and their support staff could not sit in the Sycamore Room in Government Buildings for more than two hours at a time. The parties agreed a process of a series of parallel sectoral meetings between party spokespeople and a member of the negotiation teams, which would feed into the plenary of negotiators for approval and clarification. The results might go to the three deputy leaders, or where there were identifiable disagreements between the teams, these would be put up to party leaders for resolution. These too were subject to two-hour rules, which slowed the process down. The Green team was made up of Martin and TDs Neasa Hourigan, Ossian Smyth, Roderic O'Gorman, and Marc Ó Cathasaigh; Fianna Fáil's team of Calleary, with Barry Cowen, Anne Rabbitte, Michael McGrath, and Jack Chambers; and Fine Gael's of Coveney, with Paschal Donohoe, Hildegarde Naughton, Heather Humphreys, and Richard Bruton.

Progress was 'glacially slow for the first three weeks', in the words of one participant. Partly due to cabinet commitments several sessions were cancelled. The Greens were concerned that this might be an attempt to pressure them into conceding at the last minute when time had run out. Fine Gael sources say that it was because 'the Greens came to the negotiations with slogans, and it took time to convert these into workable policies.' They felt that some Green policies were unworkable, and it took time to convince them of the trade-offs.

Though Fine Gael and Fianna Fáil had conceded on some key Green demands in advance of the formal negotiations, there were still discussions about *how* to achieve targets such as a 7 per cent reduction in carbon emissions while protecting the interests of farmers. The two bigger parties were anxious to ensure that tax rises (beyond the carbon tax) were not in the agreement, and Fine Gael was particularly concerned around the language of the budget deficit. Other issues reported as causing difficulties were the planned increase in the pension age (see Chronology and Chap. 4), whether private developers should build on public land, and an Occupied Territories Bill backed by the Greens and Fianna Fáil, which sought to ban trade with areas that are illegally occupied, relating particularly to the West Bank.

Some proposals were vetoed because there was a sense that they would make getting the PfG passed by the membership more difficult. So Fine Gael vetoed a programme of Seanad reform on this basis, while Fianna Fáil, while saying it accepted the principle of allowing councils to adjust the local property tax upwards by 30 per cent, refused to agree this on the grounds that it would make it harder for the party's councillors to support the PfG if it were introduced. This was because Fianna Fáil felt it would indicate the state would move away from direct funding of local authorities.

Who gets what in negotiations depends to a large degree on the parties' *patience* and *outside options*.[23] A negotiating party that is willing to wait is usually likely to concede less than those who are impatient to conclude a deal, because the more patient can simply sit and wait. The outside options, or best alternative to a deal, are also important. Whether a party has a good alternative to concluding a deal will influence its likelihood to concede in coalition bargaining.

In this case there was an agreement that Fianna Fáil was the most impatient to conclude a deal: 'Both the Greens and Fine Gael say that Fianna Fáil's impatience to conclude a deal at any price is jarring.'[24] Fianna Fáil said it was anxious to get a deal because of the logistical challenge of carrying out a vote among their estimated 15,000 members. But it was also the case that they 'know Micheál Martin has to become Taoiseach soon to prevent internal unrest'.[25] Martin was fighting for his political life. Without being elected Taoiseach he might find it hard to lead Fianna Fáil into a fourth election and risked becoming the first Fianna Fáil leader never to become Taoiseach.[26] This was also being played out against the backdrop of changing opinion poll numbers, which showed Fianna Fáil's support dropping and Fine Gael's surging.[27] In that context Fine Gael felt it had less to fear from government formation negotiations breaking down and a resultant election. The Greens found that even on issues where they were on the same side as Fianna Fáil, they had to do most of the heavy lifting. Fianna Fáil would argue that as the centre party of the three, it was often mediating between the Greens and Fine Gael.

In the absence of Fianna Fáil agreeing a coalition deal with Sinn Féin, something Martin had ruled out, an election was the most likely outcome of a failure to form a government. The significantly changed opinion polls put more pressure on Martin. The fall in the party's polling figures, and the rise for Fine Gael, meant the prospect of an election was much less appealing for Fianna Fáil.

Fine Gael's negotiators were described as much firmer by one person in the room. The impression was that Fine Gael ministers were not worried by the prospect of a collapse of the talks, as long as this could not be blamed on them, or even if they were blamed, it was an issue they could take to the electorate. People in Fine Gael remained sceptical throughout the process that any agreement between the negotiating teams could be reached, and even if it were, Fine Gael thought it would be difficult to get all three parties to ratify the agreement. The negotiations had a further complication. Catherine Martin indicated that she would challenge Éamon Ryan for the leadership of the party once the process was over. Ryan's use of a racial slur, albeit in the context of condemning it, caused more disquiet in the party. This did not cause real problems for Fianna Fáil or Fine Gael, and after time the 'chemistry between the teams had improved, as we got to know each other.'

The negotiations pushed on into June, and the 'two-hour rule' was abandoned as impractical in the need to get a deal. The absence of a fully constituted Seanad meant some key legislation, such as the Offences Against the State Act, would lapse by the end of that month, creating an imperative to have a new Taoiseach, able to appoint the remaining 11 senators, in place before this happened. An artificial deadline of Friday 12 June was set, and missed. By Sunday night, 14 June, the negotiating teams had agreed to most elements of the document, leaving a small number of issues to the party leaders. But still on Monday morning additions and amendments were being made to outstanding issues, such as the Occupied Territories Bill. Later that day the three parties' parliamentary parties met to discuss the proposed programme for government. Though there was some unhappiness in Fianna Fáil and Fine Gael, the parliamentary parties approved them by large margins. Within the Green Party nine of the 12 TDs, and all the rest of the parliamentary party except one member of the Northern Ireland Assembly, voted to approve the programme, agreeing to put it to the party's membership. Crucially Catherine Martin, who had opposed the initial decision to enter talks, supported it, saying that while it was not without risk, the agreement was the best achievable in the circumstances. Others feared the deal would make the party 'complicit' in regressive policies.[28]

PROGRAMME FOR GOVERNMENT

The programme for government, *Our Shared Future*, was based on the themes that Fianna Fáil and Fine Gael had earlier agreed. However, unlike in 2007, there was a sense that the Greens won many of the battles in the negotiations. The document is just over 50,000 words long, the longest ever Irish PfG (2016's was about 42,000 words, 2011's was 23,000 words, and 2007's was 33,000 words). Its length is in part due to the input of the civil service. Both Fianna Fáil and the Greens were given multiple briefings by each department and were forthcoming with requests for information, clarification, and costings.

While long, and detailed in places, the programme is quite vague at times. Critics highlighted the number of 'reviews' and 'commissions' the PfG contained and noted that it was not costed. According to Leo Varadkar this was deliberate: 'we were careful not to make very definitive promises on spending ... while there are some clear promises ... by and large because of the [Covid-19 and Brexit] risks there are actually very few definitive spending promises in there.'[29] Some of the vague language was because of late night drafting; so a commitment to have a 'referendum on housing' represented, in the minds of the negotiators, a commitment to a referendum on a right to housing.

Our Shared Future proposes a big increase in carbon taxes, something Fine Gael in government resisted for years. There is a major shift in focus from private transport to public transport, and a significant investment in walking and cycling. It proposes to invest in capital projects on renewable energy with the intention of halving Ireland's carbon emissions by 2030.

Micheál Martin said that if anyone compared the Fianna Fáil manifesto with the programme for government, there is 'a lot of overlap'. Indeed there are plenty of issues that Fianna Fáil and Fine Gael wanted—especially the emphasis on small businesses and supports for agriculture—and, in line with those parties' wishes, there are no planned income tax rises. Fianna Fáil got a commitment to defer an increase in the pension age to 67 until a commission had reported. There is also a key emphasis on the reduction in the deficit, as opposed to increasing spending, a product of Fine Gael pressure. For some in the Green Party this was a problem, as it suggested to them the continuation of austerity policies.

In some regards *Our Shared Future* reads like a wish list of the left. The PfG promises to progress towards a living wage, it will maintain social welfare rates, it promises to extend paid parental leave, and it says the government will implement Sláintecare, a plan to introduce universal healthcare. On housing, it promises to increase the stock of social housing by 50,000, built mainly by the state, and to introduce a cost rental model. It will increase the number of non-religious schools. It promises to end the system of direct provision for asylum seekers. It says it will bring in an action plan against racism and introduce measures to help people with disabilities, Travellers, and Roma. It will introduce hate crime legislation. It aims to hit the development aid target of 0.7 per cent of Gross National Income by 2030.

PARTY BACKING

All three parties have a requirement that a special conference pass any coalition agreement (because of Covid-19 restrictions, postal votes were instead proposed). In Fine Gael's case this was a result of a change to the party's constitution made at the 2018 ard-fheis (conference). It provides for a special delegate conference constituting an electoral college, with four components, each with a different weight: members of the parliamentary party (50 per cent), ten representatives from each constituency (25 per cent), Council of Local Public Representatives (15 per cent), and members of the executive council (10 per cent). In all 710 people were eligible to vote, and 674 did so.

Within Fianna Fáil there would be a special ard-fheis that all 14,345 members could attend. There was some doubt that such a body would pass a coalition agreement with Fine Gael as a number of party members and groups indicated their opposition. Some, such as Éamon Ó Cuív, were annoyed that the party had not explored the possibility of coalition with Sinn Féin.[30] There were fears that Fianna Fáil might lose its identity or become squeezed out in a new right versus left party system dominated by Fine Gael and Sinn Féin. In the event, 11,071 of the members cast a ballot.

The Green Party's rules stipulate that a decision on whether to approve a programme for government takes place at a party conference, which all members (including those based in Northern Ireland) can attend and vote at. Crucially, however, the party's constitution states that approval requires a two-thirds majority of those voting, an unusually demanding requirement whose origins date back to the earliest days of the party. As such, the party was considered the least likely to pass the deal, and so it put a great deal of care into having a day-long online debate. In addition, those on both sides maintained a strong social media presence. Opponents feared that the party would be a mere 'mudguard' for what they termed right-wing parties' austerity policies. Of the 1991 members who registered to vote, 1904 cast a ballot.

The results of each vote were announced on Friday 26 June. All three parties easily endorsed the programme. Most surprisingly, the Green Party membership's vote in favour was the highest of the three parties. It gave 76 per cent in favour (1435 to 457), compared to 74 per cent in favour by Fianna Fáil members (8154 to 2864). The weighted Fine Gael electoral college supported the PfG by 80 per cent, breaking down as constituency delegates, 71 per cent yes; Council of Local Representatives, 57 per cent yes; parliamentary party, 90 per cent yes; executive council, 85 per cent yes.

The Dáil was finally in a position to elect a Taoiseach, and given the urgency around renewing the Offences against the State legislation, the Dáil was summoned to meet the following day, 27 June. Because of Covid-19 restrictions, this took place away from Leinster House (the seat of parliament), in the National Convention Centre. There were two nominees for Taoiseach, Micheál Martin, and Mary Lou McDonald, but only one vote took place because Martin's nomination was passed by 93 votes to 63. As well as the 37 Fianna Fáil, 35 Fine Gael, and 12 Green Party TDs, Martin was also supported by nine independent TDs (Cathal Berry, Peter Fitzpatrick, Noel Grealish, Marian Harkin, Michael Lowry, Michael McNamara, Verona Murphy, Richard O'Donoghue, and Matt Shanahan). Some of these TDs have ties to Fianna Fáil or Fine Gael, while McNamara is a former Labour TD. Sixty-three TDs (from Sinn Féin, Labour, Social Democrats, Solidarity–PBP, Aontú and eight independents) voted against his nomination, and three independents abstained (see Appendix C for details).

The number of independents who supported Micheál Martin meant he could have been elected Taoiseach even without Green Party participation. However the government made clear that it had done no deals with any independent to secure their votes, and so any support would be on a case-by-case basis. Given that some of the independents are on the right of the spectrum, the new government probably has the median TD on most policy dimensions—a key expectation of democracy and coalition formation—though we have no firm evidence to confirm this.

CABINET ALLOCATION

An unusual aspect of the coalition agreement was the introduction of the idea of a 'rotating Taoiseach', with party leaders of the two main government parties sharing the office. The plan is that Micheál Martin takes office until December 2022, and Leo Varadkar, assuming he is still Fine Gael leader, will return to the office in the remaining two-and-a-bit years of the government's expected term. This idea was first mooted in 1989 by Alan Dukes when he was Fine Gael leader. There is very little comparative precedent for this; it has been used only in Israel twice (including 2020) to solve a problem of government formation.

Any Taoiseach in a rotating arrangement is likely to be much weakened, given the need to bring two other parties along on each decision and given that the office of the Tánaiste (deputy prime minister) is bulked up to monitor progress in the PfG. Some of a Taoiseach's powers are constitutional, not based on the political power of the party he or she leads. For example, Martin could choose to call an election early, though it would no doubt damage his reputation as a credible partner for government. But many of these powers, such as the right to hire and fire ministers, are related to the ability to command a majority in the Dáil.

With the Fianna Fáil, Fine Gael, and Green Party leaders choosing, respectively, six, six, and three ministers each from their parliamentary parties, the Greens received a bonus in representation given that they contributed only a seventh of the coalition's Dáil seats (see Appendix C for the composition of the government). Small parties typically do well out of the allocation of jobs in government. One person in Fianna Fáil described the scene of the changeover of power as 'chaotic and febrile'. There might have been a need to co-ordinate the balance of ministers, but that did not happen for the cabinet posts. Geography has long been thought to be an important consideration in cabinet selection, so even if there is not an even spread, at least most parts of the country are represented.[31] One independent TD who had voted for Martin as Taoiseach, Marian Harkin, told the Dáil: 'Earlier I stated I would work constructively with this Government and hold it to account. To be honest, I did not believe I would have reservations quite so soon. Like many others ... I am extremely disappointed there are no senior Ministers appointed from Connacht, Donegal or Clare.'[32]

It was unavoidable that three of the four Cork-South Central TDs were in government, but it is unusual that two ministers are from the same town in Wicklow. Dublin is less over-represented than in recent Fine Gael-dominated cabinets; six of the 15 ministers are from the capital, compared to seven in 2016 and nine in 2011. There were also complaints that the cabinet did not have a balance in the sex of the ministers. Just as the proportion of women in the Dáil did not change (see Chap. 8), so, as in the previous two governments, four of the 15 government ministers were women. Of course, given that just 13 of the 84 government party TDs were women, it would have been difficult to achieve the parity some called for.

As part of the government negotiations a new Department for Higher Education, Innovation and Science was set up at the request of Fianna Fáil. Defence and the Department of Foreign Affairs were given the same minister. Some of the demands for departments, and for the need to be seen to have government departments 'for' certain issues, mean that the names of departments are becoming unwieldy. For instance, there is now a Department of Media, Tourism, Arts, Culture, Sport and the Gaeltacht.

The constitution is clear that the government consists of just 15 people, and by law the government may appoint up to 20 ministers of state (often termed 'junior ministers'). The innovation of so-called super-juniors was introduced in 1994 to solve a coalition problem; these are ministers of state who sit at the cabinet table. In theory they may not speak unless specifically asked to do so, though it is unclear whether this principle is enforced. They may not vote in cabinet decisions given that they are not cabinet members, but since cabinet decisions are hardly ever decided by votes, this does not matter. The government chief whip always sat at cabinet even before 1994; in 2020 this position went to Dara Calleary, which caused much surprise and displeasure within Fianna Fáil given that Calleary, as party deputy leader and leader of the government negotiating team, had been thought certain of a full cabinet post. Calleary's exclusion was a surprise, and he made clear that he was angry about this decision. As it happened, an opportunity to soothe the discontent arose surprisingly early: only 17 days after the government took office Martin sacked his Agriculture minister, Barry Cowen, after Cowen refused to clarify matters relating to his arrest for driving while over the alcohol limit in 2016, and Calleary was promoted to replace him. Jack Chambers, who had also been a member of the party's negotiating team, became the new government chief whip. (In a further twist, Calleary himself had to resign from government just 37 days later after attending an Oireachtas Golf Society dinner that breached Covid-19 social distancing guidelines.) The other two parties also insisted on having a super-junior. Both their selections were women, including Pippa Hackett from the Seanad; she became the first senator to fill a junior ministerial post, and the first since James Dooge in 1981 to fill any ministerial post. Altogether, Fianna Fáil and Fine Gael each received eight junior ministerial positions and the Greens four. The appointment of junior ministers did little to improve the representation of women in government, as just five of the 20 were women. Most junior ministers might be thought to be 'marking' their senior minister from another party. In at least one case this was done explicitly; Hildegarde Naughton was put in as a 'minister for roads' in a department controlled by the Green Party.

The cabinet is younger than any before, with an average age of under 47 years. Micheál Martin, aged 59 on appointment, is the oldest member of the government, with just three other government ministers (two after the sacking of Cowen) in their 50s. There was much turnover in departments; only five of the cabinet were retained from the immediate outgoing one, and only the Ministers for Finance and for Foreign Affairs stayed in their roles. But the Fine Gael leader and new Tánaiste, Leo Varadkar, chose a generational clear-out as nearly all the older ministers were removed; only one of the demoted ministers was made a junior minister, the rest going to the backbenches. Outgoing housing minister, Eoghan Murphy, whose narrow survival in a confidence motion in December 2019 had been the proximate cause of the election (see Chap. 1), was always likely to be dropped. Another outgoing minister, Simon Harris, had also been considered likely to see demotion, but his handling of the Covid-19 crisis was perceived as adept, which possibly saved him.

Fianna Fáil had requested that it get the departments of both Housing and Health, the central areas of discontent with the outgoing government (see Chaps. 1 and 10). Martin chose the existing party spokespeople for Housing, Darragh O'Brien, and Health, Stephen Donnelly. These choices caused some unhappiness within the party, especially as Donnelly had previously been elected as a Social Democrat TD and had joined Fianna Fáil only in 2017. Martin defended the choices: 'the challenge facing the three leaders was that there was a limited number of portfolios, and in the ones we got I wanted people who could hit the ground running.'[33] Several backbench FF TDs indicated that they were unhappy that they or their constituency had no representative in government. One saw his exclusion as having 'insulted both me and my community'.[34] One TD who was offered a position as a junior minister, Jim O'Callaghan, turned it down and in a statement suggested he would act as a voice for Fianna Fáil that might be critical of the government, which was widely interpreted as implying that he might pose a threat to Martin's leadership. As a new Taoiseach Micheál Martin is unlikely to be under any immediate threat, but it might also suggest that TDs think that Martin will be making no more appointments in his career and so might feel less need to remain loyal to him.

CONCLUSION

The 140 days it took to form the government seems to be part of a trend in some countries where fragmentation of the party system has occurred. The need to have PfGs ratified by the party membership is also a factor. This government marked a break with the past in that for the first time the two 'civil war' parties are in coalition together. This may have made it necessary that members be given time to accept the need for certain compromises and be given the sense that all other options were exhausted. If there is a trend towards slower government formation, the state may want to consider ways to enable the process to be speeded up.

There seemed no urgency on the part of any of the parties to form the government quickly. Ireland lacks any mechanism to encourage parties to form a government. Many European countries allow the head of state to appoint a *formateur* (to lead the process of the formation of a government) or an *informateur* (to identify and facilitate a possible viable coalition). Though in 1987 the president had apparently informally spoken to outgoing Taoiseach, Garret FitzGerald, if it was needed that he act as an *informateur*,[35] the president sought no involvement in government formation in 2020. The drawn-out process of government formation in 2020 might lead to some thought about how the process can be expedited in the future.

The government came to office at a time of unprecedented health and economic emergencies. Unemployment rates were at a level unseen even in Ireland's deep recession in the 1980s. There was little certainty about when the restriction imposed because of the Covid crisis might be fully lifted. The PfG deal anticipates that the government would last up until the Dáil must legally be dissolved, in February 2025. The rotating Taoiseach deal limits the incentive Fine Gael has to bring down the government early. The long process of formation brought the parties together in ways that was unusual. They have a better sense of each other, and so the government might be expected to last its full term.

The key relationships are between the three leaders. Martin and Varadkar's relationship is often described as 'business-like', usually a euphemism for cold. There will be the added complication of Varadkar being the first former Taoiseach to sit at cabinet as a minister, which might be awkward, at least at first. The electoral incentives for Fianna Fáil and Fine Gael, which are close on many policies, might be to distinguish themselves in other ways, which could cause conflicts. That it is a three-party coalition should help. For only the second time ever (the first was in 1948) no party has a majority in cabinet, and for the first time ever the largest two parties are of equal strength. John Bruton, the Taoiseach in a three-party government argued: 'A three-party government is fundamentally more stable than a two-party government. In a two-party government there is a sort of binary conflict. If any issue comes up, which party has won on this issue? If you have three parties, the third party on any given issue will be able to broker the compromise.'[36] On that basis the 2020 coalition government might be expected to run more smoothly, between the parties at least.

NOTES

1. Hugh O'Connell, Philip Ryan and Cormac McQuinn, 'Leo Varadkar and Micheal Martin go head-to-head in first TV debate', *Irish Independent* 23 January 2020.
2. By tradition, most government ministers travel abroad for St Patrick's Day (17 March) to take part in official celebrations in other countries.
3. Eoin O'Malley, 'Punchbags for heavyweights? Minor parties in Irish government', *Irish Political Studies* 25:4 (2010), pp. 539–61.
4. Fiach Kelly, Marie O'Halloran and Pat Leahy, 'Sinn Féin "will talk to all parties" on forming a government', *Irish Times* 3 February 2020.
5. Michelle Hennessy, ' "We want a new government": Martin rules out grand coalition floated by Taoiseach during debate', *The Journal.ie*, 23 January 2020.
6. Juno McEnroe, 'Fianna Fáil leader Micheál Martin rules out "grand coalition" with Fine Gael', *Irish Examiner* 24 January 2020.
7. *The Irish Times* IpsosMRBI poll, 3 February 2020 https://www.irish-times.com/news/politics/poll.
8. Pat Leahy, 'Howlin wants to build "progressive alliance" before coalition talks', *Irish Times* 3 February 2020.

9. See Eoin O'Malley and Shane Martin, 'The government and the Taoiseach', pp. 243–69 in John Coakley and Michael Gallagher (eds), *Politics in the Republic of Ireland*, 6th ed (Abingdon: Routledge and PSAI Press, 2018).
10. Eoin O'Malley, '70 days: government formation in 2016', pp. 255–76 in Michael Gallagher and Michael Marsh (eds), *How Ireland Voted 2016: the election that nobody won* (Cham: Palgrave Macmillan, 2016), pp. 260–2.
11. Pat Leahy, Fiach Kelly, Jennifer Bray, ' "The numbers aren't there": Sinn Féin's preferred left-leaning coalition gets a cool reception', *Irish Times* 12 February 2020.
12. Seán Murray, 'Eoin Ó Broin says Sinn Féin cannot form government without either Fianna Fáil or Fine Gael', *The Journal.ie*, 14 February 2020.
13. RTÉ Radio 1, *Drivetime*, 11 February 2020.
14. RTÉ Radio 1, *Morning Ireland*, 17 February 2020.
15. 'Fianna Fáil and Fine Gael seeking a carve-up of political power to block change—Mary Lou McDonald', Sinn Féin press statement 21 February 2020.
16. RTÉ Radio 1, *'Today with Seán O'Rourke'*, 4 March 2020.
17. For a good overview see Michael Laver and Norman Schofield, *Multiparty Government: the politics of coalition in Europe* (Ann Arbor, MI: University of Michigan Press, 1998).
18. That view was subsequently tested in the High Court, which refused an application by ten senators on the grounds that Article 18.1 clearly and unambiguously means that the institution, Seanad Éireann, created by the constitution must comprise 60 members (Senator Ivana Bacik & ors -v- An Taoiseach & ors [2020] IEHC 313).
19. Paul Cunningham, 'Greens seek to "establish baseline" with 17 questions for Fianna Fáil and Fine Gael', *RTÉ News* website, 23 April 2020.
20. Alfred G. Cuzán, 'Five laws of politics', *PS: Political Science & Politics* 48:3 (2015), pp. 415–19; Heike Klüver and Jae-Jae Spoon, 'Helping or hurting? How governing as a junior coalition partner influences electoral outcomes', *The Journal of Politics* 82: 4 (2020), pp. 1231–42. As noted above (p. 298), part of the reason why small parties tend to fall back after a spell in government is that they often received above-average support at the previous election, which is how they earned a place in government.
21. Daniel McConnell, 'Simon Coveney: "Farming can't be decimated for Greens' 7% emissions demand" ', *Irish Examiner* 1 May 2020.
22. RTÉ Radio 1, *'Today with Seán O'Rourke'*, 1 May 2020.
23. See Abhinay Muthoo, 'A non-technical introduction to bargaining theory', *World Economics* 1:2 (2000), pp. 145–66 for an accessible introduction to bargaining theory.
24. Pat Leahy and Fiach Kelly, 'Public patience sorely tested as parties crawl towards a deal', *Irish Times* 30 May 2020.

25. Hugh O'Connell, 'More heat than light as talks drag on', *Sunday Independent* 31 May 2020.
26. Laurenz Ennser-Jedenastik and Gijs Schumacher find that party leaders stay in office even when they deliver poor electoral results if they are able to join the government. See their 'What parties want from their leaders: how office achievement trumps electoral performance as a driver of party leader survival', *European Journal of Political Research* 60:1 (2021), pp. 114–30.
27. A RedC poll published on 3 May showed Fine Gael on 35 per cent and Fianna Fáil on 14 per cent.
28. Hugh O'Connell and Cormac McQuinn, 'Martin's backing pushes Greens a step closer to deal', *Irish Independent* 19 June 2020.
29. 'Varadkar: no Plan B if the programme for government is rejected', *The Pat Kenny Show*, Newstalk, 23 June 2020.
30. Aoife Moore, 'Ó Cuív: unwise to assume Fianna Fáil's membership will support coalition with Fine Gael', *Irish Examiner* 5 April 2020.
31. See Eoin O'Malley, 'Ministerial selection in Ireland: limited choice in a political village', *Irish Political Studies* 21:3 (2006), pp. 319–36.
32. Dáil Éireann debate, vol. 994, no. 3, 27 June 2020.
33. '"All systems go" for new Taoiseach Micheál Martin's historic coalition government', *Irish Examiner* 29 June 2020.
34. Paul Hosford, 'Martin "insulted both me and my community"—Moynihan', *Irish Examiner* 2 July 2020.
35. Garret FitzGerald, *All in a Life* (Dublin: Gill and Macmillan, 1991), pp. 644–5.
36. John Bruton on '*The Tonight Show*', Virgin Media One, 24 June 2020.

CHAPTER 14

The Election in Context

John Coakley

The concluding chapter in the first volume of the *How Ireland Voted* series highlighted certain distinctive features of the 1987 general election. First, while the traditional party system survived, it was severely dented by dramatic support for a new party of the right, the Progressive Democrats, which, alongside a slow advance by the Workers' Party on the left, seemed to herald 'movement towards a redefinition of Irish politics along left–right lines'. Second, inter-party relations remained dominated by a tense relationship between the largest two parties, Fianna Fáil and Fine Gael, whose very similarity in respect of policy and ideology, and the fact that 'each finds its raison d'etre in attacking the other', paradoxically made coalition between them more difficult, since this would threaten the identity of each. The outcome was a delay of several hours following the convening of the newly elected Dáil before a new government could be appointed.[1]

In the decades that have elapsed since the 1987 election there have been big changes in each of these areas. Few now remember the Progressive

J. Coakley (✉)
Queen's University Belfast, Belfast, UK

University College Dublin, Dublin, Ireland
e-mail: john.coakley@ucd.ie

© The Author(s), under exclusive license to Springer Nature
Switzerland AG 2021
M. Gallagher et al. (eds.), *How Ireland Voted 2020*,
https://doi.org/10.1007/978-3-030-66405-3_14

Democrats who, following an eventful history, dissolved in 2009; the Workers' Party, still formally in existence, has faded away, its representation confined to a single councillor in Cork City; and there has been a dramatic surge in support for new challenger parties. Fianna Fáil and Fine Gael have seen their combined support slump from a peak of 85 per cent in February 1982 to 43 per cent in 2020—a drop of 42 percentage points, even greater than that suffered by their counterparts in Western Europe's other established two-party systems, such as Greece, Austria, Germany and Spain, and entirely out of line with the relative electoral stability of Portugal and the UK.[2]

While electoral turbulence is a common phenomenon that invites comparison with other countries, the idiosyncratic relationship between Ireland's two traditionally dominant parties is unique in Europe, and worthy of further analysis. Indeed, discomfiture at inter-party haggling that would delay the formation of a new government for a few hours now seems quaint, in a context where the negotiations may extend over several months. These developments raise two questions about long-term stability and change in Irish elections, addressed in the two sections of this chapter: about the demise of the electoral duopoly of the two large traditional parties, and about the peculiar political paralysis that followed the 2020 election.

ELECTORAL INSTABILITY

It makes sense to look behind the headline figures discussed above by addressing three dimensions of the pattern of electoral change in Ireland: the level of electoral volatility, the degree of party system fragmentation, and the relationship between government and parliament. The rest of this section describes the position in Ireland in the context of a group of similar Western European countries with a relatively long democratic tradition.[3]

The first big issue is that of electoral volatility, conventionally defined as 'the average vote-level shift from one election to the next'. This simple measure usefully tracks net shifts between parties, but necessarily overlooks the totality of vote switching, since a flight of voters from one party is commonly balanced by an influx of refugees from other parties, obscuring the level of disloyalty displayed by individual voters. The index may be measured relatively easily: as the sum of the absolute changes in the percentage of the vote won by each party from one election to the next, divided by two (to take account of the fact that deviations take place in two directions, both from and to particular parties).[4]

Figure 14.1 summarises the changing value of the volatility index in Ireland over the past half-century (1970–2020; see also Chap. 10 on recent individual-level volatility). To provide a basis for comparison, the position in two other Western European states has been juxtaposed with this: the most volatile, France (median index, 16.9), and the least volatile, the UK (median index, 6.7). The Irish median was very low (8.9), but it has fluctuated wildly over this period. Up to 2007, Irish voters, like their British counterparts, showed a relatively high level of net party loyalty; the volatility index remained close to, or below, the 10 per cent level. The index jumped sharply to 29.6 in 2011, as voters abandoned Fianna Fáil, before dropping by five points in 2016 (with Fine Gael and Labour now receiving harsh punishment), and further, to 17.4, in 2020. Irish voters, once among the least volatile in Western Europe, are now among the most volatile, a belated change driven by the economic crisis of the early 2000s,

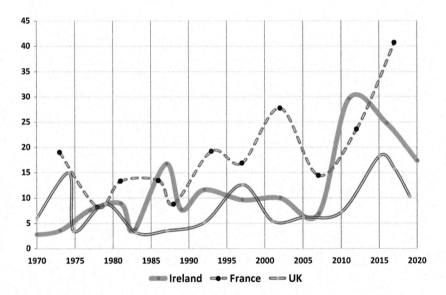

Fig. 14.1 Index of electoral volatility, Ireland, France and UK, 1970–2020
Source: Computed, with thanks, from Vincenzo Emanuele, Dataset of electoral volatility and its internal components in Western Europe since 1945, and new release, 15 December 2019. Rome: Italian Center for Electoral Studies, https://doi.org/10.7802/1112; and Chap. 8

whereas the fall of communism in the early 1990s was the initial stimulus that shaped developments elsewhere in Europe.[5]

The impact of shifting voting habits on the structure of the party system (and, specifically, on its degree of fragmentation, the second aspect of electoral change addressed here) is reported in Fig. 14.2. This summarises the position over the five decades since 1970, again setting Ireland in the context of two extremes: the most and the least fragmented party system in Western Europe. The measure of fragmentation here is the widely used index of the 'effective number of parties' (notwithstanding its name, this is a conventional index of diversity, not an approximation of any notional number of parties).[6] By this measure, the Belgian party system is by far the most fragmented, with three traditional parties each splintering along linguistic lines in the 1970s and new parties mushrooming later. The British party system is the least fragmented, in part because the plurality electoral system raises a formidable barrier to the entry of new parties.

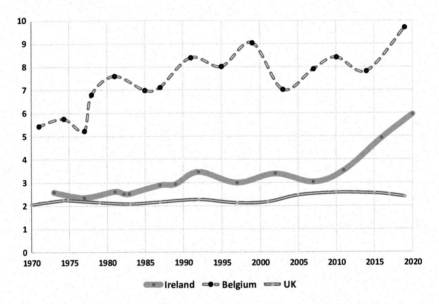

Fig. 14.2 Index of parliamentary party fragmentation ('effective number of parties'), Ireland, Belgium and UK, 1970–2020

Source: Computed, with thanks, from Michael Gallagher, Election indices dataset at http://www.tcd.ie/Political_Science/people/michael_gallagher/ElSystems/index.php, accessed 10 June 2020; and author's calculations

For long, Ireland followed a path similar to the British one, with the system dominated by two long-established parties, but with a sharp departure from this pattern from 2011 onwards. Before this point, the three parties that traditionally dominated the system were always returned to the Dáil in the same order of popularity. This is tracked in greater detail in Fig. 14.3. The four left-hand bars (which summarise the position over 23 elections from 1932 to 2002, grouping them to smooth change over time) show little variation from one period to the next. Fianna Fáil won 49 per cent of all Dáil seats that were filled at general elections over this period, with Fine Gael winning 31 per cent and Labour trailing on 10 per cent. The results of the 2007 election show a continuation of this trend (see right-hand bars in Fig. 14.3). But the collapse of this configuration following the economic crisis emerges clearly. First, the seat share for Fianna Fáil, the incumbent government, collapsed to 12 per cent in 2011, with the position of Fine Gael and Labour improving dramatically. But in 2016 it was the turn of the Fine Gael–Labour coalition to suffer severely; and the outcome in 2020, as indicated in Chap. 8, saw the collective seat

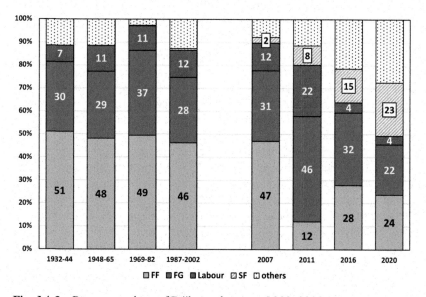

Fig. 14.3   Percentage share of Dáil seats by party, 1932–2020
Note: Data in bars refer to percentage of Dáil seats at all general elections over the relevant period

share of the three traditional parties falling just below 50 per cent (between them, they won just 79 seats out of 160). The big winner was Sinn Féin, which secured roughly the same level of support as the two other large parties, Fianna Fáil and Fine Gael.

Having considered the issues of electoral volatility and parliamentary fragmentation, we turn to the third broad matter that arose in the context of the general election: government formation difficulties. There is a case for detaching this question from that of parliamentary election, since European constitutions (including the Irish one) typically define these as separate processes, even if in Irish discourse they are seen as one and the same. In several countries, governments routinely fall and are replaced by other governments without any general election. To cite some examples where this is normally the case, in Belgium, Finland and Italy over the period 1945–2013 the mean duration of parliaments was respectively 3.7, 4.1 and 3.2 years, but the mean duration of governments was only 1.3, 1.1 and 1.5 years, due to mid-term government formation processes.[7] This has happened in Ireland on only one occasion, aside from instances where a Taoiseach has handed office over to a party colleague in mid-term: in 1994, when a 'rainbow coalition' headed by John Bruton took office from Albert Reynolds's Fianna Fáil–Labour coalition in the middle of the term of the 1992–97 Dáil.

The assumption underlying inter-party talks after every election was, then, that any new government would have a lifespan coextensive with that of the Dáil, since either it would last for five years or both Dáil and government would come to an end simultaneously. In certain countries, there is no provision for early parliamentary dissolution (as in Norway and Switzerland, where the parliamentary term is precisely four years). Normally, though, the constitution specifies a maximum term (typically, of four or five years) and early dissolution is permitted. Sometimes, as in Germany and Luxembourg, parliaments run their full term unless exceptional circumstances intervene. But more commonly, as in Belgium and Greece, parliaments almost never run their full term, and this is the category to which Ireland belongs: only the Dála elected in 1938, 2002 and 2011 ran for their full terms, though that of 1997 fell just a few weeks short of this.

The right to call an election at will indeed places a powerful instrument in the hands of the Taoiseach. In the course of the normal Dáil and government term, parliamentarians may be forced to choose between offering continuing support to the government or facing the risk of an election.

But while negotiations on the formation of a new government are under way, as after the 2020 election, the position of the incumbent Taoiseach is greatly weakened. Although fears were expressed by Fianna Fáil TDs that Fine Gael might have been planning a snap election to boost its Dáil support, at times like this the Taoiseach's authority is compromised. The President may be asked to grant a dissolution, but if a Taoiseach's bid for re-nomination has been voted down by the Dáil—as happened after the 2020 election, since Leo Varadkar explicitly failed to secure re-election as Taoiseach when the Dáil voted against him by 107 to 36 votes on 20 February—then the right to determine whether any election takes place becomes a joint decision of the Taoiseach (who may suggest a date) and the President (who makes the decision). In any case, the Irish experience offers mixed evidence of the value of a snap election in resolving parliamentary deadlock very soon after a previous election.[8]

An eccentric provision of the Irish constitution reinforces the position of the government in relation to the Dáil: the requirement that all cabinet ministers also be members of parliament. This in effect converts the government into being a committee of parliament.[9] In continental Europe, by contrast, typically there is no requirement that ministers be parliamentarians, though they are answerable to parliament; in a growing number of countries, parliamentarians are precluded from being ministers, and must resign their parliamentary seats if they wish to take up ministerial office, as in France and the Netherlands. This provision is of limited relevance during the government formation process, but had some significance after the election. The fact that some ministers continued in office for several months—admittedly in a caretaker capacity—after losing their Dáil seats in the 2020 election clashes with political cultural expectations that require ministers to be parliamentarians.

These constitutional provisions will, however, not take us very far in seeking to explain the prolonged stand-off between the parties after the February 2020 election. Neither will the unprecedented Covid-19 crisis account for this, though it might help to explain why politicians were unable to give their full attention to negotiation. Instead, we need to look at subtle aspects of the relationships between the three main parties, the topic to which we now turn.

POLITICAL STALEMATE

The features of the 2020 Irish general election discussed above would be recognisable to observers elsewhere. The electoral turmoil of the turn of the twenty-first century left its imprint right across Europe, though its expression in Ireland followed a different trajectory, peaking in the 2010s rather than two decades earlier. There is some similarity between the resurgence in support for independent candidates in Ireland and the appearance of 'pop-up' and frequently 'populist' parties elsewhere, while other beneficiaries of the revolt against the traditional parties—the Greens, Social Democrats and Solidarity–People Before Profit—match political traditions elsewhere in Europe.

How, though, are we to explain the prolonged stalemate over government formation that followed the election? The answer cannot lie merely in political arithmetic; party political fragmentation is the norm in Western European parliaments, and coalition is the mainstream government form. In seeking to explain the stand-off between the three main Irish parties we may look at three areas: *policy disagreement*, perhaps rooted in ideological divergence; *subcultural differentiation*, based on contrasting contemporary political visions and conflicting narratives of the past; and *electoral strategising*, or attempts to combine short-term tactical victories with long-term strategic calculations.

At the policy or ideological level, the three now-dominant parties may be linked formally to long-standing political traditions or 'families' in Europe: Fianna Fáil is aligned to the Liberal group (now Renew Europe), Fine Gael to the Christian Democratic group (now the European People's Party) and Sinn Féin to the European United Left–Nordic Green Left. While these alignments may point in the direction of particular ideologies or policy programmes, they are largely marriages of convenience. In reality, the three Irish parties grew out of distinctive Irish political circumstances quite different from typical Western European ones and dating back to the independence movement of the early twentieth century.

Observers have encountered particular difficulties in explaining the difference between Fianna Fáil and Fine Gael. Analysis of their election manifestos over the decades has failed to identify any enduring policy divergences, apart from a tendency for Fianna Fáil to be more 'nationalist' on certain issues.[10] Not surprisingly, then, it has been argued that the differences between them 'constitute perhaps the greatest puzzle of contemporary Irish politics to outsiders, and indeed to some insiders too'.[11] They have been compared with the two parties in Swift's *Gulliver's Travels*, which were apparently separated by animosities so deep 'that they will neither eat, nor drink, nor talk with each other', even though in reality Swift's parties were almost indistinguishable (only the length of their shoe heels set them apart).[12] Fianna Fáil and Fine Gael have been labelled 'the Tweedledee and Tweedledum of Irish politics'.[13] The second stanza of the relevant nursery rhyme, rarely cited, is worth recalling:

> Tweedledum and Tweedledee
> Agreed to have a battle;
> For Tweedledum said Tweedledee
> Had spoiled his nice new rattle.

> Just then flew down a monstrous crow,
> As black as a tar-barrel;
> Which frightened both the heroes so,
> They quite forgot their quarrel.[14]

The identity of the monstrous black crow in this case is clear: the new Sinn Féin party, which finally propelled Fianna Fáil and Fine Gael into contemplating coalition in April 2020. Sinn Féin was for some time relatively distant from the two other parties in ideological and policy terms. But since the 1990s it has been softening its nationalist position in respect of Northern Ireland, and later also its left-leaning socio-economic policies in the Republic.[15] By 2011, Sinn Féin had defined itself as a party of the left, committed to rescuing the country from policies of austerity, though analysis of its campaign pledges suggests that there was a good deal of overlap in the positions of all of the bigger parties.[16] At the 2020 election Sinn Féin maintained this position, advocating an expensive strategy in such areas as pension reform and housing policy. By this time, Fianna Fáil had shifted slightly to the left of Fine Gael.[17] Analysis of party responses in a fascinating dataset of 27 issue areas compiled for a voting advice application for the 2020 election generated some surprising findings: there were relatively few policy disagreements between Fianna Fáil and Fine Gael (with clashes in only 9 of the 27 areas); these two parties had more clashes with Sinn Féin (14 and 11 respectively); and the differences were greatest between these two parties and the Greens (16 in each case).[18] Of necessity, this approach gives all issue areas the same weight, but it offers a useful pointer to the potential pitfalls facing negotiators during the coalition bargaining process.

So what is monstrous about the black crow? If policy differences are of limited value in explaining the tense relationships between the three parties, we may consider a second type of explanation—one that rests on matters of social psychology and culture rather than on ideology and policy. Two aspects of this less tangible set of relationships need to be considered: the parties' collective self-definition, and their historical relationship with the state (reflected in particular in their distinctive narratives of the past).

There is a sense in which Fine Gael, Fianna Fáil and Sinn Féin present themselves not merely as political parties, but as close-knit social entities. Their very names offer a hint of this, given their implications of familial exclusiveness, with Fine Gael pointing to association with the Gaelic *fine* or kin-group, Fianna Fáil with the mythical standing army of Gaelic Ireland, the *Fianna*, led by the legendary warrior Fionn Mac Cumhaill, and Sinn Féin as also exclusive, since the label means simply 'ourselves', an identity no doubt to be equated with the Irish nation.[19]

Indeed, the parties may, in varying degrees over time, be seen as 'moral communities'—collectivities with a broader mission than mere electoral competition.[20] Central to this mission, in the manner of populist movements, is the struggle against conspiratorial enemies with a view to 'redeeming the nation from its alleged crisis'.[21] The classic complaint of such movements is that the elites have failed to represent the interests of ordinary people and have not protected national identity.[22] This was the criticism that the old Sinn Féin movement levelled at the Irish Nationalist Party in the 1918 election, though Sinn Féin's successor, the pro-Treaty party, quickly found a new mission for itself as the national state-building party. It was also the criticism that Fianna Fáil used against Fine Gael in its early years. Fianna Fáil specifically identified itself as no mere political party, but as a 'national movement'. Sinn Féin, in turn, criticised the two older parties along similar populist lines, presenting itself as a new, cleansing force.

Hostile attitudes and negative stereotyping of rival parties continue to be reciprocated, reflecting attitudes to be found widely in the two traditionally dominant parties. Fianna Fáil leader Micheál Martin denounced Sinn Féin in the Dáil as undemocratic, anti-Semitic and bullying, disposed to cover up serious crimes and prepared to legitimise 'a murderous sectarian campaign'.[23] Fine Gael, in turn, had for long shared a self-perception of honesty, integrity and progressive thought as differentiating it from the more populist, unprincipled and backward-looking Fianna Fáil.[24]

A further feature distinguishes these three parties from the others in the Dáil: historically, each originated as the political wing of a militant nationalist paramilitary movement, though the three were differentiated by their subsequent relationship with political violence. The pro-Treaty party that would form the core of Fine Gael inherited the pro-Treaty section of the IRA (later to become the national army) as its military ally, and in 1933 merged with a uniformed, fascist-type body, the Blueshirts, and a centrist grouping, to form the new Fine Gael party. The anti-Treaty side, rejecting the legitimacy of the Irish Free State, had proclaimed Éamon de Valera as 'President of the Republic' as it fought against the state during the civil war of 1922–23, and the anti-Treaty IRA never decommissioned its arms; they were simply 'dumped'—hidden, but available for future use. The much-cited words of Seán Lemass during a Dáil debate in 1928 described Fianna Fáil as 'a slightly constitutional party', willing to take up arms against the state once again should this make strategic sense.[25] The relationship with the IRA continued after Fianna Fáil came to power in 1932, coming to an abrupt end only in the late 1930s.

The legacy of Sinn Féin's relationship with the IRA is much more recent, and the list of deaths, injuries, damage to property and other suffering for which the IRA was responsible is a long one. But its radical change in direction seems clear, as noted by the several independent bodies that verified the final decommissioning of the IRA's arsenal in 2005, and the end of the IRA as a paramilitary group in 2011.[26] A joint MI5–PSNI investigation in 2015 concluded that although IRA structures, including its Army Council, continued to exist 'in a much reduced form' and IRA members 'believe that the [Army Council] oversees both [the IRA] and Sinn Féin with an overarching strategy', this strategy was purely political: the IRA had definitively left the field, and its leadership 'remains committed to the peace process'.[27]

But there were also reminders, from as recently as the 2020 election, of the survival of aspects of Sinn Féin that appeared to challenge the state: calls for support for the IRA, for instance, and derisive references to the 'Free State', a term used by many Sinn Féin members to refer to the Republic of Ireland. These references are not minor linguistic infelicities: they emerge from a culture that implicitly (at least) rejects the legitimacy of the state as a British-controlled entity, set up as 'a colonial state destined to rule the greatest part of Ireland in the interests of Britain'.[28] As former

Justice Minister Michael McDowell has pointed out, this worldview also extended to acceptance that authority to govern the country was vested in the 'second Dáil', which in 1938 transferred this to the IRA Army Council.[29] This authority was seen as being further transferred to the Provisional Army Council established by those who broke away from the 'Official' IRA in December 1969. In the eyes of IRA traditionalists, then, the legitimacy of the Irish state continues to be open to question.

Their revolutionary origins have left an uneven mark on the three main parties. Each began as a counter-state political force and, as mentioned earlier, saw itself in its early years as a 'moral community'. The pro-Treaty side was, however, quickly forced to take responsibility for the establishment and running of a new state, and had donned the cloak of political legitimacy already in the 1920s. Fianna Fáil was forced down a similar path following its assumption of control over the same state in 1932. But, notwithstanding its role as a governing party in Northern Ireland since 1999, Sinn Féin remains 'outside the pale' in the eyes of its two main rivals in the Republic; memory of its underground, revolutionary past continues to colour its contemporary image, in part because this is so recent. The stalled government formation process after the election was thus shaped by a number of diverging political perspectives: a legacy of Sinn Féin prevarication in respect of state institutions, a tradition of deep Fianna Fáil and Fine Gael hostility towards that party, and a culture of profound mistrust between the two older parties themselves.

The third aspect of the hostile relationship between the three main parties lies in the domain of electoral strategy. Notwithstanding the complex historical track record of all three parties in their perspectives on political violence and the subtleties of the management of the Northern Ireland peace process that had resulted in painful political compromises, Sinn Féin's recent links with the IRA were raised as an issue during the election campaign. Firmly ruling out a possible coalition with Sinn Féin after the election, Fianna Fáil leader Micheál Martin alleged that that party's elected representatives did not control the party, where decisions were made by 'shadowy figures' and 'unelected officials'. Taoiseach Leo Varadkar similarly argued that Sinn Féin was 'not a normal party', since decision making involved consultation with the party's national executive and 'key decisions are not necessarily made by elected politicians'.[30] This argument was given legs after the election, when the findings of the MI5–PSNI report of 2015 were revived; the Garda Commissioner commented that he accepted the 2015 assessment as still valid, but most commentators now interpreted this as meaning that the IRA Army Council 'oversees' Sinn Féin, not—as the report put it—that this was the belief of IRA members. This was used by the leaders of the two other large parties as further justification for refusing to share power with Sinn Féin.[31]

To what extent is the argument that Sinn Féin is controlled by sinister external forces a convenient electoral ploy to exclude it from power? In one respect, it resembles other parties. Political sociology has recognised for the past century that political parties typically function as centrally directed machines to fight elections, and that they are inherently open to autocratic rule—'who says organisation, says oligarchy', as Robert Michels rather bluntly put it.[32] In general, there is a tension within parties between electoral effectiveness and democratic management, and Sinn Féin shares with other parties the pre-eminence of its central secretariat and the influence of powerful policy advisors. It is true that the party is distinctive in the significant role of former paramilitary figures and the culture of secrecy in decision making within the party, but these features are not surprising in a post-revolutionary party that has only recently renounced militaristic methods; and they have not prevented Northern Ireland's unionist parties, whose supporters suffered greatly at the hands of the IRA, from sharing power with Sinn Féin in Stormont.

There are indeed particular circumstances relating to the Northern Ireland peace process that shape Sinn Féin's relationship with the IRA. It does not require any access to intelligence information to raise questions about the allegation that Sinn Féin is controlled by the IRA Army Council. Only a limited number of resources provide access to power: wealth or capacity to purchase influence, for example; coercive methods such as armed force; and electoral pressure such as victory at the ballot box. But the first of these is now heavily controlled in most democracies, including Ireland; the second no longer operates in respect of the Sinn Féin–IRA relationship since the IRA ceasefire and its confirmation that its war is over; and the party's future appears to be determined primarily by the third, the ballot box. Any influence by such bodies as a vestigial or nominal IRA Army Council would have to be based on some kind of fragile and transient historical deference, of limited effectiveness in the short term and incapable of surviving in the long term.

In fact, the peculiar survival of the Army Council has been explained by Michael McDowell, who was Minister for Justice in 2005 when the IRA decommissioned its final major tranche of weapons and formally announced the end of its campaign. From the perspective of the British and Irish governments, there were two options: first, to allow IRA structures to survive and become 'an inert, unarmed and withering husk'; or, second, to see it dissolved, and thus to allow the 'ideological torch' to be passed to republican dissidents, by providing 'an open-goal opportunity for dissidents to re-form an Army Council as the legitimate heir of the body that had been "treacherously" wound up'.[33] On the basis of 'a clear political calculus', the governments opted for the first of these, preferring to retain existing structures that would progressively waste away. Other commentators have also noted that it was precisely centralised organisation that made possible the profound shift in Sinn Féin from a military to a political strategy.[34] How much all of this mattered to the electorate in the Republic in 2020 is unclear. The vociferous objections of Fianna Fáil and Fine Gael to coalition with Sinn Féin may have emanated from horror at that party's militaristic past, but it may also have reflected electoral insecurity and the risk that the older parties' support base would be undermined. Sinn Féin's left-leaning policies no doubt helped it to outflank the Labour Party in the past, and its nationalist position was likely to be attractive to many Fianna Fáil supporters, leading to intense electoral rivalry. The fears of both Fianna Fáil and Fine Gael were no doubt also driven by a big shift in Sinn Féin's geopolitical support base. When the party first dipped its toe in the electoral waters in 1982, its support came overwhelmingly from Northern Ireland (amounting to 79 per cent of its combined 81,000 votes in the Dáil and Assembly elections of that year). By 2019–20, this pattern had been entirely reversed: the party won a total of 717,000 votes in the Dáil and UK House of Commons elections, but only 25 per cent of this came from Northern Ireland. This trend is likely to have hastened the Fianna Fáil–Fine Gael rapprochement that lay behind the post-election negotiations on government.

CONCLUSION

Two general points, one comparative and one historical, emerge in this chapter. The first is that insights from the electoral experience of comparable Western European countries shed useful light on Irish voting behavioural patterns. Levels of electoral volatility and party fragmentation show similarities to those in other European countries, but with Irish patterns of voting for long remaining quite stable, and the traditional party system surviving with little change until 2011; electoral revolt and party system transformation struck rather later than in other European countries. Levels of governmental stability are relatively high, with the lifespan of government and parliament generally coinciding. There are other areas—such as shifting strands in political ideology, changing social bases of party support and slowly increasing levels of women's representation—that have not been considered here, but where there is no reason to assume any radical departure from European patterns.[35]

The really distinctive feature of the 2020 election was not the continuing high level of electoral volatility, or the increased fragmentation of the party system; it was the character of inter-party relations that the election threw up, with three parties of unusual ideological provenance sharing 69 per cent of Dáil seats: a new Sinn Féin party, and two elderly offshoots of the old Sinn Féin parent party of the early twentieth century. Far from facilitating a comfortable coalition arrangement, however, this configuration ushered in an extended period of political paralysis in the middle of the Covid-19 crisis. Fine Gael and Fianna Fáil each rejected the idea of including Sinn Féin in government, painting it as unduly nationalist, excessively socialist, insufficiently democratic, and too close to the legacy of IRA violence.[36] But vehement rejection of Sinn Féin left the two parties only with each other. There had been signs that efforts to forge a shared narrative of the revolutionary past risked instead the reopening of old wounds (e.g., in January 2020 the government was forced by grassroots opposition from across the political spectrum to drop plans to commemorate the Royal Irish Constabulary). But, a century after the civil war, it was not so much lingering bitterness about the conflict between earlier generations that mattered, as the very fact that so little separated the two parties in ideological or policy terms. Coalition between the two is likely to endanger the identity of each, as the parties recognise in varying degrees, but it appeared after the election that, given the doors to Sinn Féin participation that the parties had shut, there was little alternative.

NOTES

1. John Coakley, 'The general election in context: historical and European perspectives', pp. 153–72 in Michael Laver, Peter Mair and Richard Sinnott (eds), *How Ireland Voted: the Irish general election 1987* (Dublin: Poolbeg Press, 1987), pp. 171–2.
2. The levels of decline in combined support for the two dominant parties over four decades in these countries were as follows (election years in brackets): Greece (1981–2019), -36 per cent; Austria (1979–2019),

-34 per cent; Germany (1976–2017), -29 per cent; Spain (1982–2019), -26 per cent; and UK (1979–2019), -5 per cent. In Portugal there was a small increase (1976–2019), +5 per cent.

3. These 17 countries include the 15 member states of the EU that had joined by 1995, plus Norway and Switzerland.

4. William Ascher and Sidney Tarrow, 'The stability of communist electorates: evidence from a longitudinal analysis of French and Italian aggregate data', *American Journal of Political Science* 19:3 (1975), pp. 475–99, at p. 480. The index was popularised by Mogens Pedersen; see 'The dynamics of European party systems: changing patterns of electoral volatility', *European Journal of Political Research* 7:1 (1979), pp. 1–26.

5. For discussion of trends across Europe, see Alessandro Chiaramonte and Vincenzo Emanuele, 'Party system volatility, regeneration and de-institutionalization in Western Europe (1945–2015)', *Party Politics* 23:4 (2017), pp. 376–88, and 'Towards turbulent times: measuring and explaining party system (de-)institutionalization in Western Europe (1945–2015)', *Italian Political Science Review* 49:1 (2019), pp. 1–23.

6. For the original discussion of this measure, see Markku Laakso and Rein Taagepera, '"Effective" number of parties: a measure with application to West Europe', *Comparative Political Studies* 12:1 (1979), pp. 3–27.

7. Data on governments used here are derived, with thanks, from the data collection of Staffan Andersson, Torbjörn Bergman and Svante Ersson, The European Representative Democracy Data Archive, Release 3, 2014. Main sponsor: Riksbankens Jubileumsfond (In2007-0149:1-E). (www.erdda.se)

8. In 1933, 1938 and 1944 snap elections saw support for the Fianna Fáil government rise, but in early elections in February and November 1982 support for the governing parties fell. Comparative evidence suggests that early dissolutions are often (but by no means always) to the advantage of the government; see Petra Schleiter and Margit Tavits, 'The electoral benefits of opportunistic election timing', *Journal of Politics* 78:3 (2016), pp. 836–50, at p. 848; Kaare Strøm and Stephen M. Swindle, 'Strategic parliamentary dissolution', *American Political Science Review* 96:3 (2002), pp. 575–91.

9. For development of this point, see John Coakley, *Reforming Political Institutions: Ireland in comparative perspective* (Dublin: Institute of Public Administration, 2013), pp. 227–31.

10. For comprehensive analysis of the differences between the parties in the past, see Michael Gallagher, *Political Parties in the Republic of Ireland* (Dublin: Gill and Macmillan, 1985), pp. 140–5; Peter Mair, *The Changing Irish Party System: organisation, ideology and electoral competition* (London: Pinter, 1987), pp. 138–206; Richard Sinnott, *Irish Voters Decide: voting*

behaviour in elections and referendums since 1918 (Manchester: Manchester University Press, 1995), pp. 81–2; Michael Laver, 'Are Irish parties peculiar?', *Proceedings of the British Academy* 79 (1992), pp. 359–81; and Michael Gallagher and Michael Marsh, *Days of Blue Loyalty: the politics of membership of the Fine Gael party* (Dublin: PSAI Press, 2002), pp. 180–90.

11. Gallagher, *Political Parties*, p. 140; a similar point is made in R. K. Carty, *Party and Parish Pump: electoral politics in Ireland* (Waterloo: Wilfrid Laurier University Press, 1981), p. 43. See also Chap. 11.

12. Liam Weeks, 'Parties and the party system', pp. 111–36 in John Coakley and Michael Gallagher (eds), *Politics in the Republic of Ireland*, 6th ed (London: Routledge and PSAI Press, 2018), p. 114.

13. Michael Gallagher, 'The changing nature of electoral competition in Ireland', pp. 110–28 in Niall Ó Dochartaigh, Katy Hayward and Elizabeth Meehan (eds), *Dynamics of Political Change in Ireland: making and breaking a divided island* (Abingdon: Routledge, 2017), at p. 123. The same labels were frequently used against the two parties by Sinn Féin during the 2020 election campaign; see Chap. 4.

14. Lewis Carroll, *Through the Looking Glass* [1872], pp. 126–254 in *The Complete Illustrated Lewis Carroll* (Ware: Wordsworth Editions, 1996), at p. 166.

15. See James Tilley, John Garry and Neil Matthews, 'The evolution of party policy and cleavage voting under power-sharing in Northern Ireland', *Government and Opposition* 56:2 (2021), pp. 226–44, and Sean D. McGraw, *How Parties Win: shaping the Irish political arena* (Ann Arbor: University of Michigan Press, 2015), pp. 84–7.

16. Jane Suiter and David M. Farrell, 'The parties' manifestos', pp. 29–46 in Michael Gallagher and Michael Marsh (eds), *How Ireland Voted 2011: the full story of Ireland's earthquake election* (Basingstoke: Palgrave Macmillan, 2011), pp. 42–3; Rory Costello, Paul O'Neill and Robert Thomson, 'The fulfilment of election pledges by the outgoing government', pp. 27–45 in Michael Gallagher and Michael Marsh, *How Ireland Voted 2016: the election that nobody won* (Cham: Palgrave Macmillan, 2016), pp. 30–2.

17. Luke Field, 'Irish general election 2020: two-and-a-half party system no more?', *Irish Political Studies*, 35:4 (2020), pp. 623–36.

18. See the site developed by Rory Costello of the University of Limerick, www.whichcandidate.ie/, with data available at dataverse.harvard.edu/dataverse/ines2020; and Thomas Däubler's post, 'We only agree to disagree: forming a government after the 2020 election', Connected Politics Lab, University College Dublin, 4 March 2020. Available www.ucd.ie/connected_politics/.

19. John Coakley, 'The significance of names: the evolution of Irish party labels', *Études Irlandaises* 5 (1980), pp. 171–81.

20. See Carty, *Party and Parish Pump*, pp. 102–3.
21. See Jose Pedro Zúquete, 'Populism and religion', pp. 445–66 in Cristóbal Rovira Kaltwasser, Paul Taggart, Paulina Ochoa Espejo and Pierre Ostiguy (eds), *The Oxford Handbook of Populism* (Oxford: Oxford University Press, 2017), at p. 453.
22. Rogers Brubaker, 'Between nationalism and civilizationism: the European populist moment in comparative perspective', *Ethnic and Racial Studies* 40:8 (2017), pp. 1191–226, at p. 1205.
23. *Dáil Debates* 992, 20 February 2020.
24. Gallagher and Marsh, *Days of Blue Loyalty*, p. 183.
25. *Dáil Debates* 22: 1615–16, 21 March 1928.
26. Report of the Independent International Commission on Decommissioning, 26 September 2005, in Annex K in Final Report of the IICD, 28 March 2011; http://www.justice.ie/en/JELR/Pages/IICD-Final-Rpt; Twenty-Sixth and Final Report of the Independent Monitoring Commission, p. 12; http://www.justice.ie/en/JELR/Final IMC Report.pdf/Files/Final IMC Report.pdf.
27. Paramilitary Groups in Northern Ireland: An Assessment Commissioned by the Secretary of State for Northern Ireland on the Structure, Role and Purpose of Paramilitary Groups Focusing on Those Which Declared Ceasefires in Order to Support and Facilitate the Political Process, 19 October 2015; https://www.mi5.gov.uk/mi5-in-northern-ireland.
28. Ruairí Ó Brádaigh, 'Introduction', in *Aisling 1916–1976* (Dublin: Sinn Féin, 1976), p. 2.
29. Michael McDowell, 'Sinn Féin's problem with names much more than mere wordplay', *Irish Times*, 26 February 2020. A small number of those elected to the second Dáil at the 1921 election, all of whom opposed the Anglo–Irish Treaty signed later that year, refused to accept that this Dáil had ever been validly dissolved, and maintained that consequently the 1922 election, and all following elections, had no validity and that the second Dáil, personified by them alone, continued to exist. While most anti-Treaty TDs followed de Valera into Fianna Fáil in 1926, seven refused to compromise and participated in the 'transfer' of authority in 1938; see Richard English, *Armed Struggle: The History of the IRA* (London: Macmillan, 2003), p. 401, n. 47. This group's moral authority was undermined by the fact that, although all had been returned in 1921, they subsequently contested elections to the constitutionally established Dáil; two were defeated in 1923 and four in June 1927. The remaining member, Tom Maguire, stood down in 1927 and played a political role in 'legitimising' the Provisional IRA and Sinn Féin in 1969–70 and later.
30. Simon Carswell, 'Why are Varadkar and Martin refusing to go into coalition with Sinn Féin?', *Irish Times* 27 January 2020.

31. Pat Leahy, Conor Lally and Fiach Kelly, 'Parties still talking to SF despite IRA link', *Irish Times* 22 February 2020.
32. Robert Michels, *Political Parties: a sociological study of the oligarchical tendencies of modern democracy* (Glencoe: Free Press, 1958 [1911]), p. 418.
33. Michael McDowell, 'Abolition of Provisional IRA was never on the cards', *Irish Times* 26 August 2015.
34. Sophie Whiting, 'Mainstream revolutionaries: Sinn Féin as a "normal" political party?', *Terrorism and Political Violence* 28:3 (2016), pp. 541–60, at pp. 551–2, 555.
35. See earlier volumes in the *How Ireland Voted* series, and also: Michael Marsh, David M. Farrell and Gail McElroy (eds), *A Conservative Revolution? Electoral Change in Twenty-First-Century Ireland* (Oxford: Oxford University Press, 2017); Michael Marsh, David M. Farrell and Theresa Reidy (eds), *The Post-Crisis Irish Voter: voting behaviour in the Irish 2016 general election* (Manchester: Manchester University Press, 2018); Fiona Buckley and Yvonne Galligan, 'The 2020 general election: a gender analysis', *Irish Political Studies*, 35:4 (2020), pp. 602–14.
36. On differences in Sinn Féin policy in the two parts of the island, see Gary Murphy, *Electoral Competition in Ireland since 1987: the politics of triumph and despair* (Manchester: Manchester University Press, 2016), pp. 116–18; John Garry, 'Nationalist in the North and socialist in the South? Examining Sinn Féin's support base on both sides of the border', pp. 145–56 in Ó Dochartaigh et al., *Dynamics of Political Change*. See also Chap. 13.

APPENDICES

Samuel A. T. Johnston

M. Gallagher et al. (eds.), *How Ireland Voted 2020*,
https://doi.org/10.1007/978-3-030-66405-3

Appendix A: Results of the General Election, 8 February 2020

Table A1.1 Electorate, valid votes and votes for each party

Constituency	Electorate	Valid votes	Sinn Féin	Fianna Fáil	Fine Gael	Green	Labour	SocDems	S–PBP	Aontú	Others
Carlow–Kilkenny	114,343	73,643	17,493	27,459	15,999	4942	2208	0	1558	0	3984
Cavan–Monaghan	110,190	72,183	26,476	18,161	19,233	2501	983	0	830	3840	159
Clare	91,120	59,495	8987	20,254	13,375	5624	0	0	1196	0	10,059
Cork East	89,998	54,544	12,587	14,440	10,697	3749	6610	0	0	1337	5124
Cork North-Central	87,473	51,778	13,811	12,714	7802	3205	2561	1121	3703	1325	5536
Cork North-West	71,685	46,370	0	18,279	15,403	3495	0	3845	0	3877	1471
Cork South-Central	90,916	57,140	14,057	20,259	12,155	5379	1263	1077	764	1350	836
Cork South-West	69,127	44,338	4777	10,339	8391	1647	0	4696	427	515	13,546
Donegal	125,911	77,452	34,935	15,816	10,677	1656	0	0	0	2382	11,986
Dublin Bay North	112,047	71,606	21,344	10,294	13,435	5042	8127	6229	2131	973	4031
Dublin Bay South	80,764	39,591	6361	5474	10,970	8888	3121	1801	1002	0	1974
Dublin Central	61,998	31,435	11,223	3228	4751	3851	1702	2912	977	583	2208
Dublin Fingal	101,045	63,440	15,792	13,634	9493	8400	4513	2206	1161	0	8241
Dublin Mid-West	74,506	45,452	19,463	5598	7988	2785	1541	0	3572	0	4505
Dublin North-West	54,885	32,386	14,375	3902	3579	1548	848	6124	1215	0	795
Dublin Rathdown	67,012	42,403	4926	5435	13,225	8958	3179	0	1498	1413	3769
Dublin South-Central	79,460	43,291	17,015	4782	5078	4041	2095	1595	4753	0	3932
Dublin South-West	109,517	67,565	20,077	12,193	11,380	4961	3603	2761	6130	0	6460
Dublin West	70,337	43,628	12,456	6892	10,348	4901	2096	817	4353	1062	703
Dún Laoghaire	99,811	62,293	6002	9911	20,828	9300	3009	1382	9632	1185	1044
Galway East	69,233	42,520	7108	10,694	12,332	1924	845	848	0	582	8187
Galway West	104,825	60,341	8464	13,697	10,893	3650	1548	3623	932	1058	16,476
Kerry	116,885	77,666	15,733	16,054	14,270	4122	0	0	0	1109	26,378
Kildare North	81,884	50,945	8705	13,365	9068	5100	2751	9808	861	0	1287
Kildare South	77,719	47,260	10,155	9507	8069	1639	5899	1338	598	697	9358
Laois–Offaly	110,839	69,422	16,654	22,130	11,982	3494	2011	0	910	0	12,241
Limerick City	77,643	46,129	11,006	11,957	9587	3252	2729	1799	701	1553	3545
Limerick County	72,165	46,090	6916	13,586	15,038	2503	0	0	0	714	7333

APPENDICES 343

Longford–Westmeath	94,835	56,383	11,848	16,997	14,362	2325	1904	0	632	0	8315
Louth	113,128	70,667	29,694	9692	10,822	5418	5824	0	1120	0	8097
Mayo	98,165	64,353	14,633	15,536	25,429	4177	255	0	721	2574	1028
Meath East	66,507	41,945	10,223	7980	11,871	3251	874	0	569	1634	5543
Meath West	67,982	41,504	12,652	6742	10,268	1935	0	2376	0	7322	209
Roscommon–Galway	69,598	45,612	8003	7898	5466	1413	0	0	422	504	21,906
Sligo–Leitrim	97,170	60,680	15,035	16,003	10,098	1791	1178	0	1746	368	14,461
Tipperary	126,781	81,788	10,004	14,255	11,132	3170	7857	0	0	0	35,370
Waterford	84,978	53,758	20,569	9298	8881	3996	3498	0	1153	1049	5314
Wexford	116,155	75,073	18,717	19,920	12,809	2028	9223	0	1116	1518	9742
Wicklow	101,332	71,320	17,297	9940	18,384	5634	1727	7039	1037	1051	9211
Dublin	911,382	543,090	149,034	81,343	111,075	62,675	33,834	25,827	36,424	5216	37,662
Rest of Leinster	944,724	598,162	153,438	143,732	123,634	35,766	32,421	20,561	8401	12,222	67,987
Munster	978,771	619,096	118,447	161,435	126,731	40,142	24,518	12,538	7944	12,829	114,512
Connacht–Ulster	675,092	423,141	114,654	97,805	94,128	17,112	4809	4471	4651	11,308	74,203
Total	3,509,969	2,183,489	535,573	484,315	455,568	155,695	95,582	63,397	57,420	41,575	94,364

Notes: The number of votes obtained refers to first preference figures. A further 17,703 votes were deemed invalid. S–PBP includes People Before Profit (40,220), Solidarity (12,723), and Rise (4477). In this and all other tables 'Others' includes Independents 4 Change (8421), the Irish Freedom Party (5495), Renua (5473), National Party (4773), Irish Democratic Party (2611), Workers' Party (1195), United People (43), and Independents (266,353).

Table A1.2 Turnout and percentage votes for each party

Constituency	Turnout	Sinn Féin	Fianna Fáil	Fine Gael	Green	Labour	SocDems	S-PBP	Aontú	Others
Carlow–Kilkenny	64.9	23.8	37.3	21.7	6.7	3.0	0.0	2.1	0.0	5.4
Cavan–Monaghan	66.1	36.7	25.2	6.6	3.5	1.4	0.0	1.1	5.3	0.2
Clare	65.9	15.1	34.0	22.5	9.5	0.0	0.0	2.0	0.0	16.9
Cork East	61.1	23.1	26.5	19.6	6.9	12.1	0.0	0.0	2.4	9.4
Cork North-Central	59.7	26.7	24.6	15.1	6.2	4.9	2.2	7.1	2.6	10.6
Cork North-West	65.4	0.0	39.4	33.2	7.5	0.0	8.3	0.0	8.4	3.2
Cork South-Central	63.2	24.6	35.4	21.3	9.4	2.2	1.9	1.3	2.4	1.5
Cork South-West	64.6	10.8	23.3	18.9	3.7	0.0	10.6	1.0	1.2	30.5
Donegal	62.0	45.1	20.4	13.8	2.1	0.0	0.0	0.0	3.1	15.5
Dublin Bay North	64.5	29.8	14.4	18.8	7.0	11.3	8.7	3.0	1.4	5.6
Dublin Bay South	52.1	16.1	13.8	27.7	22.5	7.9	4.5	2.5	0.0	5.0
Dublin Central	51.2	35.7	10.3	15.1	12.2	5.4	9.3	3.1	1.9	7.0
Dublin Fingal	63.2	24.9	21.5	15.0	13.2	7.1	3.5	1.8	0.0	13.0
Dublin Mid-West	61.6	42.8	12.3	17.6	6.1	3.4	0.0	7.9	0.0	9.9
Dublin North-West	59.6	44.4	12.0	11.1	4.8	2.6	18.9	3.8	0.0	2.4
Dublin Rathdown	63.7	11.6	12.8	31.2	21.1	7.5	0.0	3.5	3.3	9.0
Dublin South-Central	55.1	39.3	11.0	11.7	9.3	4.8	3.7	11.0	0.0	9.1
Dublin South-West	62.3	29.7	18.0	16.8	7.3	5.3	4.1	9.1	0.0	9.6
Dublin West	62.4	28.6	15.8	23.7	11.2	4.8	1.9	10.0	2.4	1.6
Dún Laoghaire	62.8	9.6	15.9	33.4	14.9	4.8	2.2	15.5	1.9	1.7
Galway East	61.9	16.7	25.2	29.0	4.5	2.0	2.0	0.0	1.4	19.2
Galway West	60.3	14.0	22.7	18.1	6.0	2.6	6.0	1.5	1.8	27.3
Kerry	66.9	20.2	20.7	18.4	5.3	0.0	0.0	0.0	1.4	34.0
Kildare North	62.7	17.1	26.2	17.8	10.0	5.4	19.3	1.7	0.0	2.5
Kildare South	61.4	21.5	20.1	17.1	3.5	12.5	2.8	1.3	1.5	19.8
Laois-Offaly	63.2	24.0	31.9	17.3	5.0	2.9	0.0	1.3	0.0	17.6
Limerick City	59.9	23.9	25.9	20.8	7.0	5.9	3.9	1.5	3.4	7.7

Limerick County	64.4	15.0	29.5	32.6	5.4	0.0	0.0	0.0	1.6	15.9
Longford–Westmeath	60.0	21.0	30.1	25.5	4.1	3.4	0.0	1.1	0.0	14.8
Louth	63.1	42.0	13.7	15.3	7.7	8.2	0.0	1.6	0.0	11.5
Mayo	66.1	22.7	24.1	39.5	6.5	0.4	0.0	1.1	4.0	1.6
Meath East	63.4	24.4	19.0	28.3	7.7	2.1	0.0	1.4	3.9	13.2
Meath West	61.5	30.5	16.2	24.7	4.7	0.0	5.7	0.0	17.7	0.5
Roscommon–Galway	66.0	17.5	17.3	12.0	3.1	0.0	0.0	0.9	1.1	48.0
Sligo–Leitrim	63.0	24.8	26.4	16.6	3.0	1.9	0.0	2.9	0.6	23.8
Tipperary	65.0	12.2	17.4	13.6	3.9	9.6	0.0	0.0	0.0	43.2
Waterford	63.8	38.3	17.3	16.5	7.4	6.5	0.0	2.1	2.0	9.9
Wexford	66.9	24.9	26.5	17.1	2.7	12.3	0.0	1.5	2.0	13.0
Wicklow	70.9	24.3	13.9	25.8	7.9	2.4	9.9	1.4	1.5	12.9
Dublin	59.9	27.4	15.0	20.5	11.5	6.2	4.8	6.7	1.0	6.9
Rest of Leinster	63.5	25.7	24.0	20.7	6.0	5.4	3.4	1.4	2.0	11.4
Munster	63.3	19.1	26.1	20.5	6.5	4.0	2.0	1.3	2.1	18.5
Connacht–Ulster	63.1	27.1	23.1	22.2	4.0	1.1	1.1	1.1	2.7	17.5
Total	62.9	24.5	22.2	20.9	7.1	4.4	2.9	2.6	1.9	13.5

Notes: S–PBP includes People Before Profit (1.8%), Solidarity (0.6%), and Rise (0.2%). Others includes Independents 4 Change (0.4%), the Irish Freedom Party (0.3%), Renua (0.3%), National Party (0.3%), Irish Democratic Party (0.2%), Workers' Party (0.1%), United People (0.05%), and Independents (12.2%).

Table A1.3 Seats and candidates by party

Constituency	Total	Sinn Féin	Fianna Fáil	Fine Gael	Green	Labour	SocDems	S-PBP	Aontú	Others
Carlow–Kilke	5–14	1–1	2–3	1–3	1–1	0–1	0–0	0–1	0–0	0–4
Cavan–Mon	5–13	2–2	2–3	1–3	0–1	0–1	0–0	0–1	0–1	0–1
Clare	4–15	1–1	1–3	1–3	0–1	0–0	0–0	0–1	0–0	1–6
Cork East	4–13	1–1	1–2	1–2	0–1	1–1	0–0	0–0	0–1	0–5
Cork NC	4–18	1–1	1–3	1–2	0–1	0–1	0–1	1–1	0–1	0–7
Cork NW	3–9	0–0	2–2	1–2	0–1	0–0	0–1	0–0	0–1	0–2
Cork SC	4–14	1–1	2–2	1–2	0–1	0–1	0–1	0–1	0–1	0–4
Cork SW	3–12	0–1	1–2	0–2	0–1	0–0	1–1	0–1	0–1	1–3
Donegal	5–13	2–2	1–2	1–2	0–1	0–0	0–0	0–0	0–1	1–5
Dublin Bay N	5–18	1–1	1–2	1–2	0–1	1–1	1–1	0–2	0–0	0–7
Dublin Bay S	4–15	1–1	1–1	1–2	1–1	0–1	0–1	0–1	0–1	0–7
Dublin Central	4–16	1–1	0–1	1–2	1–1	0–1	1–1	0–2	0–0	0–6
Dublin Fingal	5–16	1–1	1–2	1–2	1–1	1–1	0–1	0–2	0–0	0–6
Dublin MW	4–12	2–2	0–2	1–2	0–1	0–1	0–0	1–1	0–0	0–3
Dublin NW	3–10	1–1	1–1	0–1	1–1	0–1	1–1	0–1	0–0	0–3
Dub Rathdown	3–11	0–1	0–2	2–2	1–1	0–1	0–0	0–1	0–1	0–2
Dublin SC	4–13	1–1	0–1	0–1	1–1	0–1	0–1	1–1	0–0	1–6
Dublin SW	5–16	1–1	1–3	1–2	1–1	0–1	0–1	1–2	0–0	0–5
Dublin West	4–12	1–1	1–1	1–2	1–1	0–1	0–1	0–1	0–1	0–3
Dún Laoghaire	4–13	0–1	1–2	1–3	1–1	0–1	0–1	1–1	0–1	0–2
Galway East	3–12	0–1	1–2	1–2	0–1	0–1	0–1	0–0	0–1	1–3
Galway West	5–15	1–1	1–2	1–2	0–1	0–1	0–1	0–2	0–1	2–4
Kerry	5–13	1–1	1–3	1–2	0–1	0–0	0–0	0–0	0–1	2–5
Kildare North	4–12	1–1	1–2	1–2	0–1	0–1	1–1	0–1	0–1	0–3
Kildare South	4–12	1–1	1–3	1–1	0–1	0–1	0–1	0–1	0–0	1–2
Laois–Offaly	5–15	1–1	2–4	1–2	0–1	0–1	0–0	0–1	0–0	1–5
Limerick City	4–12	1–1	1–2	1–2	1–1	0–1	0–1	0–1	0–1	0–2

Limerick Co	3-12	0-1	1-2	1-2	0-1	0-0	0-0	0-0	0-1	1-5
Lfrd-Wmeath	4-15	1-1	2-2	1-3	0-1	0-1	0-0	0-2	0-0	0-5
Louth	5-15	2-2	0-2	1-2	0-1	1-1	0-0	0-1	0-0	1-6
Mayo	4-15	1-1	1-2	2-3	0-1	0-1	0-0	0-1	0-1	0-5
Meath East	3-12	1-1	1-2	1-2	0-1	0-1	0-0	0-1	0-1	0-3
Meath West	3-9	1-1	0-1	1-3	0-1	0-0	0-1	0-0	1-1	0-1
Rosc-Galway	3-11	1-1	0-2	0-1	0-1	0-0	0-0	0-1	0-1	2-4
Sligo-Leitrim	4-19	1-1	1-3	1-2	0-1	0-1	0-0	0-1	0-1	1-9
Tipperary	5-14	1-1	1-3	0-2	1-1	1-1	0-0	0-0	0-0	2-6
Waterford	4-11	1-1	1-2	0-2	0-1	0-1	0-0	0-1	0-1	1-2
Wexford	5-15	1-1	1-4	1-2	0-1	1-1	0-0	0-1	0-1	1-4
Wicklow	5-20	1-1	1-2	1-3	1-1	0-1	1-1	0-1	0-1	0-9
Dublin	45-152	10-12	7-18	10-21	8-11	2-11	3-9	4-15	0-5	1-50
Rest of Leinster	43-139	11-11	11-25	10-23	2-10	2-9	2-4	0-10	1-5	4-42
Munster	43-143	8-10	13-26	8-23	2-11	2-6	1-5	1-6	0-9	8-47
Conn–Ulster	29-98	8-9	7-16	7-15	0-7	0-5	0-2	0-6	0-7	7-31
Total	160-532	37-42	38-85	35-82	12-39	6-31	6-20	5-37	1-26	20-170

Figures include outgoing Ceann Comhairle Seán Ó Fearghaíl (FF), automatically re-elected in Kildare South. They also include one independent candidate who stood in two constituencies and another independent candidate who stood in 11 constituencies

Notes: S–PBP includes 27 People Before Profit (three elected), nine Solidarity (one elected), and one Rise (one elected) candidates. Others includes 4 Independents 4 Change (one elected), 11 Irish Freedom Party (none elected), 11 Renua (none elected), 10 National Party (none elected), 1 Irish Democratic Party (none elected), 4 Workers' Party (none elected),1 United People (none elected), and 128 Independent (19 elected) candidates

Appendix B: Members of the 33rd Dáil

TD (constituency)	Party	Occupation	Date of birth	First elected	Times elected	First preference vote 2020
Chris Andrews (Dublin Bay South)	SF	Business owner	Jun-65	2007	2	6361
Mick Barry (Cork North-Central)	S-PBP	Journalist	Sep-64	2016	2	3703
Richard Boyd Barrett (Dún Laoghaire)	S-PBP	Teacher	Nov-67	2011	3	9632
Cathal Berry (Kildare South)	Ind	Medical doctor, army ranger	Jun-77	2020	1	5742
John Brady (Wicklow)	SF	Carpenter	Jul-73	2016	2	17,297
Colm Brophy (Dublin South-West)	FG	Company director	Jun-66	2016	2	8269
James Browne (Wexford)	FF	Barrister	Nov-75	2016	2	8058
Martin Browne (Tipperary)	SF	Unknown	May-65	2020	1	10,004
Richard Bruton (Dublin Bay North)	FG	Economist	Mar-53	F1982	11	11,156
Pat Buckley (Cork East)	SF	Builder	Jul-68	2016	2	12,587
Colm Burke (Cork North-Central)	FG	Solicitor	Jan-57	2020	1	6646
Peter Burke (Longford–Westmeath)	FG	Accountant	Oct-82	2016	2	6617
Mary Butler (Waterford)	FF	Retailer	Sep-66	2016	2	6644
Thomas Byrne (Meath East)	FF	Solicitor	Jun-77	2007	3	6039
Jackie Cahill (Tipperary)	FF	Farmer	Aug-63	2016	2	7940
Holly Cairns (Cork South-West)	SD	Farmer and businesswoman	Nov-89	2020	1	4696
Dara Calleary (Mayo)	FF	Regional coordinator Chambers Ireland	May-73	2007	4	9163
Seán Canney (Galway East)	Ind	Quantity surveyor, lecturer	Apr-60	2016	2	7815
Ciaran Cannon (Galway East)	FG	Publican	Sep-65	2011	3	6298
Joe Carey (Clare)	FG	Accountant	Jun-75	2007	4	5684
Jennifer Carroll MacNeill (Dún Laoghaire)	FG	Policy advisor	Sep-80	2020	1	7754
Matt Carthy (Cavan–Monaghan)	SF	Political organiser	Jul-77	2020	1	16,310
Jack Chambers (Dublin West)	FF	Medical student	Nov-90	2016	2	6892
Sorca Clarke (Longford–Westmeath)	SF	Accountant, business owner	n/a	2020	1	11,848

Joan Collins (Dublin South-Central)	I4C	Clerk, An Post	Jun-61	2011	3	2831
Michael Collins (Cork South-West)	Ind	Farmer	Feb-68	2016	2	11,712
Niall Collins (Limerick County)	FF	Accountant, lecturer	Mar-73	2007	4	8436
Catherine Connolly (Galway West)	Ind	Barrister	Nov-55	2016	2	5439
Rose Conway–Walsh (Mayo)	SF	Community project leader	Oct-69	2020	1	14,633
Patrick Costello (Dublin South-Central)	Green	Social worker	May-80	2020	1	4041
Simon Coveney (Cork South-Central)	FG	Manager of family business	Jun-72	B-1998	6	9327
Barry Cowen (Laois-Offaly)	FF	Auctioneer	Aug-67	2011	3	8677
Michael Creed (Cork North-West)	FG	Farmer	Jun-63	1989	7	8338
Réada Cronin (Kildare North)	SF	Social worker	1965	2020	1	8705
Cathal Crowe (Clare)	FF	Teacher	Oct-82	2020	1	8355
Seán Crowe (Dublin South-West)	SF	Printing operative	Mar-57	2002	4	20,077
David Cullinane (Waterford)	SF	Car parts manager	Jul-74	2016	2	20,569
Pa Daly (Kerry)	SF	Solicitor	1970	2020	1	15,733
Cormac Devlin (Dún Laoghaire)	FF	Publishing company employee	Aug-80	2020	1	5715
Alan Dillon (Mayo)	FG	Company director	Sep-82	2020	1	5198
Pearse Doherty (Donegal)	SF	Civil engineer	Jul-77	B-2010	4	21,044
Paul Donnelly (Dublin West)	SF	Community outreach worker	Nov-68	2020	1	12,456
Stephen Donnelly (Wicklow)	FF	Management consultant	Feb-75	2011	3	5467
Paschal Donohoe (Dublin Central)	FG	Sales & marketing director	Sep-74	2011	3	4181
Francis Noel Duffy (Dublin South-West)	Green	Architect, lecturer	Apr-71	2020	1	4961
Bernard Durkan (Kildare North)	FG	Agricultural contractor	Mar-45	1981	11	5447
Dessie Ellis (Dublin North-West)	SF	Television repairman	Oct-52	2011	3	14,375
Damien English (Meath West)	FG	Accountant	Feb-78	2002	5	5499
Alan Farrell (Dublin Fingal)	FG	Estate agent	Dec-77	2011	3	6213
Mairéad Farrell (Galway West)	SF	Financial services employee	Jan-90	2020	1	8464
Frankie Feighan (Sligo–Leitrim)	FG	Newsagent, businessman	Jul-62	2007	3	5338
Michael Fitzmaurice (Roscommon–Galway)	Ind	Contractor, farmer	Sep-69	B-2014	3	13,077
Peter Fitzpatrick (Louth)	Ind	Businessman	May-62	2011	3	6085

(continued)

(continued)

TD (constituency)	Party	Occupation	Date of birth	First elected	Times elected	First preference vote 2020
Joe Flaherty (Longford–Westmeath)	FF	Managing director newspaper group	Jul-69	2020	1	7666
Charlie Flanagan (Laois–Offaly)	FG	Solicitor	Nov-56	1987	8	7463
Seán Fleming (Laois–Offaly)	FF	Accountant	Feb-58	1997	6	7636
Norma Foley (Kerry)	FF	Teacher	1970	2020	1	6856
Kathleen Funchion (Carlow–Kilkenny)	SF	Trade union organiser	Apr-81	2016	2	17,493
Gary Gannon (Dublin Central)	SD	Career guidance advocate	Feb-87	2020	1	2912
Thomas Gould (Cork North-Central)	SF	Logistics manager	Jul-68	2020	1	13,811
Noel Grealish (Galway West)	Ind	Company director	Dec-65	2002	5	8043
Brendan Griffin (Kerry)	FG	Publican	Mar-82	2011	3	10,296
Johnny Guirke (Meath West)	SF	Construction worker	Jan-65	2020	1	12,652
Marian Harkin (Sligo–Leitrim)	Ind	Teacher	Nov-53	2002	2	6972
Simon Harris (Wicklow)	FG	Political aide	Oct-86	2011	3	8765
Seán Haughey (Dublin Bay North)	FF	Student	Nov-61	1992	6	6651
Danny Healy-Rae (Kerry)	Ind	Businessman, contractor	Jul-54	2016	2	8663
Michael Healy-Rae (Kerry)	Ind	Shop and plant hire owner	Jan-67	2011	3	16,818
Martin Heydon (Kildare South)	FG	Farmer	Aug-78	2011	3	8069
Emer Higgins (Dublin Mid-West)	FG	Senior manager PayPal	Mar-85	2020	1	4487
Neasa Hourigan (Dublin Central)	Green	Architect, lecturer	Oct-80	2020	1	3851
Brendan Howlin (Wexford)	Lab	Teacher	May-56	1987	9	9223
Heather Humphreys (Cavan–Monaghan)	FG	Credit union manager	May-63	2011	3	12,808
Paul Kehoe (Wexford)	FG	Sales representative	Jan-73	2002	5	6337
Alan Kelly (Tipperary)	Lab	Semi-state e-business manager	Jul-75	2011	3	7857
Gino Kenny (Dublin Mid-West)	S–PBP	Care assistant	Jun-72	2016	2	3572
Martin Kenny (Sligo–Leitrim)	SF	Community project coordinator	Oct-71	2016	2	15,035

Claire Kerrane (Roscommon–Galway)	SF	Political advisor	Apr-92	2020	1	8003
John Lahart (Dublin South-West)	FF	Psychotherapist	Nov-64	2016	2	5503
James Lawless (Kildare North)	FF	Barrister	Aug-76	2016	2	7029
Brian Leddin (Limerick City)	Green	Engineer	Jan-80	2020	1	3252
Michael Lowry (Tipperary)	Ind	Company director	Mar-54	1987	9	14,802
Paul McAuliffe (Dublin North-West)	FF	Communications executive	Feb-77	2020	1	3902
Charlie McConalogue (Donegal)	FF	Farmer, political organiser	Oct-77	2011	3	8347
Mary Lou McDonald (Dublin Central)	SF	Productivity consultant	May-69	2011	3	11,223
Helen McEntee (Meath East)	FG	Political aide, bank employee	Jun-86	B-2013	3	7691
Mattie McGrath (Tipperary)	Ind	Plant hire contractor	Sep-58	2007	4	9321
Michael McGrath (Cork South-Central)	FF	Accountant	Aug-76	2007	4	9236
John McGuinness (Carlow-Kilkenny)	FF	Transport company director	Mar-55	1997	6	10,558
Joe McHugh (Donegal)	FG	Teacher	Jul-71	2007	4	7621
Pádraig MacLochlainn (Donegal)	SF	Community activist, campaigner	Jun-73	2011	2	13,891
Michael McNamara (Clare)	Ind	Barrister, farmer	Mar-74	2011	2	7332
Marc MacSharry (Sligo–Leitrim)	FF	Estate agent	Jul-73	2016	2	7004
Joespha Madigan (Dublin Rathdown)	FG	Solicitor	May-69	2016	2	6482
Catherine Martin (Dublin Rathdown)	Green	Teacher	Dec-72	2016	2	8958
Micheál Martin (Cork South-Central)	FF	Teacher	Aug-60	1989	8	11,023
Steven Matthews (Wicklow)	Green	Irish Rail signal engineer	Jul-70	2020	1	5634
Denise Mitchell (Dublin Bay North)	SF	Shop steward	Nov-76	2016	2	21,344
Aindrias Moynihan (Cork North-West)	FF	Engineer	Oct-67	2016	2	9628
Michael Moynihan (Cork North-West)	FF	Farmer	Jan-68	1997	6	8651
Imelda Munster (Louth)	SF	Optician shop assistant	Feb-68	2016	2	17,203
Jennifer Murnane O'Connor (Carlow-Kilk)	FF	Shop assistant	May-66	2020	1	9351
Catherine Murphy (Kildare North)	SD	Clerical worker	Sep-53	B-2005	4	9808
Eoghan Murphy (Dublin Bay South)	FG	Speechwriter	Apr-82	2011	3	6346
Paul Murphy (Dublin South-West)	S-PBP	Political aide to MEP	Apr-83	B-2013	3	4477

(continued)

(continued)

TD (constituency)	Party	Occupation	Date of birth	First elected	Times elected	First preference vote 2020
Verona Murphy (Wexford)	Ind	Head of road haulage organisation	Oct-71	2020	1	5825
Johnny Mythen (Wexford)	SF	ESB Technician	May-58	2020	1	18,717
Ged Nash (Louth)	Lab	Public relations consultant	Dec-75	2011	2	5824
Denis Naughten (Roscommon–Galway)	Ind	Research scientist	Jun-73	1997	6	8422
Hildegarde Naughton (Galway West)	FG	Teacher	May-77	2016	2	5609
Carol Nolan (Laois–Offaly)	Ind	School principal	May-78	2016	2	5436
Malcolm Noonan (Carlow–Kilkenny)	Green	Graphic designer, horticulturalist	Sep-66	2020	1	4942
Darragh O'Brien (Dublin Fingal)	FF	Insurance firm manager	Jul-74	2007	3	10,111
Joe Ó Brien (Dublin Fingal)	Green	Integration policy officer	May-77	B-2019	2	8400
Eoin Ó Broin (Dublin Mid-West)	SF	Policy advisor	Sep-72	2016	2	11,842
Cian O'Callaghan (Dublin Bay North)	SD	Political organiser	May-79	2020	1	6229
Jim O'Callaghan (Dublin Bay South)	FF	Senior Counsel	Jan-68	2016	2	5474
Marc Ó Cathasaigh (Waterford)	Green	Teacher	Jan-77	2020	1	3996
James O'Connor (Cork East)	FF	Student, political aide	Jun-97	2020	1	7026
Éamon Ó Cuív (Galway West)	FF	Cooperative manager	Jun-50	1996	7	8522
Willie O'Dea (Limerick City)	FF	Accountant, barrister	Nov-52	F1982	11	9198
Kieran O'Donnell (Limerick City)	FG	Accountant	May-63	2007	3	6589
Richard O'Donoghue (Limerick County)	Ind	Building contractor	May-70	2020	1	6021
Patrick O'Donovan (Limerick County)	FG	Teacher	Mar-77	2011	3	9228
Fergus O'Dowd (Louth)	FG	Teacher	Sep-48	2002	5	6380
Seán Ó Fearghaíl (Kildare South)	FF	Farmer	Apr-60	2002	5	—
Roderic O'Gorman (Dublin West)	Green	Lecturer DCU	Dec-81	2020	1	4901
Donnchadh Ó Laoghaire (Cork SC)	SF	Political aide	Feb-89	2016	2	14,057
Ruairí Ó Murchú (Louth)	SF	Political aide	May-78	2020	1	12,491
Louise O'Reilly (Dublin Fingal)	SF	Trade unionist	Sep-73	2016	2	15,792

Name	Party	Occupation	DOB	Year	No.	Votes
Aodhán Ó Ríordáin (Dublin Bay North)	Lab	School principal	Jul-76	2011	2	8127
Darren O'Rourke (Meath East)	SF	Medical scientist	Jun-80	2020	1	10,223
Aengus Ó Snodaigh (Dublin South-Central)	SF	Teacher	Aug-64	2002	5	17,015
Christopher O'Sullivan (Cork South-West)	FF	Whale-watching guide	Jun-82	2020	1	6262
Pádraig O'Sullivan (Cork North-Central)	FF	Teacher	May-84	B-2019	2	8158
John Paul Phelan (Carlow–Kilkenny)	FG	Barrister	Sep-78	2011	3	6396
Thomas Pringle (Donegal)	Ind	Water treatment plant manager	Aug-67	2011	3	5472
Maurice Quinlivan (Limerick City)	SF	Travel agency manager	Nov-67	2016	2	11,006
Anne Rabbitte (Galway East)	FF	Financial advisor	Oct-70	2016	2	5762
Neale Richmond (Dublin Rathdown)	FG	Political aide, project manager	Mar-83	2020	1	6743
Michael Ring (Mayo)	FG	Auctioneer	Dec-53	B-1994	7	14,796
Eamon Ryan (Dublin Bay South)	Green	Environmental consultant	Jul-63	2002	4	8888
Patricia Ryan (Kildare South)	SF	Shop steward	Mar-63	2020	1	10,155
Matt Shanahan (Waterford)	Ind	Marketing consultant	Jun-64	2020	1	4990
Seán Sherlock (Cork East)	Lab	Political aide	Dec-72	2007	4	6610
Róisín Shortall (Dublin North-West)	SD	Teacher of the deaf	Apr-54	1992	7	6124
Brendan Smith (Cavan–Monaghan)	FF	Ministerial advisor	Jun-56	1992	7	7354
Bríd Smith (Dublin South-Central)	S–PBP	Trade unionist	Sep-61	2016	2	4753
Duncan Smith (Dublin Fingal)	Lab	Parliamentary assistant, student	May-83	2020	1	4513
Niamh Smyth (Cavan–Monaghan)	FF	Arts and Education Officer	Apr-78	2016	2	5745
Ossian Smyth (Dún Laoghaire)	Green	Project manager in hospital	May-71	2020	1	9300
Brian Stanley (Laois–Offaly)	SF	Truck driver, builder	Jan-61	2011	3	16,654
David Stanton (Cork East)	FG	Teacher	Feb-57	1997	6	6143
Peadar Tóibín (Meath West)	Aontú	Management consultant	Jun-74	2011	3	7322
Robert Troy (Longford–Westmeath)	FF	Postmaster	Jan-82	2011	3	9331

(continued)

(continued)

TD (constituency)	Party	Occupation	Date of birth	First elected	Times elected	First preference vote 2020
Pauline Tully (Cavan–Monaghan)	SF	Teacher	n/a	2020	1	10,166
Leo Varadkar (Dublin West)	FG	Medical doctor	Jan-79	2007	4	8478
Mark Ward (Dublin Mid-West)	SF	Behavioural therapist	1975	B-2019	2	7621
Jennifer Whitmore (Wicklow)	SD	Policy analyst	Jul-74	2020	1	7039
Violet-Anne Wynne (Clare)	SF	Home help provider	1988	2020	1	8987

Source: previous *How Ireland Voted* volumes, newspapers, personal enquiries, and Tim Ryan (ed.), *The Irish Times Nealon's Guide to the 33rd Dáil and 26th Seanad* (Dublin: Grand Canal Publishing, 2020)

Notes: Most TDs are full-time public representatives. For such TDs, the occupations given here are those previously followed. Eoghan Murphy resigned his seat on 27 April 2021

Seán Ó Fearghaíl was returned automatically as the outgoing Ceann Comhairle

There were two general elections in 1982, in February (F) and November (N). 'B-' indicates that the deputy was first elected at a by-election

Appendix C: The Government and Ministers of State

A government was elected by the Dáil on 27 June 2020, 140 days after election day. It consisted of ministers from Fianna Fáil, Fine Gael, and the Green Party. Micheál Martin's nomination as Taoiseach was supported by 93 TDs: 37 Fianna Fáil, 35 Fine Gael, 12 Green Party, plus independents Cathal Berry, Peter Fitzpatrick, Noel Grealish, Marian Harkin, Michael Lowry, Michael McNamara, Verona Murphy, Richard O'Donoghue, and Matt Shanahan. It was opposed by 63 TDs. Three independents (TDs Mattie McGrath, Denis Naughten, and Carol Nolan) abstained on the vote.

The government subsequently appointed was:

Micheál Martin	FF	Taoiseach
Leo Varadkar	FG	Tánaiste and Minister for Enterprise, Trade and Employment
Simon Coveney	FG	Minister for Foreign Affairs and Minister for Defence
Barry Cowen	FF	Minister for Agriculture, Food and the Marine (replaced by Dara Calleary on 15 July, in turn replaced by Charlie McConalogue on 2 September)
Stephen Donnelly	FF	Minister for Health
Paschal Donohoe	FG	Minister for Finance
Norma Foley	FF	Minister for Education
Simon Harris	FG	Minister for Further and Higher Education, Research, Innovation and Science
Heather Humphreys	FG	Minister for Social Protection and Minister for Rural and Community Development
Helen McEntee	FG	Minister for Justice
Michael McGrath	FF	Minister for Public Expenditure and Reform
Catherine Martin	Grn	Minister for Tourism, Culture, Arts, Gaeltacht, Sport and Media
Darragh O'Brien	FF	Minister for Housing, Local Government and Heritage
Roderic O'Gorman	Grn	Minister for Children, Equality, Disability, Integration and Youth
Eamon Ryan	Grn	Minister for the Environment, Climate and Communications, and Minister for Transport
(Paul Gallagher		Attorney General)

Ministers of state, their departments, and areas of special responsibility

Dara Calleary	FF	Taoiseach (Government Chief Whip); Tourism, Culture, Arts, Gaeltacht, Sport and Media—replaced by Jack Chambers on 15 July
Colm Brophy	FG	Foreign Affairs (Overseas Development Aid, Diaspora)

(*continued*)

(continued)

Peter Burke	FG	Housing, Local Government and Heritage (Local Government and Planning)
Mary Butler	FF	Health (Mental Health, Older People)
Thomas Byrne	FF	Taoiseach, Foreign Affairs (European Affairs)
Jack Chambers	FF	Finance (Financial Services, Credit Unions and Insurance)—replaced by Seán Fleming (FF) on 15 July
Niall Collins	FF	Further and Higher Education, Research, Innovation and Science (Skills and Further Education)
Damien English	FG	Enterprise, Trade and Employment (Employment Affairs, Retail Businesses)
Frank Feighan	FG	Health (Public Health, Well Being, National Drugs Strategy)
Pippa Hackett	Grn	Agriculture, Food and the Marine (Land Use and Biodiversity)
Martin Heydon	FG	Agriculture, Food and the Marine (Research and Development, Farm Safety, New Market Development)
Charlie McConalogue	FF	Justice (Law Reform)—replaced by James Browne on 3 September
Josepha Madigan	FG	Education (Special Education and Inclusion)
Hildegarde Naughton	FG	Transport (International and Road Transport and Logistics); Environment, Climate and Communications (Postal Policy and Eircodes)
Malcolm Noonan	Grn	Housing, Local Government and Heritage (Heritage and Electoral Reform)
Joe O'Brien	Grn	Social Protection; Rural and Community Development (Community Development and Charities)
Patrick O'Donovan	FG	Public Expenditure and Reform (Office of Public Works)
Anne Rabbitte	FF	Health; Children, Equality, Disability, Integration and Youth (Disability)
Ossian Smyth	Grn	Public Expenditure and Reform (Public Procurement and eGovernment)
Robert Troy	FF	Enterprise, Trade and Employment (Trade Promotion)

Appendix D: The Electoral System

Ireland uses proportional representation by the single transferable vote (PR-STV) as its electoral system for Dáil, Seanad, local, and European Parliament elections. PR-STV is a relatively rare electoral system, with Malta being the only other country that employs it for national elections to the lower house of parliament, although it is also used for elections to the Australian Senate and to the Northern Irish Assembly. All citizens of Ireland and the United Kingdom who are resident in Ireland are entitled to vote.

For the 2020 election the country was divided into 39 constituencies, with the district magnitude of these constituencies varying between three and five seats. Article 16.2.6° of Bunreacht na hÉireann (the Irish Constitution) states that the minimum district magnitude is three, but it does not state a maximum district magnitude. However, since 1948 no constituency has had a district magnitude greater than five. In 2020, there were 9 three-seat constituencies, 17 four-seat constituencies, and 13 five-seat constituencies, returning 160 deputies, one of these being the Ceann Comhairle (speaker), who is deemed automatically re-elected.

The ballot paper is arranged in alphabetical order by candidate surname, with each candidate's name accompanied by their photograph, party label (if applicable), address, and usually their occupation. Independents may use the designation 'non-party'. Candidates are able to describe their occupation as they wish, and many state this as 'public representative' or provide a description that conveys little about their previous career. Voters rank order candidates, writing '1' next to the most preferred candidate, '2' next to their second choice, and so on. The voter needs only to provide a first preference for the vote to be rendered valid and can provide preferences for as many or as few candidates as they desire. Voters are free to vote across party lines and can use whatever criteria they like as their basis for ranking the candidates. Polling stations were open from 7:00 AM to 10:00 PM, with voting before the day restricted to those living on offshore islands and those few entitled to postal ballots.

A candidate is deemed elected if their number of votes equals the Droop quota in any of the counts. The Droop quote is calculated as the smallest integer greater than the result of dividing the total number of votes cast by the number of seats in the constituency plus one. For example, in a five-seat constituency where 60,000 votes were cast, the quota would be $(60,000 / (5 + 1)) + 1 = 10,001$. This quota is the minimum number of votes that only five candidates can attain.

Rather than beginning to count immediately after polls close, the ballot boxes are taken to a count centre, and the count begins at 9:00 AM the following day. The constituency returning officer announces the result at the end of each stage of the counting process. If a candidate exceeds the quota on that count, they are deemed elected, and their surplus votes (i.e., the number of votes they had over and above the quota) are calculated and distributed according to the proportion of second preferences marked for each of the remaining candidates. If no candidate reaches the quota, the candidate with the lowest number of votes is eliminated, and each of their votes is distributed according to the next preference marked on the ballot. This process continues until all seats are filled, either by candidates reaching the quota or by it becoming mathematically impossible for the highest-placed candidate under the quota to be overtaken (see 'Further reading' below for a full explanation of how the electoral system operates). In 2020, the shortest count was Cork North-West (5 stages) and the longest were Sligo–Leitrim and Wicklow (both had 15 stages). Candidates whose total vote reached a quarter of a quota at any point in the count may claim back expenses, to a maximum of €8700.

The transfer of votes is the distinctive feature of PR-STV, allowing voters to convey detailed information on their preferences, unconstrained by any criteria, including party lines. This feature enables us to examine many factors that are otherwise difficult to measure, including how close parties are to each other in the minds of voters, and how important voters regard non-party candidate characteristics such as geography or gender.

Further Reading

Department of Housing, Planning, and Local Government, *A Guide to Ireland's PR-STV Voting System*, available online at https://www.housing.gov.ie/sites/default/files/publications/files/pr-stv_guide.pdf.

Farrell, David M. and Sinnott, Richard, 'The electoral system', pp. 89–110 in John Coakley and Michael Gallagher (eds.), *Politics in the Republic of Ireland*, 6th ed (Abingdon: Routledge and PSAI Press, 2018).

Gallagher, Michael, 'Ireland: The discreet charm of PR-STV', pp. 511–32 in Michael Gallagher and Paul Mitchell (eds.), *The Politics of Electoral Systems* (Oxford: Oxford University Press, 2008).

APPENDIX E: RETIREMENTS AND DEFEATED INCUMBENTS FROM THE 32ND DÁIL

Members of the 32nd Dáil who did not contest the election to the 33rd Dáil

Gerry Adams	Louth	SF
Maria Bailey	Dún Laoghaire	FG
Seán Barrett	Dún Laoghaire	FG
Tommy Broughan	Dublin Bay North	I4C
Jim Daly	Cork South-West	FG
John Deasy	Waterford	FG
Martin Ferris	Kerry	SF
John Halligan	Waterford	Ind
Michael Harty	Clare	Ind
Enda Kenny	Mayo	FG
Tony McLoughlin	Sligo–Leitrim	FG
Finian McGrath	Dublin Bay North	Ind
Dara Murphy[a]	Cork North-Central	FG
Michael Noonan	Limerick City	FG
Jonathan O'Brien	Cork North-Central	SF
Caoimhghín Ó Caoláin	Cavan–Monaghan	SF
Maureen O'Sullivan	Dublin Central	Ind
Willie Penrose	Longford–Westmeath	Lab
Brendan Ryan	Dublin Fingal	Lab

[a]Murphy had resigned his seat in December 2019, and it was vacant at the time of the 2020 general election

Members of the 32nd Dáil who were defeated at the 2020 election

Bobby Aylward	Carlow–Kilkenny	FF
John Brassil	Kerry	FF
Declan Breathnach	Louth	FF
Pat Breen	Clare	FG
Joan Burton	Dublin West	Lab
Catherine Byrne	Dublin South-Central	FG
Malcolm Byrne	Wexford	FF
Pat Casey	Wicklow	FF
Shane Cassells	Meath West	FF
Lisa Chambers	Mayo	FF
Ruth Coppinger	Dublin West	S–PBP
Marcella Corcoran–Kennedy	Laois–Offaly	FG
John Curran	Dublin Mid-West	FF
Michael D'Arcy	Wexford	FG
Pat Deering	Carlow–Kilkenny	FG
Regina Doherty	Meath East	FG

(*continued*)

(continued)

Timmy Dooley	Clare	FF
Andrew Doyle	Wicklow	FG
Pat 'the Cope' Gallagher	Donegal	FF
Séamus Healy	Tipperary	Ind
Seán Kyne	Galway West	FG
Mary Mitchell O'Connor	Dún Laoghaire	FG
Kevin 'Boxer' Moran	Longford–Westmeath	Ind
Eugene Murphy	Roscommon–Galway	FF
Margaret Murphy O'Mahony	Cork South-West	FF
Tom Neville	Limerick County	FG
Kate O'Connell	Dublin Bay South	FG
Kevin O'Keeffe	Cork East	FF
Fiona O'Loughlin	Kildare South	FF
Frank O'Rourke	Kildare North	FF
Jan O'Sullivan	Limerick City	Lab
Noel Rock	Dublin North-West	FG
Shane Ross	Dublin Rathdown	Ind
Éamon Scanlon	Sligo–Leitrim	FF
Katherine Zappone	Dublin South-West	Ind

Index[1]

---

[1] Note: Page numbers followed by 'n' refer to notes.

Laffan, Brigid, 104
Laffoy, Mary, 12
Lally, Conor, 273n19
Laver, Michael, 319n17, 337n10
Leahy, John, 212, 213
Leahy, Pat, xx, 108n9, 133n6,
    273n16, 295n42, 318,
    319, 339n31
Left–right spectrum, 238–241, 256,
    259, 261, 269, 272n9
Lemass, Seán, 331
Leonard, Tom, 69n16
Lewis-Beck, Michael S., 250n1
Leyden, Orla, 48
Leyden, Terry, 48
Libertas, 102
Linehan Foley, Mary, 142, 144
Local government
    elections, 15–16, 19, 44, 50, 51,
        54, 55, 57–59, 72, 74, 76, 78,
        80, 81, 98, 123, 130, 139,
        172, 176, 177, 179, 220
    as route to parliament, 64, 65,
        143–145, 150, 157, 159,
        192, 198
    and Seanad, vi, 155–157, 282–284
Localism, 46, 197, 198, 203, 204,
    216, 247–248
Looney, Dermot, 89
Lord, Miriam, 87, 121
Loughlin, Elaine, 39n11, 69n15
Loughnane, Joe, 60
Lowry, Michael, 6, 313, 355
Lutz, Georg, 252n24
Luxembourg, 326
Lynch, Catherine, 20n13
Lyons, John, 59

M
MacCarthaigh, Muiris, 292n2, 293n7
Mac Cumhaill, Fionn, 330

MacKuen, Michael B., 133n14
MacLochlainn, Pádraig, 200
MacNeill, Hugo, 289
McQuinn, Cormac, 273n20,
    318n1, 320n28
Maguire, Sinéad, 51
Maguire, Tom, 338n29
Mair, Peter, 194n3, 336n10
Malta, 357
Manifestoes, xx, xxi, 15, 25–27,
    29–35, 38, 87, 97, 98, 106, 115,
    121, 151, 222, 255, 257, 265,
    267, 270, 292, 311, 328
Manning, Maurice, 294n31
Manning Report, 292
Marien, Sofie, 21n26
Marsh, Michael, 20n5, 22n34, 68,
    101, 110n30, 173, 195n13,
    243–245, 250–253, 337n10,
    338n24, 339n35
Marshall, Ian, 290
Martin, Catherine, xxiv, xxvi, 66, 153,
    307, 310
Martin, Micheál, xix–xxiii, 1, 2, 5–7,
    13, 19, 77–79, 85, 86, 89, 90,
    97–99, 114, 121, 124, 128, 140,
    243–245, 298–301, 303, 304,
    307–309, 311, 313–318, 330,
    332, 355
Martin, Shane, 292n2, 319n9
Martin, Vincent P., 66, 290
Matthews, Neil, 337n15
May, Theresa, 95, 96
Mbugua Henry, Salome, 280
McCabe, Maurice, 8, 9, 11, 12,
    20n15, 43
McCallion, Elisha, 287
McCarthy, Justine, 293n16
McCloskey, Anne, 64
McConnell, Daniel, 20n1, 22n35,
    69n18, 319n21
McCourt, David, 15

Printed by Printforce, United Kingdom